WRITINGS ON SLAVERY

and the

AMERICAN CIVIL WAR

Harriet Martineau statue.

(Courtesy of Wellesley College Archives)

Writings on *Slavery* and the *American Civil War*

HARRIET MARTINEAU

Edited by Deborah Anna Logan

Northern Illinois University Press / DeKalb

© 2002 by Northern Illinois University Press
Published by the Northern Illinois University Press, DeKalb,
Illinois   60115
Manufactured in the United States using acid-free paper
All Rights Reserved
Design by Julia Fauci

Library of Congress Cataloging-in-Publication Data
Martineau, Harriet, 1802–1876.
Writings on slavery and the American Civil War / Harriet Martineau ; edited by Deborah Anna Logan.
p.   cm.
Includes bibliographical references (p.) and index.
ISBN 0-87580-292-3 (acid-free paper)
1. Slavery—Social aspects—United States—History—19th century.
2. Antislavery movements—United States—History—19th century.
3. United States—History—Civil War, 1861–1865. 4. United
States—Social conditions—To 1865. 5. Martineau, Harriet,
1802–1876—Political and social views. I. Logan, Deborah Anna,
1951– . II. Title.

E449. M388 2002
973.7—dc21   2001051413

❖ ❖ ❖

CONTENTS

❖ ❖ ❖

ACKNOWLEDGMENTS

I am most grateful to Western Kentucky University for its generous support of my research on Harriet Martineau. This support includes the Junior Faculty Scholarship Program (1998) and two Faculty Scholarship Awards (1999 and 2000) for travel, both granted by the Graduate Studies Committee. I thank the Potter College Professional Development Committee for two Faculty Summer Fellowships (2000 and 2001) and for generous supplemental travel funding. In addition, I thank Dr. Jane Olmsted and the Women's Studies Department for a travel grant (1999) and for the department's overall support of research activities contributing to new scholarship on women.

The English Department at Western has been most generous in its support, providing me with student assistants to help in preparing this book and contributing to the all-important travel funding. Graduate student Karen White contributed many hours of technical expertise, and I am greatly indebted to her for her careful work and scrupulous attention to detail. Perhaps best of all is the Willson Wood Professorship awarded to me by the department, which facilitated the completion of this project. I am highly honored to have received this award, which in itself so eloquently expresses the support I have enjoyed from my colleagues. In particular, I thank Dr. Linda Calendrillo for her strong and consistent encouragement of my research and writing.

In the Interlibrary Borrowing Office at Western's Helm Library, I thank Debra Day for her good humor and friendliness, her efficiency, and her patience with the heavy demands I've placed on her office. Also, the staff and facilities at the Kentucky Library Reading Room on Western's campus afforded me many hours of research in a very pleasant environment.

For reading portions of this manuscript, I am grateful to Professor Valerie Sanders of the University of Hull and Dr. Ted Hovet of Western Kentucky University. Their comments and suggestions were invaluable in helping me to make this book a worthy representative of the enormous body of writing Harriet Martineau produced on behalf of the anti-slavery movement—as she would say, "on both sides the Atlantic." I thank Valerie for her advice on Martineau and on the history of British periodicals, and I thank Ted for his advice on American Civil War literary history, particularly Martineau's connection with Catharine Sedgwick.

Any Martineau scholar today owes a significant debt to the scholarly work on Harriet Martineau produced by Valerie Sanders, Elisabeth Arbuckle, and

R. K. Webb, all of whom have prepared the way for this and other scholarship on this quintessential woman writer.

For permission to quote from manuscript letters to, from, and about Harriet Martineau, I thank the Houghton Library, Harvard University; the Boston Public Library, Manuscript Collection, with special thanks to curator Bill Faucon; and the Bancroft Library, Reinhard Speck Collection, University of California at Berkeley. These three sources were very helpful in facilitating my research and in suggesting some useful "leads." I am grateful also for having access to Harriet Martineau material at the University of Birmingham (U.K.), the National Library of Scotland, Harris-Manchester College Library (Oxford), the British Library, and the Kendall Record Office in Cumbria (U.K.).

Finally, I thank my primary source of inspiration, my family—Jacob, Lauren, and Zachary.

And thanks, Dad.

. . .

In memory of my father, Darrell Logan

❖ ❖ ❖

INTRODUCTION

The Theory and Practice of Society in America[1]

From its inception as a British colony in the New World, America represented to many in the Old World exciting opportunities for a fresh start politically and socially. The headiness generated by the New World's seemingly infinite potential was caused as much by peoples' desire for social freedom as by the race between European nations to establish claims to New World wealth and politically strategic territory. The trends best characterizing the discovery of the New World—exploration, emigration, and colonization—continued throughout the Victorian era, when the British Empire was at its greatest height, despite having lost its American colonies a century earlier. But independence always comes with a price, and the institution of slavery that America inherited from its Old World forebears soon came to represent the single most decisive—and divisive—issue on which the success or failure of the Republic rested.

Historically, expansionism has relied on the exploitation and even decimation of native peoples powerless to resist political and military forces technologically superior to their own. Humanity's greatest barbarism is the traffic in human beings in the name of civilization; history's most vivid example was offered by nineteenth-century America, when the "land of the free" was forced to choose between perpetuating or eradicating the slave system. Because of America's self-proclaimed ideals of individual liberty and freedom from tyranny, the world's attention was fixed on the young country, anticipating its choice between human rights and economics, curious to learn what precedent it would set. Throughout this period, when its practices so blatantly conflicted with its stated values, America represented a proving ground for shaping world attitudes toward human rights.

Transatlantic abolitionism generated lively debates, as politicians and social activists on both sides of the Atlantic grappled with the issue that best symbolized the disjunctive relations between capitalism and humanism. The career of British writer Harriet Martineau (1802–1876) is intimately implicated in what she terms America's "reign of terror" and "martyr age," its "Second Revolution." Strong ties united England and America over the slavery issue during the Victorian period, dramatizing a transcontinental "triangle trade" in abolitionism aimed at subverting and eliminating a far more notorious triangle—that involving the trade in human lives.[2]

The abolitionist movement has a history as long as the history of America itself. From 1652, when Rhode Island became the first state to abolish slavery, to 1688, when Pennsylvania Quakers first protested the practice, and from a 1739 slave insurrection in South Carolina to the controversy over the wording of the Constitution in 1787, the question of humans as "real estate" was central to the period's urge to clarify the parameters of American ideology. The issue intensified: by 1793, the first Fugitive Slave Act was passed, and the 1800 census—which revealed a population of one million blacks, most of them slaves—made clear that the "problem" or "question" of slavery in America had more immediately profound and far-reaching effects than any of the country's founders could have imagined.

The year 1808 was a banner year for abolitionism: the United States instituted a ban on further importation of slaves, and Britain officially prohibited slave trading. One inventive solution to the "problem" of blacks in America was presented by the American Colonization Society, organized in 1816 and chartered by Congress to promote the emigration of blacks to Africa. Another landmark was the 1820 Missouri Compromise, which sought to achieve a balance between slavery and anti-slavery interests, although the pretense of "compromise" soon proved woefully inadequate for handling the passions driving the slavery debates. Following a decade of increasing agitation on both sides, William Lloyd Garrison launched his abolitionist newspaper, the *Liberator,* in 1831, the same year as the Nat Turner Insurrection in Southampton, Virginia. By 1834, when Harriet Martineau arrived in America, tension was high, as pro-slavers sought to protect their economic interests while anti-slavers sought emancipation on moral grounds. This distinction between economic and moral interests is essential for understanding Martineau's writing on these issues: as a political economist who was also a positivist, she was motivated not by numbers—although she did employ census figures in her analyses—but by the positive, forward movement of social evolution leading to a moral state worthy of the human race. The prerequisite, of course, is universal emancipation.

History repeatedly illustrates that colonization is rarely an end in itself and is often followed by rebellion against the "mother" country. Rebellion typically manifests itself as a revolution designed either to establish independence for the first time, as in the case of America in 1776, or to reinstate native rule displaced by colonial invasion, as in the case of India nearly two centuries later. America's audacity in bringing the great British Empire to its knees ushered in a period in world history defined by revolution and change. In Europe, the French Revolution in 1789 and Italy's mid-nineteenth-century drive for unification and independence bookended various other political revolutions as well as a different, further-reaching revolution: the Industrial Revolution that marked the end of agrarian societies and the beginning of the modern era.

The cultural upheavals generated by the pervasive revolutionary mood of the period resulted in Britain's controversial Reform Bill of 1832, which initiated a series of legislation designed to benefit the working class and rising middle classes. The Reform Bill's long overdue recognition of the problems suffered by the politically unrepresented reflects both the Romantic period's celebration of the individual and the prevailing mood of democracy, which increased as the century unfolded.[3] Having come of age during this era of revolutions, Harriet Martineau began her literary apprenticeship with a remarkable political acuity, a mind eager for reform, and a vision of social equity that sustained her for her entire career.

Essentially marking the shift from the Romantic to the Victorian era, this historic moment was aptly met with the publication of a work now virtually unknown but then of unprecedented significance: Harriet Martineau's *Illustrations of Political Economy* (1832–1834).[4] The perfect timeliness of Martineau's innovative series, which aimed to bridge the class gap in terms of understanding and correcting the inequities of political and economic systems, propelled her into international fame. For the purposes of this study, of the many reverberations created by the sudden celebrity of this provincial, unknown writer—quaintly referred to by Lord Brougham as "the little, deaf woman from Norwich"—the most important is her love for and affiliation with American society. The *Illustrations,* however inadvertently, established the foundation for what would become one of the primary defining ethics of Martineau's nearly fifty-year career as a writer: the disparity between America's progressive human rights principles and the culture of slavery and racism that directly compromised those principles. *Writings on Slavery and the American Civil War* presents the collected history of Martineau's lifelong relationship with America and her "beloved Americans," told in her own words as a journalist, sociologist, political economist, historian, travel writer, philosopher, and biographer.

Seeking to recuperate following her exhausting composition of the *Illustrations,* Martineau—idiosyncratic in all her choices—opted to forego the more conventional European tour believed to make one a well-rounded, culturally educated individual, choosing instead the far more rigorous and demanding American journey. What made America a dangerous choice at this time has little to do with the long (forty-two days) ocean journey, or with the hazards and inconveniences of travel through the countryside by riverboat, stagecoach, and horseback, or even with the threat of native attacks along the western frontier. The real danger America posed to Martineau was that her arrival in the United States coincided with the vigorous rise of the abolitionist movement that had been gathering momentum for decades, sparking a violent pro-slavery backlash. Martineau might have been small, plain, deaf, and provincial, yet her reputation as an abolitionist sympathizer preceded her visit to America, a reputation based primarily on her compassionate treatment of the plight of black slaves on a West Indian plantation in the 1832 *Illustrations* tale, "Demerara."

Unlike other abolitionist literature, which was typically sentimental,

"Demerara" aims to shock its readers, employing both logic and emotion to do so. This dual approach, which characterizes all Martineau's social problem writing, is outlined in the preface to "Demerara":

> If I had believed . . . that strong feeling impairs the soundness of reasoning, I should assuredly have avoided the subject of the following tale, since SLAVERY is a topic which cannot be approached without emotion. But [since] . . . the most stirring eloquence issues from the calmest logic . . . I have not hesitated to bring calculations to bear on a subject which awakens the drowsiest, and fires the coldest. (1832, vi–vii)

"Demerara" begins with the arrival from England of the plantation owner's young adult children, who are appalled by the demeaning quality of life and pervasive ennui bred by slavery. This culture-shock device aims to educate British readers, whose perception of plantation life was purely imaginary, few of them having witnessed empirically the institution of slavery.[5]

Interestingly, both blacks and whites are shown to be dehumanized by the system, as whites tyrannize their slaves yet live in perpetual fear of retaliatory insurrection, and blacks turn against each other in the struggle to obtain food and to earn freedom (a remote possibility). The shabby conditions of plantation life mirror the economic fallacies of a system that fosters apathy in its workers rather than loyalty and commitment, much less the healthy competitiveness of a free market economy. A final device typical of Martineau highlights the demoralization caused by slavery, specifically the system's affront to two institutions sacred to most Victorians: Christianity and marriage. Even her chapter titles invite readers' comprehension of the immorality of slavery on both counts: "Christianity: Difficult in Demerara," for example, and "No Haste to the Wedding in Demerara," the latter dramatizing that the sexual standards demanded of white women were forbidden to black women, who were prevented from legitimate marriage although used sexually by white men for breeding purposes. Martineau's conclusion asserts two main principles, one ethical—"Man has no right to hold man in property" (141)—and the other economic—"The slave system inflicts an incalculable amount of human suffering, for the sake of making a wholesale waste of labour and capital" (143). She ends, radically, by placing the blame squarely on the government: "Since the slave system is only supported by legislative protection, the legislature is responsible for the misery." In this cryptic tale she offers, significantly, all the elements guiding her subsequent analysis and critique of American society.

Because slavery was outlawed in Britain a year later, in 1833, "Demerara"'s politics caused little stir in a country already committed to eliminating slavery.[6] But the climate in America was far different, emancipation being three decades in the future—three decades of political posturing, economic manipulation, bloody insurrections, and atrocities such as lynching blacks and abolitionist whites. It was in this pre–Civil War atmosphere of heated passions on all sides of the argument that Martineau became a British witness to American society.[7] From shipboard gossip about her probable fate upon landing in 1834 (fearing she might be lynched, the captain tried to dissuade her from going ashore in New York)[8] to the hate mail sent her from America (postage due and heavily weighted with dirt and rocks) after her return two years later, Martineau's insistence on race, gender, and class equality set the tone for a lifetime of controversy evoking responses that ranged from animosity to virtual beatification. It is typical of Harriet Martineau that she regarded the timing of her arrival in America as particularly fortuitous, and not, as the circumstances suggest, especially dangerous. For the second time in her life, then, Martineau's perfect timing, coupled with her unerring fidelity to truth and morality, succeeded in placing her prominently in the public eye. There she remained throughout the next thirty years, an expert to whom many looked for guidance during America's confrontation with its most painful social issue.

Slavery was the primary topic of interest on both sides of the ocean at the time of Martineau's transatlantic journey in 1834. In July, just before her embarkation, an abolitionist meeting attended by blacks and whites in New York City was mobbed by pro-slavers, who continued rioting, looting, and burning for eight days. By the time she landed in America in September, Britain had officially emancipated its slaves. In October, shortly before her arrival in Philadelphia, the city was wracked by pro-slavery riots protesting abolitionist activities. The following letter from American abolitionist Ellis Gray Loring[9] heralds Martineau's arrival, attesting to the influence of "Demerara"'s politics, to its author's celebrity, and to the controversy into which she so willingly entered:

> The apologists for slavery in this country are thoroughly alarmed. . . . The author of "Demerara" is a formidable personage in the Southern States. . . . You are received with the most marked attention, writer as you are of the best anti-slavery tale ever written,—while a New England man who should have written that work would have been . . . indicted and imprisoned. (Chapman 1877, 129)

Loring concludes with a warning to beware of both physical danger and the aggressive censorship likely to impede her observations of America's theory and practice: "Miss Martineau is the world's property, and as she cannot be crushed, she must, if possible, be blinded." Too famous, perhaps, to be lynched, Martineau had to aggressively avert various hosts' tactics to limit her exposure to the realities of slavery. Accordingly, she visited wherever she could obtain admittance, from Congress and the White House to factories, hospitals, schools, prisons, and asylums; and from northern and southern mansions to the fields and hovels inhabited by slaves.

Martineau's travel itinerary (see appendix) began in New York and the mid-Atlantic states and continued through the southern states and up the western frontier (then the Mississippi River)[10] through the northern states.

She originally planned a return visit to the South but, for reasons discussed below, this part of the itinerary was abandoned. Throughout, Martineau remained determined to stay out of American politics and simply to record, as objectively as possible, her empirical observations of American society. In this, she is as instinctual a sociologist as she is a sharp political analyst: her aim to remain a neutral observer accords with the now-accepted sociological practice of noninterference with the culture being studied. In December 1834 Martineau wrote to Ezra Stiles Gannett: "I am heartily glad I came, and quite happy in the conviction that I shall find . . . much that may avail to higher and remoter purposes." She declined to offer her opinions but asserted that her "*impressions* are highly agreeable, and I see no reason, at present, for altering my hope and belief that you will, as a people, work yourselves through some folly and perhaps some tribulation, into a state of yet unattained and private virtue."[11]

Whereas the tendency in the modern era is either to obscure the boundary between personal and political arenas or to privilege one over the other, Martineau argued that grassroots activism—like abolitionism—is superior to political machinery in that it more accurately reflects, in true democratic form, the will of the people. Her perspective reflects a period in history when no women had the vote, no nonwhites had the vote, and no white men beneath a certain class and economic level had the vote: in short, the political realm was controlled by a small minority, although it claimed to act in the interests of the majority. Far from political naivete or ignorance, Martineau—an acknowledged expert on the operations of political economy—presents the abolitionists' approach to social change as vastly superior to a corrupt, self-serving political hegemony. Accordingly, as she writes in *A History of the American Compromises,* the abolitionists are superior because they are "a moral sect, not a political party," and as such stand outside of political institutions. Whereas politics and politicians represent special interest groups and are motivated primarily by economics, abolitionists sacrificed their incomes and reputations to a human rights cause that might drive them into poverty and infamy or even cost them their lives.

Writing to Lord Brougham, Martineau praised the abolitionists' "nonpolitical character," emphasizing the inferiority of politics to activism in social reform movements: "The American Abolitionists have succeeded admirably in giving its highest aspect to their cause,—that of general humanity instead of national politics."[12] This is not to say, however, that she dismisses politics as irrelevant, since most of her writing on slavery in America sublimates sentimentalism to shrewd analyses of political parties, presidential campaigns, and legislation, reflecting her view that political institutions should be held accountable for failing to uphold the will of the people. Nevertheless, this letter anticipates her acute distress when, just before the Civil War, America's great social crisis, the abolition of slavery, became trivialized through party politics, both within, as well as outside of, the abolitionist movement.

Accordingly, despite her professed abolitionism in "Demerara," Martineau was determined to give all sides of the slavery debates a fair hearing, in effect abiding by her assertion that "the most stirring eloquence issues from the calmest logic," whether one is pro- or anti-slavery. As she toured America, she listened to slaveholders and slaves, colonizationists and free blacks, politicians and clergy, humanists and philanthropists, feminists and abolitionists—all having an opinion on the institution of slavery.[13] Throughout she had managed to preserve, at least outwardly, the spirit of objectivity she believed necessary to her credibility as a writer. But events conspired to prevent her anticipated return visit to the South, in the process sealing Martineau's fate as an abolitionist writer and activist and transforming her initial caution into a radicalism that increased with age.

Two Americans were responsible for Martineau's decision to compromise her objectivity by pronouncing publicly her opinions on American slavery: William Lloyd Garrison and Maria Weston Chapman (popularly dubbed "Garrison's lieutenant").[14] While in Lexington, Kentucky, as the guest of Congressman Henry Clay (famed as the "architect" of the Missouri Compromise), who strove with all his political vigor to convince Martineau "in favour of slavery" (Martineau 1983, 2:22), she received a letter from Boston abolitionist Maria Weston Chapman. It was the first contact between the two women—another remarkable instance of timing. Curiously, Martineau initially rejected her future biographer as "rather intrusive, and not a little fanatical," an opinion fueled, no doubt, by her charismatic host, who dismissed Chapman as "one of the 'fanatics.'"[15] Eerily echoing the warning of Ellis Gray Loring, Chapman wrote that she feared Martineau was "blinded and beguiled by the slave-holders," arguing it was time for the British writer to give the abolitionists "a candid hearing." Stung by Chapman's implication, Martineau claimed not to remember the reply she dashed off in anger, other than "I am sure it was repulsive, cold and hard." Such uncharacteristic chilliness was based, she wrote in retrospect, on her ignorance of the true state of American affairs: "I knew nothing of what was before her eyes,—the beginning of the reign of terror in New England on the slave question. . . . I was not aware of the danger of the Colonisation snare. I was, in short, though an English abolitionist, quite unaware of the conditions of abolitionism in America" (1983, 2:22–23). Despite this inauspicious beginning to their relationship, Chapman proved to be "one in a thousand" for her patience and persistence in winning Martineau as a political ally and as a lifelong friend. Indeed, Martineau's contributions to Chapman's abolitionist activities (both in writing and in needlework for the annual Anti-Slavery Bazaars) were aptly met with Chapman's rigorous defense of her controversial friend, a defense that continued well after her death.

Chapman's letter set the stage for Martineau's full profession of abolitionism while touring New England. Contrary to popular expectations, Martineau found that "[i]t was not in the south that I saw or heard any thing to remind me of personal danger: nor yet in the west" (1983, 2:20); rather, it was in the streets of America's oldest, most venerated, and most intellectually cultivated city that she first witnessed lynch law in action: Boston.[16] Like the summer before, when she had first landed in America, the summer of 1835 bore witness to the intensifying conflict. In July, a mob seized and burned abolitionist literature in Charleston, South Carolina, while Georgia passed a law calling for the death sentence for anyone caught with material that could be construed as abolitionist—a category in which Martineau's "Demerara" cleary belonged. Some Georgians had their eye on Garrison as publisher of the *Liberator,* while in South Carolina there was actually a price on his head. In August, a New Hampshire academy was destroyed by white mobs because it enrolled black students, and at a Boston town meeting, prominent citizens vowed aggressively to prevent all abolitionist activities in their city. October was also a busy month, with a Boston pro-slavery riot protesting a speech by British abolitionist George Thompson, with whom Martineau's name was soon linked as a foreign meddler.

But the turning point for Martineau was when William Lloyd Garrison was dragged through the streets of Boston with a noose around his neck, a boiling tar kettle awaiting him—acts perpetrated not by low-class thugs, she noted with surprise, but by well-dressed "gentlemen" (1837, 112–14). She actually saw the crowd from her coach and was told, ludicrously, that these gentlemen were rushing to collect their mail on foreign-post day; she soon after learned that what she had witnessed was a mob bent on lynching Garrison.[17] Rescued from this "gentlemen's" mob by a "stout truckman" who bludgeoned his way through the crowd, Garrison was spared that day (ironically, he was put in jail to protect him from the mob, which continued to roam free and wreak havoc). Garrison remained a devoted radical activist through the entire slavery conflict and beyond (after the war, he was a temperance and female suffrage activist).[18]

For Martineau, this event—the abuse of Garrison with impunity by those whose violence contrasted with his pacifism and whose passions were trivialized by his sacrifices for the abolitionist cause—provided her with the fullest perspective on 1830s America. On 21 October, the Boston Female Anti-Slavery Society (BFASS) met despite these recent events, "well knowing that it might cost them their lives" (Martineau 1983, 2:23). Shocked by the pro-slavers' "subservience to opinion . . . [which] seemed a sort of mania" (2:39), Martineau found the Boston abolitionists' bravery and defiance infectious and, when invited to attend the BFASS meeting of 18 November, she was quick to accept.

Martineau's party arrived safely, despite threatening crowds gathered to harass the abolitionists. Her hosts' assurance that an escape route had been arranged should the crowds grow more aggressive indicates the real danger posed by this threat. During the meeting, Martineau was asked to offer words of encouragement to those whose recent feats had so impressed her. She struggled with her conscience, fearing that if she spoke the truth the many doors open to her in America would be reduced to those of abolitionists only, a serious limitation to this social observer eager to obtain a comprehensive view of American society. Speaking the truth might even involve personal risk; her compatriot George Thompson had barely escaped with his life. "[T]he fury against 'foreign incendiaries' ran high . . . and there was no safety for any one, native or foreign, who did what I was now compelled to do" (Martineau 1983, 2:30). On the other hand, she reasoned, returning to England was an option the American abolitionists did not have; the price they paid on a daily basis far exceeded mere disappointed writing agendas. When the moment of truth arrived—"I felt that I could never be happy again if I refused what was asked of me"—Martineau spoke out, her words dramatically accompanied by the protesters' shouts as they pelted the windows with dirt and mud:

> I will say what I have said through the whole South, in every family where I have been; that I consider Slavery as inconsistent with the law of God, and as incompatible with the course of his Providence. I should certainly say no less at the North than at the South concerning this utter abomination—and I now declare that in your *principles* I fully agree. (2:31)

An anonymous article in the *American Anti-Slavery Almanac for 1841* has this to say about principles: "Abolitionism is—anti-slavery principles ACTED OUT. The only true profession of a creed is, *the practice of it.* . . . [S]how your abolitionism is not mere theory . . . not mere sentimentalism . . . [but] a *principle* dwelling out from your very life-spring" (1841, 15). Measuring principles against practice, interestingly, is the motivation outlined in Martineau's 1833 letter to publisher William Tait—she aims to study "the *principles* of American institutions"—an idea informing both her professional observations and her personal standards. Every conversation, every event, and every experience of Martineau's American tour since—or even before—landing in New York seemed to point to the necessity of her doing precisely that which she had determined not to do, a determination based on the idea that acting on her private principles as a public person constituted interference in, rather than observation of, American society. But the situation in 1830s America demanded more than sterile investigative reporting, especially from one whose professed aim was assessing the disjunction between American theory and practice.

Ironically, then, the BFASS meeting turned the tables on Martineau by confronting her with a challenge—reconciling the differences between her private theory and her public practice and between sympathy for and active promotion of a cause. The process culminating in Martineau's public "confession" seems most appropriately consistent with the rhetoric of martyrdom and apocalypticism typical of abolitionist writing—including, for a time, her own (see *The Martyr Age of the United States*). As a result of this public avowal, she admits, "I was unexpectedly and very reluctantly, but necessarily, implicated in the struggle" (1983, 2:25). Later, her perception of this pivotal moment was more philosophical: "Having thus declared on the safe side of the Atlantic [in "Demerara"], I was bound to act up to my declaration on the unsafe side" (1838c, 1:163).

These experiences generated the writing that is the source for this collection, attesting to the idea that, while in a sense her opportunities for seeing America were curtailed as a result of the BFASS avowal, her career now assumed a depth and breadth of shape, character, and direction that sustained her for the remainder of her long life. Reflecting the religious underpinnings of the abolitionist movement, Martineau must survive baptism by fire—the public confession—before being capable of bearing witness to America's *principles,* a quite different sort of credibility than that required of an objective reporter.

In her *Memorials* of Martineau's life, Maria Weston Chapman claims that, until Martineau's visit,

> [n]o English traveller had before visited the country with so brilliant a prestige. . . . There was not an eminent statesman or man of science, not an active politician or leading partisan, not a devoted philanthropist, not a great jurist, nor university professor, nor merchant-prince, nor noted divine, nor distinguished woman in the whole land who did not to the fullest measure of their natures pay homage to the extraordinary compass of hers. (1877, 98, 105)

Chapman's hyperbole aside, it is true that Martineau's extraordinary fame as the author of *Illustrations of Political Economy* resulted in her celebrity status in America. Her literary accomplishments opened doors for her at every level of American society—socially, institutionally, politically—gratifying her every request to explore the culture. In fairness, her American hosts did not lack an agenda: people from all perspectives in the slavery debates understood the desirability of claiming Martineau's endorsement; for her part, Martineau, who could not help "seeing things through author spectacles" (1983, 2:3), gleaned enough material for several books on her American experiences.[19] But fame, as she well knew, is transitory, and the backlash resulting from her pronouncement at the Boston Female Anti-Slavery Society meeting, once it was exploited in the press throughout the country, earned her social rejection and even death threats. Following the press's "declaration of hostilities," she remarked, "the abuse of me ran through almost every paper in the Union" (1983, 2:35, 46).[20] She did not return to the South as she had originally planned; instead, southern newspapers offered "mock invitations to me to come and see how they would treat foreign incendiaries. They would hang me: they would cut my tongue out, and cast it on a dunghill, and so forth."

Shortly after the BFASS meeting, Ellis Grey Loring wrote to Garrison about the "storm of abuse" Martineau endured as a result of her "independent conduct." Although pressed for an explanation, she insisted none was needed, adding that the only truthful newspaper account of the affair was to be found in the *Liberator.* By highlighting a central tenet of Martineau's social activism—that grassroots activism was superior to politics and that individual and communal efforts outweigh the institutional—Loring pinpoints an idiosyncracy of this energetic and prolific social reformer. On the other hand, he noted, "she goes even further than *some* of us" in her insistence on immediate and complete emancipation without compensation to slaveholders. "Respecting, as I do, Miss M's pronounced judgment and wide information (second only to the truth and sweetness of her moral character,)" concluded Loring, "I am gratified at her adhering to *immediate* emancipation as well in an economical as in a moral point of view."[21]

Garrison wrote to Samuel May:

> I have just read the scandalous attack upon Miss Martineau, in the Daily Advertiser. . . . It will confirm her in the faith, for it is too passionate to convince or alarm a steadfast and enlightened mind like hers. . . . We ought not to be surprised, however, that the attendance of Miss Martineau at the anti-slavery meeting creates a stir among our opponents, for it is as if a thunderbolt had fallen upon their heads. I believe, could they have foreseen this event, to prevent its occurrence they would have permitted even George Thompson to address the ladies without interruption.[22]

The significance of the event is clearly indicated by Garrison's assertion that the influence of the "little, deaf woman from Norwich" far eclipsed even that of the famous George Thompson, although she, like all women of the time, was "politically invisible."[23]

The remainder of Martineau's stay in America was marked by public infamy, private snubs, and the likelihood that vigilante "justice" might triumph over her status as a woman, a foreigner, and a celebrity. In her only concessions to threats, she arranged for the safety of her travel journals and altered her itinerary. She abandoned plans to travel down the Ohio River after learning that some who had "sworn vengeance" aimed to check all steamboats to arrest and prosecute a trumpet-wielding Englishwoman.[24] "Much worse things were contemplated at the slaveholding city of Louisville," she observes cryptically, but the ambiguity is resolved by Loring's grave assertion: "They mean to lynch you" (Martineau 1983, 2:48). Outwardly calm "in the midst of a clamour which left me scarcely any quietness for reflection," she was in fact quite shaken by "the hubbub of censure in which I was living,—enough to confound the soberest senses" (2:43–44).[25]

Interestingly, there were still those (other than the abolitionists) who saw in Martineau a useful ally despite her notoriety. Adding to the political chaos of the period, the "Texas Question" perplexed many as secessionists threatened to diminish the Union while other states sought annexation. Both secession and annexation were predicated on individual states' positions on slavery issues. The Texas territory—fighting against Mexico, seeking annexation to the United States, struggling between pro- and anti-slavery factions—became a focal point for much of the period's social and political agitation. These "adventurers," as Martineau called them, saw in her a link that might win them British support and draw English immigrants to help settle the land as well as promote the annexation bid. To that end, they offered her an estate of several thousand acres, along with "every aid and kindness that could be rendered, if I would bind myself to live for five years in Texas, helping to frame their Constitution, and using my influence to bring over English settlers," an offer she rejected as "most ludicrous" (1983, 2:51–52). Although assured that Texas would remain free of slavery and the slave trade, she was aware of the already existing trade in southern blacks, who were kidnapped from other states and brought to Texas, where their servitude was termed an "apprenticeship": "apprentices for ninety-nine years! I gave my visitors a bit of my mind, in return for their obliging offer." After years of political posturing on all sides, Texas was annexed in 1845, without Martineau's assistance, only to secede with the slave states in 1861.[26]

The remaining months of her tour through the Great Lakes states were marked by constant rumors of lynchings. Anyone even suspected of abolitionist sympathies was subject to harassment and lynching, yet Martineau seemed strangely determined to court disaster by using every opportunity to promote the anti-slavery agenda: "Our Abolitionism could be no secret, ready as we always were to say what we knew and thought" (1983, 2:54). Once having declared herself publicly, she defiantly and somewhat recklessly discounted the threat of being "bullied" by thugs. She records spending an evening with the governor of Michigan, promoting Garrison's cause and securing the governor's promise to protect abolitionists in his state. The woods of the northern states are sublimely beautiful, she asserts, yet they conceal vigilantes ready to kill anyone expressing sympathy for blacks. Even less provocation was needed in cities like Pittsburgh, where Martineau and her companions witnessed, from their lodgings, neighboring houses burned to the ground because they belonged to free blacks.

She also found, particularly in such urban centers as Philadelphia and New York, a concentrated myopia at work in those who denied the seriousness of the American situation in the 1830s, a situation that continued to worsen for several decades before the Civil War settled the slavery question definitively. Contrasting with such complacent tunnel vision is this remarkable admission:

> There were times when I was sorry that I was not the victim of the struggle, instead of Lovejoy, or some other murdered citizen. I was sorry, because my being a British subject would have caused wider and deeper consequences to arise from such a murder than followed the slaughter of native Abolitionists,—despised and disowned by their government for their very Abolitionism. The murder of an English traveller would have settled the business of American Slavery (in its federal sense) more speedily than perhaps any other incident. (1983, 2:56)[27]

Her comments signal an outspokenness that increased proportionately with every instance of social apathy, violence, and censorship she witnessed in America; this orientation became a pattern in her life and work.

Writing of these events twenty years later in the *Autobiography*, Martineau critiques the negative aspects of "literary lionism" (in American parlance, being "Lafayetted") she was famous for guarding against: "I am told that many people who were panic-stricken during that reign of terror are heartily ashamed now of their treatment of me. I should be glad if they were yet more ashamed of the flatteries and worship with which the Americans received and entertained me, *till I went to that meeting*" (2:37; emphasis added). On a lighter note, she quips: "I am pleased to find, however, . . . that in the South I am still reviled, as I was twenty years ago, and held up, in the good company of Mrs. Chapman and Mrs. Stowe, to the abhorrence of the South" (2:40).

It seems most appropriate that, in the process of studying the disjunction between America's theory and practice, Martineau was faced with her own inconsistencies, which, once confronted, infused her writing with both passion and sociological clarity. Her claim that "[t]he accident of my arriving in America in the dawning hour of the great conflict accounts for the strange story I have had to tell about myself" (1983, 2:61) is borne out in her life's work, most of which stems from an idiosyncratic union of empirical observation, intense self-scrutiny, and an appreciation for the significance of the historical moment.[28] While engaged in focusing her "author spectacles" on America, she was amazed to find the lens turned on herself when presented with one of the most pivotal decisions of her life. What preceded and what followed Martineau's American tour is perfectly symbolized by that decisive moment at the BFASS meeting when she chose to act on her principles rather than simply write about them. And that decision, far from resulting in a limited or diminished access to American society, imbued Martineau's experiences with a higher value precisely because she herself became the target of political passions intense enough to threaten her well-being and endanger her life. Exhilarated by that intensity, she found that, both personally and professionally, her own resistance to familial, social, and literary tyranny dovetailed perfectly with the spirit of the American "experiment" manifesting itself throughout the 1830s.[29] Far from becoming limited in her opportunities as a result of the Boston meeting, Martineau instead had the great privilege and good fortune of experiencing America as it truly was in the 1830s: a land of sublime beauty and infinite promise, an ideology rooted in the very finest human values, a culture in anguished conflict with itself, a New World society striving to break away from Old World tyranny.

· · ·

The two books most readily associated with Martineau's American travels are *Society in America* and *Retrospect of Western Travel*. Martineau justifies the seemingly repetitive account of her American tour presented in volume 2 of the *Autobiography* by highlighting an issue she grappled with throughout her career: clarifying the boundaries between her personal and her professional lives. In *Society in America*, she strove to produce the definitive account of

America from an objective, sociological perspective; in contrast, *Retrospect of Western Travel* is the more anecdotal, conventional travelogue—and thus the more subjective of the two. But when writing the *Autobiography* twenty years later, prompted by the urgency of what she believed was imminent death, she was troubled by the rumors, lies, and exaggerations still circulating about her American experiences and determined to set the record straight for posterity.

While admitting she has had plenty to say in print about the American tour, "one subject remains nearly untouched in those books" still needing to be addressed: "I refer to my own personal connexion with the great controversy on negro slavery which was then just beginning to stir the American community" (1983, 2:7). In both earlier accounts, she "said as little as possible" about that "connexion" because "some undeserved suspicion of resentment on my own account might attach to my historical narrative; and because it was truly my object to present an impartial view, and by no means to create an interest in my personal adventures. In this place I feel it right to tell my story" (2:7–8). Now, her enduring concern that subjective bias would compromise her credibility as a writer was overridden by the more pressing possibility that she might die before recording her own near martyrdom while in America. Central to Martineau's keen sense of timing is her understanding of the significance of the historical moment even as it is unfolding and the importance of recording both the event and her place in its context. Twenty years after her American tour, her literary influence continued to be relevant; more importantly, it continued so for another twenty years.

Rather than reprinting the account of her American tour from the *Autobiography,* I have employed it in this introduction in the same spirit in which it was composed: "that it may afford material for an instructive comparison between the state of the cause, (and of American society as determined by it,) in 1835 and 1855," when the *Autobiography* was written (2:57). Of particular interest to this woman journalist who viewed the world "through author spectacles" was the rampant censorship marking those twenty years. Earlier, despite its association with freedom of speech and of the press, American society was crippled by "a rigid censorship . . . [that] expunged . . . every reference to Slavery, and every perilous aspiration after freedom. . . . Every liberty, personal and social, was sacrificed in the attempt to enforce silence on that one sore subject" (2:58). Now, in 1855, "the whole world rings with it. Congress can, in fact, talk about nothing else."

Martineau's concern with censorship also dictated the publishing history of the *Autobiography.* Faced with what she believed was terminal illness, she wrote the autobiography in 1855. Her eagerness to commit the manuscript to print was prompted by a desire to prevent any editing and censoring by meddling family members like her estranged brother, James. In addition, she secured Chapman as her biographer rather than leaving that important decision to her survivors, some of whom were likely to suppress her more controversial idiosyncracies.

These precautions proved to be appropriate, as James aggressively contested various accounts by Martineau (and Chapman) after her death just as he had during her life. Ironically, the *Autobiography* was in storage for over twenty years before its posthumous distribution in 1877, long after the conclusion of America's civil conflict; thus, it lacks Martineau's personal account of the Civil War years. Nonetheless, her professional account of those years, written as the American affairs expert for London's *Daily News* and other periodicals, produced some of the finest work of her career. Because the *Autobiography*'s purpose was as a memoir rather than (during her life, at least) to influence public opinion, as her periodical articles were intended to do, the selections that follow aim to illustrate her public persona as a pro-abolitionist writer on American affairs rather than her personal dramas, fascinating though they are.

To facilitate an understanding of Martineau's role in a gradually unfolding history, the selections are arranged chronologically within genres, beginning with excerpts pertaining to slavery from the American travel journals. Written in response to the popularity of the sociological *Society in America* (1837), the anecdotal *Retrospect of Western Travel* (1838) addresses the travel-memoir audience; it, too, enjoyed great popular success. *The Martyr Age of the United States* (1839), based on Maria Weston Chapman's yearly reports for the Boston Female Anti-Slavery Society and Martineau's own recent experiences in America, compiles a brief history of the abolitionist movement through biographical sketches of prominent activists. These three publications stemmed directly from her only American tour and served as the foundation for her work on American issues over the next three decades. Martineau's affiliations with the "movers and shakers" of American politics and society placed her at the forefront of Anglo-American relations on the slavery issue.[30] In effect, her journey and the publications immediately resulting from it, the celebrity status that earned her introductions to prominent people wherever she went, and her close, long-term relationships with key abolitionists combined to establish a career based on her commitment to the abolition of slavery.

The remaining readings reflect Martineau's richly textured career as "the first and greatest of women journalists" (Arbuckle 1994, xviii). The content, style, and length of journalistic writing proved to be especially suited to Martineau's literary abilities, from her interest in contemporary issues to her reluctance to revise or edit her work (even her most sustained work, she claimed, was dashed off "like a letter"). The amazing array of journals and periodicals for which she wrote attests to the immense quantity and versatility of the work produced by this writer. The periodicals' selections are arranged in two categories. The first is series publications, such as her work as a regular contributor to the *Daily News* over a period of approximately fifteen years (1852–1866), her 1858 series in the *Spectator,* her regular articles in *Once a Week* in 1861–1862, and her column as European correspondent to the *National Anti-Slavery Standard* printed between 1859 and 1862. Also included in this section is a selection from Martineau's contributions to Maria Weston Chapman's annual, the *Liberty Bell*, for which she wrote between 1839 and 1858. The second category features more in-depth, occasional articles about slavery issues written during the greatest intensification of America's civil conflict in such periodicals as *Edinburgh Review, Westminster Review, Household Words,* and *Macmillan's*.

Both categories of selections—"series" and "occasional"—are chosen to illustrate the range of Martineau's expertise on a wide variety of topics. They demonstrate that understanding her role in American abolitionism as a literary liaison between Britain and America is essential for any comprehensive understanding of Anglo-American relations during this crucial period in United States history.

WRITINGS ON SLAVERY

and the

AMERICAN CIVIL WAR

Till now ye have gone on and filled the time

With all licentious measure, making your wills

The scope of justice: till now, as many such

As slept within the shadow of your power,

Have wandered with their traversed arms, and breathed

Their sufferance vainly. Now the time is flush

When crouching marrow, in the bearer strong,

Cries of itself—NO MORE.

—Shakespeare, *Timon of Athens*
  (epigraph to "Demerara")

❖ ❖ ❖

ꟼart One

THE AMERICAN
TRAVEL WRITINGS

Excepting it be Fanny Wright or Harriet Martineau there is not a sane
woman in the world, much less in the United States, who has a desire to
enlarge her sphere of action beyond the limits of her domestic home.[31]

Travel writing was an enormously popular genre throughout the nineteenth century
and seemed especially suited to women writers—as long as their accounts were
anecdotal rather than analytical. As industry and technology broadened European
horizons, America was increasingly the subject of curiosity and fascination, appealing to those jaded by the conventional European tour. What travelers—and the
reading public—sought was something fresh, new, and relatively untried, and
America offered the perfect venue. Although hardly a jaded traveler, Martineau, determined to uproot any inclination in herself toward middle-class complacency fostered by professional success, proposed a radical antidote: an extended tour of the
wild, idealistic New World instead of visiting the monuments to ancient civilization
in the Old. Martineau's 1833 letter to publisher William Tait, written in the midst of
her three series' projects (Illustrations of Political Economy; Poor Laws and Paupers
Illustrated; and Illustrations of Taxation), reveals her awareness of the potential dangers of such a journey—a point apparently in its favor—and, significantly, under-
scores her desire to write the definitive account of the country: "If I am spared to
come back, this country shall know something more than it does of the principles
of American institutions. I am tired of being left floundering among the details
which are all that a Hall or a Trollope can bring away. . . . What I have said seems
presumptuous. But the thing should be done, and I will do it."[32]

     Her careful distinction—principles over descriptive details—proved to be a cru-
cial impetus in the development of the social sciences disciplines as we know them
today. Typically, most of the period's travel writing served to entertain rather than to
instruct. Superficial descriptions of American people, places, and events supplied
the demand for escapist fare and fostered the illusion that armchair traveling was a

viable alternative to the real experience. Ever striving against established boundaries, Martineau aimed for greater depth than that permitted by material descriptions alone, a depth more appropriate to the seriousness of the social issues facing
nineteenth-century America. Her focus on American *principles* illustrates her conviction that description is passive and one-dimensional, contributing little or nothing to cultural understanding, international relations, or social reform.

In contrast, measuring principles against practice initiated a more relevant av-
enue of exploration characteristic of an age in which inquiry based on scientific
method was increasingly becoming the accepted standard of authority. Preferring
to view the world through "author spectacles" rather than rose-colored glasses,
Martineau in her American travel writing heralded the birth of a genre designed
more to instruct than entertain, a "presumption" for which she was as roundly criticized then as she is highly praised now. Distressed by the controversy surrounding
the publication of her American books, Martineau wrote to Charles Sumner, asking
that he bear testimony "to my love for your country, and to my friends in it, and . . .
to my hearty forgiveness of the unkindness with which I am treated there by those
who do not know me. I am deeply indebted to large numbers of your countrymen
and women and for their sakes, I am willing to pardon the injustice which my
name suffers from others."[33]

❖ ❖ ❖

S O C I E T Y   I N   A M E R I C A

1837

I became fully convinced that I could not live for any other purpose than
ascertaining and avowing truth: and the witnessing and being implicated in
the perils and struggles of the abolitionists in the present martyr age of
America has, of course, strengthened my convictions.[34]

A 1938 pamphlet by Walter Brownlow Posey, *Alabama in the 1830s as Recorded
by British Travellers,* presents six travel accounts by British visitors, only one of
which was written by a woman. That woman was Harriet Martineau. Composed a
century after her American tour, Posey's introduction to relevant excerpts from
Society in America highlights the odd spectacle presented by an unmarried
woman traveler who, although her abolitionist sympathies were widely known,
proposed to study empirically the South's "peculiar institution." Attesting to the
unusual degree of celebrity Martineau enjoyed, Posey observes: "During her first
winter in this country she made a tour through the South and was hospitably received despite the fact that she had already written against slavery" (1938, 3). His
comment, relevant in the American South of both the 1830s and the 1930s, highlights Martineau's position as a British writer on American society. Posey's comparative analysis of the period's travel writers notes that "foreign travellers, hur-
riedly passing through a region, usually leave a poor word picture," but he singles
out Martineau's account as distinct from the others on one crucial issue: "Miss
Martineau was the only one of the six travellers who gave especial attention to the
condition of the Negro in slavery. This was her chief interest in Alabama and despite her admiration for many sides of plantation life, she felt that this state of society was 'false and hollow'" (3).

Long before personally witnessing slavery, she vehemently rejected the ownership of humans under any circumstances, an attitude met by an array of pro-slavery
arguments from the religious to the political and economic. Martineau's decidedly
humanistic view of the world reflects her apparently rare capacity to perceive what
seemed invisible to some travelers: the spectacle of one race enslaving another or,
at least, the capacity to apprehend that spectacle as an atrocity. As the depth of the
problem became clear to her over the two years of her tour, the many exciting
promises and challenging problems of American culture seemed reducible to one

primary idea: that the freedoms enjoyed by white America depended on the enslavement of nonwhites and the persecution of free blacks.

Other examples reveal that many travel writers developed a blind spot when it came to accounting for slavery in America. Frances Trollope traveled throughout the southern states but declined to "dilate" on the topic of slavery in her *Domestic Manners of the Americans* (1832). Another Martineau contemporary, French traveler Alexis de Tocqueville, published his travel journals as *Democracy in America* (1835). Although Martineau's assessment of de Tocqueville's perspectives on America avoids direct comparison with an obvious competitor, her own *Society in America*, the analogy is implicit and inevitable. Citing his "logical treatment of an idealised theme" as "too plain" to highlight cultural problems or yield sociological insights, Martineau demonstrates that de Tocqueville shares an essential flaw with other famous travel writers: "He saw few people, *he did not go southwards beyond Washington,* and conversed very little; and the remark was that his book might have been written in his own library, without the trouble of the voyage" (1861b, 293; emphasis added).[35] De Tocqueville's failure to witness the South's "peculiar institution" results in a distorted and partial picture of American democracy. As a philosopher and political sage, de Tocqueville merely theorizes about democracy, making it inevitable that his account of the country pales next to Martineau's innovative sociological approach with its aggressive critiques of American slavery.[36] In her view, the very title of de Tocqueville's book, *Democracy in America,* was a contradiction in terms as long as slavery remained integral to American society.

That Martineau's intended title for *Society in America* was *Theory and Practice of Society in America* reveals the primary quality distinguishing her book from those of her contemporaries. According to sociologist Seymour Lipset, of the various American travel accounts circulating during the 1830s, Martineau's is distinguished as "one of the most important of the early efforts to describe and account for seemingly constant aspects of American society" (1962, 9). In developing a system by which to measure the "science of morals and manners"—her methodology was published as *How to Observe Morals and Manners* (1838)—and employing it in her observations of and writings on America, Martineau effectually put into practice the theories underpinning modern sociology.[37] Lipset equates Martineau's perception of the term "morals" with a value system or ideology. Identifying America's ideology as based on individual freedom, for example, establishes an essential perspective through which to assess the implications of the country's political elections and congressional legislation; the efficacy of such institutions as hospitals, prisons, and schools; and the functioning of social organizations like nuclear families and the feudal plantation structure. In this, notes Lipset, "Martineau was an early precursor of one of the major sociological orientations, an approach that attempts to analyze the effect of values on structure and change" (10).

Contemporary reactions to *Society in America* illustrate two primary points: first, the eagerness with which Martineau's pronouncements on the "American experiment" were anticipated on both sides of the Atlantic and second, the vigor with which her innovative analysis was critically denounced. The book's reception depended, of course, on the degree to which her accounts supported or undermined various agendas. In the midst of a storm of praise and condemnation, Martineau wrote ruefully: "The newspapers and the Boston aristocracy are perfectly frantic against me" (Burchell 1995, 47), while Chapman affirmed that the media's general reaction was even more violent than that following the Boston Female Anti-Slavery Meeting: "The press of the United States was well-nigh unanimous in taunting England with her goodness and greatness, which is called by every abusive name, and took the occasion to brand her personally with every ill epithet which she least deserved. She was a 'hard,' 'cold,' 'pitiless,' 'Amazonian,' 'masculine,' 'incendiary,' 'radical,' 'amalgamationist'" (1877, 183).

But not all American reviewers responded negatively: "It would be doing injustice to the editors at that time in the towns of Plymouth, Lowell, Salem, Lynn, and Haverhill in Massachusetts, and Keene in New Hampshire, besides the anti-slavery journals, not to remember that they paid sensible and able tributes to Harriet Martineau as having 'rightly divided the word of truth'" (Chapman 1877, 183). The predominance of New England cities in this list clearly reflects the centers of abolitionist sympathy arising at the time. The topic was also discussed between private correspondents: "Almost everything has been put out of my head this last week, by Miss Martineau's book," wrote C. Smith to Caroline Weston. "What tirades the Newspaper Editors are making against her. Is it not shameful, abominable? . . . She speaks her mind with great freedom and boldness, and . . . she certainly speaks in the highest terms of our country, our institutions, and our destiny."[38]

Of course, negative responses to *Society in America* are the ones most clearly demonstrating cultural anxieties over the intensifying slavery question. In its thirty-page condemnation of the book, the *American Quarterly Review* predicts rather threateningly that Martineau "will hear from us more than once; for she cuts right and left, sparing none but abolitionists and negroes" (Chapman 1877, 172). Relying on anti-British sentiment, the reviewer demands: "Does a woman of circumscribed education and recluse habits feel herself competent to teach a whole nation,—a nation that did not think the wisest and the greatest in *her* land capable of giving them sound instruction?" (175) After ridiculing at length Martineau's deafness, the *Quarterly* condemns the book as a "precious patchwork" comprised of "agrarianism, abolition, amalgamation, Malthusianism, and radicalism, with a strong dash of egg-and-milk-ism . . . ; humbugism . . . ; conceit and maudlinism" (176). But after thirty pages of this sort of pseudoanalysis, the exhausted reviewer pleads that he is not equal to critiquing "every point on which this Malthusian butterfly—no, dragonfly has alighted" (177).

Another reviewer (quoted in a review by a writer identified only as Boyle), who admits to not having read *Society in America*, demonstrates the sort of journalistic levity Martineau most deprecates:

> Well, Miss Martineau was hailed by our good friends, the ladies, as not only the mere representative of Old England, but the actual Genius of Britannia incarnate. . . . [She is] more arrogant than ever, and has now published a book . . . [containing] many truths, many lies, many compliments, many slanders, much stupidity, more ignorance, and some wisdom. (Quoted in Boyle 1837, 6)

Boyle counters, interestingly, that Martineau's negative reputation results from the "shameful" and "wilfull" misrepresentation of her in the American press. Part of this misrepresentation relies on hackneyed stereotypes designed to discredit Martineau as a spinster: "[T]he only natural situations of woman are those of wife and mother. . . . [U]nless she be a mother, she is neutral. . . . She is simply an accidental visitor . . . , and in this capacity she can have no political character. It is as a mother, therefore, that she is entitled to our consideration—this being her natural situation" (quoted in Boyle 1837, 33). As long as she produces books instead of babies, Martineau challenges the political invisibility expected of all women.

Another review, "by a South Carolinian," employs even more personal insults: "[S]he is too talkative to listen, and too dogmatical to learn" ("*Slavery in America*" 1838, 28), while her physical disability again provides a target for criticism: "She gets nothing from her hearer, for she does not hear him. . . . That she has never listened while in America, is evident from these volumes" (58). Despite its own plea for brevity, the review is eighty pages long, attesting to the anxiety sparked by Martineau's influence. The writer charges Martineau with "pre-existing prejudice" and proceeds to correct the ignorance of this "leveller" by reasserting some of the more notorious arguments in favor of slavery. This includes the "natural" inferiority of blacks, who are cast as whites' divinely appointed burden; slaves must be protected from themselves, argues the writer, because of their innate propensity toward insanity, theft, and promiscuity. Hailing the proliferation of mulattoes as the prototype for a new and superior workforce—rather than, as Martineau charges, proof of white men's sexual exploitation of black women—the writer concludes that slaves, particularly in the American South, are happy and content in their circumstances.

Such "criticisms" of Martineau's work reveal a lack of serious engagement with the deeper ideological issues at work in her critique of American society. Although lacking the transparent pro-slavery bias demonstrated in the American reviews, the London *Times* review is significant for criticizing the very qualities singled out by modern scholars as sociologically innovative. Complaining of the absence of the "simple and vivid description" typical of the period's travel writing by women, the reviewer charges that "the parade of what is called philosophy is indeed one of the most preposterous and burlesque exhibitions that we have long met with." The criticism that the text is "essentially fragmentary" highlights her application of the scientific methodology employed by biologists, astronomers, and geologists—studying individual increments and their interrelationships as a precursor to comprehending the whole—to her study of society. In its dismissal of Martineau's deviation from contemporary norms, the *Times* claims that her "mapping out 'the morals' of America . . . as they ought to figure according to the principles which she imbibed before her visit"—actually, a perfectly sound scientific principle—is the book's worst flaw. Dubbing her a "she apostle," the reviewer demonstrates an ignorance of scientific innovation as well as the sort of sexist and elitist bias that came to define decades of antagonistic exchanges between the *Times* and Harriet Martineau.[39]

Some members of the press came to her defense with vigor, animated by the controversy stirred up by one who spoke her mind so fearlessly. To quote Boyle's spirited defense of Harriet Martineau once more:

Were we to collect all the slanders that have been uttered against Miss M, since her work has been published, the catalogue would make her out, as one of the worst women, that ever remained within the pale of society. . . . [But] she is a lady of unblemished moral reputation—her life has been spent in alleviating the miseries of mankind—she is beloved by all who have been favored by her intercourse—and her literary character is beyond the reach of all the denunciations that our press can utter. (4)

Other contemporary responses include an endorsement by Ralph Waldo Emerson, who preferred *Society in America* to *Retrospect of Western Travel.* Margaret Fuller, however, flatly condemned *Society in America* as "an abolition book" (Martineau 1983, 2:70). British abolitionist George Thompson wrote, "Well done, Harriet!" while Charles Dickens, who read Martineau's American travel books in preparation for his own journey to America in 1842, pronounced them "the best . . . that had been written on America."[40] And Maria Weston Chapman, writing forty years after the publication of *Society in America,* lends her authority as an American and an abolitionist:

[It] is not only by far the best book of travels in that country, in the judgment of the best qualified Americans and Englishmen, but it must needs remain of permanent value as a picture of the United States towards the middle of the nineteenth century. . . . Its fairness, its largeness and accuracy, the truth and beauty of its impartial reprehension of all that was bad and its sympathetic admiration of all that was good, are not only universally acknowledged among intellectual Americans at the present time, but they were so at the very period of publication, when moral opposition was at its hottest. (Chapman 1877, 168–69)

Aware that measuring practices against principles was an innovative and therefore potentially controversial approach likely to disappoint some readers' expectations, Martineau "had little hope of being at first understood by more than a few" (Martineau 1983, 2:103). Yet, if the intensity of these transatlantic responses is any indication, Martineau's *Society in America* illustrates that her rightful position in Victorian culture ranges far beyond the role of a mere "populariser," as she dubbed herself in her self-composed obituary. On the contrary, her acute synthesis of timely issues and topics repeatedly attests to an almost prophetic ability to anticipate currents in public and political thought. Her sense of historical significance was impressive by any standards; she was, in modern parlance, a genuine "mover and shaker" in the period's world events.

. . .

Introduction

. . . In seeking for methods by which I might communicate what I have observed in my travels, without offering any pretension to teach the English, or judge the Americans, two expedients occurred to me; both of which I have adopted. One is, to compare the existing state of society in America with the principles on which it is professedly founded; thus testing Institutions, Morals, and Manners by an indisputable, instead of an arbitrary standard, and securing to myself the same point of view with my readers of both nations. . . . .

The other method by which I propose to lessen my own responsibility, is to enable my readers to judge for themselves, better than I can for them, what my testimony is worth. For this purpose, I offer a brief account of my travels, with dates in full; and a report of the principal means I enjoyed of obtaining a knowledge of the country.

At the close of a long work which I completed in 1834 [*Illustrations of Political Economy*], it was thought desirable that I should travel for two years. I determined to go to the United States, chiefly because I felt a strong curiosity to witness the actual working of republican institutions; and partly because the circumstance of the language being the same as my own is very important to one who, like myself, is too deaf to enjoy anything like an average opportunity of obtaining correct knowledge, where intercourse is carried on in a foreign language. I went with a mind, I believe, as nearly as possible unprejudiced about America, with a strong disposition to admire democratic institutions, but an entire ignorance how far the people of the United States lived up to, or fell below, their own theory. I had read whatever I could lay hold of that had been written about them; but was unable to satisfy myself that, after all, I understood anything whatever of their condition. As to knowledge of them, my mind was nearly a blank: as to opinion of their state, I did not carry the germ of one. [Here follows her itinerary and discussion of how she handled the combined challenges of traveling and deafness.]

It has been frequently mentioned to me that my being a woman was one disadvantage. . . . In this I do not agree. . . . I am sure, I have seen much more of domestic life than could possibly have been exhibited to any gentleman travelling through the country. The nursery, the boudoir, the kitchen, are all excellent schools in which to learn the morals and manners of a people: and, as for public and professional affairs,—those may always gain full information upon such matters, who really feel an interest in them,—be they men or women. No people in the world can be more frank, confiding and affectionate, or more skilful and liberal in communicating information, than I have ever found the Americans to be. I never asked in vain; and I seldom had to ask at all; so carefully were my inquiries anticipated, and my aims so completely understood. I doubt whether a single fact that I wished to learn, or any doctrine that I desired to comprehend, was ever kept from me because I was a woman.

Citizenship of People of Colour

Before I entered New England, while I was ascending the Mississippi, I was told by a Boston gentleman that the people of colour in the New England States were perfectly well-treated; that the children were educated in schools provided for them; and that their fathers freely exercised the franchise. This gentleman certainly believed he was telling me the truth. That he, a busy citizen of Boston, should know no better, is now as striking an exemplification of the state of the case to me as a correct representation of the facts would have been. There are two causes for his mistake. He was not aware that the schools for the coloured children in New England are, unless they escape by their insignificance, shut up, or pulled down, or the schoolhouse wheeled away upon rollers over the frontier of a pious State, which will not endure that its coloured citizens should be educated. He was not aware of a gentleman of colour, and his family, being locked out of their own hired pew in a church, because their white brethren will not worship by their side. But I will not proceed with an enumeration of injuries, too familiar to Americans to excite any feeling but that of weariness; and too disgusting to all others to be endured. The other cause of this gentleman's mistake was, that he did not, from long custom, feel some things to be injuries, which he would call anything but good treatment, if he had to bear them himself. Would he think it good treatment to be forbidden to eat with fellow-citizens; to be assigned to a particular gallery in his church; to be excluded from college, from municipal office, from professions, from scientific and literary associations? If he felt himself excluded from every department of society, but its humiliations and its drudgery, would he declare himself to be "perfectly well treated in Boston?" Not a word more of statement is needed.

A Connecticut judge lately declared on the bench that he believed people of colour were not considered citizens in the laws. He was proved to be wrong. He was actually ignorant of the wording of the acts by which people of colour are termed citizens. Of course, no judge could have forgotten this who had seen them treated as citizens: nor could one of the most eminent statesmen and lawyers in the country have told me that it is still a doubt, in the minds of some high authorities, whether people of colour are citizens. He is as mistaken as the judge. There has been no such doubt since the Connecticut judge was corrected and enlightened. The error of the statesman arose from the same cause; he had never seen the coloured people treated as citizens. "In fact," said he, "these people hold an anomalous situation. They are protected as citizens when the public service requires their security; but not otherwise treated as such." Any comment would weaken this intrepid statement.

The common argument, about the inferiority of the coloured race, bears no relation whatever to this question. They are citizens. They stand, as such, in the law, and in the acknowledgment of every one who knows the law. They are citizens, yet their houses and schools are pulled down, and they can obtain no remedy at law. They are thrust out of offices, and excluded from the most honourable employments, and stripped of all the best benefits of society by fellow-citizens who, once a year, solemnly lay their hands on their hearts, and declare that all men are born free and equal, and that rulers derive their just powers from the consent of the governed.

This system of injury is not wearing out. Lafayette,[41] on his last visit to the United States, expressed his astonishment at the increase of the prejudice against colour. He remembered, he said, how the black soldiers used to mess with the whites in the revolutionary war. The leaders of that war are gone where principles are all,—where prejudices are nothing. If their ghosts could arise, in majestic array, before the American nation, on their great anniversary and hold up before them the mirror of their constitution, in the light of its first principles, where would the people hide themselves from the blasting radiance? They would call upon their holy soil to swallow them up, as unworthy to tread upon it.[42] But not all. It should ever be remembered that America is the country of the best friends the coloured race has ever had. The more truth there is in the assertions of the oppressors of the blacks, the more heroism there is in their friends. The greater the excuse for the pharisees of the community, the more divine is the equity of the redeemers of the coloured race. If it be granted that the coloured race are naturally inferior, naturally depraved, disgusting, cursed,—it must be granted that it is a heavenly charity which descends among them to give such solace as it can to their incomprehensible existence. As long as the excuses of the one party go to enhance the merit of the other, the society is not to be despaired of, even with this poisonous anomaly at its heart.

Happily, however, the coloured race is not cursed by God, as it is by some factions of his children. The less clear-sighted of them are pardonable for so believing. Circumstances, for which no living man is answerable, have generated an erroneous conviction in the feeble mind of man, which sees not beyond the actual and immediate. No remedy could ever have been applied, unless stronger minds than ordinary had been brought into the case. But it so happens, wherever there is an anomaly, giant minds rise up to overthrow it: minds gigantic, not in understanding, but in faith. Wherever they arise, they are the salt of their earth, and its corruption is retrieved. So it is now in America. While the mass of common men and women are despising, and disliking, and fearing, and keeping down the coloured race, blinking the fact that they are citizens, the few of Nature's aristocracy are putting forth a strong hand to lift up this degraded race out of oppression, and their country from the reproach of it. If they were but one or two, trembling and toiling in solitary energy, the world afar would be confident of their success. But they number hundreds and thousands; and if ever they feel a passing doubt of their progress, it is only because they are pressed upon by the meaner multitude. Over the sea, no one doubts of their victory. It is as certain as that the risen sun will reach the meridian. Already are there overflowing colleges, where no distinction of colour is allowed;—overflowing, *because* no distinction of colour is allowed. Already have people of colour crossed the thresholds of many whites, as guests, not as drudges or beggars. Already are they admitted to worship, and to exercise charity, among the whites.

The world has heard and seen enough of the reproach incurred by America, on account of her coloured population. It is now time to look for the fairer side. The crescent streak is brightening towards the full, to wane no more. Already is the world beyond the sea beginning to think of America, less as the country of the double-faced pretender to the name of Liberty, than as the home of the single-hearted, clear-eyed Presence which, under the name of Abolitionism, is majestically passing through the land which is soon to be her throne.

Morals of Economy

. . . What is life in the slave States, in respect of work?

There are two classes, the servile and the imperious, between whom there is a great gulf fixed. The servile class has not even the benefit of hearty toil. No solemn truths sink down into them, to cheer their hearts, stimulate their minds, and nerve their hands. Their wretched lives are passed between an utter debasement of the will, and a conflict of the will with external force.

The other class is in circumstances as unfavourable as the least happy order of persons in the old world. The means of educating children are so meagre . . . that young people begin life under great disadvantages. The vicious fundamental principle of morals in a slave country, that labour is disgraceful, taints the infant mind with a stain which is as fatal in the world of spirits as the negro tinge is at present in the world of society. It made my heart ache to hear the little children unconsciously uttering thoughts with which no true religion, no true philosophy can co-exist. . . . When children at school call everything that pleases them "gentlemanly," and pity all (but slaves) who have to work, and talk of marrying early for an establishment, it is all over with them. A more hopeless state of degradation can hardly be conceived of, however they may ride, and play the harp, and sing Italian, and teach their slaves what they call religion. . . .

There are a few unhappy persons in the slave States, too few, I believe, to be called a class, who strongly exemplify the consequences of such a principle of morals as that work is a disgrace. There are a few, called by the slaves "mean whites"; signifying whites who work with the hands. Where there is a coloured servile class, whose colour has become a disgrace through their servitude, two results are inevitable: that those who have the colour without the servitude, are disgraced among the whites; and those who have the servitude without the colour are as deeply disgraced among the coloured. More intensely than white work-people are looked down upon at Port-au prince, are the "mean whites" despised by the slaves of the Carolinas. They make the most, of course, of the only opportunity they can ever have of doing what they see their superiors do,—despising their fellow-creatures. No inducement would be sufficient to bring honest, independent men into the constant presence of double-distilled hatred and contempt like this; and the general character of the "mean whites" may therefore be anticipated. They are usually men who have no prospect, no chance elsewhere; the lowest of the low.[43]

Morals of Slavery

This title is not written down in a spirit of mockery; though there appears to be a mockery somewhere, when we contrast slavery with the principles and the rule which are the test of all American institutions:—the principles that all men are born free and equal; that rulers derive their just powers from the consent of the governed; and the rule of reciprocal justice. This discrepancy between principles and practice needs no more words. But the institution of slavery exists; and what we have to see is what the morals are of the society which is subject to it.

What social virtues are possible in a society of which injustice is the primary characteristic? in a society which is divided into two classes, the servile and the imperious? . . .

This mercy, indulgence, patience, [of masters toward slaves] was often pleaded to me in defence of the system, or in aggravation of the faults of intractable slaves. The fallacy of this is so gross as not to need exposure anywhere but on the spot. I was heart-sick of being told of the ingratitude of slaves, and weary of explaining that indulgence can never atone for injury: that the extremest pampering, for a life-time, is no equivalent for rights withheld, no reparation for irreparable injustice. What are the greatest possible amounts of finery, sweetmeats, dances, gratuities, and kind words and looks, in exchange for political, social, and domestic existence? for body and spirit? Is it not true that the life is more than meat, and the body than raiment?

This fallacious plea was urged upon me by three different persons, esteemed enlightened and religious, in relation to one case. The case was this. A lady of fortune carried into her husband's establishment, when she married, several slaves, and among them a girl two years younger than herself, who had been brought up under her, and who was employed as her own maid. The little slaves are accustomed to play freely with the children of the family,—a practice which was lauded to me, but which never had any beauty in my eyes, seeing, as I did, the injury to the white children from unrestricted intercourse with the degraded race, and looking forward as I did to the time when they must separate into the servile and imperious.[44] . . . [Here follows a narrative of the slave, who poisoned the childhood "friend," now her mistress; as a result, the lady sold her.]

Little can be said of the purity of manners of the whites of the south; but there is purity. Some few examples of domestic fidelity may be found: few enough, by the confession of residents on the spot; but those individuals who have resisted the contagion of the vice amidst which they dwell are pure. Every man who resides on his plantation may have his harem, and has every inducement of custom, and of pecuniary gain,[45] to tempt him to the common practice. Those who, notwithstanding, keep their homes undefiled may be considered as of incorruptible purity.

Here, alas! ends my catalogue of the virtues which are of possible exercise by slave-holders towards their labourers. The inherent injustice of the system extinguishes all others, and nourishes a whole harvest of false morals towards the rest of society.

The personal oppression of the negroes is the grossest vice which strikes a stranger in the country. It can never be otherwise when human beings are wholly subjected to the will of other human beings, who are under no other external control than the law which forbids killing and maiming;—a law which it is difficult to enforce in individual cases. . . .

There are, as is well known throughout the country, houses in the free States which are open to fugitive slaves, and where they are concealed till the search for them is over. I know some of the secrets of such places; and can mention two cases, among many, of runaways, which show how horrible is the tyranny which the slave system authorises men to inflict on each other. A negro had found his way to one of these friendly houses; and had been so skilfully concealed, that repeated searches by his master, (who had followed for the purpose of recovering him,) and by constables, had been in vain. After three weeks of this seclusion, the negro became weary, and entreated of his host to be permitted to look out of the window. His host strongly advised him to keep quiet, as it was pretty certain that his master had not given him up. When the host had left him, however, the negro came out of his hiding-place, and went to the window. He met the eye of his master, who was looking up from the street. The poor slave was obliged to return to his bondage.

A young negress had escaped in like manner; was in like manner concealed; and was alarmed by constables, under the direction of her master, entering the house in pursuit of her, when she had had reason to believe that the search was over. She flew up stairs to her chamber in the third story, and drove a heavy article of furniture against the door. The constables pushed in, notwithstanding, and the girl leaped from the window into the paved street. Her master looked at her as she lay, declared she would never be good for anything again, and went back into the south. The poor creature, her body bruised, and her limbs fractured, was taken up, and kindly nursed; and she is now maintained in Boston, in her maimed condition, by the charity of some ladies there.

The following story has found its way into the northern States (as few such stories do) from the circumstance that a New Hampshire family are concerned in it. It has excited due horror wherever it is known. . . . [Here follows the story of a man whose attempt to bring his newly orphaned nieces home to New Hampshire from the South was thwarted by their father's creditors. Although white in appearance, the sisters were born to a mulatto woman and thus regarded as black; the uncle's offers to redeem his nieces were rejected.] It was said that there were other purposes for which the girls would bring more than for field or house labour. . . . [T]hey were taken into the New Orleans slave-market. There they were sold, separately, at high prices, for the vilest of purposes: and where each is gone, no one knows. They are, for the present, lost. But they will arise to the light in the day of retribution.

It is a common boast in the south that there is less vice in their cities than in those of the north. This can never, as a matter of fact, have been ascertained; as the proceedings of slave households are, or may be, a secret, and in the north, what licentiousness there is may be detected. But such comparisons are bad. Let any one look at the positive licentiousness of the south, and declare if, in such a state of society, there can be any security for domestic purity and peace. The Quadroon connexions in New Orleans are all but universal, as I was assured on the spot by ladies who cannot be mistaken. The history of such connexions is a melancholy one: but it ought to be made known while there are any who boast of the superior morals of New Orleans, on account of the decent quietness of the streets and theatres.

The Quadroon girls of New Orleans were brought up by their mothers to be what they have been; the mistresses of white gentlemen. The boys are some of them sent to France; some placed on land in the back of the State; and some are sold in the slave-market. They marry women of a somewhat darker colour than their own; the women of their own colour objecting to them, "ils sont si degoutants!" [they are so disgusting!] The girls are highly educated, externally, and are, probably, as beautiful and accomplished a set of women as can be found. Every young man early selects one, and establishes her in one of those pretty and peculiar houses, whole rows of which may be seen in the Ramparts. The connexion now and then lasts for life: usually for several years. In the latter case, when the time comes for the gentleman to take a white wife, the dreadful news reaches his Quadroon partner, either by a letter entitling her to call the house and furniture her own, or by the newspaper which announces his marriage. The Quadroon ladies are rarely or never known to form a second connexion. Many commit suicide: more die broken-hearted. Some men continue the connexion after marriage. Every Quadroon woman believes that her partner will prove an exception to the rule of desertion. Every white lady believes that her husband has been an exception to the rule of seduction.

What security for domestic purity and peace there can be where every man has had two connexions, one of which must be concealed; and two families, whose existence must not be known to each other; where the conjugal relation begins in treachery, and must be carried on with a heavy secret in the husband's breast, no words are needed to explain. If this is the system which is boasted of as a purer than ordinary state of morals, what is to be thought of the ordinary state? It can only be hoped that the boast is an empty one.

There is no occasion to explain the management of the female slaves on estates where the object is to rear as many as possible, like stock, for the southern market: nor to point out the boundless licentiousness caused by the practice: a practice which wrung from the wife of a planter, in the bitterness of her heart, the declaration that a planter's wife was only "the chief slave of the harem." Mr. Madison avowed that the licentiousness of Virginian plantations stopped just short of destruction; and that it was understood that the female slaves were to become mothers at fifteen.[46]

A gentleman of the highest character, a southern planter, observed, in conversation with a friend, that little was known, out of bounds, of the reasons of the new laws by which emancipation was made so difficult as it is. He said that the very general connexion of white gentlemen with their female slaves introduced a mulatto race whose numbers would become dangerous, if the affections of their white parents were permitted to render them free. The liberty of emancipating them was therefore abolished, while that of selling them remained. There are persons who weakly trust to the force of the parental affection for putting an end to slavery, when the amalgamation of the races shall have gone so far as to involve a sufficient number! I actually heard this from the lips of a clergyman in the south. Yet these planters, who sell their own offspring to fill their purses, who have such offspring for the sake of filling their purses, dare to raise the cry of "amalgamation" against the abolitionists of the north, not one of whom has, as far as evidence can show, conceived the idea of mixture of the races. It is from the south, where this mixture is hourly encouraged, that the canting and groundless reproach has come. I met with no candid Southerner who was not full of shame at the monstrous hypocrisy.

It is well known that the most savage violences that are now heard of in the world take place in the southern and western States of America. Burning alive, cutting the heart out, and sticking it on the point of a knife, and other such diabolical deeds, the result of the deepest hatred of which the human heart is capable, are heard of only there. The frequency of such deeds is a matter of dispute, which time will settle.[47] The existence of such deeds is a matter of no dispute. Whether two or twenty such deeds take place in a year, their perpetration testifies to the existence of such hatred as alone could prompt them. There is no doubt in my mind as to the immediate causes of such outrages. They arise out of the licentiousness of manners. The negro is exasperated by being deprived of his wife,—by being sent out of the way that his master may take possession of his home. He stabs his master; or if he cannot fulfil his desire of vengeance, he is a dangerous person, an object of vengeance in return, and destined to some cruel fate. If the negro attempts to retaliate, and defile the master's home, the faggots are set alight about him. Much that is dreadful ensues from the negro being subject to toil and the lash: but I am confident that the licentiousness of the masters is the proximate cause of society in the south and south-west being in such a state that nothing else is to be looked for than its being dissolved into its elements, if man does not soon cease to be called the property of man. This dissolution will never take place through the insurrection of the negroes; but by the natural operation of vice. But the process of demoralisation will be stopped, I have no doubt, before it reaches that point. There is no reason to apprehend serious insurrection; for the negroes are too degraded to act in concert, or to stand firm before the terrible face of the white man. Like all deeply-injured classes of persons, they are desperate and cruel, on occasion, kindly as their nature is; but as a class, they have no courage. The voice of a white, even of a lady, if it were authoritative, would make a whole regiment of rebellious slaves throw down their arms and flee. Poison is the weapon that suits them best: then the knife, in moments of exasperation. They will never take the field, unless led on by free blacks. Desperate as the state of society is, it will be rectified, probably, without bloodshed.[48]

It may be said that it is doing an injustice to cite extreme cases of vice as indications of the state of society. I do not think so, as long as such cases are so common as to strike the observation of a mere passing stranger; to say nothing of their incompatibility with a decent and orderly fulfilment of the social relations. Let us, however, see what is the very best state of things. Let us take the words and deeds of some of the most religious, refined, and amiable members of society. It was this aspect of affairs which grieved me more, if possible, than the stormier one which I have presented. The coarsening and hardening of mind and manners among the best; the blunting of the moral sense among the most conscientious, gave me more pain than the stabbing, poisoning, and burning. A few examples which will need no comment, will suffice.

. . . A southern lady, of fair reputation for refinement and cultivation, told the following story in the hearing of a company, among whom were some friends of mine. She spoke with obvious unconsciousness that she was saying anything remarkable: indeed such unconsciousness was proved by her telling the story at all. She had possessed a very pretty mulatto girl, of whom she declared herself fond. A young man came to stay at her house, and fell in love with the girl. "She came to me," said the lady, "for protection; which I gave her." The young man went away, but after some weeks, returned, saying he was so much in love with the girl that he could not live without her. "I pitied the young man," concluded the lady; "so I sold the girl to him for 1,500 dollars." . . .

Of course, in a society where things like these are said and done by its choicest members, there is a prevalent unconsciousness of the existing wrong. The daily and hourly plea is of good intentions towards the slaves; of innocence under the aspersions of foreigners. They are as sincere in the belief that they are injured as their visitors are cordial in their detestation of the morals of slavery. Such unconsciousness of the milder degrees of impurity and injustice as enables ladies and clergymen of the highest character to speak and act as I have related, is a sufficient evidence of the prevalent grossness of morals.

. . . A woman of strong mind, whose strenuous endeavours to soften the woes of slavery to her own dependents, failed to satisfy her conscience and relieve her human affections, has shaken the blood-slaked dust from her feet, and gone to live where every man can call himself his own: and not only to live, but to work there, and to pledge herself to death, if necessary, for the overthrow of the system which she abhors in proportion to her familiarity with it. Whether we are to call her Genius or Calamity, or by her own honoured name of Angelina Grimke, certain it is that she is rousing into life and energy many women who were unconscious of genius, and unvisited by calamity, but who carry honest and strong human hearts. This lady may ere long be found to have materially checked the "advance towards orientalism."[49]

Of course, the children suffer, perhaps the most fatally of all, under the slave system. What can be expected from little boys who are brought up to consider physical courage the highest attribute of manhood; pride of section and of caste its loftiest grace; the slavery of a part of society essential to the freedom of the rest; justice of less account than generosity; and humiliation in the eyes of men the most intolerable of evils? What is to be expected of little girls who boast of having got a negro flogged for being impertinent to them, and who are surprised at the "ungentlemanly" conduct of a master who maims his slave? Such lessons are not always taught expressly. Sometimes the reverse is expressly taught. But this is what the children in a slave country necessarily learn from what passes around them; just as the plainest girls in a school grow up to think personal beauty the most important of all endowments, in spite of daily assurances that the charms of the mind are all that are worth regarding.

The children of slave countries learn more and worse still. It is nearly impossible to keep them from close intercourse with the slaves, and the attempt is rarely made. The generality of slaves are as gross as the total absence of domestic sanctity might be expected to render them. They do not dream of any reserves with children. The consequences are inevitable. The woes of mothers from this cause are such that, if this "peculiar domestic institution" were confided to their charge, I believe they would accomplish its overthrow with an energy and wisdom that would look more like inspiration than orientalism. Among the incalculable forces in nature is the grief of mothers weeping for the corruption of their children.

. . . Another of my reasons for supposing that the gentry of the south do not know what freedom is, is that many seem unconscious of the state of coercion in which they themselves are living; coercion, not only from the incessant fear of [slave insurrection] . . . ,—a fear which haunts their homes, their business, and their recreations; coercion, not only from their fear, and from their being dependent for their hourly comforts upon the extinguished or estranged will of those whom they have injured; but coercion also from their own laws. The laws against the press are as peremptory as in the most despotic countries of Europe[50]: as may be seen in the small number and size, and poor quality, of the newspapers of the south. I never saw, in the rawest villages of the youngest States, newspapers so empty and poor as those of New Orleans. It is curious that, while the subject of the abolition of slavery in the British colonies was necessarily a very interesting one throughout the southern States, I met with planters who did not know that any compensation had been paid by the British nation to the West India proprietors. The miserable quality of the southern newspapers, and the omission from them of the subjects on which the people most require information, will go far to account for the people's delusions on their own affairs, as compared with those of the rest of the world, and for their boasts of freedom which probably arise from their knowing of none which is superior. They see how much more free they are than their own slaves; but are not generally aware that liberty is where all are free.

. . . Passing over the perils, physical and moral, in which those are involved who live in a society where recklessness of life is treated with leniency, and physical courage stands high in the list of virtues and graces,—perils which abridge a man's liberty of action and of speech in a way which would be felt to be intolerable if the restraint were not adorned by the false name of Honour,—it is only necessary to look at the treatment of the abolitionists by the south, by both legislatures and individuals, to see that no practical understanding of liberty exists there.

Upon a mere vague report, or bare suspicion, persons travelling through the south have been arrested, imprisoned, and, in some cases, flogged or otherwise tortured, on pretence that such persons desired to cause insurrection among the slaves. More than one innocent person has been hanged; and the device of terrorism has been so practised as to deprive the total number of persons who avowedly hold a certain set of opinions, of their constitutional liberty of traversing the whole country. It was declared by some liberal-minded gentlemen of South Carolina, after the publication of Dr. Channing's work on Slavery, that if Dr. Channing were to enter South Carolina, with a bodyguard of 20,000 men, he could not come out alive.[51] I have seen lithographic prints, transmitted in letters to abolitionists, representing the individual to whom the letter was sent hanging on a gallows. I have seen the hand-bills, purporting to be issued by Committees of Vigilance, offering enormous rewards for the heads, or for the ears, of prominent abolitionists.

If it be said that these acts are attributable to the ignorant wrath of individuals only, it may be asked whence arose the Committees of Vigilance, which were last year sitting throughout the south and west, on the watch for any incautious person who might venture near them, with antislavery opinions in his mind? How came it that high official persons sat on these committees? How is it that some governors of southern States made formal application to governors of the northern States to procure the dispersion of anti-slavery societies, the repression of discussion, and the punishment of the promulgators of abolition opinions? How is it that the governor of South Carolina last year recommended the summary execution, without benefit of clergy, of all persons caught within the limits of the State, holding avowed anti-slavery opinions; and that every sentiment of the governor's was endorsed by a select committee of the legislature?

All this proceeds from an ignorance of the first principles of liberty. It cannot be from a mere hypocritical disregard of such principles; for proud men, who boast a peculiar love of liberty and aptitude for it, would not voluntarily make themselves so ridiculous as they appear by these outrageous proceedings. Such blustering is so hopeless, and, if not sincere, so purposeless, that no other supposition is left than that they have lost sight of the fundamental principles of both their federal and State constitutions, and do now actually suppose that their own freedom lies in crushing all opposition to their own will. No pretence of evidence has been offered of any further offence against them than the expression of obnoxious opinions. There is no plea that any of their laws have been violated, except those recently enacted to annihilate freedom of speech and the press: laws which can in no case be binding upon persons out of the limits of the States for which these new laws are made.

The amended constitution of Virginia, of 1830, provides that the legislature shall not pass "any law abridging the freedom of speech or of the press." North and South Carolina and Georgia decree that the freedom of the press shall be preserved inviolate; the press being the grand bulwark of liberty. The constitution of Louisiana declares that "the free communication of thoughts and opinions is one of the invaluable rights of man; and every citizen may freely speak, write, and print, on any subject, being responsible for the abuse of that liberty." The Declaration of Rights of Mississippi declares that "no law shall ever be passed to curtail or restrain the liberty of speech, and of the press." The constitutions of all the slave states contain declarations and provisions like these. How fearfully have the descendants of those who framed them degenerated in their comprehension and practice of liberty, violating both the spirit and the letter of their original Bill of Rights! They are not yet fully aware of this. In the calmer times which are to come, they will perceive it, and look back with amazement upon the period of desperation, when not a voice was heard, even in the legislatures, to plead for human rights; when, for the sake of one doomed institution, they forgot what their fathers had done, fettered their own presses, tied their own hands, robbed their fellow-citizens of their right of free travelling, and did all they could to deprive those same fellow-citizens of liberty and life, for the avowal and promulgation of opinions.

Meantime, it would be but decent to forbear all boasts of superior knowledge and love of freedom.

Here I gladly break off my dark chapter on the Morals of Slavery.

Morals of Commerce

The gravest sin chargeable upon the merchants of the United States is their conduct on the abolition question. This charge is by no means general. There are instances of a manly declaration of opinion on the side of freedom, and also of a spirit of self-sacrifice in the cause, which can hardly be surpassed for nobleness. There are merchants who have thrown up their commerce with the south when there was reason to believe that its gains were wrung from the slave; and there are many who have freely poured out their money, and risked their reputation, in defence of the abolition cause, and of liberty of speech and the press. But the reproach of the persecution of the abolitionists, and of tampering with the fundamental liberties of the people, rests mainly with the merchants of the northern States.

It is worthy of remembrance that the Abolition movement originated from the sordid act of a merchant. While Garrison was at Baltimore, studying the Colonisation scheme, a ship belonging to a merchant of Newburyport, Massachusetts, arrived at Baltimore to take freight for New Orleans. There was some difficulty about the expected cargo. The captain was offered a freight of slaves, wrote to the merchant for leave and received orders to carry these slaves to New Orleans. Garrison poured out, in a libel, (so called,) his indignation against this deed, committed by a man who, as a citizen of Massachusetts, thanks God every Thanksgiving Day that the soil of his State is untrod by the foot of a slave. Garrison was fined and imprisoned; and after his release, was warmly received in New York, where he lectured upon Abolition; from which time, the cause has gained strength so as to have now become unconquerable.[52]

The spirit of this Newburyport merchant has dwelt in too many of the same vocation. The Faneuil Hall meeting was convened chiefly by merchants; and they have been conspicuous in all the mobs. They have kept the clergy dumb: they have overawed the colleges, given their cue to the newspapers, and shown a spirit of contempt and violence, equalling even that of the slave-holders, towards those who, in acting upon their honest convictions, have appeared likely to affect their sources of profit. At Cincinnati, they were chiefly merchants who met to destroy the right of discussion; and passed a resolution directly recommendatory of violence for this purpose. They were merchants who waited in deputation on the editor of the anti-slavery newspaper there, to intimidate him from the use of his constitutional liberty, and who made themselves by these acts answerable for the violences which followed. This was so clear, that they were actually taunted by their slave-holding neighbours, on the other side of the river, with their sordidness in attempting to extinguish the liberties of the republic for the sake of their own pecuniary gains.

The day will come when their eyes will be cleansed from the gold-dust which blinds them. Meanwhile, as long as they continue active against the most precious rights of the community, as long as they may be fairly considered more guilty on this tremendous question of Human Wrongs than even the slave-holders of the south,—more guilty than any class whatever, except the clergy,—let them not boast of their liberality and their benevolence. Generosity loses half its grace when it does not co-exist with justice. Those can ill be esteemed benefactors to the community in one direction, who are unfaithful to their citizenship in another. Till such can be roused from their delusion, and can see their conduct as others see it, the esteem of the world must rest on those of their class who, to the graces of enterprise, liberality, and taste, add the higher merit of intrepid, self-sacrificing fidelity to the cause of Human Rights.

Morals of Economy II

. . . We saw to-day, the common sight of companies of slaves travelling westwards; and the very uncommon one of a party returning into South Carolina. When we overtook such a company proceeding westwards, and asked where they were going, the answer commonly given by the slaves was, "Into Yellibama" [*sic*]. Sometimes these poor creatures were encamped, under the care of the slave-trader, on the banks of a clear stream, to spend a day in washing their clothes. Sometimes they were loitering along the road; the old folks and infants mounted on the top of a wagon-load of luggage; the able-bodied on foot, perhaps silent, perhaps laughing; the prettier of the girls, perhaps with a flower in the hair, and a lover's arm around her shoulder. There were wide differences in the air and gait of these people. It is usual to call the most depressed of them brutish in appearance. In some sense they are so; but I never saw in any brute an expression of countenance so low, so lost, as the most degraded class of negroes. There is some life and intelligence in the countenance of every animal; even in that of "the silly sheep," nothing so dead as the vacant, unheeding look of the depressed slave is to be seen. To-day, there was a spectacle by the roadside, which showed that this has nothing to do with negro nature; though no such proof is needed by those who have seen negroes in favourable circumstances, and know how pleasant an aspect those grotesque features may wear. To-day we passed, in the Creek Territory, an establishment of Indians who sold slaves. Negroes are anxious to be sold to Indians, who give them moderate work, and accommodations as good as their own. Those seen to-day among the Indians, were sleek, intelligent, and cheerful-looking, like the most favoured house-slaves, or free servants of colour, where the prejudice is least strong. . . .

We visited the negro quarter; a part of the estate which filled me with disgust, wherever I went. It is something between a haunt of monkeys and a dwelling-place of human beings. The natural good taste, so remarkable in free negroes, is here extinguished. Their small, dingy, untidy houses, their cribs, the children crouching round the fire, the animal deportment of the grown-up, the brutish chagrins and enjoyments of the old, were all loathsome. There was some relief in seeing the children playing in the sun, and sometimes fowls clucking and strutting round the houses; but otherwise, a walk through a lunatic asylum is far less painful than a visit to the slave quarter of an estate. The children are left, during working hours, in the charge of a woman; and they are bright, brisk, and merry enough, for the season, however slow and stupid they may be destined to become.

❖ ❖ ❖

R E T R O S P E C T   O F
W E S T E R N   T R A V E L

1838

Slavery was a question of humanity, not of country or race; a moral, not a merely political question; a general affair, and not one of city, state, party, or nation. (Martineau 1838, 2:156)

Despite (or perhaps because of) the impressive originality of *Society in America*, its controversial reception was one of the factors compelling Martineau to produce another, more conventional version aimed at a more mainstream audience. But although *Retrospect of Western Travel* serves as a travelogue, it is, if anything, more strident on the topic of slavery than its predecessor. Her laudable concern with assessing the country according to its own standards, rather than to inappropriate European standards, she later regards as a sign of ideological immaturity based on her own "metaphysical" state of mind: "I am well pleased that I wrote the book, though I now see how much better it might have been done if I had not been at the metaphysical period of my life when I had to treat of the most metaphysical constitution and people in the world" (1983, 2:105). She deems the style and content of *Society in America* more appropriate for American than for British readers, yet asserts: "I have never regretted its boldness of speech. I felt a relief in having opened my mind which I would at no time have exchanged for any gain of reputation or fortune."

Responding to comments that *Society in America* was too abstract for a travelogue, Martineau decided to write a "more concrete" account of her New World adventures for British readers eager to experience American culture vicariously. Far from designed to rectify its predecessor, *Retrospect of Western Travel* was prompted as much by the earlier title's lively popularity as by its controversy: "The other book succeeds so well," she wrote, "that the publishers urge me to yield to the desire of the public, and give my personal narrative. There is no reason better than false delicacy for refusing; and so I am doing it."[53] Martineau's preface to *Retrospect* suggests she considered herself finished with America as a literary topic:

> When I finished my late work on Society in America, I had not the most remote idea of writing anything more on the subject of the New World. I have since been strongly so-

licited to communicate more of my personal narrative, and of the lighter characteristics of men, and incidents of travel than it suited my purpose to give in the other work. It has also been represented to me that, as my published book concerns the Americans at least as much as the English, there is room for another which shall supply to the English what the Americans do not want—a picture of the aspect of the country, and of its men and manners. There seems no reason why such a picture should not be appended to an inquiry into the theory and practice of their society; especially as I believe that I have little to tell which will not strengthen the feelings of respect and kindness with which the people of Great Britain are more and more learning to regard the inhabitants of the Western Republic. I have, therefore, willingly acceded to the desire of such of my readers as have requested to be presented with my Retrospect of Western Travel. (1838c)

As this anthology attests, her protest—"I had not the most remote idea of writing anything more on the subject of the New World"—proved to be one of the great ironies of her career. At this point in her life, the abundance of journal material, the public demand for a "lighter" account of her travels and, significantly, what she perceived as an opportunity to promote "feelings of respect and kindness" between England and her estranged colony combine to present Martineau with a compelling case for producing another book on America.

Interestingly, Martineau's rather disparaging comments about *Society in America* in her *Autobiography*—a public document—do not accord with an attitude expressed privately. To her friend Fanny Wedgwood, Martineau wrote this of *Retrospect:* "My book thrives marvellously; I should say gloriously, except that I have not the same interest in it as in the other [*Society*]" (Arbuckle 1983, 11). As for her readers, she admits that those who "read for amusement, and skip the politics, liked my second book best" (Martineau 1983, 2:105–6).[54] As idiosyncratic as any of her writings, *Retrospect* affords lively reading, freed as it is from the objective restraint required by analytical writing. That it relies less on objectivity and methodology gives *Retrospect of Western Travel* a distinctive appeal of its own while demonstrating Martineau's remarkable flexibility as a writer who is at ease in a variety of literary modes. Style notwithstanding, however, the anti-slavery ideology shaping *Society in America* in effect finds even fuller expression in *Retrospect of Western Travel*.

· · ·

First Sight of Slavery

From the day of my entering the States till that of my leaving Philadelphia, I had seen society basking in one bright sunshine of good will. The sweet temper and kindly manners of the Americans are so striking to foreigners, that it is some time before the dazzled stranger perceives that, genuine as is all this good, evils as black as night exist along with it. I had been received with such hearty hospitality everywhere, and had lived among friends so conscientious in their regard for human rights, that though I had heard of abolition, riots, and had observed somewhat of the degradation of the blacks, my mind had not yet been really troubled about the enmity of the races. The time of awakening must come. It began just before I left Philadelphia.

I was calling on a lady whom I had heard speak with strong horror of the abolitionists (with whom I had then no acquaintance); and she turned round upon me with the question whether I would not prevent, if I could, the marriage of a white person with a person of colour. I saw at once the beginning of endless troubles in this inquiry, and was very sorry it had been made: but my determination had been adopted long before, never to evade the great question of colour; never to provoke it; but always to meet it plainly in whatever form it should be presented. I replied that I would never, under any circumstances, try to separate persons who really loved, believing such to be truly those whom God hath joined: but I observed that the case she put was one not likely to happen, as I believed the blacks were no more disposed to marry the whites than the whites to marry the blacks. "You are an amalgamationist!" cried she. I told her that the party term was new to me; but that she must give what name she pleased to the principle I had declared in answer to her question. This lady is an eminent religionist, and denunciations spread rapidly from her. The day before I left Philadelphia, my old shipmate, the Prussian physician, arrived there; and lost no time in calling to tell me, with much agitation, that I must not go a step further south; that he had heard on all hands, within two hours of his arrival, that I was an amalgamationist, and that my having published a story against slavery ["Demerara"] would be fatal to me in the slave States. I did not give much credit to the latter part of this news; and saw plainly that all I had to do was to go straight on. I really desired to see the working of the slave system, and was glad that my having published against its principles divested me altogether of the character of a spy, and gave me an unquestioned liberty to publish the results of what I might observe. In order to see things as they were, it was necessary that people's minds should not be prepossessed by my friends as to my opinions and conduct; and I therefore forbade my Philadelphia friends to publish in the newspapers, as they wished, an antidote to the charges already current against me.[55]

The next day I first set foot in a slave State, arriving in the evening at Baltimore. I dreaded inexpressibly the first sight of a slave, and could not help speculating on the lot of every person of colour I saw from the windows, the first few days. The servants in the house where I was were free blacks.

Before a week was over, I perceived that all that is said in England of the hatred of the whites to the blacks in America is short of the truth. The slanders that I heard of the free blacks were too gross to injure my estimation of any but those who spoke them. In Baltimore the bodies of coloured people exclusively are taken for dissection, "because the whites do not like it, and the coloured people cannot resist." It is wonderful that the bodily structure can be (with the exception of the colouring of the skin) thus assumed to be the pattern of that of the whites; that the exquisite nervous system, the instrument of moral as well as physical pleasures and pains, can be nicely investigated on the ground of its being analogous with that of the whites; that not only the mechanism, but the sensibilities of the degraded race should be argued from to those of the exalted order and that men come from such a study with contempt for these brethren in their countenances, hatred in their hearts, and insult on their tongues. These students are the men who cannot say that the coloured people have not nerves that quiver under moral injury nor a brain that is on fire with insult, nor pulses that throb under oppression. These are the men who should stay the hand of the rash and ignorant possessors of power who crush the being of creatures, like themselves, "fearfully and wonderfully made." But to speak the right word, to hold out the helping hand, these searchers into man have not light nor strength.

. . . A lady from New England, staying in Baltimore, was one day talking over slavery with me, her detestation of it being great, when I told her I dreaded seeing a slave. "You have seen one," said she. "You were waited on by a slave yesterday evening." She told me of a gentleman who let out and lent out his slaves to wait at gentlemen's houses and that the tall handsome mulatto who handed the tea at a party the evening before was one of these. I was glad it was over for once; but I never lost the painful feeling caused to a stranger by intercourse with slaves. No familiarity with them, no mirth and contentment on their part ever soothed the miserable restlessness caused by the presence of a deeply-injured fellow being. No wonder or ridicule on the spot avails anything to the stranger. He suffers, and must suffer from this, deeply and long, as surely as he is human and hates oppression.

The next slave that I saw, knowing that it was a slave, was at Washington, where a little negro child took hold of my gown in the passage of our boarding-house, and entered our drawing-room with me. She shut the door softly, as asking leave to stay. I took up a newspaper. She sat at my feet, and began amusing herself with my shoe-strings. Finding herself not discouraged, she presently begged play by peeping at me above and on each side the newspaper. She was a bright-eyed, merry-hearted child,—confiding, like other children, and dreading no evil, but doomed, hopelessly doomed to ignorance, privation, and moral degradation. When I looked at her, and thought of the fearful disobedience to the first of moral laws, the cowardly treachery, the cruel abuse of power involved in thus dooming to blight a being so helpless, so confiding, and so full of promise, a horror came over me which sickened my very soul. To see slaves is not to be reconciled to slavery.

At Baltimore and Washington again I was warned in various stealthy ways, of perils awaiting me in the South. I had no means of ascertaining the justness of these warnings but by going on; and turning back for such vague reasons was not to be thought of. So I determined to say no word to my companions (who were in no danger), but to see the truth for myself. The threats proved idle, as I suspected they would. Throughout the South I met with very candid and kind treatment.—I mention these warnings partly because they are a fact connected with the state of the country; and partly because it will afterwards appear that the stranger's real danger lies in the north and west, over which the south had, in my case, greatly the advantage in liberality.[56]

Country Life in the South

. . . You are overtaking a long train of negroes going to their work from dinner. They look all over the colour of the soil they are walking on: dusky in clothing, dusky in complexion. An old man, blacker than the rest, is indicated to you as a native African; and you point out a child so light as to make you doubt whether he be a slave. A glance at the long heel settles the matter.[57] You feel that it would be a relief to be assured that this was a troop of monkeys dressed up for sport, rather than that these dull, shuffling animals should be human.

There is something inexpressibly disgusting in the sight of a slave woman in the field. I do not share in the horror of the Americans at the idea of women being employed in out-door labour. It did not particularly gratify me to see the cows always milked by men (where there were no slaves); and the hay and harvest fields would have looked brighter in my eyes if women had been there to share the wholesome and cheerful toil. But a negro woman behind the plough presents a very different object from the English mother with her children in the turnip field, or the Scotch lassie among the reapers. In her pre-eminently ugly costume, the long, scanty, dirty woollen garment, with the shabby large bonnet at the back of her head, the perspiration streaming down her dull face, the heavy tread of the splay foot, the slovenly air with which she guides her plough,—a more hideous object cannot well be conceived; unless it be the same woman at home, in the negro quarter, as the cluster of slave dwellings is called.

. . . Meantime, you attempt to talk with the slaves. You ask how old that very aged man is, or that boy; they will give you no intelligible answer. Slaves never know, or never will tell, their ages; and this is the reason why the census presents such extraordinary reports on this point; declaring a great number to be above a hundred years old. If they have a kind master, they will boast to you of how much he gave for each of them, and what sums he has refused for them. If they have a hard master, they will tell you that they would have more to eat, and be less flogged, but that massa is busy, and has no time to come down, and see that they have enough to eat. Your hostess is well known on this plantation, and her kind face has been recognized from a distance; and already a negro woman has come to her with seven or eight eggs, for which she knows she shall receive a quarter dollar. You follow her to the negro quarter, where you see a tidy woman knitting, while the little children who are left in her charge are basking in the sun, or playing all kinds of antics in the road; little shining, plump, clear-eyed children, whose mirth makes you sad, when you look round upon their parents, and see what these bright creatures are to come to. You enter one of the dwellings, where every thing seems to be of the same dusky hue: the crib against the wall, the walls themselves, and the floor, all look one yellow. More children are crouched round the wood fire, lying almost in the embers. You see a woman pressing up against the wall, like an idiot, with her shoulder turned towards you, and her apron held up to her face. You ask what is the matter with her, and are told that she is shy. You see a woman rolling herself about in a crib, with her head tied up. You ask if she is ill, and are told that she has not a good temper; that she struck at a girl she was jealous of with an axe; and the weapon being taken from her, she threw herself into the well, and was nearly drowned before she was taken out, with her head much hurt.

City Life in the South

. . . I had soon reason to perceive that Charleston deserves its renown for hospitality. . . . In the midst of all this, there was no little watchfulness, among a totally different set of persons, about my proceedings with regard to the negroes. I had not been in the city twenty-four hours before we were amused with ridiculous reports of my championship on behalf of the blacks; and long after I had left the place, reported speeches of mine were in circulation which were remarkably striking to me when I at length heard them. This circumstance shows how irritable the minds of the people are upon this topic. I met with no difficulty, however, among my associates. I made it a rule to allow others to introduce the subject of slavery, knowing that they would not fail to do so, and that I might learn as much from their method of approaching the topic as from any thing they could say upon it. Before half an hour had passed, every man, woman or child I might be conversing with had entered upon the question. As it was likewise a rule with me never to conceal or soften my own opinions, and never to allow myself to be irritated by what I heard, (for it is too serious a subject to indulge frailties with,) the best understanding existed between slaveholders and myself. We never quarrelled; while I believe we never failed to perceive the extent of the difference of opinion and feeling between us. I met with much more cause for admiration in their frankness than reason to complain of illiberality. The following may serve as a specimen of this part of our intercourse:—

The first time I met an eminent Southern gentleman, a defender of slavery, he said to me (within the half hour)—

"I wish you would not be in such a hurry away. I wish you would stay a year in this city. I wish you would stay ten years; and then you would change your opinions."

"What opinions?"

"Your opinions on slavery."

"What do you know of my opinions on slavery?"

"Oh, we know them well enough: we have all read 'Demerara.'"

. . . We had engaged to dine with this gentleman the next week: it was now arranged that our party should go two hours earlier than the other guests, in order to hear this gentleman's exposition of slavery. He was well prepared; and his statement of facts and reasons was clear, ready, and enter-taining. The fault was in the narrowness of his premises; for his whole argu-ment was grounded on the supposition that human rights consist in suffi-cient subsistence in return for labour. Before he began I told him that I fully understood his wish not to argue the question, and that I came to hear his statement, not to controvert it; but that I must warn him not to take my si-lence for assent. Upon this understanding we proceeded; with some little ir-ritability on his part when I asked questions, but with no danger of any quarrel. I never found the slightest difficulty in establishing a similar clear understanding with every slave-holder I met. In the drawing-room of the boarding-house at Richmond, Virginia, three gentlemen, two of whom were entire strangers, attacked me in the presence of a pretty large company, one afternoon. This was a direct challenge, which I did not think fit to decline, and we had it all out. They were irritable at first, but softened as they went on; and when, at the end of three hours, we had exhausted the subject, we were better friends than when we began.

. . . The houses which we visited in returning calls were generally hand-some; with capacious piazzas, rich plants and bouquets, and good furniture. The political bias of the inhabitant was often discoverable from the books on the table, or the prints and casts on the walls. In no society in the world could the division of parties be more distinct, and their alienation more threatening than in Charleston, at the time I was there. The Union gentlemen and ladies were dispirited and timid. They asked one another's opinion whether there was not some mysterious stir among the Nullifiers; whether they were not concerting measures for a new defiance of the General Government. This anx-ious watchfulness contrasted strangely with the arrogant bearing of the lead-ing Nullifiers.[58] During my stay, Mr. Calhoun and his family arrived from Congress; and there was something very striking in the welcome he received, like that of a chief returned to the bosom of his clan. He stalked about like a monarch of the little domain; and there was certainly an air of mysterious un-derstanding between him and his followers; whether there was really any great secret under it or not.[59] One lady who had contributed ample amounts of money to the Nullification funds, and a catechism to Nullification lore, amused while she grieved me by the strength of her political feelings. While calling on her, one morning, the conversation turned on prints, and I asked an explanation of a strange-looking one which hung opposite my eye; the portrait of a gentleman, the top of the head and the dress visible, but the face obliterated or covered over. She was only too ready to explain. It was a por-trait of President Jackson, which she had hung up in days when he enjoyed her favour.[60] Since Nullification she had covered over the face, to show how she hated him. A stranger hardly knows what to think of a cause whose lead-ers will flatter and cherish the perpetrators of a piece of petty spite like this: yet this lady is treated as if she were a main pillar of the Nullification party.

. . . We visited the arsenal twice; the second time with Mr. Calhoun and Governor Hayne, when we saw the arms and ammunition, which were not visible the first time, because "the key was not on the premises"; a token that no invasion was immediately expected. There were two bombs brought in by Governor Hayne; and all the warlike apparatus, which was made ready during the Nullification struggle.[61] It is difficult to believe that Mr. Calhoun seriously meant to go to war with such means as his impoverished State could furnish; but there is no doubt that he did intend it. The ladies were very animated in their accounts of their State Rights Ball, held in the area of the arsenal; and of their subscriptions of jewels to the war fund. They were certainly in earnest.

The soldiers were paraded in our presence, some eleven or twelve recruits, I believe: and then Mr. Calhoun first, and Governor Hayne afterwards, uncovered and addressed them with as much gravity and effusion of patriotic sentiment, as if we had been standing on the verge of a battle-field. Some of our party were of Union politics; and they looked exceedingly arch during the speechifying. It will be too sad if this child's play should be turned into bloodshed after all, for the gratification of any man's restless ambition, or in the guilty hope of protracting slavery under the reprobation of the whole of society, except a small band of mercenaries.

. . . I was told much of the Poor House, rather in a tone of boasting; and I was anxious to see what a Poor-House could be in a region where all labourers are private property, and where pauperism would therefore seem to be obviated. Infirmity, vice, and orphanhood keep up a small amount of pauperism, even here; reducing capitalists to a state of dependence.

. . . The Orphan House has been established about forty years; and it contained, at the time of my visit, 200 children. As none but whites are admitted, it is found to be no encouragement to vice to admit all destitute children, whether orphans or not: for the licentiousness of the South takes the women of colour for its victims.

. . . Charleston is the place in which to see those contrasting scenes of human life brought under the eye which moralists gather together for the purpose of impressing the imagination. The stranger has but to pass from street to street, to live from hour to hour in this city, to witness in conjunction the extremes between which there is everywhere else a wide interval. The sights of one morning I should remember if every other particular of my travels were forgotten. I was driven round the city by a friend whose conversation was delightful all the way. Though I did not agree in all his views of society, the thoughtfulness of his mind and the benevolence of his exertions betokened a healthy state of feeling, and gave value to all he said. He had been a friend of the lamented Grimke; and he showed me the house where Grimke lived and died, and told me much of him,—of the nobleness of his character, the extent of his attainments, and how, dying at fifty-four, he had lived by industry a long life. My mind was full of the contemplation of the heights which human beings are destined to reach, when I was plunged into a new scene,—one which it was my own conscientious choice to visit, but for which the preceding conversation had ill-prepared me. I went into the slave-market,—a place which the traveller ought not to avoid, to spare his feelings. There was a table, on which stood two auctioneers; one with a hammer, the other to exhibit "the article," and count the bids. The slaves for sale were some of them in groups below; and some in a long row behind the auctioneers. The sale of a man was just concluding when we entered the market. A woman, with two children, one at the breast, and another holding by her apron, composed the next lot. The restless, jocose zeal of the auction-eer who counted the bids was the most infernal sight I ever beheld. The woman was a mulatto; she was neatly dressed, with a clean apron, and a yel-low head-handkerchief. The elder child clung to her. She hung her head low, lower, and still lower on her breast, yet turning her eyes incessantly from side to side, with an intensity of expectation which showed that she had not reached the last stage of despair. I should have thought that her agony of shame and dread would have silenced the tongue of every spectator; but it was not so. A lady chose this moment to turn to me and say, with a cheerful air of complacency;—"You know my theory,—that the one race must be sub-servient to the other. I do not care which: and if the blacks should ever have the upper hand, I should not mind standing on that table, and being sold with two of my children." Who could help saying within himself, "Would you were! so that that mother were released!" Who could help seeing in vi-sion the blacks driving the whites into the field, and preaching from the pul-pits of Christian churches the doctrines now given out there, that God has respect of persons, that men are to hold each other as property, instead of re-garding each other as brethren; and that the right interpretation of the golden rule by the slaveholder is, "Do unto your slaves as you would wish your master to do unto you, if you were a slave?" A little boy of eight or nine years old, apparently, was next put up alone. There was no bearing the child's look of helplessness and shame. It seemed like an outrage to be among the starers from whom he shrunk; and we went away before he was disposed of.

We next entered a number of fine houses where we were presented with flowers, and entertained with lively talk about the small affairs of gay society which to little minds are great. To me every laugh had lost its gaiety, every courtesy had lost its grace, all intercourse had lost its innocence. It was a re-lief to think of Grimke in his grave, escaped from the hell in which we were pent. If there be a scene which might stagger the faith of the spirit of Chris-tianity itself,—if there be an experience which might overthrow its serenity, it is the transition from the slave-market to the abodes of the slave-masters, bright with sunshine, and gay with flowers, with courtesies and mirth.

Restless Slaves

The traveller in America hears, on every hand, of the fondness of slaves for slavery. If he points to the little picture of a runaway prefixed to adver-tisements of fugitives, and repeated down whole columns of the first newspaper that comes to hand, he is met with anecdotes of slaves who have been offered their freedom, and prefer remaining in bondage. Both aspects of the question are true; and yet more may be said on both sides. The traveller finds, as he proceeds, that suicides are very frequent among slaves; and that there is a race of Africans who will not endure bondage at all, and who, when smuggled from Africa into Louisiana, are avoided in the market by purchasers, though they have great bodily strength and comeliness. When one of this race is accidentally purchased and taken home, he is generally missed, before twenty-four hours are over, and found hanging behind a door, or drowned in the nearest pond. The Cuba slave-holders have volumes of stories to tell of this race, proving their incapacity for slavery. On the other hand, the traveller may meet with a few negroes who have returned into slave-land from a state of freedom, and besought their masters to take them back.

These seeming contradictions admit of an easy explanation. Slaves are more or less degraded by slavery in proportion to their original strength of character, or educational discipline of mind. The most degraded are satisfied, the least degraded are dissatisfied with slavery. The lowest order prefer release from duties and cares to the enjoyment of rights and the possession of themselves; and the highest order have a directly opposite taste. The mistake lies in not perceiving that slavery is emphatically condemned by the conduct of both.

. . . I do not remember ever hearing of the return of a slave who, having long nourished the idea and purpose of liberty, had absconded with danger and difficulty. The prosecution of such a purpose argues a strength of mind worthy of freedom.

The stories on this side of the question are as various as the characters and fortunes of the heroes of them. Many facts of this nature became known to me during my travels, most of which cannot be published, for fear of involving in difficulty either the escaped heroes, or those who assisted them in regaining their liberty. But a few may be safely related, which will show, as well as any greater number, the kind of restlessness which is the torment of the lives of "persons held to labour,"—the constitutional description of the slave-class of the constituents of government.

Slavery is nowhere more hopeless and helpless than in Alabama. The richness of the soil and the paucity of inhabitants make the labourer a most valuable possession; while his distance from any free State,—the extent of country overspread with enemies which the fugitive has to traverse,—makes the attempt to escape desperate. All coloured persons travelling in the Slave States without a pass,—a certificate of freedom or of leave,—are liable to be arrested and advertised, and if unclaimed at the end of a certain time, sold in the market. Yet slaves do continue to escape from the farthest corners of Alabama or Mississippi. Two slaves in Alabama, who had from their early manhood cherished the idea of freedom, planned their escape in concert, and laboured for many years at their scheme. They were allowed the profits of their labour at over-hours; and by strenuous toil and self-denial, saved and hid a large sum of money. Last year, they found they had enough, and that the time was come for the execution of their purpose. They engaged the services of a "mean-white,". . . to personate a gentleman; bought him a suit of good clothes, a portmanteau, a carriage and horses, and proper costume for themselves. One night the three went off in style, as master, coachman and footman, and travelled rapidly through the whole country, without the slightest hindrance, to Buffalo. There the slaves sold their carriage, horses, and finery, paid off their white man, and escaped into Canada, where they now are in safety.

They found in Canada a society of their own colour prepared to welcome and aid them. In Upper Canada there are upwards of 10,000 people of colour, chiefly fugitive slaves, who prosper in the country which they have chosen for a refuge. Scarcely an instance is known of any of them having received alms, and they are as respectable for their intelligence as for their morals. One peculiarity in them is the extravagance of their loyalty. They exert themselves vehemently in defence of all the acts of the Executive, whatever they may be. The reason for this is obvious:—they exceedingly dread the barest mention of the annexation of Canada to the United States.

It is astonishing that, in the face of facts of daily occurrence, like that of the escape of these men, it can be pleaded in behalf of slavery that negroes cannot take care of themselves, and that they prefer being held as property. . . . [Here follow two anecdotes: one about a house servant who preferred freedom to the material comforts of her situation and another about a slave who sued unsuccessfully for his freedom.][62]

A woman once lived in Massachusetts, whose name ought to be preserved in all histories of the State, as one of its honours, though she was a slave. Some anecdotes of her were related in a Lyceum lecture delivered at Stockbridge in 1831. Others were told me by the Sedgwicks, who had the honour of knowing her best, by means of rendering her the greatest services.[63] Mum Bett, whose real name was Elizabeth Freeman, was born, it is supposed, about 1742. Her parents were native Africans, and she was a slave for about thirty years. At an early age she was purchased, with her sister, from the family into which she was born, in the State of New York, by Colonel Ashley, of Sheffield, Massachusetts. The lady of the mansion, in a fit of passion, one day struck at Mum Bett's sister with a heated kitchen shovel. Mum Bett interposed her arm, and received the blow, the scar of which she bore to the day of her death. "She resented the insult and outrage as a white person would have done," leaving the house, and refusing to return. Colonel Ashley appealed to the law for the recovery of his slave. Mum Bett called on Mr. Sedgwick, and asked him if she could not claim her liberty under the law. He inquired what could put such an idea into her head. She replied that the "Bill o' Rights" said that all were born free and equal, and that as she was not a dumb beast, she was certainly one of the nation. When afterwards asked how she learned the doctrine and facts on which she proceeded, she replied, "By keepin' still and mindin' things." It was a favourite doctrine of hers, that people might learn by keeping still and minding things. But what did she mean, she was asked, by keeping still and minding things? Why, for instance, when she was waiting at table, she heard gentlemen talking over the Bill of Rights and the new constitution of Massachusetts; and in all they said she never heard but that all people were born free and equal, and she thought long about it, and resolved she would try whether she did not come in among them.

Mr. Sedgwick undertook her cause, which was tried at Great Barrington. Mum Bett obtained her freedom, and compensation for her services from twenty-one years of age. "What shall I do with all this money of yours?" said Mr. Sedgwick. "Fee the lawyers handsomely,—pay 'em well," said she, "and keep the rest till I want it." She was offered every inducement to return to Colonel Ashley's; but she recoiled from all that reminded her of slavery. She begged the Sedgwicks to take her into their family, which they did; and with them she spent twenty years of great comfort. Her example was followed by many slaves; and from the day of her emancipation, in 1772, more and more claimants were decreed free under the Bill of Rights, till slavery was abolished in Massachusetts. . . .

The energies of slaves sometimes take a direction which their masters contrive to render profitable,—when they take to religion as a pursuit. The universal, unquenchable reverence for religion in the human mind is taken advantage of, when the imagination of the slave has been turned into the channel of superstition. It is a fact, that in the newspapers of New Orleans may be seen an advertisement, now and then, of a lot of "pious negroes." Such "pious negroes" are convenient on a plantation where the treatment is not particularly mild; as they consider non-resistance a Christian duty, and are able to inspire a wonderful degree of patience into their fellow-sufferers.

The vigour which negroes show when their destiny is fairly placed in their own hands, is an answer to all arguments about their helplessness drawn from their dullness in a state of bondage. . . .

The finest harvest field of romance perhaps in the world is the frontier between the United States and Canada. The vowed student of human na-ture could not do better than take up his abode there, and hear what fugi-tives and their friends have to tell. There have been no exhibitions of the forces of human character in any political revolution, or religious reforma-tion, more wonderful and more interesting than may almost daily be wit-nessed there. The impression on even careless minds on the spot is very strong. I remember observing to a friend in the ferry-boat, when we were crossing the Niagara, from Lewiston to Queenston, that it seemed very ab-surd, on looking at the opposite banks of the river, to think that, while the one belonged to the people who lived on it, the other was called the prop-erty of a nation three thousand miles off,—the shores looking so much alike as they do. My friend replied, with a smile, "Runaway slaves see a great dif-ference." "That they do!" cried the ferryman in a tone of the deepest earnestness. He said that the leap ashore of an escaped slave is a sight unlike any other that can be seen.

New Orleans

. . . I could never get out of the way of the horrors of slavery in this region. Under one form or another, they met me in every house, in every street,—everywhere but in the intelligence pages of newspapers, where I might read on in perfect security of exemption from the subject. In the advertizing columns, there were offers of reward for runaways, restored dead or alive; and notices of the capture of a fugitive with so many brands on his limbs and shoulders, and so many scars on his back. But from the other half of the newspaper, the existence of slavery could be discovered only by inference. What I saw elsewhere was, however, dreadful enough. In one house, the girl who waited on me with singular officiousness, was so white, with blue eyes and light hair, that it never occurred to me that she could be a slave. Her mistress told me afterwards that this girl of fourteen was such a depraved hussy that she must be sold. I exclaimed involuntarily, but was referred to the long heel, in proof of the child's being of negro extraction. She had the long heel, sure enough. Her mistress told me that it is very wrong to plead in behalf of slavery; that families are rarely separated. . . .

About the same time, the cashier of a bank in New Orleans sent one of his slaves out of the way, in order to be undisturbed in the violence which he meditated against the negro's attached wife. The negro understood the case, but dared not refuse to go where he was bid. He returned unexpectedly soon, however; found his home occupied, and stabbed the defiler of it. The cashier was the stronger man; and in spite of his wound, he so maltreated the negro that he expired on the barrow on which he was being conveyed to gaol. Nothing ensued on account of this affair; though, when the cashier was some time after found to be a defaulter, he absconded.

I would fain know what has become of a mulatto child in whom I became much interested at New Orleans. Ailsie was eight years old, perfectly beautiful, and one of the most promising children I ever saw. She was quick, obedient, and affectionate, to a touching degree. She had a kind master and mistress. Her mistress's health was delicate; and the child would watch her countenance wistfully in the constant hope of saving her trouble. She would look very grave if the lady went up stairs with a languid step, take hold of her gown, and timidly ask, "What, an't ye well?" I used to observe her helping to dress her mistress's hair, her little hands trembling with eagerness, her eye following every glance of the eye which ever looked tenderly upon her. Her master declared he did not know what to make of the child, she looked so scared, and trembled so if she was spoken to: and she was indeed the most sensitive of children. As she stood at the corner of the dinner-table to fan away the flies, she was a picture from which it was difficult to turn away. Her little yellow head-dress suited well with her clear brown complexion and large soft black eyes: nothing that she could at all understand of the conversation escaped her, while she never intermitted her waving of the huge brush of peacocks' feathers. Her face was then composed in its intelligence, for she stood by her mistress's elbow; a station where she seemed to think no harm could befall her. Alas! she has lost her kind mistress. Amidst the many sad thoughts which thronged into my mind when I heard of the death of this lady, one of the wisest and best of American women, I own that some of my earliest regrets were for little Ailsie; and when I think of her sensibility, her beauty, and the dreadful circumstances of her parentage, as told me by her mistress, I am almost in despair about her future lot; for what can her master, with all his goodness, do for the forlorn little creature's protection? None but a virtuous mistress can fully protect a female slave,—and that too seldom.

Ailsie was born on an estate in Tennessee. Her father is a white gentleman, not belonging to the family; her mother the family cook. The cook's black husband cherished such a deadly hatred against this poor child, as to be for ever threatening her life; and she was thought to be in such danger from his axe, that she was sent down the river to be taken into the family where I saw her. What a cruel world,—what a hard human life, must Ailsie find that she is born into![64]

. . . Abroad, all was, as in every other American city, hospitality and gaiety. I had rather dreaded the visit to New Orleans, and went more from a sense of duty than from inclination. . . . But my strongest impression of New Orleans is, that while it affords an instructive study, and yields some enjoyment to a stranger, it is the last place in which men are gathered together where one who prizes his Humanity would wish to live.

Signs of the Times in Massachusetts

. . . [Martineau discusses the abolitionists' successful challenge to Boston's efforts to forbid right of assembly. The next issue facing the abolitionists was the South's insistence that preservation of the Union depended on the arrest and silencing of anti-slavery advocates.] Two months before, the attorney-general of the state had advocated in council the expected demand of the South, that abolitionists should be delivered up to the Slave States for trial and punishment under Southern laws. This fact is credible to those, and, perhaps, to those only, who have seen the pamphlet in reply to Dr. Channing's work on Slavery attributed to this gentleman. The South was not long in making the demand. Letters arrived from the governors of Southern States to the new governor of Massachusetts, demanding the passing of laws against abolitionism in all its forms. The governor, as was his business, laid these letters before the legislature of his state. This was the only thing he could do on this occasion. Just before, at his entrance upon his office, he had aimed his blow at the abolitionists in the following passages of his address. The same delusion (if it be mere delusion) is visible here that is shared by all persons in power, who cannot deny that an evil exists, but have not courage to remove it; a vague hope that "fate, or Providence, or something," will do the work which men are created to perform; men of principle and men of peace, like the abolitionists; victims, not perpetrators of violence. "As the genius of our institutions and the character of our people are entirely repugnant to laws impairing the liberty of speech and of the press, even for the sake of repressing its abuses, the patriotism of all classes of citizens must be invoked to abstain from a discussion which, by exasperating the master, can have no other effect than to render more oppressive the condition of the slave; and which, if not abandoned, there is great reason to fear will prove the rock on which the Union will split. . . . A conciliatory forbearance," he proceeds to say, "would leave this whole painful subject where the Constitution leaves it, with the states where it exists, and in the hands of an all-wise Providence, who in his own good time is able to cause it to disappear, like the slavery of the ancient world, under the gradual operation of the gentle spirit of Christianity." The time is at hand. The "gradual operation of the gentle spirit of Christianity" had already educated the minds and hearts of the abolitionists for the work they are doing, but which the governor would fain have put off. It thus appears that they had the governor and attorney-general of the state against them, and the wealth, learning, and power of their city. . . . [Here follows an account of the confrontation between legislators and abolitionists; the meeting is dismissed because of spectators' rowdiness and reconvened the next day.]

The hall was crowded and shouts of applause broke forth as the pleaders demolished an accusation or successfully rebutted the insolence of the chairman. Dr. Follen was again stopped, as he was showing that mobs had been the invariable consequence of censures of abolitionism passed by public meetings in the absence of gag-laws.[65] He was desired to hold his tongue, or to be respectful to the committee; to which he replied, in his gentlest and most musical voice, "Am I, then, to understand that, in speaking ill of mobs, I am disrespectful to the committee?" The chairman looked foolish enough during the applauses which followed this question. Dr. Follen fought his ground inch by inch, and got out all he had to say. The conduct of the chairman became at last so insufferable, that several spectators attempted a remonstrance. A merchant was silenced; a physician was listened to, his speech being seasoned with wit so irresistible as to put all parties into good-humour.

The loudly-expressed opinion of the spectators as they dispersed was, that the chairman had ruined his political career, and, probably, filled the chair of a committee of the legislature for the last time. The result of the affair was that the report of the committee "spoke disrespectfully" of the exertions of the abolitionists, but rejected the suggestion of penal laws being passed to control their operations. The letters from the South therefore remained unanswered.[66]

. . . These were a few of the signs of the times in Massachusetts when I was there. They proved that, while the aristocracy of the great cities were not to be trusted to maintain the great principles on which their society was based, the body of the people were sound.

❖ ❖ ❖

THREE LETTERS
ON AMERICA

Harriet Martineau was a prolific letter writer with an amazingly broad range of correspondents throughout America and England. From personal correspondence to professional and business letters, and from letters to the editor to nonfiction written in epistolary form, Martineau employed this genre frequently throughout her career. The following two letters to the *Spectator,* written shortly after her return from America, indicate her commitment to promoting the American abolitionist cause in Britain through her role as an influential writer and public figure. The letters convey the spirit of excitement marking her return—a homecoming characterized by her desire to return to the United States and to labor in the abolitionist trenches, side by side with Garrison, Chapman, and Abby Kelley.[67] Such was not to be, as health and family matters absorbed her attention for some years to come. Her role in the abolitionist struggle was to be as a journalist, which many of those actually in the "trenches" viewed as the most effective use of her gifts. The third letter, to Abby Kelley, acknowledges her membership in the Massachusetts Anti-Slavery Society. The society honored Martineau posthumously, in 1884, with a statue commissioned of American sculptor Anne Whitney.

. . .

Harriet Martineau to the *Spectator*
14 October 1837

Sir—I have more than once observed with pain, that your paper, usually the intrepid advocate of whatever is just and ultimately true, in contempt of mere temporary expediency, exhibits a temper of flippant illiberality on the subject of Abolitionism in America, inconsistent with its prevailing tone of philosophical Radicalism. Yours is perhaps the last paper in England in which should have been found such an article as that headed "White and Black in the United States," in your number of yesterday.

The writer of that article has apparently been misled by his conviction of a principle generally true, into condemning and ridiculing the actions of persons as fully convinced as himself of the same principle, and much better informed of the circumstances by which its operation is modified in the society amidst which they live. The Abolitionists of the United States are perfectly aware that slavery was once necessary. They know that when their fathers were thrown—a handful of men—into a vast wilderness, there was no alternative between employing compulsory labour and starvation. As a body, the Abolitionists, including the women who met in Convention, are the best political economists in the country. Their perilous interest in the object they have embraced, has driven them to arm themselves with science, among other intellectual and moral weapons and defences. It is their economical science, in conjunction with their human sympathies, which has taught them that, if there has been a time when slavery must begin, there must also come a time when it must cease; and that this latter time is at hand.

. . . It is a mistake to suppose that the Abolition movement has exasperated the condition of the Blacks. I can speak confidently of this, not only from what I saw in all the Southern States, at the time of the slaveholders' greatest fury, but from the admission of the planters themselves. I learned on the spot, from the lips of the fiercest defenders of the existing system, that the condition of the slaves is materially improved by the compassionate eyes of the world being fixed upon them. . . .They are better fed, less worked, and less flogged; for the obvious reason, that it is their masters' interest to present the fairest aspect of slavery to the awakened observation of the world. If the condition of the slaves *had* been made worse, this should have animated rather than relaxed the efforts of the Abolitionists to put an end to the liability altogether—to save all future generations, if they could not help the present. But it is not so. The Negroes are less outrageously oppressed than they were. In confirmation of this, there has not been a single insurrection since the Abolition movement became important; while, before that time, there was a rising, on an average, once a month.

The mobbing by the mercenary interest of the North has already ceased. It was a necessary evil, a lion in the path of the Abolitionists. It has had its roar out, and has turned tail. The Abolitionists are carrying all before them, by that moral force beneath which the physical has quailed. The members of the first general Convention of Women had previously braved the physical force: they now confront what is perhaps more difficult to bear, the insults of the powerful, the mercenary, and the mean at home, and, it appears, the scoffs of persons three thousand miles off, who complacently assume to know their work and understand the affairs of their country better than they do themselves.

The "attempt to excite horror of slavery" is not "superfluous," while it is scarcely possible to pass a day in the United States without being informed that "the slaves are very happy," or questioned as to whether they are not so.

With regard to the exceedingly disagreeable and flippant paragraph of the article under notice, on the subject of associating with people of colour, it is enough to say, that while vicious Whites enter into all but virtuous relations with them, it must be possible for the pure to sustain all that are virtuous.

The people of colour are not all, nor nearly all, servants. Many are educated, and fit for companionship with the enlightened; and more are likely to become so in consequence of the efforts of the members of the New York Convention. Many members of that Convention, some movers and seconders of resolutions and members of committees, are ladies of colour, part of whose business of the week was drawing up addresses to one class or another of American society, on affairs which they thoroughly understand.

I need not say that I go further than "honouring the feelings" of your contemporary of the *True Sun,* whose remarks were the occasion of the article in your paper. I am confident that he has solid ground for his rejoicing. He truly sees, from the substance and framing of the resolutions of the Convention of Women, that the authors are not a set of praters, of fanatics, or sentimentalists, but women of business transacting their philanthropic affairs in rational while fervent reliance on the dictum—true before Aristotle breathed, and true for evermore—"that which is the best principle always constitutes the best polity." I am, Sir, your obedient servant, Harriet Martineau.

Harriet Martineau to the *Spectator*

21 October 1837

Sir—I have no wish to protract an argument on a subject which will probably soon be settled in a better way—by experience; but a few errors of fact have crept into the commentary on my letter of last week, which, on account of the importance of the question, must not be allowed to pass unnoticed.

The free Blacks sent to Liberia were, almost without an exception, slaves freed on condition of transportation. A reference to the Reports of the Colonization Society will confirm this. Multitudes of slaves refused freedom from the dread of removal. . . . [T]he few who did go voluntarily were . . . not Blacks previously free, but slaves freed for the express purpose of transportation.

. . . The laws against the education of slaves date from 1740 downwards, as the constitutions of Virginia and the other slave States show. Under these laws, the knowledge of the alphabet is of little or no use to slaves, since books are unattainable; and the Negroes are besides denied the education by circumstances, which is a prerequisite to education by books. The privation of education by books, great as it is to the free peasant, is not less unjustifiable in the case of the slave, but is still the lowest item in the catalogue of his tremendous injuries.

. . . [T]hat the general treatment of slaves has been eminently improved by the Abolition movement having fixed the eyes of the world upon the slaveholder and his human property, is not only just what might be expected, but what I found to be generally admitted on the spot.

"Have the Abolitionists been victorious?" They have. The first Abolition meeting, attended by five persons, took place in 1832. The number of Abolition Societies in operation last May was 1,006; being an increase of 483 since the preceding year. The Abolitionists now decide the elections in Rhode Island. The new Legislature of Massachusetts voted the Abolitionists the use of the State House at Boston last February, by a majority of 378 to

16. The Abolitionists have obtained the introduction of the question into Congress. They have established seats of learning where students of Colour are admitted as freely as Whites. Their course thus far has been a series of victories. No native Abolitionist is known to have been driven out of the country. Mr. Thompson is no longer wanted. His work of rousing the people on the question is done; but he would probably be very safe now. Persecution has ceased, partly because the cause is now too strong, and partly because a host of its former opponents have become its friends.

. . . The indication that the hour has arrived for the extension of the trial is found in that great fact of the place and time—that, whereas proprietors once found it necessary to have slaves to till their land, they are now struggling for new tracts of land to employ their slaves. The economical pretext for slavery is worn out in that region. A little time will probably show whether slavery itself be not worn out also. —Harriet Martineau

Harriet Martineau to Abby Kelley

20 June 1838

My Dear Madam, On my return from the country I find the certificate of membership of the Massachusetts Anti-slavery Society, which the members of the Lynn Society have had the kindness to forward to me. I accept the valued gift with feelings of high gratification. The generous interpretation which my American sisters put upon the small efforts of those who have done less than themselves shows that the spirit of disinterestedness is strong among them; and my great pleasure in this mark of kindness arises, not from a consciousness of merit in myself, but from an appreciation of the generosity of my correspondents. I do not wish to enlarge on the subject of myself and my doings; but I must just remind you that, in bearing my testimony in print against slavery, I have incurred no risk and no discredit. Here public sentiment is wholly with me on this subject. The only sacrifice I had to make was of the good opinion of some of my friends in America; and I cannot but trust that the time is not far distant when they will forgive and agree with me.

You and your sisters, my dear madam, have a far harder battle to wage, in which I beg to assure you that you have all my sympathy, and, I believe, the sympathy of this whole nation. Not one of your efforts is lost upon us. You are strengthening us for the conflicts we have to enter upon. We have a population in our manufacturing towns almost as oppressed, and in our secluded rural districts almost as ignorant, as your negroes. These must be redeemed. We have also negroes in our dominions, who, though about to be entirely surrendered as property, will yet, we fear, be long oppressed as citizens, if the vigilance which has freed them be not as active as ever. I regard the work of vindicating the civil standing of negroes as more arduous and dangerous than freeing them from the chain and the whip. Both you and I have a long and hard task before us there, when the first great step is, as in our colonies, safely accomplished. But this is a kind of labour which renews strength instead of causing fatigue; the reason of which is, that a sure and steadfast hope is before us. May this hope sustain you! I think it surely will; for nothing was ever to my mind more sure than that there is no delusion connected with your objects; that they are sanctioned by the calmest reason and the loftiest religion, and that in the highest condition of wisdom in which you may find yourselves in the better world to which you are tending, you will never despise your present action in your great cause.

We have heard with mingled feelings of the outrages at Philadelphia. Upon the whole, we hope for a great good from them; but, till I hear more particulars, I shall not cease to wonder at the extent and intensity of the bigotry still existing in that city. I should have supposed that your enemies had seen enough, by this time, of the fruits of persecution. While earnestly desiring that God will advance the cause in his own best way, we cannot but hope that no more struggles of this nature, involving so much guilt, may be in store for you. It is a severe pain to witness so cruel a worship of Mammon, however strong may be our faith in the persecuted. By whatever means, however, the cause is destined to advance, God's will be done!

It gives me heartfelt pleasure to remember that I am now one of your sisterhood in outward as well as inward relation. If I should ever be so blessed as to be able to assist you, you may count upon me. At least, you will always have my testimony, my sympathy, and my prayers. I fear there is no prospect of visiting your country again. I have both domestic and public duties here which I cannot decline; but my thoughts and hopes will be with your people, though I must continue to live among my own.

Believe me, dear madam, with high respect for the body in whose name you have addressed me, Gratefully and affectionately theirs and yours, Harriet Martineau.

THE MARTYR AGE OF THE UNITED STATES

1839

Maria Weston Chapman was the single most influential woman in Martineau's life. From their first contact in the spring of 1835 until Martineau's death in 1876, the two women shared a personal and professional collaboration that outlived even the Civil War and the abolition of slavery. Exemplifying yet again the uncanny timing marking the most pivotal moments of Martineau's life, Chapman's first letter to the illustrious British visitor arrived while she was in Lexington, Kentucky, where she was being pressured to support Henry Clay's colonization scheme.[68] In terms of its timeliness and apparently abrasive content, Chapman's letter—"My first intercourse with any abolitionist" (Martineau 1983, 2:22)—served to turn the tides of Martineau's tour and her life. Chapman's letter charged that Martineau's delay in hearing the abolitionists' side indicated that she already supported the pro-slavers, as she had been among them almost exclusively since her arrival in America. The energy of Martineau's "repulsive, cold and hard" response—"not one woman in a thousand" could forgive such a vindictive retaliation, she noted remorsefully—verifies she was stung by Chapman's implication. But Chapman's calm acceptance of Martineau's anger "with a spirit of generosity, disinterestedness and thorough nobleness" (Martineau 1983, 2:23) served to establish a relationship whose strength and endurance were proportionate to the very inauspiciousness of its beginning.

Officially, the literary collaboration between Martineau and Chapman began with The Martyr Age of the United States, written by Martineau and based on Chapman's compilation of the Boston Female Anti-Slavery Society (BFASS) annual reports. The collaboration ceased with Chapman's composition of the biographical Memorials volume of Martineau's autobiography, a memoir based on personal letters and journals whose privacy Martineau guarded ferociously but fully entrusted to her friend. Martineau also made regular contributions to Chapman's periodical, the Liberty Bell, a rather sentimental publication promoting abolition and sold to raise funds for the cause; further, it was at Chapman's prompting that Martineau became (for a time) a regular contributor to the National Anti-Slavery Standard. But perhaps their most important collaboration of all is the unofficial one: Chapman's regular letters and packets of newspapers to Martineau kept her so well informed of the unfolding American situation that they became an essential source of information for her Daily News articles before and during the Civil War.

Although Martineau never returned to America, Chapman and her family visited her in England periodically, and the personal and professional intimacy between the two families—one conventional, one not—centers around abolitionism. Despite their differences, the two friends—one sentimental, one not—clearly complemented each other, although their relationship was at times as prickly as their initial encounter suggests. Initially, Martineau's susceptibility to Chapman's forceful personality required her "utmost moral care," but this early power balance shifted as Martineau weathered a series of public controversies, with Chapman her tireless defender. This "susceptibility" may be seen in Martineau's writing style during the period between the American travel journals and her more mature writing of the 1840s; *The Martyr Age of the United States* reveals an evangelical, sentimentalized tone more typical of Chapman's style than Martineau's. Her choice of Chapman as her biographer—over any English writer, friend, or family member—attests to her enduring regard for the woman who first compelled her to align her practice with her principles—dramatized at the BFASS meeting in which Martineau declared her support of the cause—and aptly symbolizes her strong identification with America.

Around the time she composed *The Martyr Age of the United States*,[69] when still riding the wave of professional success marking the 1830s, Martineau wrote that Chapman was "a strong-minded abolition woman" (Arbuckle 1983, 9). The materials Chapman sent from America "send a stream of fire thro' my whole soul," particularly the information that women abolitionists such as the Grimké sisters and Martineau herself were loudly denounced by the clergy. Apparently enjoying the notoriety, she defiantly concluded, "It is already clear that the women will carry the day" in terms of the "philosophy and practice of priesthood and womanhood."

Writing to Garrison nearly thirty years after publication of *The Martyr Age*, Martineau urged him to visit her friend Matthew Arnold, whose father, Thomas, had read it aloud to his child: "The boy was too young to enter into the story; but the deep emotion of his father's voice thrilled him: and *that* has been the association with your name in his mind ever since."[70] The commitment to universal emancipation and to racial integration characterizing Garrisonian abolitionism finds expression in the history of the movement and the biographical sketches of its participants that comprise *The Martyr Age of the United States*.

. . .

1. *Right and Wrong in Boston in 1835.* Boston, U.S.: Isaac Knapp.
2. *Right and Wrong in Boston in 1836.* Boston, U.S.: Isaac Knapp.
3. *Right and Wrong in Boston in 1837.* Boston, U.S.: Isaac Knapp.[71]

There is a remarkable set of people now living and vigorously acting in the world, with a consonance of will and understanding which has perhaps never been witnessed among so large a number of individuals of such diversified powers, habits, opinions, tastes and circumstances. The body comprehends men and women of every shade of color, of every degree of education, of every variety of religious opinion, of every gradation of rank, bound together by no vow, no pledge, no stipulation but of each preserving his individual liberty; and yet they act as if they were of one heart and of one soul. Such union could be secured by no principle of worldly interest; nor, for a terms of years, by the most stringent fanaticism. A well-grounded faith, directed towards a noble object, is the only principle which can account for such a spectacle as the world is now waking up to contemplate in the abolitionists of the United States.

Before we fix our attention on the history of the body, it may be remarked that it is a totally different thing to be an abolitionist on a soil actually trodden by slaves, and in a far-off country, where opinion is already on the side of emancipation, or ready to be converted; where only a fraction of society, instead of the whole, has to be convicted of guilt; and where no interests are put in jeopardy but pecuniary ones, and those limited and remote. Great honor is due to the first movers in the anti-slavery cause in every land: but those of European countries may take rank with the philanthropists of America who may espouse the cause of the aborigines: while the primary abolitionists of the United States have encountered, with steady purpose, such opposition as might here await assailants of the whole set of aristocratic institutions at once, from the throne to pauper apprenticeship. Slavery is as thoroughly interwoven with American institutions—ramifies as extensively through American society, as the aristocratic spirit pervades Great Britain. The fate of Reformers whose lives are devoted to making war upon either the one or the other must be remarkable. We are about to exhibit a brief sketch of the struggle of the American abolitionists from the dawn of their day to the present hour, avoiding to dwell on the institution with which they are at war, both because the question of slavery is doubtless settled in the minds of all our readers, and because our contemplation is of a body of persons who are living by faith, and not of a party of Reformers contending against a particular social abuse. Our sketch must be faint, partial, and imperfect. The short life of American abolitionism is so crowded with events and achievements, that the selection of a few is all that can be attempted. Many names deserving of honor will be omitted; and many will receive less than their due: and in the case of persons who are so devoted to others as to have no thoughts to bestow on themselves, no information to proffer regarding their own lives, it is scarcely possible for their describers to avoid errors about their history. Though an extraordinary light is shed from their deeds upon their lives, it scarcely penetrates far enough into the obscurity of the past to obviate mistake on the part of a foreign observer.

Ten years ago there was external quiet on the subject of slavery in the United States. Jefferson and other great men had prophesied national peril from it; a few legislators had talked of doing something to meliorate the "condition of society" in their respective States; the institution had been abolished in some of the northern States, where the number of negroes was small, and the work of emancipation easy and obviously desirable: an insurrection broke out occasionally, in one place or another; and certain sections of society were in a state of perplexity or alarm at the talents, or the demeanor, or the increase of numbers of the free blacks. But no such thing had been heard of as a comprehensive and strenuously active objection to the whole system, wherever established. The surface of society was heaving; but no one surge had broken into voice, prophetic of that chorus of many waters in which the doom of the institution may now be heard. Yet clear sighted persons saw that some great change must take place ere long; for a scheme was under trial for removing the obnoxious part of the negro population to Africa. Those of the dusky race who were too clever, and those who were too stupid, to be safe or useful at home, were to be exported; and slaveowners who had scruples about holding man as property might, by sending their slaves away over the sea, relieve their consciences without annoying their neighbors. Such was the state of affairs, previous to 1829.

The Colonization Society originated abolitionism. It acted in two ways. It exasperated the free blacks by the prospect of exile, and it engaged the attention of those who hated slavery, though the excitement it afforded to their hopes was illusory. Its action in both ways became manifest in the year 1829. In the spring of this year the stir began at Cincinnati, where a strenuous effort was made to induce the white inhabitants to drive away the free colored people, by putting in force against them the atrocious state laws, which placed them in a condition of civil disability, and providing at the same time the means of transportation to Africa. The colored people held a meeting, petitioned the authorities for leave to remain in their present condition for sixty days, and despatched a committee to Canada, to see whether provision could be made for their residence there. The sixty days expired before the committee returned: the populace of Cincinnati rose upon the colored people, and compelled them to barricade themselves in their houses, in assailing which, during three days and nights, several lives were lost. Sir James Colebrook, Governor of Upper Canada, charged the Committee with the following message:—"Tell the Republicans on your side of the line that we do not know men by their color. If you come to us, you will be entitled to all the privileges of the rest of his Majesty's subjects." In consequence of this welcome message, the greater part of the proscribed citizens removed to Canada, and formed the Wilberforce settlement.[72] The few who remained behind were oppressed to the utmost degree that the iniquitous laws against them could be made to sanction. This was not a transaction which could be kept a secret. Meetings were held by the free blacks of all the principal towns north of the Carolinas, and resolutions passed expressive of their abhorrence of the Colonization Society. The resolutions passed at the Philadelphia meeting are a fair sample of the opinions of the class:

> Resolved,—That we view with deep abhorrence the unmerited stigma attempted to be cast upon the reputation of the free people of color by the promoters of this measure, "that they are a dangerous and useless part of the community," when, in the state of disfranchisement in which they live, in the hour of danger they ceased to remember their wrongs, and rallied round the standard of their country.

> Resolved,—That we never will separate ourselves voluntarily from the slave population in this country: they are our brethren by the ties of consanguinity, of suffering, and of wrong: and we feel that there is more virtue in suffering privations with them than in fancied advantages for a season.

Such was one mode of operation of the Colonization Society. The other was upon the minds of individuals of the privileged color who had the spirit of abolitionism in them, without having yet learned how to direct it. Of these the chief, the heroic printer's lad, the master-mind of this great revolution, was then lying in prison, undergoing his baptism into the cause.

William Lloyd Garrison is one of God's nobility—the head of the moral aristocracy whose prerogatives we are contemplating.[73] It is not only that he is invulnerable to injury—that he early got the world under his feet in a way which it would have made Zeno stroke his beard in complacency to witness, but that in his meekness, his sympathies, his self-forgetfulness, he appears "covered all over with the stars and orders" of the spiritual realm whence he derives his dignities and powers. At present he is a marked man wherever he turns. The faces of his friends brighten when his step is heard: the people of color almost kneel to him; and the rest of society jeer, pelt, and execrate him. Amidst all this, his gladsome life rails on, "too busy to be anxious, and too loving to be sad." He springs from his bed singing at sunrise; and if, during the day, tears should cloud his serenity, they are never shed for himself. His countenance of steady compassion gives hope to the oppressed, who look to him as the Jews looked to Moses. It was this serene countenance, saint-like in its earnestness and purity, that a man bought at a print-shop, where it was exposed without a name, and hung up as the most apostolic face he ever saw. It does not alter the case that the man took it out of the frame and hid it when he found that it was Garrison who had been adorning his parlour. As for his own persecutors, Garrison sees in them the creatures of unfavorable circumstances. He early satisfied himself that a "rotten egg cannot hit truth"; and then the whole matter was settled. Such is his case now. In 1829 it was very different. He was an obscure lad, gaining some superficial improvement in a country college, when tidings of the Colonization scheme reached him, and filled him with hope for the colored race. He resolved to devote himself to the cause, and went down to Baltimore to learn such facts as would enable him to lecture on the subject. The fallacies of the plan melted before his gaze, while the true principle became so apparent as to decide his mission. While this process was going on, he got into his first trouble. A Mr. Todd, a New England merchant, freighted a vessel with slaves for the New Orleans market, in the interval of his annual thanksgivings to God that the soil of his State was untrodden by the foot of a slave. Garrison said what he thought of the transaction in a newspaper; was tried for libel, and committed to prison till he could pay the imposed fine of a thousand dollars—a sum which might as well have been a million for any ability he had to pay it. . . . The imprisonment of an honest man for such a

William Lloyd Garrison

cause was an occasion for the outbreak of discontent with slavery on all hands. . . . He was freed by the generosity of an entire stranger, Mr. Arthur Tappan, a wealthy merchant of New York, whose entire conduct on the question has been in accordance with the act of paying Garrison's fine.

Garrison's lectures were now upon abolition, not colonization. He was listened to with much interest in New York; but at Boston he could obtain no place to lecture in; and it was not till it was clear that he intended to collect an audience on the Common, in the midst of the city, that a door was opened to him. He obtained a few coadjutors,—for one, a simple minded clergyman, Mr. May, who on the next Sunday prayed for slaves, among other distressed persons, and was asked, on coming down from the pulpit, whether he was mad?[74] Another of these coadjutors, William Goodell, said, in 1836, "My mind runs back to nearly seven years ago, when I used to walk with Garrison across yonder Common, and to converse on the great enterprise for which we are now met. The work then was all *future*. It existed only in the ardent prayer and the fixed resolves." It was wrought out by prompt and strenuous action. Garrison and his friend Knapp, a printer, were ere long living in a garret on bread and water, expending all their spare earnings and time on the publication of the *Liberator*, now a handsome and flourishing newspaper; then a small, shabby sheet, printed with old types. "When it sold particularly well," says Knapp, "we treated ourselves with a bowl of milk." The venerable first number, dated January 1st, 1831, lies before us in its primitive shabbiness; and on its first page in Garrison's "Address to the Public," we see proof that the vehemence of language, which has often been ascribed to personal resentment (but by none who knew him), has been from the beginning a matter of conscience with him. "I am aware," he says,

> that many object to the severity of my language, but is there not cause for severity? I *will* be as harsh as truth, and as uncompromising as justice. I am in earnest—I will not equivocate—I will not excuse—I will not retreat a single inch—AND I WILL BE HEARD. The apathy of the people is enough to make every statue leap from its pedestal, and to hasten the resurrection of the dead. It is pretended that I am retarding the cause of emancipation by the coarseness of my invective, and the precipitancy of my measures. The charge is not true. On this question my influence, humble as it is, is felt at this moment to a considerable extent, and shall be felt in coming years—not perniciously, but beneficially; not as a curse, but as a blessing; and posterity will bear testimony that I was right. I desire to thank God that he enables me to disregard the fear of man, and to speak his truth in its simplicity and power.

The time was ripe for Garrison's exertions. A pamphlet appeared in the autumn of 1829, at Boston, from the pen of a man of color, named Walker, which alarmed society not a little. It was an appeal to his colored brethren, to drown their injuries in the blood of their oppressors. Its language is perfectly appalling. It ran through several editions, though no bookseller would publish it. Not long after, the author was found murdered near his own door; but whether he had been assassinated for his book, or had been fatally wounded in a fray, is not known.[75] If the slave-owners could but have seen it, Garrison was this man's antagonist, not his coadjutor. Garrison is as strenuous a "peace-man" as any broad-brimmed Friend in Philadelphia; and this fact, in conjunction with his unlimited influence over the Negro population, is the chief reason why no blood has been shed,—why no insurrectionary movement has taken place in the United States, from the time when his voice began to be heard over the broad land till now. Every evil, however, which happened, every shiver of the master, every growl of the slave was henceforth to be charged upon Garrison. Some of the Southern States offered rewards for the apprehension of any person who might be detected in circulating the *Liberator,* or *Walker's Appeal;* and one Legislature demanded of the Governor of Massachusetts that Garrison should be delivered up to them. The fate of Walker was before his eyes; and it came to his ears, that gentlemen in stage coaches said that it was everywhere thought that he "would not be permitted to live long," that he "would be taken away, and no one be the wiser for it." His answer, on this and many subsequent occasions, was the same in spirit. "Will you aim at no higher victims than Arthur Tappan, George Thompson, and W. L. Garrison? And who and what are they? Three drops from a boundless ocean—three rays from a noon day sun—three particles of dust floating in a limitless atmosphere—nothing, subtracted from infinite fulness. Should you succeed in destroying them, the mighty difficulty still remains." As a noble woman has since said, in defence of the individuality of action of the leaders of the cause, "It is idle to talk of 'leaders.' In the contest of morals with abuses, men are but types of principles. Does any one seriously believe that if Mr. Garrison should take an appealing, protesting, backward step, abolitionists would fall back with him?" The "mighty difficulty" would still remain,—and remain as surely doomed as ever, were Garrison to turn recreant or die.

One more dreadful event was to happen before the "peace-man" could make his reprobation of violence heard over the Union. The insurrection of slaves in Southampton county, Virginia, in which eighty persons were slain—parents with their five, seven or ten children, being massacred in the night—happened in 1832.[76] The affair is wrapped in mystery, as are most slave insurrections, both from policy on the part of the masters, and from the whites being too impatient to wait the regular course of justice, and sacrificing their foes as they could catch them. In the present case many Negroes were slaughtered, with every refinement of cruelty, on the roads, or in their masters' yards, without appeal to judge, jury, or evidence. This kind of management precludes any clear knowledge of the causes of the insurrection; but it is now supposed near the spot to have been occasioned by the fanaticism of a madman, a Negro, who assured the blacks who came to him for religious sympathy that they were to run the course of the ancient Jews— slaying and sparing not. We mention this rising because it is the last on the part of the people of color. Free or enslaved, they have since been peaceable; while all the succeeding violences have been perpetrated by "gentlemen of property and standing." It was natural that those who had suffered by this slaughter or its consequences, those who mourned large families of relations thus cut off, those who for the sake of their crops feared the amendment of the system as a result of this exhibition of its tendencies, those who for the sake of their children nightly trembled in their beds, should cast about for an object on whom to vent their painful feelings; and Garrison was that object. The imputation of the insurrection to him was too absurd to be long sustained; but those who could not urge this against him still remonstrated against his "disturbing the harmony and peace of society." "Disturbing the slave holders!" replied he. "I am sorry to disturb anybody. But the slave-holders have so many friends; I must be the friend of the slaves.". . .

By this time the abolition cause was supported by twenty-six periodicals, circulating from Maine to Virginia and Indiana. Some excellent individuals had done the brave deed of publishing books in aid of the same cause. Among these was Mrs. Child, a lady of whom society was exceedingly proud before she published her *Appeal,* and to whom society has been extremely contemptuous since. Her works were bought with avidity before, but fell into sudden oblivion as soon as she had done a greater deed than writing any or all of them. Her noble-minded husband lost his legal practice, sound and respected as were his talents, from affording his counsel to citizens of color; and he was maliciously arrested on the quays of New York, for a fictitious or extremely trifling old debt, when he was just putting his foot on board a vessel for England. . . .[77] By this time the degraded free blacks began to hold up their heads; and they entered upon a new course of action,—setting out upon a principle of hope instead of despair. As they found the doors of schools shut against them, they formed associations for mutual improvement. The best minds among them sent forth urgent entreaties to the rest to labor at the work of education, pleading that the nearer the prospect of an improved social condition, the more pressing became the necessity of strengthening and enriching their minds for their new responsibilities. It was a glad day for them when they saw the assemblage in Convention at Philadelphia of anti-slavery delegates from ten States out of the twenty-four of which the Union was at that time constituted. These ten States were the six which compose New England, and New York, New Jersey, Pennsylvania, and Ohio. Some State Associations were already organized: the National one organized by this Convention bears date December 1833. There might be seen Garrison, just returned from England, refreshed by sympathy and exhilarated by hope. There was May, the mild gentleman, the liberal clergyman, who unconsciously secures courtesy from the most contemptuous of the foe, when nothing but insult was designed. There was Lewis Tappan, the grave Presbyterian, against whom violence was even then brewing, and who was soon to be despoiled of his property by the firebrands of a mob.[78] These, and many others, put their signatures to a Declaration, of which we subjoin the concluding passage:—

> Submitting this DECLARATION to the candid consideration of the people of this country; and of the friends of liberty throughout the world, we hereby affix our signatures to it; pledging ourselves that, under the guidance and by the help of Almighty God, we will do all that in us lies, consistently with this Declaration of our principles, to overthrow the most execrable system of slavery that has ever been witnessed upon earth—to deliver our land from its deadliest

curse—to wipe out the foulest stain which rests upon our national es-
cutcheon—and to secure to the colored population of the United States all the
rights and privileges which belong to them as men, and as Americans,—come
what may to our persons, our interests, or our reputation whether we live to
witness the triumph of Liberty, Justice, and Humanity, or perish untimely as
martyrs in this great, benevolent, and holy cause. . . .

The next year (1834) was a stirring year. "The Young Men" of the large
cities began to associate themselves for the cause. Those of New York pledged
their lives, their fortunes, and their sacred honor, (in the language and spirit
of the Declaration of Independence,) to overthrow slavery by moral assault,
or to die in the attempt. The most remarkable accession of young men to the
cause was from Lane Seminary, Cincinnati,—a Presbyterian college of high
reputation, with the eminent Dr. Beecher to preside over it.[79] The students,
most of whom were above one-and-twenty, and fifty of whom were above
five-and twenty years of age, discussed the abolition and colonization questions for eighteen evenings, and decided unanimously in favor of the former.
The alarmed Faculty forbade discussion and association on the question, and
conferred an irresponsible power of expulsion on the Executive Committee.
The students refused to be tongue-tied, and preferred expulsion. Those who
were not formally expelled, withdrew; so that of forty theological students,
only two returned the next term; and of classical students, only five out of
sixty. It is strange that the Faculty did not foresee the consequences. Almost
every one of these dispersed young men became the nucleus of an abolition
society. Some distributed themselves among other colleges; and some set
about establishing a seminary where freedom of thought and speech might
be secured, and whose doors should be open to students of all complexions.
Ere long, President Beecher's two sons were active abolitionists; several colleges had invited students of color to enter; and five establishments belonging to the noble Oberlin Institute were overflowing with students of both
sexes, and any color that might please Heaven. Out of the forlornness of
Lane Seminary arose the prosperity of the Oberlin Institute.[80]

While these things were doing in the West, a strange thing was happening
in the South. In the midst of the hot fields of Alabama, where the negro
drinks the last dregs of his cup of bitterness, and sees his family "killed off,"
before his eyes, in securing for one whom he hates, the full abundance of a
virgin soil;—from among the raw settlements where white men carry secret
arms, and black men secret curses, a great man rose up before the public eye,
and declared himself an abolitionist. Mr. Birney was a great man in a worldly
as well as a moral sense,—not only "a gentleman of property and standing,"
but Solicitor-General of the State, and in the way to be Judge of its Supreme
Court. But he was also an honest and a moderate man. It was he who, being
asked about investment for capital in the West, smiled, and said, "I am the
worst person you could ask. My family and I are happy with what we have: we
do not know that we should be happier with more; and therefore we inquire

nothing about investments." None can be fully aware of the singularity of this answer who have not witnessed the prevalence and force of the spirit of speculation in the Western States.—Mr. Birney removed from Alabama, emancipated and settled all his slaves, giving them education in defiance of the laws of Kentucky, and himself setting up a newspaper in Cincinnati, standing his ground there against many and awful attempts upon his life, and at length gaining a complete victory, and establishing freedom of speech and the press.[81] This is the gentleman to whom Mr. Channing wrote his splendid letter (on liberty of speech and the press): and to that letter Mr. Birney acknowledges himself under great obligations—Dr. Channing's name effecting in some minds changes which angelic truth could not achieve. Mr. Birney is he to whom Southern Members of Congress now address themselves—now that they are compelled to stoop to address abolitionists at all:—he is addressed as the *gentleman* of the party—a distinction at which he would be the first to smile. The whole South felt the shock of such a man coming forth against its "peculiar domestic institutions": and all the more from Mr. Birney's having been an active colonizationist—a bountiful and influential friend to that society—even a collector of funds for it—till experience convinced him, first of its inefficiency, and then of its wickedness. There was much sensation about Mr. Birney in many a house. His name was carefully avoided before strangers, as it was well that they should not hear the story ("strangers could not understand it") but here were men gnashing their teeth at him for "loosening the bonds of society": there women horror-struck lest he should introduce "insubordination" (meaning midnight massacre); and children . . . agreeing that he could be no gentleman to think of putting notions into the heads of "people," and turning them adrift to take care of themselves. Silence brooded over the cotton-fields where slaves were within earshot; but within the dwellings, multitudes of whites were whispering about Mr. Birney.

The cities of the North were at the same time in commotion. From disturbing meetings and inflicting petty social wounds, the enemies of the colored race proceeded to gross outrage. The fear for the purses of the merchants and ship-owners of the North was becoming exasperated into panic. The panic was generously shared by those who had no ships, and conducted no commerce. The lawyers and clergy, "gentlemen of property and standing" of every sort, and the press, gave their sympathy to the merchants, and the result was presently visible in the reflection of flames upon the midnight sky. The American reign of terror now began. In Philadelphia forty-four houses and two churches were besieged: some few greatly damaged, and the rest sacked and destroyed. The forty four houses belonged to the people of color. In New York the mob hunted higher game. On the fourth of July, (the anniversary of the day when liberty was guaranteed to all American citizens by the declaration of Independence,) the house of Mr. Lewis Tappan was sacked, and the furniture burned in the street. A certain bureau, in which his children kept their little keepsakes and other treasures, was thrown upon the heap, and was soon crackling in the flames; an early taste of persecution for the young creatures, and a circumstance exceedingly well adapted to perpetuate their father's spirit in them. The house of Dr. Cox was seriously damaged, and the African school-house in Orange street, with twelve adjacent houses, chiefly belonging to people of color, was destroyed. St. Philip's church was sacked, and several others much damaged. The abolitionists not only suffered the destruction of their property and the peril of their lives, but the revilings of the press were poured out upon them. They were upbraided as the cause of the riots and were told that, though *they* were served rightly enough, they had no business to scare the city with the sight of their burning property and demolished churches.

Next followed the virtual accession of a great northern man to the cause, for though Dr. Channing continued to censure the abolitionists for two years after this, it was in the autumn of 1834 that his mind's eye was fixed upon the question on which he has since acted a brave part. It was at the close of this summer, in the parlor of his Rhode Island retreat, that the memorable conversation with Mr. Abdy took place by which Dr. Channing's attention was aroused to the wrongs of the colored race.[82] Scarcely any other man of his heart and his principles could have remained so long unaware of the actual state of the case: but there are circumstances of health, habit, and environment which account for the fact to those who know Dr. Channing. As soon as Mr. Abdy had quitted him, he applied himself to learn the truth of the case, and in the month of October preached a thorough-going abolition sermon, as to its principles at least, though many months elapsed before he learned fully to recognize the merits of the men who were teaching and practising them at the hazard of all that ordinary men most value. But the ray of doubt which was thus carried into that country retreat has now brightened into the sunshine of perfect conviction; it did so in time to dispel the dark clouds which had gathered above the morals of the Texas question. It is owing to Dr. Channing, finally and chiefly (though in the first instance to Mr. Child) that the United States have been saved the crime and the shame of annexing Texas to the Union, for the purpose of the protraction of slavery.

At the close of this busy year it was found that the Auxiliary anti-Slavery Societies had increased from sixty to about two hundred. . . .

In the month of July, 1835, one of the dismissed students of the Lane Seminary, Amos Dresser by name, travelled southward from Cincinnati, for the purpose of selling bibles and a few other books, as a means of raising funds for the completion of his education; a very common practice in the west, and highly useful to the residents of new settlements. At Nashville, Tennessee, he was arrested on suspicion of being an abolition agent; which was not the fact, and in support of which there was positively no evidence whatever. He had not spoken with slaves, or distributed books among free persons of color. He was brought before a Committee of Vigilance, consisting of sixtytwo of the principal citizens, among whom were seven elders of the Presbyterian church. His examination lasted from between four and five in the afternoon till eleven at night. His trunk was brought before the Committee and emptied. In it were found three volumes, written by abolitionists, put in by Dresser for his private reading; and some old newspapers of the same character, used as stuffing to prevent the books from rubbing. His private journal was examined; but as it was in pencil, consisting only of memoranda, and those put in abbreviation, little could be made out of it. The Mayor gave up the attempt to read it aloud, observing, as he laid it down, that it was "evidently very hostile to slavery." Private letters from friends were then read aloud, and wise looks were exchanged among the judges at every expression which could be laid hold of as indicating a different way of thinking from theirs. At eleven o'clock the young man was sent into an adjoining room to await the judgment of the Committee. He had not conceived the idea of any very serious issue of the examination; and it was, therefore, with horror that he heard from the principal city officer that the Committee were debating whether his punishment should be thirtynine lashes, or a hundred (a number considered fatal, in the way in which abolitionists are flogged,) or death by hanging. The Committee acknowledged, through the whole proceeding, that Dresser had broken no law; but pleaded that if the law did not sufficiently protect slavery against the assaults of opinion, an association of gentlemen must make law for the occasion. Dresser was found guilty of three things: of being a member of an anti-Slavery Society in another State,—of having books of an anti-Slavery tendency in his possession, and of *being believed* to have circulated such in his travels. He was condemned to receive twenty lashes on his bare back in the market place. To the market place he was marched, amidst the acclamation of the mob; and there by torchlight, and just as the chimes were about to usher in the Sunday, he was stripped and flogged with a heavy cow-hide. At the close, an involuntary exclamation of thanksgiving escaped his lips that it was over, and that he had been able to bear it. "God d...n him, stop his praying!" was shouted on all hands. Twentyfour hours were allowed him to leave the city; but it was thought unsafe for him to remain a moment longer than was absolutely necessary, or to return to his lodgings. Some kind person or persons, entire strangers to him, drew him into a house, bathed his wounds, gave him food, and furnished him with a disguise, with which he left the place on foot, early in the morning. Neither clothes, books, nor papers were ever returned to him, though he made every necessary application. There is little in the excitement of annual or quarterly meetings which can sustain a young man under an ignominious public whipping, in a strange city, where there was not one familiar face to look upon. Dresser has some other support, which has prevented his shrinking from the consequences of his opinions then and ever since. . . . It was about this time that the Attorney General of Massachusetts, Austin by name, gave advice to the Governor in Council that any abolitionists demanded by the South should be delivered up for trial under Southern laws, (the sure result of which is known to be death.) A pamphlet by a leading lawyer of Boston, named Sullivan, followed on the same side, offering a legal opinion that those who discussed the subject of slavery (an act injurious to the peace of society) might be brought under the penal laws of Massachusetts; *ex post facto* laws, if no others could be found. A friend of Dr. Channing's wrote to him that it was now time for him to come forward: and he obeyed the suggestion. During the Autumn he wrote his tract on Slavery, and published it at Christmas. During the interval some remarkable events had taken place.

Our historical review has now brought us up to the date of the first of the works whose titles we have prefixed to this article, and which are, substantially, annual Reports of the proceedings of the Massachusetts Female Anti-Slavery Society. We have arrived at the most remarkable period of the great struggle, when an equal share of its responsibility and suffering came to press upon women. We have seen how men first engaged in it, and how young men afterwards, as a separate element, were brought in. Many women had joined from the first, and their numbers had continually increased: but their exertions had hitherto consisted in raising funds, and in testifying sympathy for the colored race and their advocates. Their course of political action, which has never since been checked, began in the autumn of 1835.

The Female Anti-Slavery Society in Boston is composed of women of every rank, and every religious sect, as well as of all complexions. The president is a Presbyterian; the chief secretary is a Unitarian; and among the other officers and members may be found Quakers, Episcopalians, Methodists, and Swedenborgians. All sectarian jealousy is lost in the great cause; and these women have, from the first day of their association, preserved, not only harmony, but strong mutual affection, while differing on matters of opinion as freely and almost as widely as if they had kept within the bosom of their respective sects. Upon such a set of women was the responsibility thrown of vindicating the liberty of meeting and of free discussion in Boston; and nobly they sustained it.

Before we proceed, it is necessary to say a few words upon the most remarkable of these women,—the understood author of the books whose titles stand at the head of our article. Maria Weston was educated in England, and might have remained here in the enjoyment of wealth, luxury, and fashion: but with these she could not obtain sufficient freedom of thought and action to satisfy her noble nature; and, no natural ties detaining her, she returned to New England, to earn her bread there by teaching, and breathe as freely as she desired. She has paid a heavy tax of persecution for her freedom; but she has it. She is a woman of rare intellectual accomplishment, full of reading, and with strong and well exercised powers of thought. She is beautiful as the day, tall in her person, and noble in her carriage, with a voice as sweet as a silver bell, and speech as clear and sparkling as a running brook. Her accomplishments have expanded in a happy home. She has been for some years the wife of Mr. Henry Chapman, a merchant of Boston, an excellent man, whose spirit of self-denial is equal to his wife's, and is shown no less nobly in the same cause. A woman of genius like her's cannot but take the lead wherever she acts at all; and she is the life and soul of the enterprise in Boston. The foes of the cause have nicknamed her "Captain Chapman"; and the name passes from mouth to mouth as she walks up Washington street,—not less admired, perhaps, all the while than if she were only the most beautiful woman in the city. The lady, with all her sisters, took her ground early, and has always had sober reason to plead for every one of her many extensions of effort. She is understood to have drawn up the petition which follows,—a fair specimen of the multitudes of petitions from women which have been piled up under the table of Congress, till the venerable John Quincy Adams has been roused to the remarkable conflict which we shall presently have to relate:[83]

> *Petition. To the Honorable Senate and House of Representatives in Congress assembled,* The undersigned, women of Massachusetts, deeply convinced of the sinfulness of slavery, and keenly aggrieved by its existence in a part of our country over which Congress possess exclusive jurisdiction in all cases whatsoever, do most earnestly petition your honorable body immediately to abolish slavery in the District of Columbia, and to declare every human being free who sets foot upon its soil.
>
> We also respectfully announce our intention to present the same petition yearly before your honorable body, that it may at least be a "memorial of us," that in the holy cause of Human Freedom "we have done what we could."

In answer to objections against such petitioning, the author of *Right and Wrong in Boston* says—

> If we are not enough grieved at the existence of slavery to ask that it may be abolished in the ten miles over which Congress has exclusive jurisdiction, we may rest assured that we are slave-holders in heart, and indeed under the endurance of the penalty which selfishness inflicts,—the slow but certain death of the soul. We sometimes, but not often, hear it said, "It is such an odd, *unladylike* thing to do!" We concede that the human soul, in the full exercise of its most god-like power of self-denial and exertion for the good of others, is, emphatically, a very unladylike thing. We have never heard this objection but from that sort of woman who is dead while she lives, or to be pitied as the victim of domestic tyranny. The woman who makes it is generally one who has struggled from childhood up to womanhood through a process of spiritual suffocation. Her infancy was passed in serving as a convenience for the display of elegant baby-linen. Her youth, in training for a more public display of braiding the hair, and wearing of gold, and putting on of apparel; while the ornament of a meek and quiet spirit,—the hidden man of the heart, is not deemed worthy the attainment. Her summers fly away in changes of air and water; her winters in changes of flimsy garments, in inhaling-lampsmoke, and drinking champagne at midnight with the most dissipated men in the community. This is the woman who tells us it is *unladylike* to ask that children may no longer be sold away from their parents, or wives from their husbands, in the district of Colum-

bia, and adds, "They ought to be mobbed who ask it." . . . O how painful is the contemplation of the ruins of a nature a little lower than the angels!—*Right and Wrong in Boston in 1836*, p. 27.

"We feel," she elsewhere declares,

> that we may confidently affirm that no woman of Massachusetts will cease to exercise for the slaves the right of petition (her only means of manifesting her civil existence) for which Mr. Adams has so nobly contended. Massachusetts women will not forget in their petitions to Heaven the name of him who upheld their prayer for the enslaved of the earth, in the midst of sneers and wrath, bidding oppressors remember that *they,* too, were women-born, and declaring that he considered the wives, and mothers, and daughters of his electors, as his constituents. . . . What immediate effect would be produced on men's hearts, and how much they might be moved to wrath before they were touched with repentance, we have never been careful to inquire. We leave such cares with God; we do so with confidence in his paternal providence; for what we have done is right and womanly.—*Right and Wrong in Boston in 1837*, p.84.

To consult on their labors of this and other kinds, the ladies of the Boston Anti-Slavery Society intended to meet at their own office, Washington street, on the 21st of October. Handbills had been circulated and posted up in different parts of the city the day before, offering a reward to any persons who would commit certain acts of violence,—such as "bringing Thompson to the tar-kettle before dark." The ladies were informed that they would be killed; and when they applied at the Mayor's office for protection to their lawful meeting, the City Marshal replied,—"You give us a great deal of trouble." This trouble, however, their consciences compelled them to give. They could not decline the duty of asserting their liberty of meeting and free discussion. But Mrs. Chapman felt that every member should have notice of what might await her; and she herself carried the warning from house to house, with all discretion and quietness. Among those whom she visited was an artizan's wife, who was sweeping out one of her two rooms as Mrs. Chapman entered. On hearing that there was every probability of violence, and that the warning was given in order that she might stay away if she thought proper, she leaned upon her broom and considered for awhile. Her answer was—"I have often wished and asked that I might be able to do something for the slaves; and it seems to me that this is the very time and the very way. You will see me at the meeting and I will keep a prayerful mind, as I am about my work, till then."

Twentyfive reached the place of meeting by presenting themselves three-quarters of an hour before the time. Five more struggled up the stairs, and a hundred were turned back by the mob. It is well known how these ladies were mobbed by some hundreds of gentlemen in fine broad-cloth—(Boston broad-cloth has become celebrated since that day.)[84] It is well known how those gentlemen hurraed, broke down the partition, and threw orange-peel at the ladies while they were at prayer; but Mrs. Chapman's part in the lessons of that hour has not been made public. [Here follows Chapman's confrontation with the mayor, after which the women adjourn, having finished their business. When the mob comes to her home later that night seeking George Thompson, Chapman turns them away.]

The women who were at the meeting of this memorable day were worthy of the occasion, not from being strong enough to follow the lead of such a woman as Maria Chapman, but from having a strength independent of her. The reason of Garrison being there was, that he went to escort his young wife, who was near her confinement. She was one of the last to depart, and it could not be concealed from her that her husband was in the hands of the mob. She stepped out of the window upon a shed, in the fearful excitement of the moment. He was in the extremest danger. His hat was lost, and brick-bats were rained upon his head, while he was hustled along in the direction of the tar-kettle, which was heating in the next street. The only words which escaped from the white lips of the young wife were,—"I think my husband will not deny his principles: I am sure my husband will never deny his principles." Garrison was rescued by a stout truck-man, and safely lodged in jail (the only place in which he could be secure,) without having in the least flinched from the consequences of his principles. The differences in the minds of these women, and the view which they all agree to take of the persecution to which they are subjected, may be best shown in the eloquent words of the author of *Right and Wrong:* . . .

> A few more years of danger and intense exertion, and the South and the North will unite in reading the Constitution by the light from above, thrown on it by the Declaration of Independence, and not by the horrible glare of the slave code. The cause of freedom will ere long become the popular one; and a voice of regret will be heard throughout the land from those who will have forgotten these days of misrepresentation and danger—"Why was not I among the early abolitionists!" Let us be deeply grateful that we are among the early called. Let us pray God to forgive the men who would deface every feature of a Christian community by making it personally dangerous to fulfil a Christian woman's duty; to forgive the man who sneers at the sympathy for the oppressed implanted by the Spirit of God in the heart of the mother that bore and cherished his infancy—of the wife, the helpmate of his manhood, and of the daughter whom that same quality of womanly devotedness would lead to shield his grey head with her own bosom. . . .—*Right and Wrong,* vol. ii. pp. 81–83.

"Angelina E. Grimke." Who is she? She and her sister Sarah are Quaker ladies of South Carolina. Our author says of their visit to Boston, to act and speak in this cause—"It might have been anticipated that they would have met with a friendly reception from those calling themselves the better sort, for they were highly connected. Unfortunately they were but women, though the misfortune of that fact was greatly abated by their being sisters of the Hon. Thos. S. Grimke." This gentlemen was, in point of scholarship, the greatest ornament of the United States, and his character was honored by the whole community. After his death his sisters strove by all the means which could be devised by powerful intellects and kind hearts to meliorate the condition of the slaves they had inherited. In defiance of the laws, they taught them, and introduced upon their estates as many as possible of the usages of free society. But it would not do. There is no infusing into slavery the benefits of freedom. When these ladies had become satisfied of this fact, they surrendered their worldly interests instead of their consciences. They freed their slaves, and put them in the way of providing for themselves in a free region, and then retired to Philadelphia, to live on the small remains of their former opulence. It does not appear that they had any intention of coming forward publicly, as they have since done; but the circumstance of their possessing the knowledge, which other abolitionists want, of the minute details and less obvious workings of the slavery system, was the occasion of their being applied to, more and more frequently and extensively, for information, till they publicly placed their knowledge at the service of all who needed it, and at length began to lecture wherever there was an audience who requested to hear them. Their Quaker habits of speaking in public rendered this easy to them; and the exertion of their great talents in this direction has been of most essential service to the cause. It was before they adopted this mode of action that the public first became interested in these ladies, through a private letter written by Angelina to her friend Garrison—a letter which he did his race the kindness to publish, and which strengthened even the great man's strong heart. We give the greater part of it:—

> I can hardly express to thee the deep and solemn interest with which I have viewed the violent proceedings of the last few weeks. Although I expected opposition, yet I was not prepared for it so soon—it took me by surprise, and I greatly feared the abolitionists would be driven back in the first onset, and thrown into confusion. So fearful was I, that though I clung with unflinching firmness to our principles, yet I was afraid of even opening one of thy papers, lest I should see some indications of a compromise, some surrender, some palliation. Under these feelings I was induced to read thy appeal to the citizens of Boston. Judge, then, what were my feelings, on finding that my fears were utterly groundless, and that thou stoodest firm in the midst of the storm, determined to suffer and to die, rather than yield one inch. . . .
>
> My mind has been especially turned towards those who are standing in the forefront of the battle; and the prayer has gone up for their preservation—not the preservation of their lives, but the preservation of their minds in humility and patience, faith, hope, and charity—that charity which is the bond of perfectness. If persecution is the means which God has ordained for the accomplishment of this great end, Emancipation, then, in dependence upon him for strength to bear it, I feel as if I should say, let it come; for it is my deep, solemn, deliberate conviction, that this is a cause worth dying for.

At one time I thought this system would be overthrown in blood, with the confused noise of the warrior; but a hope gleams across my mind that our blood will be spilt, instead of the slaveholders'; our lives will be taken, and theirs spared:—I say a hope, for of all things I desire to be spared the anguish of seeing our beloved country desolated with the horrors of a servile war. A.E. Grimke.

In answer to an overwhelming pressure of invitations, these ladies have lectured in upwards of sixty towns of the United States to overflowing audiences. Boston itself has listened to them with reverence. Some of the consequences of their exertions will be noticed as we proceed: meantime we must give our author's report of this novelty in the method of proceeding:—

The idea of a woman's teaching was a startling novelty, even to abolitionists; but their principled and habitual reverence for the freedom of individual action induced them to a course unusual among men—to examine before they condemned. Only a short examination was needed to convince them that the main constituents in the relation of teacher and taught are ignorance on one side and knowledge on the other. They had been too long accustomed to hear the Bible quoted in defence of slavery, to be astonished that its authority should be claimed for the subjugation of women the moment she should act for the enslaved. The example and teaching of the Grimkes wrought conviction as to the rights and consequent duties of women in the minds of multitudes. Prejudices and ridiculous associations of ideas vanished. False interpretations of scripture disappeared. Probably our children's children, our sons no less than our daughters, will dwell on the memory of these women, as the descendants of the bondman of to-day will cherish the name of Garrison.—*Right and Wrong*, Vol. iii. P. 61. . . .

A gentleman of the class from which the Grimkes have emerged, Mr. M'-Duffie, Governor of South Carolina, wrote a remarkable message to the legislature of his State the same year, 1835. He declared therein that freedom can be preserved only in societies where work is disreputable, or where there is a hereditary aristocracy, or a military despotism, and that he preferred the first, as being the most republican. He further declared—

"No human institution, in my opinion, is more manifestly consistent with the will of God than domestic slavery; and no one of his ordinances is written in more legible characters than that which consigns the African race to this condition, as more conducive to their own happiness than any other of which they are susceptible." . . .

Domestic slavery, therefore, instead of being a political evil, is the cornerstone of our republican edifice. No patriot who justly estimates our privileges will tolerate the idea of emancipation, at any period, however remote, or on any conditions of pecuniary advantage, however favorable. I would as soon think of opening a negotiation for selling the liberty of the State at once, as of making any stipulations for the ultimate emancipation of our slaves. So deep is my conviction on this subject, that if I were doomed to die immediately after recording these sentiments, I would say, in all sincerity, and under all the sanctions of Christianity and patriotism, "God forbid that my descendants, in the remotest generations, would live in any other than a community having the institution of domestic slavery, as it existed among the patriarchs of the primitive Church, and in all the states of antiquity!"—*Governor M'Duffie's Message*, 1835.

When this message, endorsed by a committee of the South Carolina Legislature, with General Hamilton for its chairman, arrived in New England, Dr. Channing observed in conversation that, but for the obligation to preserve peace and good humor, he should have liked to ask the yeomanry of his State (that body of whom Washington exclaimed in a paroxysm of admiration and gratitude, "God bless the yeomanry of Massachusetts!") what they thought of the doctrine that freedom can be preserved only where the efficient classes of society are slaves, where work is disreputable, and where slavery is cherished as "the cornerstone of the republican edifice."

The other events which attracted the most attention during this year were two. The first was a desperate and cruel massacre of upwards of twenty persons on the gibbet at Vicksburg on the Mississippi, on a vague and unfounded suspicion of an intended rising among the slaves. The other remarkable event was the "disinterring of the law of Massachusetts," in defence of two women who had been kidnapped, in order to be carried into southern slavery. . . .

In Massachusetts alone there was an accession of twenty societies during this year. The report says:

> Five of them are of females. Our opposers affect to sneer at their co-operation; but we welcome, and are grateful for it. The influence of woman never was, never will be, insignificant; it is dreaded by those who would be thought to contemn it. Men have always been eager to secure their cooperation. We hail it as most auspicious of our success that so many faithful and zealous women have espoused the anti-slavery cause in this republic. Events of the past year have proved that those who have associated themselves with us will be helpmates indeed; for they are animated by a spirit that can brave danger, endure hardship, and face a frowning world.

It is impossible, in a sketch like the present, to enumerate the acts of violence, or to describe the mobs with which the abolitionists have had to contend. At Canaan, in New Hampshire, there was an academy, to which some benevolent persons had procured admission for about twelve young men of color. All seemed to be going on well, when a town meeting was called, and it was resolved to put a stop to the instruction of people of color. Three hundred citizens assembled one morning, provided with ropes and rollers, and fairly rolled away the Noyes Academy over the boundary of the State. At Cincinnati the gentry disgraced themselves by a persecution of Mr. Birney, which caused the destruction of his office, press, and types, but which terminated in the triumph of his moral power over their brute force. At St. Louis, in Missouri, a mulatto, named M'Intosh, was burned alive under circumstances of deep atrocity; and because he was heard to pray as his limbs were slowly consuming, he was pronounced by the magistrates to be in league with the abolitionists. The gentlemen of Charleston broke open the post-office, and burned the mails in the street, on the charge of their containing anti-slavery papers. Such were a few of the events of the year 1836. . . .

The President had now taken the matter in hand. General Jackson, the people's man, who talked of liberty daily, with energetic oaths and flourishes of the hand, inquired of Congress whether they could not pass a law prohibiting, under severe penalties, the transmission through the mails of anti-slavery publications, or,—as he worded it, of publications "intended to excite the slaves to insurrection." Mr. Calhoun, the great bulwark of slavery, declared in Congress that such a measure would be unconstitutional; but that a bill which he had prepared would answer the purpose. This was the celebrated Gag Bill. We insert it as amended for the third reading, as we could not expect of our readers that they should credit our report of its contents! Here stands the Bill which in 1836 was read a third time in the Senate of a Republican Congress—

"A Bill" For prohibiting deputy postmasters from receiving or transmitting through the mail to any State, Territory, or District, certain papers therein mentioned, the circulation of which, by the laws of said State, Territory, or District, may be prohibited, and for other purposes. . . .

Mr. Van Buren, now President of the United States, was then Vice President and held the casting vote in the Senate.[85] Every one knows his terror of committing himself. What must have been his feelings when his casting vote was called for as to the third reading of this bill? He was standing behind a pillar, talking, when the votes were declared to be eighteen to eighteen. "Where's the Vice President?" shouted Mr. Calhoun's mighty voice. Mr. Van Buren came forward and voted for the third reading. "The Northern States are sold!" groaned the New England senators with one voice. By their strenuous efforts the bill was thrown down the third reading. If it had passed it would have remained to be seen, as the abolitionists remarked, "whether seven millions of freemen should become slaves, or two and a half millions of slaves should become free?"

For men and women engaged in a moral enterprise so stupendous as that under notice, there is no rest. It is well for them that the perspective of their toils is shrouded from them when they set forth; for there is perhaps no human soul that could sustain the whole certainty. Not a day's repose can these people snatch. If they were to close their eyes upon their mission for even the shortest interval, they would find that new dangers had gathered, and that their work was in arrear. Towards the end of 1836 the abolitionists felt their prospects were darker than ever. The annexation of Texas to the Union seemed an evil scarcely possible to be averted: and, if it were not averted, their enterprise was thrown back centuries. Instead of sinking in despair at seeing the success of their foes in flattery, not only the worldly interests of the sordid and ambitious part of society, but the best feelings of the superficial and thoughtless, they made a tremendous effort. Mr. Child began with an admirable exposure of the Texas scheme in the *Anti-Slavery Quarterly Magazine,* and Dr. Channing finished the business (for the present) by his noble tract. As for the rest they sounded a tocsin of alarm that aroused the land to a sense of its danger; they sent their appeals, warnings, and remonstrances into every part of the republic; they held meetings by day and by night, with reference solely to this momentous question; they covered the entire surface of the nation with tracts, circulars, and papers, revealing the design of the southern planters; in short, they put into motion all that has been done for the perpetual exclusion of Texas from the American confederacy. At the extra session of Congress in September, through their instrumentality, in the course of a few weeks, many thousand petitions, signed by hundreds of thousands of men and women, were received by that body, remonstrating against the annexation in strong and emphatic language. Never before had the people made such a demonstration of their will in the form of petition." It was a noble spectacle—the bulk of a nation protesting against an acquisition of territory, on the ground of its being wrong.

In August of this year it became known to the abolitionists in Boston that a child was in the city, brought as a slave from New Orleans, and to be carried back thither as a slave. They determined to attempt the rescue of this child by law. If they failed, she was only as she was before; if they succeeded, the case would be a parallel one with that of Sommersett in England, under Lord Mansfield's famous decision.[86] The laws of Massachusetts were appealed to, as had been proposed, without good result, in similar cases before. This time the case was in the hands of sound lawyers, and tried before a courageous judge, Chief Justice Shaw. The child was declared free; and her happy fate decides that of all slaves (except fugitives) who shall henceforth touch the soil of Massachusetts. The Newspapers opened out in full cry against her protectors, for having separated her from her mother. They overlooked the fact that parental claims merge in those of the master; that a slave child is not pretended to belong to its parents; and that if the owner of this particular child views the relation in the right light, he has nothing to do but to emancipate the mother. . . . The decision of Judge Shaw in the case of this slave-child was presently followed in Connecticut; and, within a very short time, the abolitionists obtained right of jury trial for persons arrested as fugitive slaves in the states of Massachusetts, New Jersey and Vermont.

At the beginning of the remarkable year 1837, great confusion was excited in Congress by Mr. Adams's management of a low jest aimed at him by the Southern members. A petition was sent to him signed by nine slaves, requisitioning of the House of Representatives to expel him, on the ground of the countenance he afforded to the petitions of persons who would put an end to the blessed institution of slavery. Mr. Adams presented this document as if it was a *bona fide* petition. The uproar in the House was tremendous; but the attention of the members was fairly fixed upon the right of petition as held by slaves, and the venerable ex-President has since been acting a more heroic part than any of his predecessors on that floor have ever been called to go through. The name of John Quincy Adams will stand out bright from the page of American history for ever, as the vindicator of the right of petition in the perilous times of the republic. We pass over, as well known, the conflict on Mr. Pinckney's resolutions, the speeches of the Southern members, (after their late complacent assurances that the subject of slavery would never be breathed in Congress) and the new President's somewhat fool-hardy declaration against any relaxation of the present state of things in regard to slavery, in his inaugural address, on the 4th of March. Our space is only too narrow for the two other great events of the year, which are less widely understood.

During the second week of May was held the first General Convention of Women that was ever assembled. Modest as were its pretensions, and quietly as it was conducted, it will stand as a great event in history—from the nature of the fact itself, and probably from the importance of its consequences. "This," says the Report, reasonably enough, "was the beginning of an examination of the claims and character of their clergy, which will end only with a reformation, hardly less startling or less needed than that of Luther."

The Convention met at New York, and consisted of one hundred and seventyfour delegates, from all parts of the Union. Lucretia Mott, an eminent Quaker preacher of Philadelphia,—a woman of an intellect as sound and comprehensive as her heart is noble—presided.[87] The Convention sat for three successive days; and, by means of wise preparation, and the appointment of sub-committees, transacted a great deal of business. Some fine addresses, to different classes interested in the question, were prepared by the sub-committees, and a plan of political action and other operations fixed on for the year. One resolution was passed to the effect that it was immoral to separate persons of color from the rest of society, and especially in churches; and that the members of the Convention pledged themselves to procure for the colored people, if possible, an equal choice with themselves of sittings in churches; and, where this was not possible, to take their seats with the despised class. Another resolution was to this effect, "that whereas our fathers, husbands, and brothers have devoted themselves to the rescue of the enslaved, at the risk of ease, reputation, and life, we, their daughters, wives and sisters, honoring their conduct, hereby pledge ourselves to uphold them by our sympathy, to share their sacrifices, and vindicate their characters." After having discharged their function, and gained some strength of heart and enlightenment of mind by their agreement in feeling and differences of opinion, these women went home, to meet again the next year at Philadelphia.

On the 27th of June the orthodox clergy took up their position against the abolitionists. The occasion was the General Association of Massachusetts Clergymen. They had long shown themselves to be uneasy at the improvements in certain of their flocks in self-reliance; and their anger and fear blazed out at the meeting of this association. Their causes of complaint were two fold: that there was a decay of deference to the pastoral office, and that an alteration was taking place in the female character. On the first point they alleged that discussion of moral questions was promoted among their people independently of the pastors, and that

> topics of reform were presented within the parochial limits of settled pastors without their consent. If there are certain topics upon which the pastor does not preach with the frequency, or in the manner which would please his people, it is a violation of sacred and important rights to encourage a stranger to present them. Deference and subordination are essential to the happiness of society, and peculiarly so in the relation of a people to their pastor.

The complaint regarding the women of the age urged that female influence should be employed in bringing minds to the pastor for instruction, instead of presuming to give it through any other medium. The movement begun by these Resolutions, worthy of the dark ages, was kept up by a set of sermons, in which this magnanimous clergy came out to war against women— the Misses Grimke in particular. It is wonderful how many of these sermons ended with a simile about a vine, a trellis and an elm.[88]

It does not appear that the parties most interested would have thought of mixing up the question of the Rights of Women with that of the Rights of Man in Slavery: but the clergy thus compelled the agitation of it. The women themselves merely looked into their own case, and went on doing what they found to be their duty. But men had more to do regarding it; more to learn upon it; and the result of the examination to which they have been driven is, that many newspapers,[89] and a large proportion of the Anti-Slavery body, have come out boldly and without reservation for the political rights of women:—the venerable Adams has pertinaciously vindicated their right of petition on the floor of Congress, and the clergy are completely foiled.[90] Long before all this took place, there was a clergyman who advocated the agency of woman in social questions, in words which are worthy of preservation. At a public meeting in 1835, Dr Follen spoke as follows. He is not, like his clerical brethren, of the same mind with Rabbi Eliezur, who said, "Perish the Book of the Law rather than it should be expounded by a woman!"

> And now, Mr. President, I come to the last topic of my resolution. I maintain that, with regard to the Anti-Slavery cause, *men* and *women* have the same duties and the same rights. The ground I take on this point is very plain. I wish to spare you, I wish to spare myself the worthless and disgusting task of replying, in detail, to all the coarse attacks and flattering sophisms, by which men have endeavored to entice or to drive women from this, and from many other spheres of moral action. "Go home and spin!" is the well-meaning advice of the domestic tyrant of the old school. "Conquer by personal charms and fashionable

attractions!" is the brilliant career marked out for her by the idols and the idolaters of fashion. "Never step out of the bounds of decorum and the *customary* ways of doing good," is the sage advice of maternal caution. "Rule by obedience, and by submission sway!" is the saying of the moralist poet, sanctioning female servitude, pointing out a resort and compensation in female cunning. What with the fear of the insolent remarks about women, in which those of the dominant sex, whose bravery is the generous offspring of conscious impunity, are particularly apt to indulge; and with the still stronger fear of being thought unfeminine—it is indeed, a proof of uncommon moral courage, or of an overpowering sense of religious duty and sympathy with the oppressed, that a woman is induced to embrace the unpopular, unfashionable, obnoxious principles of the abolitionists. Popular opinion, the habits of society, are all calculated to lead women to consider the place, the privileges and the duties which etiquette has assigned to them, as their peculiar portion, as more important than those which nature has given them in common with men. Men have at all times been inclined to allow to women peculiar privileges, while withholding from them essential rights. In the progress of civilization and christianity, one right after another has been conceded, one occupation after another has been placed within the reach of women. Still are we far from a practical acknowledgment of the simple truth, that the rational and moral nature of man is the foundation of all rights and duties, and that women as well as men are rational and moral beings. It is on this account that I look upon the formation of Ladies' Anti-Slavery Societies as an event of the highest interest, not only for its direct beneficial bearing on the cause of emancipation, but still more as an indication of the moral growth of society. Women begin to feel that the place which men have marked out for them, is but a small part of what society owes to them, and what they themselves owe to society, to the whole human family, and to that Power to whom each and all are indebted and accountable, for the use of the powers entrusted to them. It is indeed, a consoling thought, that such is the providential adaptation of all things, that the toil and the sufferings of the slave, however unprofitable to himself, and however hopeless, are not wholly thrown away and vain—that the master who has deprived him of the fruits of his industry, of every motive and opportunity for exercising his highest faculties, has not been able to prevent his exercising, unconsciously, a moral and spiritual influence all over the world, breaking down every unnatural restraint, and calling forth the simplest and deepest of all human emotions, the feeling of man for his fellow man, and bringing out the strongest intellectual and moral powers to his rescue. It is, indeed, natural that the cry of misery, the call for help, that is now spreading far and wide, and penetrating the inmost recesses of society, should thrill, with peculiar power, through the heart of woman. For it is woman, injured, insulted woman, that exhibits the most baneful and hateful influences of slavery. But I cannot speak of what the free woman ought and must feel for her enslaved sister—because I am overwhelmed by the thought of what we men, we, who have mothers, and wives, and daughters, should not only feel, but do, and dare, and sacrifice, to drain the marshes whose exhalations infect the moral atmosphere of society.

As no degree of violence directed to break up the meetings of the Ladies' Society, was too strong for the consciences of certain of the gentlemen of Boston, so no device was clearly too low for their purpose of hindering utterance. When they found they could not stop the women's tongues by violence, they privily sprinkled cayenne-pepper on the stove of their place of meeting, thus compelling them to cough down their own speakers. . . . [discusses clergy's resistance to women abolitionists, followed by Chapman's response]:

"Women of New England! We are told of our powerful *indirect* influence; our claim on man's *gallantry* and *chivalry.* We would not free all the slaves in Christendom by indirection—*such* indirection. We trust to be strengthened for any sacrifices in their cause; but we may not endanger our own souls for their redemption. Let our influence be open and *direct:* such as *our* husbands will not blush to see us exercise."—["]When clergymen plead usage and immemorial custom in favor of unutterable wrong, and bid us keep silence for courtesy, and put the enginery of church organization in play as a hindrance to our cause, and not as a help, our situation calls for far more strenuous exertion than when, in 1835, the freedom of the women of Boston was vilely bartered away in the merchant-thronged street. Our situation is as much more perilous now, as spiritual is more dreadful than temporal outrage. We have no means to strengthen and nourish our spirits but by entertaining and obeying the free Spirit of God."—"As yet our judgment is unimpaired by hopes of the favor, and our resolution undamped by the fear of the host who oppose us. As yet our hearts are not darkened by the shadow of unkindness. We listen to clerical appeals, and religious magazines, and the voices of an associated clergy, as though we heard them not, so full on the ear of every daughter among us falls the cry of the fatherless and those who have none to help them—so full in every motherly heart and eye rises the image of one pining in captivity, who cannot be comforted because her children are not."—*Right and Wrong in Boston,* iii. pp. 73, 75, 86.

If the orthodox clergy are wise, they will let matters rest where they are.[91]

The other great event of the year concerned the freedom of the press, and was as remarkable in its consequences as it was interesting in itself. Never was there a case of martyrdom more holy than that which we are about to relate. Never was there more complete evidence that a man in the prime of life, attached to the world by the tenderest ties, and of a calm, rational mind, was able long to sustain the apprehension of violent death, and to meet it at last, rather than yield up a principle which he knew to be true. He could not give up truth for safety and life—no not even for wife and child,—Elijah P. Lovejoy was a native of Maine, a graduate of Waterville College. He settled at St. Louis, Missouri, and attained a high reputation as editor of a newspaper there. He became a clergyman, and at length an abolitionist. After the burning of M'Intosh, at St. Louis, he spoke out in his newspaper about the atrocity of the deed, and exposed the iniquities of the district judge, and of the mob which overawed Marion College and brought two of the students before a Lynch Court. For this, his press and types were destroyed, and he established himself on the opposite side of the river, in the free State of Illinois. But the town of Alton, in which he set up his press, was as dangerous to him as if it had stood in a slave State. It was the resort of slave-traders and river-traders, who believed their interests to depend on the preservation of slavery. For some time after his settlement at Alton, he did not think it necessary to enter into express discussion of the slavery question. At length he saw it to be his duty to do so: he called together the supporters of the paper, and laid his views before them. They consented to let his conscience have free course: he did his duty, and his press was again destroyed by a mob. Twice more was his property annihilated in the same manner, without the slightest alteration of conduct on his part. His paper continued to be the steady, dispassionate advocate of freedom and reprover of violence. In October 1837, he wrote to a friend in New York, to unburden his full head and heart. After having described the fury and murderous spirit of his assailants, and the manner in which for weeks his footsteps had been tracked by assassins, he proceeded—

> And now, my dear brother, if you ask what are my own feelings at a time like this, I answer, perfectly calm, perfectly resigned. Though in the midst of danger, I have a constant sense of security that keeps me alike from fear and anxiety, I read the Bible, and especially the Psalms, with a delight, a refreshing of soul I never knew before. God has said, "As thy day is, so shall thy strength be"; and he has made his promise good. Pray for me.—We have a few excellent brethren here, in Alton. They are sincerely desirous to know their duty at this crisis, and to do it: but as yet they cannot see that duty *requires* them to maintain their cause here, at all hazards. Of this be assured, the cause of truth still lives in Illinois and will not want defenders. Whether our paper starts again will depend on our friends, East, West, North, and South. So far as it depends on me, it shall go forward. By the blessing of God, I will not abandon the enterprise so long as I live, and until success has crowned it. And there are those in Illinois who join me in this resolution. And if I am to die, it cannot be in a better cause. Your's, till death or victory, E. P. Lovejoy.

Death and victory were now both at hand. Two or three weeks after this letter was written, he was called before a large meeting of the townsmen on a singular affair. A committee of gentlemen was appointed to mediate between the editor of the *Alton Observer* and the mob. They drew up a set of "Compromise Resolutions," so called, which yielded everything to the mob, and required of Lovejoy to leave the place. One member of the committee, Mr. Gilman, remonstrated: but he was overborne. Lovejoy was summoned, and required to leave the place. He listened till the chairman had said what he had to say, and then stepped forward to the bar. There, with grisly Murder peeping over his shoulder, he bore his last verbal testimony in the following unpremeditated address, reported by a person present. . . . [Here follows Lovejoy's speech.]

A few days after this he was murdered. His office was surrounded by an armed mob, and defended from within by a guard furnished by the Mayor of Alton. When the attack was supposed to be over, Lovejoy looked out to reconnoitre. He received five bullets in his body, was able to reach a room on the first floor, declared himself fatally wounded, and fell on his face dead. His age was thirtytwo. . . .

In a note to his tract on Slavery, Dr Channing had said, a year before this, "One kidnapped, murdered abolitionist would do more for the violent destruction of slavery than a thousand societies. His name would be sainted. The day of his death would be set apart for solemn, heart stirring commemoration. His blood would cry through the land with a thrilling voice, would pierce every dwelling, and find a response in every heart." These latter clauses have come true. The anniversary of Lovejoy's death will be a sacrament day to his comrades till slavery shall be no more: and as for the community,—the multitudes who were too busy eating and drinking, planting, trading, or amusing themselves, to know the pangs that were rending the very heart of their society,—those who considered abolitionism too "low" a subject for their ears, and the abolitionists too "odd" a set of people for their notice,—the shock of murder has roused even these from their apathy, and carried into their minds some notion that they are living in remarkable times, and that they have some extraordinary neighbors. We believe that no steps have been taken to punish the murderers; but such punishment was urged by the newspapers even in the slave States; and the cry of reprobation of the deed was vehement from all the more enlightened parts of the Union. Dr Channing did his duty well. The rioters at Alton were heard encouraging one another by reference to old Boston. The time was at hand for them to learn that there was a right as well as wrong in the time honored city.

It was proposed to hold a meeting in Boston, where there should be no distinction of sect or party, and no reference to any anti-slavery organization, to express the alarm and horror of the citizens at the view of the prostration of civil liberty, and at the murder of a Christian minister for daring to maintain his inalienable and constitutional rights. Application was made to the authorities for the use of Faneuil Hall for the occasion,—Dr Channing's name being placed at the head of the requisition. The authorities were intimidated by a counter-petition, and refused the use of the Hall, on the ground of the request not being in accordance with public sentiment! . . .

A spontaneous meeting of citizens was held to discuss the refusal of the authorities, and Dr Channing's strictures on it. The consequence was that the very same requisition was again tendered to the authorities, with such a mass of signatures to it that its prayer was granted with an obsequiousness as remarkable as the previous insult. Faneuil Hall was thrown open on the 8th of December, and crowded. The chair was taken by a respected citizen, who was allied with no party,—Mr. Jonathan Phillips. The resolutions were prepared by Dr. Channing. Neither he, nor the chairman, nor any one but the organized abolitionists (who have good reason to know their townsmen) was fully aware of the crisis to which this meeting brought the fate of the abolitionists throughout the community. It hung at last for the space of

three minutes upon the lips one very young speaker, who was heard only because of his rank. It came to the turn of a hair whether the atrocious mob-
speech of the Attorney General should be acted upon, or whether he should
be overwhelmed with the reprobation of society; whether the abolitionists
should have the alternative of being murdered at home, and being driven
into the wilderness, or whether liberty of speech and the press should prevail. Happily, the eloquence of the young Wendell Phillips secured the victory.[92] Among other discoveries, the Attorney General announced that Lovejoy died "as a fool dieth," and that his murderers were patriots of the same
order as the Tea Party of the Revolution. An extract from a private letter will
best describe this critical meeting.

> You will have heard of Dr. Channing's recent exploit. The massacre of one of
> our beloved friends in the West for being an abolitionist and acting up to his
> principles, induced Dr. C. to sign a call for a public indignation meeting in Fa-
> neuil Hall. It was a noble sight,—that hall on that day. The morning sunlight
> never streamed in over such a throng. By night it has been closer packed; but
> never, they tell me, by day. I went (for the Woman Question), with fifteen oth-
> ers. The indignation at us was great. People said it gave the meeting the air of
> an abolition gathering to have women there; it hung out false colors. Shame!
> when it was a free discussion meeting, and nothing more, that women should
> have "given color to the idea that it was for abolition purposes." Good, is it not,
> that sixteen women can give a character to a meeting of twentyfive hundred
> men? O that you had been there! A hundred women or so in a drawing room,
> gathered together by a new application of religious and democratic, viz: Chris-
> tian principles, was all that Boston had to show you when you were here. But
> this Faneuil Hall gathering, to *protect* the minority in the application of their
> principles was an imposing spectacle. . . . Dr. Channing did not know how dan-
> gerous an experiment (as people count danger) he adventured. *We* knew that
> we must send the children out of town, and sleep in our garments that night,
> unless free discussion prevailed. Lovejoy stood upon the defensive, as the Bill of
> Rights and New England Divinity bear him out in having done. His death lies,
> in a double sense, at the door of the church; for she trained him to self-defence,
> and then attacked him. This new aspect of the cause, orthodox church opposi-
> tion to it as a heresy, has presented itself since you were here, and a most per-
> ilous crisis it has been. I think the ship has righted; but she was on her beam-
> ends so long, that I thought all was over for "this 200 years," as Dr. Beecher
> says. I have just sent off 55,000 women's signatures for the abolition in the Dis-
> trict of Columbia—a weary labor. My brain turns with the counting and indors-
> ing. I wrote well on them for the honor of Massachusetts, which is the reason I
> write so badly to you now. I am thoroughly tired. God be with you evermore!

The second General Convention of Women was held, as appointed, at
Philadelphia, in the spring of the present year. Once, again, has the intrepidity of these noble Christian women been put to the proof; the outrages in

this "city of brotherly love" having been the most fearful to which they have yet been exposed. The cause of the extraordinary violence of this year is to be found in the old maxim that men hate those whom they have injured. The State Convention, which had been employed for many previous months in preparing a new constitution for Pennsylvania, had deprived the citizens of color of the political rights which they had held (but rarely dared to exercise) under the old constitution. Having done this injury, the perpetrators, and those who assented to their act, were naturally on the watch against those whom they had oppressed, and were jealous of every movement. When the abolitionists began to gather to their Convention, when the liberal part of the Quaker population came abroad, and were seen greeting their fellow-emancipators in the city of Penn—when the doors of the fine new building, Pennsylvania Hall, were thrown open, and the people of color were seen flocking thither, with hope in their faces, and with heads erect, in spite of the tyranny of the new laws, the hatred of their oppressors grew too violent for restraint. It was impossible to find reasonable and true causes of complaint against any of the parties concerned in the Convention, and falsehoods were therefore framed and circulated. Even these falsehoods were of a nature which makes it difficult for people on this side of the Atlantic to understand how they should be used as a pretext for such an excess of violence as succeeded. The charge against the abolitionists was that they ostentatiously walked the streets arm-in-arm with people of color. They did not do this, because the act was not necessary to the assertion of any principle, and would have been offensive; but if they had, it might have been asked what excuse this was for firing Pennsylvania Hall?

The delegates met and transacted their business, as in the preceding year, but this time with a yelling mob around the doors. The mild voice of Angelina [Grimké] Weld was heard above the hoarse roar; but it is said that the transient appearance of Maria Chapman was the most striking circumstance of the day. She was ill, and the heat of the weather was tremendous; but, scarcely able to sustain herself under an access of fever, she felt it her duty to appear on the platform, showing once more that where shame and peril are, there is she. Commenting upon the circumstances of the moment, the strain of her exhortation accorded well with the angelic beauty of her countenance, and with the melting tones of her voice, and with the summary of duty which she had elsewhere presented: "Our principles teach us how to avoid that spurious charity which would efface moral distinctions, and that our duty to the sinner is, not to palliate, but to pardon; not to excuse, but to forgive, freely, fully, as we hope to be forgiven." To these principles she has ever been faithful, whether she gathers her children about her knees at home, or bends over the pillow of a dying friend, or stands erect amidst the insults and outrages of a mob, to strengthen the souls of her fellow-sufferers. Her strain is ever the same—no compromise, but unbounded forgiveness.

If the authorities had done their duty, no worse mischief than threat and insult would have happened; but nothing effectual was done in answer to a demonstration on the part of the mob, repeated for three or four nights; so at last they broke into Pennsylvania Hall, heaped together the furniture and books in the middle of the floor, and burned them and the building together. The circumstance which most clearly indicates the source of the rage of the mob, was their setting fire to the Orphan Asylum for colored children; a charity wholly unconnected with abolitionism, and in no respect, but the complexion of its inmates, on a different footing from any other charitable institution in the Quaker city. The Recorder interposed vigorously; and, after the burning of the Hall, the city firemen undertook the protection of all the buildings in the place, public and private. The morning after the fire the abolitionists were asked what they intended to do next. Their answer was clear and ready. They had already raised funds and engaged workmen to restore their Hall, and had issued their notices of the meeting of the third General Convention in the spring of 1839. They have since applied for damages, which we believe the city agreed, without demur, to pay. It is astonishing that the absurdity of persecuting such people as these has not long been apparent to all eyes. Their foes might as well wage a pop-gun war against the constellations of the sky.

It appears as if each State had to pass through riot to rectitude on this mighty question. Every State which has now an abolition legislature, and is officered by abolitionists, has, we believe, gone through this process. The course of events seems to be this: the abolitionists are first ridiculed as a handful of insignificant fanatics; then the merchants begin to be alarmed for their purses, and the aristocracy for their prerogatives; the clergy and professional men act and speak for the merchant-interest, and engage authorities to discountenance the movement, which they do by threatening penal laws, or uttering warnings of mobs. A mob ensues, of course; the apprehensions of the magistracy furnishing the broadest hint. The business is brought home to the bosom of every citizen. All, especially the young men, look into the matter, rally in defence of the law, elect a good legislature, look carefully to their magistracy, and the right prevails. Such seems to have been the process in every State disgraced by an anti-abolition riot. We trust it may be so in Pennsylvania. Mrs. Child said long ago that this evil spirit having so long intimately possessed the nation, we cannot expect that it should be cast out without much rending and tearing.

The abolitionists, as a body, are now fairly recognized by the South. Mr. Birney has been applied to by Mr. Elmore, a southern member of Congress, under the sanction of Mr. Calhoun himself, for a fulfilment of his offer to lay open all the affairs of the anti-slavery body. The affairs of the abolitionists have from the beginning been open to all the world; the evil has been that the world would not attend to them. Now, however, "the South desires to learn the depth, height and breadth of the storm which impends over her." She has learned what she wants, for Mr. Birney has forwarded exceedingly full replies to the fourteen queries proposed by the southern representatives and senators. This may be regarded as an extremely fortunate event.

It is a most cheering testimony to the progress of the cause; and it affords some hope that the South will take warning in time, and present an honorable exception to the conduct and catastrophe of a struggle for and relinquishment of irresponsible power. The hope is faint; for instances are rare, if not unknown, of privileged bodies surrendering their social privileges on a merely moral summons. But again, instances are rare, if not unknown, of a privileged class appealing to a magnanimous foe for an exposure of his forces, his designs, and his expectations. Whatever irritability may display itself in the conduct of the appeal, the fact is highly honorable to both parties. To our minds, it is one of the most striking circumstances of this majestic story. Mr. Birney's reply is far too long to be given here, even in the briefest abstract. It is extremely interesting, from the honorable accuracy and candor of its statements, and its abstinence from all manifestation of the triumph which its facts might well justify. These important papers go by the name of the "Elmore Correspondence."

The most melancholy feature of the struggle—more so than even the conduct of the clergy (which has been far more extraordinary than we have had space to relate) is the degeneracy of Congress. The right of petition has been virtually annihilated for these three years past; and the nation has been left unrepresented on the most important question which has been occupying the nation's mind. The people hold their remedy in the ballot box. The elections are now going forward; and we doubt not the electors will take care that such a suspension of their rights does not happen again. We understand, indeed, that the usual federal and democratic questions are in many cases laid aside at the present elections for the all-important one of the abolition of slavery in the District of Columbia, and the prohibition of the inter-state slave trade. Happen what may, it will not be forgotten in future times that there was one man who did his duty. Several others tried, but found circumstances too strong for them. John Quincy Adams has conquered circumstances. Speculation has for some years been busy on a fact of this gentleman being a Massachusetts representative after having been President of the United States. While some honored the succession of offices as a proof of the highest patriotism, others magnanimously interpreted it is an indication of vain, restless ambition. His late conduct must convince all fairminded observers of the intrepidity and purity of his patriotism. At his years it is impossible that he can look to the anti-slavery party for any rewards adequate to what he has risked and undergone in defence of their rights. Inch by inch has he maintained alone the ground of constitutional rights; month after month has he painfully struggled for speech, and been gagged by unconstitutional resolutions and *ex-post facto* rules. We will not enter upon the grievous tale of the insults that have been heaped upon his revered head, and the moral inflections by which his noble heart has been wrung. This man was (by universal acknowledgment) the purest of the American Presidents, except Washington; and he has lived to see the nation he governed virtually deprived (however temporarily) of their rights of petition and free discussion; and when he protested against this privation, one member started up to say that he considered Mr. Adams to be in the wane of his intellect, and another to call him a sort of stormy petrel, delighting in commotion. (This is of a piece with the assurance that the abolitionists *like* to be persecuted.) The more pertinaciously his mouth was stopped, the more vigilantly did Mr. Adams watch for an opportunity to speak. At last he found it. Under cover of remarks on the Report of the Committee of Foreign Affairs in relation to Texas, he delivered himself of all his protests and all his opinions on the vicious legislation of the last two sessions on slavery, Texas, and the reception of petitions. For an hour a day during twelve days he spoke, under perpetual calls to order, but with power to proceed till he chose to stop. We subjoin an extract from that hour-long oratory, which will not be forgotten by any of the hundreds who heard it, or by any of the millions who owe to him the patient and intrepid assertion of their constitutional rights in the martyr-age of the republic.

Thursday, June 28, 1838. Mr. Adams resumed the floor in support of his resolution respecting the admission of Texas to the Union.

> When I last addressed the House I was engaged in discussing the principle asserted by the Chairman of the Committee on Foreign Affairs; the practical effect of which must be to deprive one half of the population of these United States of the right to petition before this House. I say it goes to deprive the entire female sex of all right of petition here. The principle is not an abstract principle. It is stated abstractedly, in the report of his remarks, which I have once read to the House. I will read it again; it is highly important, and well deserving of the attention of this House, and its solemn decision. It referred to all petitions on the subject of the annexation of Texas to this Union which come from women:—
>
> "Many of these petitions were signed by women. He always felt regret when petitions thus signed were presented to the House relating to political matters. He thought these females could have a sufficient field for the exercise of their influence in the discharge of their duties to their fathers, their husbands, or their children, cheering the domestic circle, and shedding over it the mild radiance of the social virtues, instead of rushing into the fierce struggles of political life. He felt sorrow at this departure from their proper sphere, in which there was abundant room for the practice of the most extensive benevolence and philanthropy, because he considered it discreditable, not only to their own particular section of the country, but also to the national character, and thus giving him a right to express this opinion."
>
> Now, I say, in the first place, that this principle is erroneous, vicious. As a moral principle it is vicious; and in its application the chairman of the committee made it the ground of a reproach to the females of my district; thousands of whom, besides those 238 who signed the first petition I presented here, have signed similar petitions. That is his application. And what is the consequence intended to follow? Why, that petitions of that sort deserve no consideration,

and that the committee are, therefore, fully justified in never looking into one of them. And this, because they come from *women;* and women, departing from their own proper sphere, in the domestic circle, do what is discreditable, not only to their own particular district of country, but to the national character. There is the broad principle, and there is its application. This has compelled me to probe it to the bottom, and to show that it is fundamentally wrong, that it is vicious, and the very reverse of that which should prevail.

Why does it follow that women are fitted for nothing but the cares of domestic life? for bearing children, and cooking the food of a family? devoting all their time to the domestic circle—to promoting the immediate personal comfort of their husbands, brothers, and sons? Observe, sir, the point of departure between the chairman of the committee and myself. I admit that it is their duty to attend to these things. I subscribe fully to the elegant compliment passed by him upon those members of the female sex who devote their time to these duties. But I say that the correct principle is, that women are not only justified, but exhibit the most exalted virtue when they do depart from the domestic circle, and enter on the concerns of their country, of humanity, and of their God. The mere departure of women from the duties of the domestic circle, far from being a reproach to her, is a virtue of the highest order, when it is done from purity of motive, by appropriate means, and towards a virtuous purpose. There is the true distinction. The motive must be pure, the means appropriate, and the purpose good. And I say that woman, by the discharge of such duties, has manifested a virtue which is even above the virtues of mankind, and approaches to a superior nature. That is the principle I maintain, and which the chairman of the committee has to refute, if he applies the position he has taken to the mothers, the sisters, and the daughters of the men of my district who voted to send me here. Now I aver, further, that in the instance to which his observation refers, viz. in the act of petitioning against the annexation of Texas to this Union, the motive was pure, the means appropriate, and the purpose virtuous, in the highest degree. As an evident proof of this, I recur to the particular petition from which this debate took its rise, viz. to the first petition I presented here against the annexation—a petition consisting of three lines, and signed by 238 women of Plymouth, a principal town in my own district. Their words are—

"The undersigned, women of Plymouth (Mass.), thoroughly aware of the sinfulness of slavery, and the consequent impolicy and disastrous tendency of its extension in our country, do most respectfully remonstrate, with all our souls, against the annexation of Texas to the United States, as a slave-holding territory."

Those are the words of their memorial. And I say that, in presenting it here, their motive was pure, and of the highest order of purity. They petitioned under a conviction that the consequence of the annexation would be the advancement of that which is sin in the sight of God, viz. slavery. I say, further, that the means were appropriate, because it is Congress who must decide on the question; and, therefore, it is proper that they should petition Congress if they wish to prevent the annexation. And I say, in the third place, that the end was virtuous, pure, and of the most exalted character, viz. to prevent the perpetuation and spread of slavery through America. I say, moreover, that I subscribe, in my own person, to every word the petition contains. I do believe slavery to be a sin before God, and that is the reason, and the only insurmountable reason, why we should refuse to annex Texas to this Union. For, although the amendment I have moved declares that neither Congress nor any other portion of this Government is of itself competent to make this annexation, yet I hold it not impossible, with the consent of the people of the United States and of the people of Texas, that a Union might properly be accomplished. It might be effected by an amendment of the Constitution, submitted to the approval of the people of the United States, as all other amendments are to be submitted, and by afterwards submitting the question to the decision of the people of both States.—I admit that in that way such a union might be, and may be, formed. But not with a State tolerating slavery; not with a people who have converted freemen into slaves; not so long as slavery exists in Texas. So long as that continues, I do not hold it practicable, in any form, that the two nations should ever be united. Thus far I go. I concur in every word of the petition I had the honor to present; and I hold it to be proof of pure patriotism, of sincere piety, and of every virtue that can adorn the female character.

With regard to this principle I am willing it shall be discussed. I hope it will be discussed, not only in this House, but throughout this nation.

I should not have detained the House so long in establishing this position, had I not felt it a duty I owed to my constituents to vindicate the characters of their wives and sisters and daughters, who were assailed by the sentiment I have opposed. . . .

During the last year, several Halls of State Legislature have been granted to the abolitionists for their meetings, while the churches have remained closed against them. The aspect of these assemblages has been very remarkable, from the union of religious and political action witnessed there. But the most extraordinary spectacle of all—a spectacle perhaps unrivalled in the history of the world—was the address of Angelina Grimke before a Committee of the Legislature of Massachusetts. Some have likened it to the appeal of Hortensia to the Roman Senate; but others have truly observed that the address of Angelina Grimke was far the nobler of the two, as she complained not as the voice of a party remonstrating against injuries done to itself, but as the advocate of a class too degraded and helpless to move or speak on its own behalf. The gentle dignity of the speaker's manner, and the power of statement and argument shown in her address, together with the righteousness of her cause, won the sympathies of as large an audience as the State House would contain, and bore down all ridicule, prejudice, and passion. Two emotions divided the vast assemblage of hearers;—sympathy in her cause, and veneration for herself. The only fear entertained by the abolitionists with regard to the cause in the leading State of Massachusetts, is lest it should become too flourishing, and lose something of its rectitude in its prosperity.

The history of this struggle seems to yield a few inferences which must, we think, be evident to all impartial minds; and which are as important as they are clear. One is, that this is a struggle which cannot subside till it has prevailed. If this be true, the consequence of yielding to it would be the saving of a world of guilt and woe. Another is, that other sorts of freedom, besides emancipation from slavery, will come in with it, that the aristocratic spirit in all its manifestations is being purged out of the community;—that with every black slave a white will be also freed. Another is, that republicanism is in no degree answerable for the want of freedom and of peace under which the American nation is now suffering;—that, on the contrary, the turbulence and tyranny are the immediate offspring of the old-world, feudal, European spirit which still lives in the institution assailed, and in the bosoms of the aristocracy of the country, while the bulwarks of the Constitution, the true republicans, are the "peacemen," the sufferers, the moral soldiers, who have gone out armed only with faith, hope, and charity. Another is, that the colored people have a promising *morale* on which to ground their civilization. Their whole conduct affords evidences of generosity, patience, and hopefulness, from which fine results of character may be anticipated, whenever this unfortunate race shall have leave to exert their unfettered energies under circumstances of average fairness.

It is a wide world that we live in, as wonderful in the diversity of its moral as of its natural features. A just survey of the whole can leave little doubt that the abolitionists of the United States are the greatest people now living and moving in it. There is beauty in the devotedness of the domestic life of every land; there is beauty in the liberality of the philosophers of the earth, in the laboriousness of statesmen, in the beneficence of the wealthy, in the faith and charity of the poor. All these graces flourish among this martyr company, and others with them, which it is melting to the very soul to contemplate. To appreciate them fully, one must be among them. One must hear their diversity of tongue—from the quaint Scripture Phraseology of the Pilgrims to the classical language of the scholar—to estimate their liberality. One must witness the eagerness with which each strives to bring down the storm upon his own head to save his neighbor, and to direct any transient sunshine into his friend's house rather than his own, to understand their generosity. One must see the manly father weeping over his son's blighted prospects, and the son vindicating his mother's insulted name, to appreciate their disinterestedness. One must experience something of the soul-sickness and misgiving caused by popular hatred, and of the awful pangs of an apprehended violent death, to enter fully into their heroism. Those who are living in peace afar off can form but a faint conception of what it is to have no respite, no prospect of rest, of security, of success, within any calculable time. The grave, whether it yawns beneath his feet, or lies on the far horizon, is, as they well know, their only resting-place; adversity is all around them, like the whirlwind of the desert. But, if all this can be scarcely conceived of at a distance, neither can their bright faces be seen there. Nowhere but among such, can an array of countenances be beheld so little lower than the angels'. Ordinary social life is spoiled to them; but another which is far better has grown up among them. They had more life than others to begin with, as the very fact of their enterprise shows: and to them that have much shall more be given. They are living fast and loftily. The weakest of them who drops into the grave worn out, and the youngest that lies murdered on his native republican soil, has enjoyed a richer harvest of time, a larger gift out of eternity, than the octogenarian self-seeker, however he may have attained his ends. These things, as branches of general truths, may be understood at the distance of half the globe. Let us not, therefore, wait, as it has been the world's custom to wait, for another century to greet the confessors and martyrs who stretch out their strong arms to bring down Heaven upon our earth; but even now, before they have stripped off care and sorrow with their mortal frame,—even now, while sympathy may cheer and thanks may animate, let us make our reverent congratulations heard over the ocean which divides us from the spiritual potentates of our age. H. M.

❖ ❖ ❖

Part Two

N E W S P A P E R S
A N D   P E R I O D I C A L S

Writing of the central role of journalism in Victorian culture, Susan Drain notes: "The history of journalism is the history of the Victorian age. Not just as a vivid contemporary record, but in its huge quantity and vast range, its penetration of all levels of society, . . . the work of the journalists . . . is of unprecedented and unequaled significance" (1988, 415). Far from modern associations with hackwork and unscrupulous tactics, Victorian journalism frequently exhibits a superior level of writing that exceeds today's readers' expectations of daily and weekly publications.

The suggestion (by Elizabeth Barrett Browning, for one) that Harriet Martineau compromised her literary talent by writing for periodicals fails to account for the changing view of journalism over the course of the nineteenth century. Early in the century, newspaper journalism was regarded as a rather low occupation for any man—much less any woman—who aspired to respectability. "High" journalism, like the quarterlies discussed in part III, was more respectable; it implied a degree of gentility denied to weekly or daily papers because the quarterlies allowed extended treatments of lofty topics compared to the necessarily briefer treatments of current, often "coarse" events in dailies and weeklies. But although the profession began in ignominy, it grew in stature and respectability as the century progressed. Drain writes that journalism was not "just a literary career; it was a major part of intellectual activity in all areas. Historians, scientists, politicians, theologians, and critics all wrote for the periodicals," resulting in an "intellectual cross-fertilization" quite unlike what we find in modern journalism (416). She observes also that the common practice of anonymity allowed women and other "unknowns" access to writing careers that might otherwise have been denied them.

Of the variety of genres and styles produced by Harriet Martineau throughout her career, the most prominent is her periodicals writing. Beginning with her writing debut in 1821 in the Unitarian *Monthly Repository,* the success of which won her family's approval while providing her with a necessary, although unusually brief, literary apprenticeship, Martineau wrote for *Athenaeum, Chambers' Journal, Cornhill Magazine, Daily News, Edinburgh Review, Household Words, Leader,*

London and Westminster Review, Macmillan's Magazine, New Monthly Magazine, Once a Week, Pall Mall Gazette, Penny Magazine, People's Journal, Quarterly Review, Spectator, Tait's Edinburgh Review, Westminster Review, and the American periodicals National Anti-Slavery Standard, Liberty Bell, and Atlantic Monthly.

The selections in this section begin with the Liberty Bell, in which Martineau's use of a spiritualized style and the rhetoric of martyrdom is typical of the period that also produced The Martyr Age of the United States. A comparison of her Liberty Bell contributions with her mature journalism charts her growth as a journalist who ultimately handled the slavery issue with mature gravity, philosophical insight, historical and political acuity, and a commanding rhetorical presence. Harriet Martineau's participation in the extraordinarily rich and lively discourse of nineteenth-century journalism is central both to the development of the genre and to her role as a social reformer.

❖ ❖ ❖

T H E *L I B E R T Y B E L L*

1839–1856

The *Liberty Bell,* an annual published in Boston for the Massachusetts Anti-Slavery Fair and edited by Maria Weston Chapman, featured poetry, fiction, letters, and short nonfiction pieces. Chapman learned publishing and editing skills through her work on Garrison's *Liberator.* Originally modeled after the elegantly bound gift books that were fashionable at the time, the *Liberty Bell* "reflected the popular culture of the day, containing a quantity of melodramatic stories, verse . . . , improving tales and topical articles" (Taylor 1995, 88). Martineau contributed to the *Liberty Bell* for twenty years, along with such high-profile abolitionists as Lydia Maria Child, Lucretia Mott, Maria Weston Chapman, William Lloyd Garrison, Frederick Douglass, Wendell Phillips, and George Thompson.

The tone of this periodical is typical of the abolition movement's evangelical sentimentalism, to which the practical concerns of emancipation tend to be sublimated. As a survey of her work on American issues demonstrates, Martineau's abolitionism was distinguished by its attention to practical matters—politics, economy, psychology, health, and sociology—all presented in the context of a fundamental ethic: that ownership of humans is morally wrong. Proving Charles Dickens's disgruntled charge that she evidently aimed to enlighten all of humankind, Martineau is best characterized as a social-problem writer eager to address all sides of an argument from a variety of ideological perspectives. As is true of all her writing, her periodical articles typically speak to both economic concerns and human rights issues, endeavoring to strike common ground without compromising the latter.

Yet, interestingly, her contributions to the *Liberty Bell* are more in the sentimental than the pragmatic vein. One reason for this may be Chapman's early influence over Martineau, which seemed to threaten the latter's identity: "My relation to Mrs. Chapman required my utmost moral care. . . . I felt that it must be morally perilous to lean on any one mind as I could not but lean on hers" (1983, 2:84–85). The identity struggle is evidenced in some of Martineau's more sentimental contributions, like "The Elixir Vitae" (1841), "A Child's Thought" (1842), and a poem entitled "Pity the Slave" (1844).

Subsequent articles reflect the dramatic shift in Martineau's theological thinking following her 1846 tour of the Middle East—for example, "Incidents of Travel" (1848) and "Letter from Harriet Martineau" (1849), which boldly compare the sexual slavery of "hareems" with slavery in the American South. Another original approach to the topic of slavery is an article about black Haitian liberator Toussaint L'Ouverture, the subject of Martineau's 1841 historical biography, *The Hour and the Man.*

Maria Weston Chapman
(Boston Public Library/Rare Books Department.
Courtesy of The Trustees)

Departing somewhat from the usual sentimentalism of the *Liberty Bell,* the follow-ing entry is significant as a response to the 1840 ideological split in the abolitionist movement; the resulting hostilities and fragmentation remained unhealed through the end of the Civil War. Reprinted here is a letter from "Harriet Martineau to Elizabeth Pease" (written 1841, published 1845) addressing those differences as outlined in John Collins's *Right and Wrong among the Abolitionists of the United States.*[93] By 1839–1840, some American Anti-Slavery Society members began to have serious dif-ferences with Garrison, arguing against the participation of women in abolitionist ac-tivities and urging more aggressive political involvement than grassroots activism per-mitted. Mirroring the threat of secession from the Union posed by the southern states, Arthur and Lewis Tappan and others broke away from the society to form the American and Foreign Anti-Slavery Society and the Liberty Party, whose candidates ran in several presidential elections; the Massachusetts Anti-Slavery Society was also formed at this time, permitting only men to join. Aside from grassroots versus political activism, then, women's rights are here sharply revealed as another primary proving ground; together, the two dramatize Martineau's distinction between politics (official hegemonic institu-tions) and morality (human rights issues). Martineau's letter makes clear her allegiance to Garrisonian abolitionism, with its recognition of women's parallel enslavement.

Martineau was an extremely prolific letter writer who employed this essentially pri-vate genre in many of her professional writings intended for publication. She favored the epistolary form for the atmosphere of intimacy and sincerity it evoked; this exam-ple illustrates that Martineau's fame and influence were such that an ostensibly private letter between herself and abolitionist Elizabeth Pease served as a suitable introduction for Collins's pamphlet. In another letter to Pease, Martineau wrote: "It seems to me that there is no longer a choice about publishing the Correspondence. . . . It sickens one's heart to learn of their proceedings; but they are now so flagrant that it appears neces-sary to tell the whole story. . . . We may yet hope that the truth will shine out from be-hind all defects in the medium of convenance."[94]

Martineau's final contribution to the *Liberty Bell* is undoubtedly the most cryptic of her career. Entitled "Truth," the full text reads: "Among the few things absolutely sure, is the obligation of them that search for truth to communicate what they ob-tain" (1858: 328). Written in the midst of the most serious and professionally grati-fying literary engagements of her life, her words suggest that now, freed from the early influences that stymied her development, this "first and greatest of women journalists" is her own best influence and source of truth.

. . .

"Harriet Martineau to Elizabeth Pease"
1845

(The date of this Letter [the composition date of 1841] shows it to have been written soon after the attempt to destroy the American Anti-Slavery Society in 1840. As long as the warfare then begun against the American

Abolitionists, by the organization of a hostile society, and carried on under the name of a "Liberty Party," shall continue, so long will this Letter be as useful to the cause of the Slave, as it is beautiful and true in general principle, and noble and faithful in individual deed. [Chapman])

My Dear Friend: I have read the statements in *Right and Wrong among the Abolitionists of the United States*, with respect to the differences between the two Anti-Slavery Societies of America, with a strong and painful interest. I wish I could adequately express my sense of the duty of every one interested in the cause of the Negro—of human freedom at large—to read and deeply meditate this piece of history. I am not more firmly persuaded of any thing, than that those who, on the present occasion, listen to one side only, or refuse to hear either, are doing the deepest injury in their power to the Anti-Slavery cause, and sowing the seeds of a bitter future repentance.

I am aware how distasteful are the details of a strife. I know but too well, from my own experience, how natural it is to turn away, with a faint and sickening heart, from the exposure of the enmities of those whose first friendship sprang up in the field of benevolent labors. I fully understand the feelings of offended delicacy which would close the ears and seal the lips of those who have been fellow-workers with both the parties now alienated. Among all these causes of recoil, I see how it is but too probable that the Anti-Slavery parties on the other side of the Atlantic may be left by many of their British brethren to "settle their own affairs," to "fight their own battles." But if I had a voice which would penetrate wherever I wished, I would ask, in the depths of every heart that feels for the Slave, whether it should be so;—whether such indifference and recoil may not be as criminal in us as dissension in them;—whether, in declining to do justice to the true friends of the Slave, (on whichever side they may appear to be,) we may not be guilty of treachery as fatal as compromising with his enemies.

Those who devote themselves to the redemption of an oppressed class or race, do, by their act of self-devotion, pledge themselves to the discharge of the lowest and most irksome offices of protection, as much as to that of the most cordial and animating. We are bound not only to fight against foes whom we never saw, and upon whom our sympathies never rested; not only to work for millions of poor creatures, so grateful for our care that they are ready to kiss the hem of our garments—this kind of service, however lavish it may require us to be of our labor, our time, our money, is easy enough in comparison with one which is equally binding upon us—it is also our duty to withdraw our sympathy and countenance from our fellow-laborers, (however great their former merits and our love,) when they compromise the cause. It is our duty to expose their guilt, when, by their act of compromise, they oppress and betray those brethren whose nobleness is a rebuke to themselves. This painful duty may every friend of the Negro in this country now find himself called upon to discharge, if he give due attention to the state of Anti-Slavery affairs in America. If he does NOT give his attention, it would be better for him that he never named the Negro and his cause; for it is surely better to stand aloof from this philanthropic enterprise, than to mix up injustice with it.

The first movers in the Anti-Slavery cause in America, those who have stood firm through the fierce persecutions of many years, who have maintained their broad platform of catholic principles, who have guarded their original Constitution from innovation and circumscription,—Garrison, and his corps of devout, devoted and catholic fellow-laborers, with the Bible in their heart of hearts, and its spirit in all their ways, are now in a condition in which they need our support. They have been oppressed, betrayed, pillaged, and slandered. Not they, but their foes, are the innovators, the bigots, the unscrupulous proselyters, the preachers of a new doctrine, modified to propitiate the pro-slavery spirit of the country in which they live. No one will call my words too strong, my accusations exaggerated, who will read the evidence relating to the transfer of the *Emancipator* [the organ of the American Anti-Slavery Society], (for one instance,) or, casting an eye upon the statement of accounts of the American Anti-Slavery Society, will perceive who voted into their own pockets the money by which the *Emancipator* might have been sustained, under whose commission the assailants of the old organization crossed the Atlantic, and at whose expense they travelled throughout our country, sowing calumnies against Garrison and his faithful companions throughout the length and breadth of our land. When the friends of the Slave here are told of treachery, pillage, and slander, will they hazard being a party to the guilt, for want of enquiry, even though the London Anti-Slavery Committee, and their organ, the *Reporter,* at present appear to stand in that predicament? If they would avoid such a liability, let them read and consider the statement by which the case is placed fully before them.

No one is more ready than I to make allowance for lapse in the friends of the Negro in America. I have seen too much of the suffering (not conceivable here) consequent upon a profession of Anti-Slavery principles, to wonder that there are but few who can endure, from year to year, the infliction from without, the probing of the soul within, which visits the apostles of Freedom in a land which maintains Slavery on its soil. From my heart I pity those who, having gone into the enterprise, find that they have not strength for it, and that they are drawn by their weakness into acts of injustice towards such as are stronger than themselves;—for those who are not with the thorough-going are necessarily against them. We must regard with even respectful compassion the first misgivings, before they have become lapse. But what then must we feel,—what ought we to do—for those who *have* strength,—for those who *can* suffer to the end,—for those who are, after the pelting of a ten years' pitiless storm, as firm, as resolved, as full of vital warmth as ever,—as prepared still to abide the tempest, till the deluge of universal conviction shall sweep away the iniquity of Slavery from the earth? Shall we refuse to hear the tale of their injuries, of their justification, because others have refused, or because the story is painful? May we dare to call ourselves workers in the Anti-Slavery cause while thus deserting the chief of its apostles now living in the world?

All believe that the truth will finally prevail; and you and I, dear friend, have a firm faith that therefore the old organization, with Garrison at its head, will prevail, at length, over the base enmity of the seceders. But we ought not to be satisfied with their prevailing *at length,* till we see whether they cannot be enabled to stand their ground *now.* Not a moment is to be lost. Not for a moment should their noble hearts be left uncheered;—not for a moment should the Slave-holder be permitted to fan his embers of hope;— not for a moment should the American Slave be compelled to tremble at the adversity of his earliest and staunchest friends, if we can, by any effort, obtain a hearing for the cause. Let us urge and rouse all who are about us,—not to receive our mere assertions, not to take our convictions upon trust,—but to read, search out, and weigh the evidence, and judge for themselves.

This is all that is needed; for I believe there is not a friend of the Slave, in any part of the world, who, knowing the facts, would not make haste to offer his right hand to Garrison and his company, and his voice and purse to their cause. I am yours very truly, Harriet Martineau.

❖ ❖ ❖

L O N D O N ' S   D A I L Y   N E W S

1852–1866

Martineau's most prolific, sustained periodical engagement—"the greatest literary engagement of my life" (1983, 2:389)—was her affiliation with London's *Daily News*, for which she wrote steadily from 1852 through 1866, with occasional pieces through 1874. Despite Martineau's remarkably broad experience in writing for periodicals, it was not until 1852 that she became a regular "leader" or editorial writer for London's *Daily News*. Invited by editor Frederick Knight Hunt to try a different tempo of writing from what she was accustomed to, she at first demurred but, typically, was willing to give the proposal a try. Martineau's success as a leader writer was immediate, and she delighted in the reading public's initial inability to guess the identity of the paper's new staff writer.

Writing topical articles for a daily newspaper presented new challenges, primarily by imposing strict time constraints between studying the issues, writing the article, and sending the copy off to London via the mail train. This phase of her career was no less idiosyncratic than any other—rather than moving to London to be in the thick of activities surrounding a major daily newspaper, she conducted this most public phase of her career from her Ambleside home in the Lake District.[95] Martineau participated in world politics from her own parlor, attesting to the continued international scope of her influence. And thus, observes Elisabeth Arbuckle, was Martineau "embarked on the last and arguably most significant phase of her career" (1994, x), the "greatest" of all her literary engagements.

As one of the *Times*'s competitors, the *Daily News* aimed at a middle- and lower-class audience and promoted progressive social reforms and humanitarian values. In contrast, the *Times,* Martineau's old nemesis, represented the American South's "old planter interest" best characterized by the British aristocracy and by the upper middle classes (like cotton mill factory owners) who were economically empowered by the 1832 Reform Bill.[96] The ideological rivalry set the stage for lively debate between two distinct factions, each claiming to present the truth about American Civil War politics. Given the *News*'s ideals, Martineau's early role as an American affairs expert (as a result of her travels and travel publications), combined with the strong ties she maintained with prominent Americans and her powerful literary reputation, found its most apt expression in her role as a leader writer. Under Thomas Walker's editorship, Martineau strove to keep shifting, often impassioned public attitudes toward American affairs balanced—although, as the *Times* employed more aggressively biased editorial tactics favoring the South, her leaders accordingly became more explicitly pro-North. A later editor eulogized Martineau as a great journalist who "alone kept public opinion on the right [i.e., pro-North] side" (quoted in Arbuckle 1994, xii). This is no small achievement, given that, for Britain, the anti-slavery cause resulted in the loss of American cotton, the near-collapse of its cotton industry, and the economic ruin of entire factory towns.[97]

The significance of Martineau's *Daily News* leaders during the Civil War years is in their synthesis of political issues affecting both sides of the Atlantic. These articles number over sixteen hundred and provide valuable accounts of the major events shaping world history during the mid-nineteenth century. But despite the eclecticism of her periodicals writing, the overwhelmingly predominant theme in these leaders is American affairs and any issues and events bearing on the question of slavery. In fact, notes Arbuckle, "[v]irtually all Martineau's *Daily News* writing on the United States attacks slavery directly or indirectly" (xiii).

The selections reprinted here reflect that predominantly American context, with examples chosen to illustrate her remarkable range of expertise over the course of fourteen years. Martineau's journalistic writing style is the best of her career: clean, crisp, and rhetorically compelling, featuring an effective balance of objective clarity with passionate commitment. Hailed by a *Daily News* editor thirty years after her death as "the first and greatest of women journalists," Martineau in her leaders and articles once again proved to be a woman in the right place at the right time as one of the era's foremost social reform writers.[98]

. . .

"Harriet Beecher Stowe"

12 May 1853

The Authoress[99] of *Uncle Tom's Cabin* was, on Saturday, welcomed to Stafford-house by the Duchess of SUTHERLAND, where, in the midst of an assemblage of ladies of rank and influence, and no small muster of public men, she received the long-talked of address. The scene was one of much interest; and as Mrs. Beecher Stowe,—slim, sun-complexioned, active, intelligent, simply dressed, and perfectly self-possessed,—was seen petted and lionised by a whole bevy of Duchesses and Countesses, who had been charmed by her marvellous book; there was afforded a gratifying proof of the incense that truth and humanity may gain from all ranks—and proof, moreover, of the admiration which the genius of the New World may win from even the most select coterie of the Old.

When the first Anti-Slavery meeting at Stafford House took place, we said as little as possible about it; because it was a fair occasion for criticism, and we could not blame those who did criticise it; while the anti-slavery cause appears to us sufficiently strong and sufficiently venerable to cover some sins of judgment in its supporters. We thought that, on the whole, the meeting was to be regretted, because those who managed the business were insufficiently informed of the facts of the case—about the relation, we

Harriet Beecher Stowe (Boston Athenaeum)

mean, of the women of America to the institution of slavery. Of all the foes of American slavery none live in such anguish of hostility to the institution as the women of the Southern States, for reasons which are obvious enough, when the morals that coexist with slavery are considered. And we certainly must dissent emphatically from the declaration in the Address, that we—we of the existing generation of Englishmen and Englishwomen, ought to humble ourselves in shame and grief, on account of England's share in the guilt of American slavery. To this coaxing statement we absolutely object. But the sacredness of the cause silenced us when it would have been easy to ridicule and blame; and it was never a part of our objection that the movement was one conducted by women. Slavery is a subject on which women may and should speak and act as freely as men, and if men do not speak and act as freely as they ought, women are quite right to choose their own method of expressing their own protest, individual or collective. All ridicule aimed at the meeting, as a woman's meeting, was below notice, and always will be on a similar occasion. The time has now come for ridicule to cease, in regard to anti-slavery business going forward at Stafford House, and all the more so that the authoress of *Uncle Tom's Cabin* has taken part in the proceedings.

Mrs. STOWE is no fine lady, come to play off fine sentiments amidst the flutter of fans and the homage of adoring listeners. She is no *Corinne*, crowned for intellectual triumphs. She is no wonderful new novelist, whose pictures of the sufferings of the heart provoke and tempt an inquisition into the personal experience of the idol of the season. She has plenty of ability, a sound head, a keen sagacity, accurate intuitions if not an always sober judgment, and charming and inexhaustible humour, such as is usually found in connexion with that united sensibility and power of expression which constitute pathos in writing. She has plenty of ability; but that is comparatively a small matter. The singularity of the case is that she has been made, unintentionally and even unconsciously, the apostle of the greatest cause now existing in the world. Two years ago, she was in her home in Ohio, the daughter and the wife of clergymen, living in the humble way which in America is justly thought the most honourable for that profession, busy in her nursery, and carrying about an anxious heart, always and increasingly burdened by a growing knowledge of the sins and sufferings attendant upon the institution of slavery. When she could bear it no longer, she spoke; and the manner in which she spoke indicates the quality of the woman, and explains the power of her speech. She did not bewail her own pain, or put forth her own opinions, or in any way make known her own presence in the scene. She told, in the most straightforward way, what happens every day in the slave states of America. She did not even give high artistical qualities to her work. *Uncle Tom's Cabin* has grave artistical faults which would have been talked about abundantly on all hands, if one order of readers had not been overwhelmed by their sympathies and another by their rage. The power of the book was in its truth, set forth in its full strength by the objective character of the work—by the absence of all self-reference on the part of one of whom the world could have afforded to hear a great deal. In natural and complete accordance with this original tone of mind, she now is the very first among those who ascribe her marvellous fame to the ripeness of the world for the subject on which she spoke, as she says, "because she could not help it": and her steady persistence in this view in the midst of such an intoxicating whirl of success of every kind as would have turned almost any other head, marks her as a greater woman than all the genius of all the women who ever lived could have made her, without her honest simplicity. We beg to call the attention of observers and critics to this. Some are trying to make out that she is saucy, and selfish, and affected, because, in their practised judgment, she must be so, after her year of unequalled feminine fame. Some say that if she is not *exigeante* now, she soon will be,—for the same excellent reason. Some look upon her passage through our country as one of the amusements of the season, and get up an enthusiasm and a criticism, as they would upon any great artist of the day. This is all wrong—all a mistake; and those who perpetrate it have no real understanding of the cause, or of this its involuntarily preacher. She has sought no suffrages, and nobody can point to any personal aim that she has ever proposed. She is eager to interest all she meets in the cause, to hasten the day of the abolition of slavery; but all sympathy that she meets here must be embittered by the shame that she, with her patriot heart, must endure, that all such sympathy is like reproach to her republican country. These are feelings in the presence of which all petty gossip, all narrow criticism, all thoughtless levity should be silent, and, if possible, be turned into respect and humility. It was not to say this that we have spoken at such length of Mrs. STOWE. It can matter little to her or her kindly and sympathising entertainers, or anybody else, how lightminded people talk. Nor is it for Mrs. STOWE's sake or that of her friends that we have spoken of her at all. It is because her fame and her presence are a portent of a serious kind. Her fame is a protest on the part of the world against slavery in a democratic republic; and her welcome here is a broad hint, if her countrymen would but take it, that that institution is doomed, and that they would be wise to see how they could best release themselves from it. They know, as well as we do, that any institution which is condemned by the most advanced nations of Europe (the condemnation being on moral and economical, as well as political, grounds) cannot be long sustained in a free, generous, growing, and wealthy nation. Whether it is a book, or a woman, or a Great Exhibition, or a Hungarian revolt, or anything else that elicits the truth, and conveys the warning, matters little; it becomes a solemnity through its use. And thus it is that Mrs. STOWE's reception in the British islands is, in the eyes of thoughtful persons, no trivial matter, to be treated with transferable sympathy, or stared at for amusement. She is the embodied rebuke of the lovers of freedom and the advocates of popular government, addressed to the brethren from whom they have hoped, and still hope, so much; and addressed, surely, in the mildest form that remonstrance ever assumed—that of grateful hospitality to the most successful of living American authors.

"Fugitive Slave Law"

8 June 1855

It is nearly a year since we had occasion to point out that there was something going forward in the Western world which might, and probably would, become as interesting as any Eastern question whatever. In the first days of June, 1854, events occurred in Boston, United States, which exhibited to the world the very remarkable spectacle of a collision between the constitutional laws of the United States and those of the leading State of the Union—Massachusetts. For many years the laws of Massachusetts, in regard to personal liberty, had been precisely the same as our own. In the case of the slave child MED, it was decided in Boston, as in the case of SOMERSETT in England, that every slave, on touching the soil of the State, became free. When the Fugitive Slave Law[100] was in the course of discussion at Washington, the State of Massachusetts declared it to be radically unconstitutional, because it was incompatible with the "Personal Liberty laws" of some of the States, and especially of Massachusetts. It was evident to all clear-minded men that the die was now cast, for revolution. Several dangerous cases of collision about State Rights had occurred before, leading (especially in the South Carolina Nullification matter) to the very verge of war; but never before has there been a conflict on the "Personal Liberty Laws" of any State— on such important rights as *Habeas Corpus*[101] and Trial by Jury. When such a discrepancy is known to exist and to be beyond mending by any sort of compromise, it does not much matter what the occasion of collision is— whence the spark comes which determines the explosion. That it would be some difficulty about fugitive slaves, however, nobody had much doubt; and when the demand was made, a year ago, for the rendition of BURNS, the fugitive slave, everybody felt that the occasion was come. And so it was, though BURNS was for the moment rendered up. The citizens were not ready. They could not, in the agitation of the moment, decide on the proper mode of sustaining the constitution of Massachusetts against the encroachments of the new federal law. They sent out placards by the early trains from Boston to every part of the State, requesting the yeomanry to hasten to Boston, to witness the transaction, in order to decide afterwards what to do for the defence of their ancient liberties. "Come then," said the appeal, "by the early trains on Monday, and rally in Court-square. Come with courage and resolution in your hearts; but *this time*, with only such arms as God gave you." Multitudes obeyed the summons; and those who remained at home tolled the church bells and hung out black flags, mourning for the lost liberties of their State. On the ensuing 4th of July, the great national holiday was spent in Massachusetts, not with rejoicings and boastings, as always before, since 1776, but with tolling of bells, and other tokens of public mourning, and humiliation, and prayer for the restoration of their constitutional privileges. It is strange if anybody who knew these things should imagine that such action and demonstration on the part of the Sons of the Pilgrims could be a mere show of displeasure, an indulgence of barren sentiment. We do not believe that in America anybody has so regarded the demonstration; and if we have heard little of it in England, it is because the British are unaware of the seriousness of the affair, and too much engrossed with Eastern transactions to attend to the significance of those of the West.[102] While Europe is thus unconscious of the critical moment for the American Union having arrived, the most thorough-going pro-slavery newspapers are admitting the fact in the broadest manner. Here is, for one, the *Richmond* (Virginia) *Examiner* saying, "There is no intelligent man, of any party, or section of the United States, who does not know and feel that the question of slavery is the vital question of the republic—more important in its bearings upon the destiny of the American people than all other questions, moral, political, and religious combined. Politicians may cry peace; but there is no peace for the slaveholder." Nor, it may be added, for any citizen, when the liberties of every white man are subordinated to the bondage of the black.

The growling of the storm has never ceased since that pregnant cloud of last June lowered upon Massachusetts; and now the explosion of the tempest seems to be very near, for the revolutionary deed is actually done. Long ago the women of Worcester sent thirty pieces of silver to the unconstitutional Judge who decreed the rendition of BURNS; and many another token of the kind reached the man who had, as the citizens thought, sold his brother's blood. The proceedings taken to procure the removal of Judge [Edward G.] LORING have elicited a refusal from the Governor of Massachusetts the only affect of which will be to banish the Governor from public life to keep company with the Judge. These functionaries are really very much to be pitied. They cannot obey the contradictory laws of the Union and the State: they have to make their choice between them. They have preferred the federal laws; and one can only say that if they expect, after that, to be permitted to hold their State offices, they are highly unreasonable. They may look to Washington for employment or recompense; but their chance is over in Massachusetts. Well: the next thing was the attempt, which has miscarried, to bring three of the most eminent and honoured of the citizens of Boston to trial on a charge of constructive treason. It was found that no jury could be depended on to find them guilty; and the trials never took place. The attempt had, however, a very serious consequence. The acute examination of the laws, old and new, affecting the personal rights of citizens, disclosed the fact that the privileges which had been transplanted from the field of Runnymede[103] into the valleys of Massachusetts, are now actually uprooted and cast abroad at the command of the slave-holding power, preponderant at Washington. This is to be set right immediately, of course. There can be no doubt about that in a case where the liberties of the Sons of the Pilgrims are involved. Thus far, it has been done without sacrifice; for poor BURNS himself, the slave who was marched down to the wharf at Boston in the presence of tens of thousands assembled to witness the sacrifice, has been sent back again. He was found very burdensome at the South, because he could not be allowed to speak to anybody of his own race, lest he should tell what had been said and done at Boston. He was sold for a very small sum, and he has been telling his story in public in Massachusetts and elsewhere. That sacrifices will have to be made, and very serious sacrifices, and very soon, there can now be little doubt; and the only question remaining is, whether the people of the State will be staunch enough to bear out their representatives in the prodigious deed which they have done.

That deed is, carrying their Declaratory Bill on the Personal Liberties of the Citizens of Massachusetts, in spite of the veto of the Governor of the State. The moment of collision has arrived and is past. It remains to be seen whether the citizens will support their representatives under the consequences. When the Governor's veto was communicated to the Senate, an earnest debate ensued on the question, "Shall this bill pass, the Governor's decision to the contrary notwithstanding"; and "the bill was passed yeas 32, nays 3." So much for the Senate, which sent down the bill to the Representatives, who report: "The Personal Liberty Bill came down, with the Governor's objections, which were read; and then the bill was read in concurrence, the veto notwithstanding—yeas 229, nays 76."

What the consequences will be, there is no saying. We wish there was ground for a hope that the central government would retrace its steps, repeal the Fugitive Slave law—so hated by the great majority of the citizens of the Union—and take very good care never again to infringe the dearest rights of the oldest and wisest and best of the States. But of this there seems to be no hope as yet. The slave power is too strong in Congress at present for any *amende* of the sort. What then? Is Massachusetts ready to withdraw from the Union, or to be declared excluded from it? If so, she may, we think, reasonably hope for the companionship of all the best States—of all that are peopled by the posterity of the Pilgrim Fathers, and probably several more. But, supported or unsupported, accompanied or lonely in her testimony, she cannot shrink from it now. It is inconceivable that she should not conquer. It is surely impossible that republicans, descended from Englishmen, should not be able to preserve, in the 19th century, personal liberties which were obtained by their ancestors in the 12th.

If the citizens give way, and expose their representatives to a vindictive retribution for their daring act, they will be unworthy of our interest and sympathy, and will have themselves pronounced their republic a sham, and their national honour extinguished. This is, we trust, even a more absurd anticipation than the conversion of the slaveholders to a creed of personal rights. But if the people of Massachusetts are resolved to hold their ground, they must prepare for conflict, and be ready to fight the battle of Independence over again. Let them remember that one kind of excommunication, the Papal, has been braved and endured till it died out, to afflict the world no more. If the thunders of the Capitol are now to rival the old thunders of the Vatican, they also may endure, in the certainty that such tyranny, while infinitely less fearful than the ancient one, may be far more easily withstood and vanquished. No man in Massachusetts knows what may be ahead. Every man feels, we trust, that, whatever be ahead, his duty is clear. For the honour of his forefathers, for the safety of his fellow-citizens, and for the benefit of his posterity, he must now, at all hazards, maintain the rights of *Habeas Corpus* and Trial by Jury in old Massachusetts.

"Kansas"

10 October 1856

The proclamations of the new Governor of Kansas present an appearance of impartiality to unpractised eyes; and thence it is that European readers of those documents presume that peace is being restored in the territory. There is, however, no present warrant for such a hope. It may be asked—What can be more fair than a declaration that the existing laws of Kansas must be obeyed till they are repealed? But the question assumes that the so-called laws are of constitutional origin, and that they can be repealed, under the ordinary conditions of legislation. Neither of these assumptions is true. We need not repeat the well-known story of the invasion of the polls in the spring of 1855, and of the way in which a troop of foreigners thrust upon the settlers a set of commands which they called laws. These dictatorial orders are what Governor Geary calls "the existing laws of Kansas." These laws, too, which he pretends to sustain, are so framed as to be secure from repeal. They deprive of the constitutional and universal right of voting every man who does not previously pledge himself to support the Kansas-Nebraska Act[104] as it stands, the Fugitive Slave Law, and all the pro-slavery legislation of recent years. They deprive of the right of jury trial, of residence, and of protection under the law, every man who is known or believed to hold antislavery opinions. In fact, these laws prevent all social action and rights whatever, except on terms which none but the Border-ruffian party can assent to. The existing laws cannot therefore be repealed while the laws themselves are in force; and the Governor's declaration that they must be obeyed is anything but a demonstration of impartiality.

Even if these laws could be, and were to be, repealed the prospects of peace would not become much brighter. The Slave power in the United States is just now offering astounding evidence that it will refuse constitutional obedience to the decision of the majority. The audacity is almost incredible with which Southern men and Southern parties declare that they will accept no man for President but their own candidate, and that unless they can have their own way, as hitherto, they will be off their constitutional bargain, and rebel or secede. In 1820, Virginia offered, by her legislature, all sympathy and aid to the inhabitants of Missouri, then seeking admission into the Union, as Kansas is now. Even to the point of resisting Congress, Virginia offered sanction and aid. Now, when the Northern States have done nothing so critical—nothing more than peopling the territory, as virtually invited by the Act of Settlement to do, and then enabling the settlers to hold their ground, the Slave power raises the cry of "Treason." On the other hand, the Northern States, discovering that an organisation is forming for preventing Fremont's taking his seat if elected, are reciprocating the cry of "Treason," and with a good deal more justice, according to the judgment of all law-and-order-loving citizens of all free countries.[105]

The question, "Who are the traitors?" is shouted now from side to side of the Union. We can gather some kind of answer from the newspapers and pamphlets, from Northern, Southern, Eastern, and Western States, which every mail now brings.

We observe, in the first place, that the Slave power has so far altered its tone as to admit that its antagonists are now the majority. It used to talk of the anti-slavery citizens as a handful of fanatics. Now it declares itself shocked to see how a "midsummer madness has seized the whole North"; and it sets itself up, as a virtuous and strong minority, to check the frantic folly of a community bent on worshipping its hewers of wood and drawers of water rather than its aristocracy. One inference from this is, that Colonel Fremont's chances have conspicuously improved. Another is, that an equally remarkable change has taken place in the Southern notion of what treason is. Hitherto, the submission of the majority to the minority has been, in the eyes of the South, a simple matter of duty when the minority was uppermost. The submission of even a small minority to the vast majority now appears to the South, not a simple matter of duty, but—somehow or other—"treason." A Virginia ministerial paper, the South Side Democrat, publishes a confession of its alarm and disgust at seeing in a contemporary the statement that the free and fair election of Fremont, however lamentable, is no violation of the constitution; and that it will be time enough for the Southern States to secede from the Union, or rebel against the Federal Government, when anything unconstitutional shall be actually proposed. In reply to this dangerous statement the South asserts that "it will never submit to be governed by the Republican party"; and that to assist the chances of Fremont by declaring "such a fellow" a constitutional candidate is treasonable. Again, several States having petitioned their governors to call an extra session of their legislatures, "for the purpose of devising some legal and constitutional way for the protection and redress of our fellow-citizens, who, in the exercise of their rights, have emigrated into Kansas," the Slave power is horrified at the treason of such petitioning, connected as it is with a proposal of intercommunication between the Executive of States which desire to resist all unlawful aggression, either in Kansas or at Washington. "So wild, and deep, and dangerous, has fanaticism got to be!" exclaim the men of the South, who are at the moment plotting to resist—not unlawful aggression, but a constitutional election. They interpret this proposed "concert of action" as an alliance of the free States against other

States, in contravention of the federal compact. They cry out, "Another Hartford convention! These are the traitors!" Another group of citizens they also point out as traitors—men who write such letters as that of a Georgia Planter, which appeared in our columns on the 3rd instant. A speech delivered in Richmond, Virginia, and much applauded there, turns out to have opened sluices of sympathy between the non-slaveholders of the South and the North. A Virginia hearer was at the time alarmed, and whispered to a neighbour that the Northern Republicans would thankfully give the reporter 10,000 dollars for his notes, if they could conceive of such a speech about social rights and constitutional law being delivered in a Slave State; and now that the Northern and Southern anti-slavery men seem likely to understand each other, there is a cry of "Treason" from the Slave power. The fact is creeping out that most, if not all, of the Southern States could support an electoral ticket in favour of Fremont, and that the contest is likely to be much less purely sectional than was at first supposed; and every time this is said the Slave power cries, "Here are the traitors!" Among so many traitors, we turn at last to the men who claim the praise of chivalrous loyalty. What do we find? We find that (in the words we quoted last week) "it is arranged to call the Legislatures of Virginia, South Carolina, and Georgia to concert measures to withdraw from the Union before Fremont can get possession of the army and navy, and the purse-strings of Government. Governor Wise is actively at work already in the matter. The South can rely on the President in the emergency contemplated." We find that South Carolina boasts that there is not a public man in the State "who is not pledged to the lips in favour of disunion." We find in the speech of Preston Brooks, delivered at Columbia on the 29th of August, and received with shouts of applause from crowds of hearers, the following passage, as reported in the *Carolina Times:* "On the first Tuesday of November next the great question would be decided. For his (the speaker's) part, if Fremont, the traitor to his section, should be successful, it was his deliberate opinion that on the 4th of March next the people of the South should rise in their might, march to Washington, and seize the archives and the treasury of the Government." The comment on this speech which the local newspapers make and repeat is this: "As to the line of policy he recommends to the people of the State, we believe it is founded in wisdom and moderation, and entitled to their adoption." It appears to us that the turn of the North has come for asking "Who are the traitors?" Whatever may be the presumed doubt as to which are the law-and-order men and which the ruffians and traitors in Kansas, the case is pretty clear in other parts of the Union.

"Dred Scott and States' Rights"

18 June 1857

The latest accounts from the United States are deeply significant, and of the strongest possible interest to Europeans who are aware how much hangs on the mutual relations of the Sovereign States during the present action of the Federal Government. The new incidents are various; but they all illustrate the progress of the so-called Revolt of the State-Rights section of the Nation against the Slave power which uses the Federal Court for its mouthpiece. The speakers at the late New England Convention declared that the word "Revolt" was not strong enough; and, adopting the reply to CHARLES X., which has become proverbial, avowed that it was not a Revolt but a Revolution. No impartial spectator can doubt that this is true; and every step taken towards an issue of such grave political and historical importance must be interesting to Europe, and especially to Great Britain, in the highest degree.

Chief Justice TANEY has published his judgment in the DRED SCOTT case,[106] thus putting an end to the disputes as to what he did, and what he did not say, in delivering his decision. It is agreed among the Reporters that some points of his address have been altered; and such modifications as there are, are clearly owing to the publication of the protest of the dissentient judges—CURTIS and MCLEAN. But the passage which has been most disputed stands out conspicuously in the official Report: that the negroes were "so far inferior as that they had no rights which the white man was bound to respect" (p. 409); and this is broad ground for a revolutionary struggle to proceed upon. Opportunity could not long be wanting. The slave, DRED SCOTT, has not afforded it. The second husband of the lady to whom Dred and his family belonged is a citizen of Massachusetts, and not at all disposed to be the owner of slaves. After all his efforts to intercept the cause, and leave the family at liberty, had failed, he succeeded by a device in freeing the victims of an unconstitutional judgment. He made over the family to a citizen of a Slave State, who had power to emancipate; and thus the SCOTTS are no longer concerned in the case. But there are fugitives every day; and those who have the courage to remain in the Northern States, instead of getting to Canada, are the real holders of the wires by which the mine may be exploded at any moment. Up to the moment of MR. BUCHANAN's accession the policy of the Central Government was to kidnap fugitives at the bidding of the South;[107] and Mr. PIERCE's last great surprise was at the completeness of the organisation by which the Northern citizens outstripped his telegraphic messages, were prepared for his searching and blockading cutters, and somehow or other had always news of flown birds for his most diligent agents.[108] The present state of things is, to all appearance, precisely opposite. The Northern States spread as widely as possible the news of fugitives being among them, and no notice is taken from Washington. This is not because a BUCHANAN has succeeded a PIERCE, but because the decision of the Supreme Court is an incitement to resistance which cannot be refused. In one striking speech at the New England Anti-Slavery Society, on the 12th of May, we observe that an eminent citizen declares the time to have arrived when institutions which were a safe-guard in their day are found to be a snare; and the first which he specifies are the Underground Railway and the Personal Liberty Laws of the Free States. The Underground Railway is simply the organisation by which the escape of slaves is rendered secure, from the respective Slave States to Canada. Instead of giving dollars to fugitives and putting them on the track, the citizens ought now to induce fugitives to remain in their own country, and to pledge the faith of the community for their security. So think the sons of the Pilgrims in this crisis. No Personal Liberty Laws should be needed, they say again—their old Constitution being enough for men of all orders and complexions, who tread the soil of New England. This recurrence to the old scope and powers of the Northern Constitutions is portentous to the last degree, because it means the same thing as denying the whole course of pro-slavery law-making at Washington, which, for the time, instigated the laws and arrangements on behalf of slaves, which are now to be cast aside as temporary expedients. We observe, at the same time, a remarkable act of defiance, of which the Senate of Massachusetts has taken the responsibility. It has ordered the Secretary of State (of Massachusetts) to give Passports to citizens of colour, about to travel abroad. The United States Minister in London cannot do this in the case of the most intelligent and accomplished Americans who have a dark skin; but old Massachusetts asserts her right to do this (as she once did with effect, to coin money), and there seems every reason to hope and expect that the passports she gives will be duly respected, wherever they are carried.

Our readers need not be told that Ohio must be in the van of such a fight as this—on the one side or the other. One frontier faces the Slave States and the other Canada, and a perpetual stream of fugitives passes through her territory. By her laws every person who touches her soil is free; and as fugitives are touching that soil every day, there could not but be a speedy and flagrant collision between the decree of the Federal Court and the laws of the State. Such a collision has happened. A Kentucky slaveowner repeatedly sent his slave, Henry Poindexter, across the river into Ohio on business. At length he agreed to let the negro purchase his freedom for 400 dollars: the man gave notes for the amount, with adequate security, and went to work on both sides the river, to earn the money. The money was not ready when the first bill became due; and Poindexter put himself into the hands of counsel, who pleaded with success that the man was free before he obtained permission to pay for his liberty, his master having repeatedly sent him into Ohio. Even under the vicious clause of the old Federal Constitution the master has no claim, because his slave did not enter Ohio as a fugitive, but was sent by his owner. The Supreme Court of Ohio has pronounced in favour of Poindexter, and against any claim of his former owner. The natural consequence has ensued. The Federal Government has attempted at once to assert its power in the defiant State, and has been so foiled that all accommodation appears to be out of the question. It has ordered its own officer in the State, Marshall Churchill, to arrest four citizens of Mechanicsburg, Champagne County, on the charge of harbouring fugitive slaves in the summer of 1856. Though writs of *habeas corpus* were obtained as quickly as possible, the Marshal, his eleven assistants, and their prisoners had passed the bounds of the County. Another writ was taken out, and served by the Sheriff, backed by the resident citizens in a body. The Federal officers unhappily resisted, and used their fire-arms, receiving shots in return. They were overpowered, and committed for trial on the charge of resisting the Sheriff in the discharge of his duty. Some telegraphic messages were passing between the Government and their imprisoned agents, and there is no doubt of this trial being prepared for as a crucial case. The Federal District Judge, meantime, has issued a writ, and it was to be served on the 29th of May. If any resistance was made to the enlargement of the prisoners, it was understood that the United States troops would be in readiness to enforce obedience to the Central Government.

The action of some of the Slave states is scarcely less suggestive than anything done at the North. The fierce controversy in Virginia about the admission of free labour in the shape of European immigration lays open the griefs of the dignified old State in a way which only necessity can justify to the pride of its citizens. But a more significant contest is going on further south, between the leading newspapers of South Carolina and Louisiana. The former State is unquestionably the great agitator; and yet it appears to be the first which is seriously alarmed. It now proposes, through its leading journals, that slavery shall give way wherever it is strongly opposed on the frontier, because if would be ungenerous and unwise in the Cotton States to allow the deteriorated frontier States to bear the brunt of the battle. The Louisiana citizens, on the other hand, see through the disguise by which South Carolina would conceal its misgivings about the stability of slavery in the border region, and declare it to be good policy to give the border States something to do in fighting the battle, while southern citizens are making the best of their time. The loyalty of the frontier States being questionable, it is proposed that their slaves shall be a prohibited article, in order to compel them to refuse admission to free labour. All this savours of fear and perplexity; and when we perceive that the Churches are ranging themselves for battle, or splitting among parties, we need say no more to prove the portentous condition of affairs. At the May anniversaries of the religious world, we observe that the Northern clergy pray for the "nominal Christian churches" of the Southern. The Romish organs, too, give out that the condition of the Republic is so alarming that there is no comfort but in contemplating the prodigious spread of the true faith in consequence. Coupled with the explanation of the spread of Romanism, which is probably the true one—that the Confessional is the best possible security against insurrection—these theological declarations are as interesting as any political avowals whatever. Everything that happens just now, in all departments, suggests the approach of the second great crisis in the history of the United States.

"Liberia"

20 November 1858

Our valued New York correspondent informed us, in a recently published letter, that President Benson, of Liberia, has been vindicating himself in

America as well as in England from the charges made against him in connexion with the *Regina Coeli* affair;[109] and our correspondent adds, "It seems now to resolve itself into a question of veracity between him and the French officials." This Liberian case must still be looked to. The American newspapers call on the Colonisation Society to explain past transactions with the French Emperor's agents; the Colonisation Society calls on the Liberian authorities to explain, in like manner; and the Liberian authorities give the lie direct to the Emperor's agents and officers, through whom the particulars have been mainly furnished. Thus stands the matter in regard to past events, when the news is given out in Paris that all is to go smoothly in Liberia henceforth, in regard to the immigration scheme; that there is to be a favouring President, who will give active assistance where the present one has afforded obstruction; and that this new President, whoever he is, will be fraternised with by Kings and Chiefs of many districts; 17 Kings, 9 Chieftains, 36 towns, and the Sovereigns of Dahomey and Benin. Such is the apparatus for supplying victims to the slave ships and the French colonies; and if this account is true, it will not do to leave Liberia and Cape Mount unwatched because the Emperor of the French is going to give up his bargain. It must be first ascertained whether or not this announcement is one of those enormous untruths—one of those items of "false news" which the Emperor's system of repression of simple news is always creating. But if it should turn out to be in any degree true, the patrons and allies of Liberia, American and European, must keep an eye on the little Republic, knowing that there will never be a lack of buyers of as many negroes as their Kings and Chiefs are tempted to sell.

Some of the circumstances look as if the story was false. "Roberts" is spoken of as the President who is not re-elected, on account of his opposition to the French scheme; whereas President Benson is the man. He has been President for two years; he now charges the French agents with gross falsehood, and declares that he opposed the exportation of negroes; and Roberts was never accused, as far as is known here, of any unwillingness to second the French Emperor's purposes. Here is, then, a mistake to begin with. But this mistake rather goes to confirm the truth of the rest. When we first heard of the case of the *Regina Coeli,* the President was represented as in entire accord with the French officials; as having sanctioned and encouraged their scheme, aided them to procure the negroes, taken their money, and even petitioned that they would draw their supply of labourers from his territory. All these allegations have been denied in the most emphatic way, as our readers have seen, by President Benson, in a letter which appeared in our columns on the 22nd. It is the misfortune of Mr. Benson, as it will long be of every ruler of Liberia, that the world is, and must for some time continue to be, distrustful of all professions against slavery and the Slave-Trade which come from that quarter. The origin of the settlement and the history of its early years are too well known to admit of an unsuspicious state of mind in the hearers of such professions; but it must strike everyone that the recent

French news, that the Liberian President has been ousted on account of his opposition to the Immigration scheme is in direct contradiction to the French narrative of the case of the *Regina Coeli*. Mr. Benson is entitled to the benefit of this evidence; and till his statements are answered it stands asserted that he refused, in letters which are producible, to permit the French to establish depots for their labourers, because such depots would be too like slave barracoons to be legal; that he repeatedly warned his visitors of the consequences of carrying away any emigrants but those who freely offered themselves; and that he cautioned the French officers against remaining more than four days at any one point of the coast, as persons brought from the interior would certainly not be voluntary emigrants. President Benson's statements have been abundantly published; they present a damning case against the French officials, and they have not, as far as we know, been replied to. Thus, we have the original French narrative first: next, the President's story, in direct opposition to almost every point of it: and now, finally, the French news that the President is ousted, on account of his impracticability in regard to the French scheme. Unless new facts arise, the world will believe President Benson.

There is another view disclosed by the same story, which will be more interesting to everybody—unless it be President Benson. If he is ousted for the reason assigned, it is clear that the public—or the leaders of the electoral body—in Liberia are strongly in favour of the French scheme. This is the broad hint to the European Powers to watch the Republic and its coasts. The readiness of the citizens to sell some of their innumerable and hopeless vagrants is an old story; and certainly the temptation is very strong. It appears that there has never yet, for any permanency, been food enough in the territory to feed the people upon it; and yet the United States keep sending shiploads of shiftless beings, without property or talents, to aggravate the misery. At one time the people are devouring green plums; at another time they are cutting down palms, to eat the cabbage at the top—as recklessly as South Sea islanders, who know neither want nor forethought. It is the very place for the headquarters of the Messrs. Regis of Europe and America; and the coast must be watched, whatever the Emperor's decision may be.

Another consideration is that the Slave Trade may be carried on otherwise than from the nearest shore. Nile travellers know that very well; and so do the explorers of Algeria. Patriotic Frenchmen boast of the prospect of Algeria being the highway by which African products of every kind will reach the other continents. Of all African products slaves are popularly reckoned the most lucrative article; and the transit of that commodity through Algeria will have to be watched. For this last consideration we have time before us. As to the other, not a day's carelessness can be permitted. The American Government has just sent to Liberia a cargo of recaptured negroes, who are no more at home there than in South Carolina, and who might just as easily have been sent to their homes, near Kabenda. While such helpless beings are sent to a colony which is underfed and bare of work, and for ever overflowed by a new deluge of hungry paupers, while slavetraders and Imperial agents are hovering round, to pick up a cargo of colonial immigrants at so much a head, to serve without wages and without hope of return, it is the duty of England and her true allies to see that there is no foul play that they can prevent.

"Black Insurrections; Harper's Ferry"

2 November 1859

If there must be a negro insurrection in the United States before the slavery question is settled, Maryland is more likely than any other place to be the scene of it, under the circumstances of the present time. It is a misfortune that the negroes should rise; and for a long interval there was hope that the transition from slave to free labour might be accomplished in a peaceful and orderly way. Up to about a quarter of a century ago the universal supposition was that slavery could come to an end by no other means than a servile war; and this was the dread which kept quiet some leading citizens, who, if they had stirred in time, might have accomplished the revolution in the labour-market long before this. There were then risings, of more or less consequence, in the Slave states so frequently that the average was set down as 12 per year. The fearful insurrection known by the name of the Southampton Massacre took place in 1832, and this was till recently called the last negro rising. The abolition movement was instituted at that time; the news of that humble beginning spread over the Slave States, in the way that news about negro interests does spread; and from the moment when Garrison was understood to have dedicated himself to their cause the negroes tacitly committed their affairs to his hands, and he and his coadjutors were non-resistant. For above twenty years, while the slaveholders kept up their alarms and cautions, suspecting incendiarism, material and moral, at every turn, the slaves never rebelled, more or less. This was one good service done by the abolitionists; and another was that the slaves were better treated, in proportion as the attention of the world was directed towards their case. By degrees there came a slackening of the alarms which prevail wherever slavery exists; and, in 1856, rash practices were adventured which are bitterly repented of now. In their horror of having an Anti-slavery President in the person of Fremont, the Southern politicians made speeches all over the country, proving that his election would doom slavery and Southern institutions altogether. These speeches were uttered in the hearing of the negroes who hang round all crowds, and of course every one of them became a worshipper of Fremont, and spread his praise up and down all the rivers of the interior. This is universally admitted to have been the cause of the so-called conspiracy of 1856, which scared whole communities out of their wits. There was certainly a wide-spread communication and sympathy. Whether there was actual conspiracy to rise, before the whites drove the negroes to it, remains a matter of dispute. What is certain is, that along the course of the great rivers the negroes believed that their day of deliverance had come, and acted accordingly; and that many died under the lash and on the gibbet as martyrs. The strongest admonitions to prudence have since been promulgated among the whites; and the speeches that have been listened to by inquisitive negroes have been full of assurances that slavery would endure for ever. The constant discussion of the topic, however, in connexion with politics, is a significant fact which the negro is able to note and reason upon. In former times slavery went on of itself, like marriage, and public worship, and magistracy; and it was no more talked about in the way of assertion and defence than the modern discussions show that it is called in question; and the prodigious amount of escape from slavery proves before all men's eyes that the whites find difficulty in maintaining the institution.

Then there is the new phase of the persecution of the free negroes—felt and resented wherever there are free negroes; and they are everywhere, in spite of all efforts to dislodge them. While in the Free States they now hold annual conventions, to consider their political and social condition, and arrange their resistance to plans of expatriation, and provide means and inducements for the elevation of their class by means of education and the rousing of an honest ambition, their brethren in the Slave Sates are sustaining a persecution which the slaves perfectly understand. While projects are brought forward in legislatures, in newspapers, and in public meetings, for selling the free blacks into slavery; for inducing them to sell themselves into slavery for terms of years; for exporting them to the West Indies; for compelling them to colonise Africa, &c., and everything that can be done by unequal taxation and by the infliction of petty hardships and gross indignities, is done to drive them out of the state or into fatal offences. Maryland has been conspicuous above perhaps every other State in the frantic character of her recent anti-negro agitation. Her position is an awkward and difficult one, requiring the utmost prudence, moderation, and forecast; and her citizens have acted like demented tyrants, in the very crisis of her fortunes. Her territory is small. Her slaves are more burdensome than profitable; and they are running away in greater numbers every year. They make such a poor figure as cultivators of the soil, in the presence of a constant influx of industrious Germans and other free labourers, that they are otherwise employed, whenever they can be let out on hire. Fugitives from the South come trooping through, on their way into Pennsylvania; and it is well known all along the road that they are going to join the twenty thousand free negroes in Canada who have travelled by the same "underground railroad." Every negro in the little State of Maryland is surrounded by excitements. There is Washington close by—standing on soil yielded by Maryland and Virginia; and for months of every year slavery is quarrelled about there by the first men in the Republic. There is Baltimore—prone to slave traffic—known to send out vessels every year to trade between the African coasts and Cuba. There is Annapolis, where the Legislature holds its sittings, and where stringent restraints on the free blacks are proposed with more vehemence from session to session, till we even hear of proposals to sell into slavery every free negro who is found in the State after a certain date. There is Pennsylvania close at hand from the rural districts, with its thriving class of free blacks, who own ships and rows of houses in Philadelphia, and are known by their good deeds in aiding wanderers from the South. There is the broad Potomac, with its abundant shipping, and its snug berths for many more fugitives than the cruel vigilance of exasperated slaveholders can track. There is Virginia all along the southern frontier, and not a little of it is Western Virginia, where slavery has long been condemned and abhorred. Nowhere is slavery more unpopular than on the table lands of Virginia, where the farmers were talking of abolishing it before the abolitionists entered upon their enterprise. There is probably not a man of any colour in Virginia who does not know that the great question of State politics is how soon Virginia shall join the free States, when she must choose between North and South: and such news is not kept in by frontier lines. In this way all influences have for some time combined to inform the negroes of Maryland that the maintenance of slavery has become a difficult task to their masters; that it is a tottering institution; that the great quarrel of the American people is about allowing it to exist; that thousands of slaves escape every year; that free labourers come in in yet greater numbers; and that their masters are growing too angry to be endured. It may be some time before we can know with certainty the origin and course of the insurrection at Harper's Ferry;[110] but, whether it is the work of free blacks or slaves, whether a conspiracy or an outbreak of sudden rage, there can be nothing wonderful in it, however regretfully it may be regarded by the best friends of humanity, white and black.

Harper's Ferry is particularly well and very daringly chosen, if chosen at all, as the seat of an insurrection. On the frontier between Virginia and Maryland, at the confluence of great rivers, and the junction of State Railways, and the centre of a net of telegraphic wires, it would have been a post of great importance even if there had not been an arsenal from which a great negro population might be armed. If the recent moods of the masters and the State politicians had been less fierce, and their language and acts less oppressive, we might have hoped that the parties might come to fair terms before much mischief is done. As it is, we cannot but dread the reflection of the tyrannical temper of the masters in the vindictive conduct of the slaves. The Negroes have shown wonderful patience, and, on occasion, a very remarkable generosity; but the Maryland slave-traders and free negro haters have not appealed to the best but the worst parts of human nature in their recent dealings with their precarious human property, and there may well be apprehension of the result. We mean only as to what may have been done in the first outbreak. No doubt the rising would be immediately put down by the Federal and State forces. This is to be hoped on every account, for the doom of slavery in the Republic, especially in the frontier States, and, above all, in Maryland, is so clear and so closely impending that every breach of order is likely to be a mere mischief—an impediment, and no furtherance. If the masters were wise they would know how to turn the occasion to advantage for getting rid of their burden and curse; but Maryland slaveholders, who cannot bear the presence of the free negro on any foot of soil in the State, are not wise; and they will doubtless make the worst of their own case.

"The Burial of John Brown"

3 January 1860

I have not sent you an account of the last hours, the death, and the burial of John Brown, because I consider it of great importance that the effects of his action in Virginia on the whole of the United States should not be mixed up with the emotions aroused by the character and bearing of the man. It is not my object to arouse in the English public the admiration of the old confessor which must now, and ever will, follow the narrative of his last hours. The story will be abundantly recorded elsewhere, and never forgotten. My business at this time is to give you some idea of the state of mind of the community in such a crisis as the present, as far as it can be judged of by the manifestations which took place wherever the coffin of the hanged man rested.

Up to this time death by hanging has been more intensely disgusting to the American community than perhaps to any other. Henceforth it has lost its degrading power. There is nothing profane in repeating what has been said from hundreds of pulpits within the last month—that it is the case of the death of the Cross over again. We have all heard from every class of preachers, all our lives, that crucifixion was once as ignominious a punishment as hanging is in our day; and that a clear understanding of this is needful to enable us to form any true conception of the story of the Gospels. Quite inevitably, this parallel has been reiterated in connexion with the recent case; and the clergy themselves, who must best feel the force of it, have not a word to say against the truth of it. On the day of Brown's execution, therefore, the cities, towns, and villages of New England, and many in the other free states, assumed mourning, and celebrated the departure of an honoured fellow-citizen as if he had died amidst the honours of victory on the battle-field. The inhabitants dressed their balconies, their churches, and their public halls in black; hung out black flags along the streets; and tolled the bells of their churches. In country towns, where there had been pride or slowness in regard to so *low* a cause as that of an enslaved race, the sons of the clergymen might be seen themselves tolling the bells. So much for the state of popular feeling. How far it was expressed in the public meetings of that night, by the reception of the speeches on both sides, you have seen by the reports of those meetings. You may be less aware what took place along the route by which the corpse of John Brown was carried from the foot of the gallows to its grave among the snows of the Vermont mountains. Harper's Ferry, you are aware, is close upon the frontier between Virginia and Maryland, and within a few miles of the Pennsylvania territory. The Vermont mountains border upon Canada. The question has often been asked why the old captain, with such a colony of sons and married daughters with their husbands, should have taken up his abode in a region where the climate is very severe and the soil scarcely capable of any cultivation at all, after the family had had experience of such a climate and soil as that of Ohio, to say nothing of Kansas. The reason assigned is that the Browns desired to aid the benevolent project of the venerable Gerrit Smith, who had assigned a large portion of his lands near the Vermont frontier for the residence of such people of colour as might desire to settle within easy reach of Canada.[111] John Brown made his abode on the bleak and barren spot where he could best guide and direct the project; and his devoted and united family were as ready as himself. Thus there was a long and dreary winter journey for the widow, conveying home her husband's body. He had no care for the destination of his remains. He even advised that his body and those of the sons and sons-in-law who perished in the enterprise should be burned together, that the remains might be the more easily and inexpensively carried home. His wife could not agree to anything so strange, and was sure that it should not be permitted; and therefore her husband indicated the spot where his coffin should be laid, if she was indeed resolved to take it home. It was for her solace that he did it; and the place named was the shadow of a rock near the dwelling-house, where he was fond of sitting when at leisure.

He was so well aware of the difficulty of the journey that, as soon as the parting with his wife was over, the night before his execution, he sat down to draw a plan of the route, and with full instructions. He named the resting-places, and so described the various roads over the mountains, now snow-covered, as to spare the party much fatigue, time, and uncertainty. Mrs. Brown was well escorted, all the way; but the gentlemen who attended her did not know the wild parts of the country. They carried this plan in their hands; and so went straight to their point.

The body was to be taken from Charlestown, near Harper's Ferry, to Mrs. Brown at Philadelphia, where she had been conveyed after parting with her husband on Thursday night. It was to arrive on Saturday morning, and to remain till Monday, not only that Mrs. Brown might have needful rest, but that an undertaker might prepare everything properly. A coffin had been provided at the jail; and Brown made it his seat on the way to the scaffold. When his body was cut down and thrown down on the platform, it fell in a heap; and while still warm and limp, it was laid in the coffin, dressed as it was, and committed to Mrs. Brown's agents. It was remarked then, and throughout, that so far from there being any occasion to cover the face, the countenance was so entirely natural and placid that his children might have satisfaction in looking upon it once more. Except a flush in a face usually pale, there was no change from his ordinary aspect in sleep. Hence the permission to friends and grateful strangers to view the body at several resting-places.

The Philadelphia plan was baffled by the Mayor of the city. His conduct otherwise had been in accordance with the best mind of the citizens; and if he was mistaken in this instance, great allowance may be made, charged as he was with the peace of the city, in which several riots occurred in earlier stages of the conflict. The Mayor himself met the two gentlemen who had charge of the coffin, on its arrival at noon on Saturday, and insisted on its being forwarded by the next train at 2 P.M. He declared that the enthusiasm of the people was so wide-spread, and the interest of even the Union party so awake, that some demonstration would certainly be made unsuitable to a funeral occasion. He declared that he would enforce his commands by the whole power of the police and military if any difficulty was made.

Though every attempt was made, for Mrs. Brown's sake, to keep the thing quiet, here, as throughout the journey, a great crowd had watched the station. They surrounded the wagon on which the coffin was removed to the station; and as the citizens gathered in the streets they formed a funeral procession. At the station they ranged themselves in long lines, through which the body passed, still attended by Mr. McKim.[112] It reached New York at night, amidst a storm of wind and rain. At 2 A.M. it was quietly conveyed to the house of an undertaker in the Bowery, where it was to be prepared, as it ought to have been at Philadelphia. But the excited citizens soon discovered that it had arrived by the Amboy boat, and traced it to its resting place. Early in the morning the house had a dense crowd before it; and it was impossible to refuse to the weeping and adoring people of colour a last sight of the face of their apostle. They had hoped that at least one day would have been allowed for a public testimony of homage to the relics of the martyr: but the children at home must be considered; and they had fixed Thursday for the interment. Early on Monday, therefore, before the city was astir, the coffin was met at the Hudson Railway by Mrs. Brown and her protectors, and the sympathising hosts by whom she had been received for the night, and the day's journey was to Troy, on the Hudson. Throughout the whole route there were no expenses. Money had been sent for the purpose to Brown himself, and he had arranged everything; but no one would touch money on this occasion, and willing services were rendered everywhere without pay.

Wendell Phillips here joined the party from Boston. Brown himself had indicated the Temperance Hotel as the resting-place. He knew it well; and the landlord treasures the repeated signatures of John Brown in his books, refusing large sums offered for any one of them. The people of colour assembled, and entreated the honour of being permitted by a deputation to take the widow by the hand. A procession of the citizens was organised for the next day; but it was stopped by gentlemen who feared that it would be too much for the mourners. At Vergennes, in Vermont, the news of their arrival spread like wildfire. The citizens waited on Mr. Phillips and Mr. McKim; carriages were brought to convey the coffin and its guardians to the steamer on Lake Champlain; and, though there was no sound of preparation, the party was escorted by the entire population of the place, the men with uncovered heads, and the bells of the churches tolling. The procession stood in silence till the widow had disappeared on board. The steamer's course had been arranged so as to land the party at a point of the shore nearest to their destination for the night. It was a stormy evening, and their arrival was not expected; yet here again the citizens formed an escort, uncovering their heads in the rain. At Elizabeth'stown, the resting place for the night, the Courthouse was offered for the deposit of the coffin; and six gentlemen watched it there through the night. They probably desired the honour, in the eyes of their children's children.

The men of the place could hardly credit that the deed was done; that such a man as their fellow-citizen could have been hanged by order of any court or government. They assembled to hear how it came to pass that a God-fearing man, of the purest life and the tenderest affections, could actually have been hanged. While they listened, one citizen did a perilous service. He took a strong and swift horse, and set off up the mountain track, to traverse twenty-five miles, to give notice to the family of the approach of the party. It was the son of the sheriff who did this; and every eminent citizen, members of the Legislature, the municipal authorities, &c., left their names and inquiries for the widow. Few or none approve Brown's deed. Those who do not think it wrong consider it unwise; but this has no apparent effect at all on their conduct now. No one excuses himself for backwardness now on the plea of disapprobation of the exploit. This is a plain proof that Brown has accurately represented the spirit and the convictions of his time and country, and fairly inaugurated the political and social reform which has been so long preparing. The final days' journey was dreary. The road was almost impassable; so that the twenty-five miles were not completed till night. At some distance from the now desolate home moving lights were seen. Men had come out in the dark night to meet the party—the delay having caused alarm at home.

Here I will stop. I am not writing, as I said before, for the sake of the domestic interest. It is enough to say that on the escorting friends devolved the task of relating to the family, assembled in a room for the purpose, the whole narrative of what had been done since the outbreak at Harper's Ferry. The group of young widows was there, and the remaining son, and the youngest child of five. Such a group as that—all with their eyes fixed on the speaker, all well disciplined in restraining emotion, an old-fashioned puritan family as they are—was a picture, not enjoyed by the eye, but burnt in upon the brain and heart of men from Philadelphia and Boston, who hardly conceived that such elements existed in modern life, even in New England.

Next day the remains of John Brown were laid beneath his rock, after his placid countenance had been once more gazed upon by children and neighbours. A stone is to be placed over it by persons who are well aware that, if the coffin is not removed hereafter, the secluded spot in the mountain wilderness will be visited by multitudes—by as many, perhaps, as the grave at Mount Vernon itself. Brown used to relieve his wife of some of her nursery cares, and was excellent at singing his infants to sleep. The hymn which he was fond of for this purpose was sung at his grave. It will be the characteristic New England hymn henceforward, "sung to the good old Puritan tune of Lenox." The services were performed by two clergymen, who, hearing at

Burlington of what was going on, achieved the passage of the mountains during the wintry night, in order to assist at the last honours.

When those honours were paid the visitors departed—the way being dangerous, and their return being eagerly awaited all along the route. Mr. Phillips had promised to deliver a lecture on the Anti-slavery cause at Vergennes, the next night. No place could contain the crowds assembled; but he was heard by a large number. I mention this lecture for the sake of a comment made upon it, which appears to many people a good expression of the state of the national mind at present over the greater part of the Republic. A venerable Deacon of the Church said, on his return from the lecture, "I have listened to seven thousand sermons in my life; and I have heard more of God's eternal truth to-night than was contained in them all."

Other sermons have been beside the mark; this one hit it. Other events have left men's hearts and consciences untouched; John Brown's life and death have touched them to the quick. The consequences will soon be seen.

"Election of Abraham Lincoln"

22 November 1860

The election of Mr. Lincoln to the office of President of the United States is an event of the highest importance.[113] In his own country it is the most important event which has occurred since the organization of the great Republic was first got into regular working order; and to the rest of the world, scarcely anything that could happen in a foreign country could involve interests so grave and so various as a radical change of policy in the American Union. The deeper the interest of the occasion, the more desirable it is that there should be no misunderstanding as to the precise grounds of the importance of the event. The tumult and confusion of mind reflected in the American newspapers from the society around them may well mislead European, as they do many American readers as to the probable results of the election of an Anti-slavery President. Instead of believing the threats, and sympathising in the terrors, of interested or agitated alarmists, it will be wise to look at the matter from a more serviceable point of view than they occupy. The chief considerations we believe to be these.

The New President is neither a Northern nor a Southern man. The election of 1860 is the nineteenth since the establishment of American institutions; and of the eighteen terms now fulfilled only four have been occupied by Northern men, and all the rest by Southern men and slaveholders. No Northern man has been re-elected, while five slaveholders have served twice. Now both sections make way for the great West, which did not exist, except as an unexplored wilderness, when Federal government was erected at Washington. That Western territory has become peopled and improved up to the point of claiming and obtaining the honour of giving a President to the Republic. It need hardly be explained that the co-operation of the North and West in this election secures the overthrow of the peculiar policy of the

South. The South, weak in itself, has retained the predominance at Washington thus long by working on the fears and the vanity of the other two sections. Now that they have thrown off its influence, it must give up the game. The South has had its turn, and a very long one, at the head of affairs; and now it must go into opposition, if indeed it cannot participate in the policy of the Republican party. Hence arise two more points of importance. The leaders of Southern policy and their organs declare that the Southern States will not go into opposition. If they cannot rule the Republic they will secede from it. It is necessary to ascertain the probable value of this threat.

It is well known that certain members of the existing government have aided the Disunion cry, and have in some places begun it. This mitigates the alarm at the cry, while increasing the general disgust at it. It was raised to affect the election; and, as it has failed in that direction, it will not be repeated by the same persons. But it is not the less true that there is a very serious agitation in several States in favour of leaving the Union. No man whose opinion is of any value believes that it can be done; but the disposition to attempt it is a grave evil. South Carolina, supported by Mississippi and Alabama, proposed, after Mr. Lincoln's election was certain, to secede before Mr. Buchanan's term expires, in order that the Federal forces might not be held by their new enemy, but by their old friend and nominee. The Southern party in Virginia promises to be ready to join, when the movement is begun, and the actual importation of arms into Virginia is so great as to cause a general expectation of civil war through the State. We hear of an universal arming of the citizens throughout several States; of plans for marching on Washington, to get possession of the departments of the Federal Government; of schemes for preventing the inauguration of Mr. Lincoln in March; and so forth. Everywhere outside the frontier of those angry States men smile at such projects; and it need not be explained that they can never be executed: but it is a melancholy truth that most of the misguided citizens suppose that they can, and that others are "ready to perish in the attempt." They imagine an anti-slavery President a sort of monster, and believe all they are told of an impending destruction of society. A few months will show them, if they will wait, that the laws of the Republic are the protection of the citizens, quite apart from the opinions of the President; and that social changes can be wrought only through legislation, in which they have a much larger share than Northern citizens, by means of their three-fifths suffrage. If they can but be induced to wait a little while, they will cease to talk of secession from the Union. If they continue to propose it, and are seen to take any steps towards it—then certain grave considerations enter into the case. The North has an overwhelming preponderance of population and wealth; and the small force of the Slave States must be so occupied in representing five millions of slaves as to have no means to oppose the authority of Government and the Free States. The plain truth is, it is nonsense talking of resisting the national will: and the menaces of civil war would not deserve notice in Europe but for their operation on commercial credit. The suspension of two or three banks, in consequence of panic about an anti-slavery President, the refusal of the Southern banks generally to discount bills till the effect of the election was seen, the sudden decline in the value of negroes to the extent of 30 per cent, and the inevitable effect on industry of such alarms, are substantial evils which belong to the history of the case.

The second consideration referred to is one of extreme importance—the sudden and open manifestation of republican opinion in the Slave States. If the slaveholders did not before know, they will now see and feel how small a minority they are in the great nation they have till now coerced for their own objects. We need but point to the growth of republican and anti-slavery opinion in Virginia, and especially in the Harper's Ferry region, since this time twelvemonth, to show what is the immediate effect of any free discussion such as was introduced by the raid of John Brown, and will now be everywhere created by a reversal of the national policy. Looking, also, at the agitation in Maryland, the demonstrations at Washington, and the undisguised purpose of the non-slaveholding states to resist any reimposition of the oligarchical yoke under which they have sunk to be what they are, there remains no doubt whatever that there is a much stronger and broader sympathy between the Free States and the inhabitants of the Southern States than has been at all supposed till within the last few weeks. If the slaveholders will abstain from meddling with others, others will let them alone; but they had better not refuse to fulfil their share of the republican compact—to abide by the decision of the majority.

The dangers of the Republic are incalculably reduced by the bringing of this great quarrel to a constitutional arbitrament. Whatever changes may occur will be very slow in coming to pass. If Mr. Lincoln were the violent fanatic he is assumed to be, he must wait upon Congress. It will take several years to renew the material of the Senate and the House of Representatives; and, till that is done, the South will have more than its share of influence at Washington. No doubt its policy will be reversed, in regard to the aim of extending the conditions of slavery over the whole country; but there will be plenty of wrangling before it is done, and abundance of delay, through the obstacles which an unreformed Legislature can interpose.

A calm review of the position leaves the result, in the shape of good and evil, something like this. To take the evil first:—The existing panic, during which the citizens are hanging their neighbours, and any stranger who may cross their sight, and suspecting and punishing their slaves, and hoarding their gold, and arming their families, and selling off their property, is an evil; but it is a less evil than the reality, in the place of the panic, would be. The universal expectation of a rising of the slaves, in case of Mr. Lincoln's failure, should almost reconcile the citizens, and their commercial correspondents, to the mischievous agitation they have created, even if it should end in a considerable crash. The negroes are less likely to rise now than at any time these thirty years past; and if there is more or less rebellion, it will be owing to the cruelties which the fears of their owners are now impelling them to inflict. There will be a period of obstructed legislation at Washington, and of virulent party strife, till the hitherto dominant party has learned to show due respect to the national will. There will be disorder and much complaint from the change of officials throughout the whole hierarchy of Government, a change indispensable in this case, on account of the reform in the principle of government, and also of the prevalent official corruption which has been so lately exposed. Finally, it is probable that all parties will complain of Mr. Lincoln. We know no more of Mr. Lincoln than all the rest of the world; but, if he were to turn out a second Washington, he would have no chance of satisfying a community like that of the United States, at the moment of its going over from a corrupt to a regenerate republican system. If it is a mystery how any man can govern, at such a moment, a nation which is living in different stages of civilization, it is no mystery that he must fail in doing at once what the people expect, and what the nation requires. One more evil may be impending—the failure of the cotton supply. It need not be so if the planters were wise; but they are, in this matter, not wise. We can only bear in mind that a servile war would have been worse for the cotton crop than a fanciful political agitation, and meantime, for our own part, make haste to create other sources of supply.

As for the good results:—the great Republic will, as soon as an improved Congress permits, transfer her testimony from the side of slavery to that of free labour and free existence. When Slavery is abolished within the congressional district of Columbia (which the inhabitants of the district are now demanding), Negro Slavery will cease to be an American institution. Any of the States in which it exists may keep it up if they like, and if they can; but it will have ceased to be a national interest. We shall have the nation on our side in our opposition to the slave trade, and in our endeavours to make industrial allies of the inhabitants of Africa. Spain must then give way about her Cuban slave trade. In America, free labour will presently supersede the more extravagant method of production, and the antagonism of race will be much softened.

The liberties of the citizens will be recovered from this day onward, after having been more and more encroached upon for a quarter of a century. The Americans will be again the free people their fathers made them. Best of all, the national character and reputation will improve and rise, as character and reputation do rise after the casting off of a great sin and sore disgrace. Both have suffered grievously; but we may hope now that they have touched their lowest point, and that their present noble awakening to duty, and rejection of the compromises of self-interest, may be in time to secure political regeneration and social peace at home, and the respect of the civilized world to institutions which make the people who live under them really free.

"Anarchy in the South"

29 January 1861

The American revolution had been so long and so clearly foreseen that it might be expected to move rapidly. The parts were prepared, and the play was ready for the moment when the curtain should rise on a new Presidential term. But something has occurred—something which ought to have been considered in the programme—which has hurried on the course of events faster than the most reckless political leader ever imagined. The movement in the Southern States is now in the hands of the mob.

Here ends all possibility of compromise. Here ends, indeed, every chance of arrangement of any kind, unless the authorities and the leading planters can recover the influence which they have certainly at present lost. As the Governor of South Carolina has appealed to private friends in the army for protection against the mob in Charleston itself; and as the planters are flying to the North as fast as they can find means of doing so, it does not appear probable that they will resume the lead in the society of their own State, so as to carry on negotiations at Washington or anywhere else. As these gentlemen themselves say, on arriving at a place of safety, or when they can send letters in some secure and secret way, the state of society is like nothing but the period of mob rule in the first French Revolution. They say that men and women are drunk with passion, under the instigation of agitators who have found the means of extorting money from the wealthier members of society. It really appears that the political phase of the movement is already merged in the social—not yet at Washington, but in the several Southern States.

Last week we should have said that the time had arrived when it was desirable to speak of the antagonists as the Constitutional and the Revolutionary party; because the distinction of Democratic and Republican no longer serves. In the Free States all men, whether democrats or republicans, are of one mind about the conduct of the Seceding States; and in the Slave States there is known to be a strong minority in favour of adhesion to the Union. Thus, till the latest flood of evidence poured in, it seemed to be necessary to change the grounds and the names of parties, and to regard them simply in their attitude towards the constitution. Even this, it appears, is now too late; and the work to be done is to deal with the anarchy which is destroying the very form of society in the planting States; and in none more than the State which has always called itself chivalrous *par excellence*—South Carolina.

Till nothing better could be had, the world (Northern and other) had to gather its notions of what was doing from the Southern newspapers; and very eagerly they were read and quoted, while understood to be written with a view to that destiny. The handing about of letters at Washington had much the same object, and the same effect, though an incident or a phrase here and there conveyed an impression that all was not so brave and fine as was pretended. Next, several agents from the South arrived in the great Northern towns (and especially at Pittsburg and other manufacturing towns in the mining districts) to purchase arms, ammunition and stores. The astonishment of these men at what they saw caused the first real disclosures of the state of affairs they had left behind. They had come in fear and perplexity about how to discharge their commission, expecting to find society convulsed by fear and hatred of the South, and even anticipating peril to their own lives. They had imagined white labourers to be like the poor whites at home, swarming in the streets, threatening fire, demanding blood, in order to get dollars. They found all quiet, everybody at work as usual—nobody desiring the perdition of anybody, and a considerable proportion of society (to use their own words) scarcely knowing or caring whether the Union were dissolved or not. They could buy any commodity that they could pay for— pistols and powder, guns or grain, without question or opposition. The natural impulse was to make friendship with people so little like enemies; and these men have made a clean breast of the tidings that were bursting their hearts. Next, families from the South began to arrive; mothers, and children, and governesses, with or without the husbands and fathers. Some of them have arrived bare of almost everything; for they had to get away when and as they could, with or without preparation and luggage. On some points of great importance these witnesses, and the letters carried by some of them, are entirely agreed, whether they come from the south-east or the south-west. They agree that the "Mean-whites" have got the upper hand of the authorities, the capitalists, and even the secession leaders; that this mob-rule is a system of pillage; that money is fast disappearing; that food is absolutely deficient in many places, and scanty in stock everywhere; and that there is no chance of a cotton crop next year. If the soil is tilled at all, it will be for food. One incident is repeated by one new comer after another, and also in letters; that one arrangement enforced in South Carolina, but carefully kept from publication in the newspapers, is that every owner of slaves shall pay a tax of sixteen dollars a head on his slaves. Many have not the means of paying; and then their slaves are confiscated; or, as there is no sale for negroes, other property is seized instead. Wealthy planters are marked men, and in some cases a special "tax," so called, of a thousand dollars is imposed, "for the good of the State." One of the sufferers was informed that his mansion would be destroyed if he did not pay. He raised the money, and despatched his family to the North instantly. Those who have not the means of paying have not the means of escape, and are awaiting the catastrophe with as much courage as they can muster. The State loan of 400,000 dollars is parceled out at Charleston among the wealthier citizens, each one of whom must take his share under penalty of being considered "disaffected." This method of alienating the main supports of the movement is so impolitic that the secret sittings of the Convention are supposed to be overruled, as the Governor himself is, by the mob. Private families are subject to intrusion by bands of poor whites, who call themselves patrols or minute men, and who demand food first, and, when they have got it, money. In Alabama, in Mississippi, and elsewhere, the course of affairs is just the same. The citizens declare that they must appear to be secessionists to save life and property. One who writes from Alabama wishes Government would blockade the port, because there is not bread enough to last sixty days, and hunger would compel submission. In Mississippi the planters are generally opposed to violent secession; but they are silenced by threats of confiscation. One who was further menaced with lynching has fled to the North, where he can say what he thinks while his landless neighbours are helping themselves out of his property. These gentlemen say that if the President and his Ministers would take a decided stand on behalf of the Constitution, and show an intention to fight vigorously, "a submissionist party would soon make itself heard."

Meantime, "there is no more business going on at noon than at twelve at night"; and it is not stagnation but annihilation of trade. There is no flour in some places, no bacon at others, no beef or pork elsewhere. Some complain that they "are living in war, famine, and pestilence." There is here food for four months, there food for six weeks; and in parts even of South Carolina no food at all. They have got some from Tennessee, but it is not paid for, and their credit is exhausted. Of course, there are the usual alarms of negro insurrection—nights fixed on which a rising is to take place, casks of powder found secreted, and so on. Not only is it always uncertain whether such rumours are true or false, but it even does not much matter. The negroes and their supposed leaders are punished and agitation is engendered in the one case as in the others. One trait gives a look of falseness to the alarm. A writer from Alabama says it is singular that all the plots that have been discovered have been headed by white men. Thus far it has always proved to be a false and absurd belief that white men head negro risings, and it probably is so now. False or true, absurd or rational, the effect of the alarm is the same. Negroes find themselves totally idle in the day, and incessantly visited by their owners or overseers; and at night they are barred into their own quarter, and the tread of the patrol is heard all night. Though it is holiday time as to work, they have bare living and no pleasure: they are sternly kept at home; and they must be wondering why. We are told that in country places they get out at night, and meet in the woods, in spite of all precautions. In the large towns the negroes are well kept under, but in planting districts security depends on the lives of a handful of owners and overseers. These are now worn out; many overseers not having had their clothes off for weeks; and they are liable to be called on to join the State forces at any hour, leaving wives and children to bar out the negroes as they can. The alarm here is real, whatever the actual peril may be; and certainly the Southern political agitators have done what they could to make the negroes suppose there was "a good time coming" for them, and to put it into the heads of the poor whites to use their grand opportunity of pillage.

It is now beyond concealment that the revolution has passed into the hands of one of the two classes of victims of the slaveholding system, and that the planters are in mortal fear of the other. Their certain retribution has overtaken them, in the mob rule of the landless whites whom they have reduced to barbarism; and they are in further dread of their own negroes. What is to be done with the social chaos?

One important view arises out of all these elements—important to us, in connexion with the prospects of our cotton manufacture. As we have said, we are warned to expect no cotton crop next year, from the sudden arrest of industry, and the pressing need of food on the spot. There are attempts at storing up cotton, in hope of high prices; but those stores will be pillaged, no doubt, like other wealth. At the same time, the Northern newspapers are emphatically directing attention to the vast flax cultivation of the Western prairies, as available both for Europe and New England. Flax is grown almost without limit on those prairies, for the sake of the seed and its oil. The fibre is likely now to be more valuable than the seed; and we observe that the men of the West are strongly appealed to from the Northern ports to hasten to suppose the falling off of cotton. They are told that England will be independent of America in five years' time, from the capabilities of her own and other territories; and that, if they can sell Western flax as cheap as the Southern cotton, while linen lasts twice as long as calico, they had better bestir themselves to send the fibre to market rather than the oil, which can be otherwise supplied. Lancashire should attend to all such indications. It is as well for Lancashire to know what Americans expect of us, in regard to our supplying ourselves with cotton from other territory than theirs.

"Emancipation Proclamation"

10 October 1862

What vile imaginations some guardians of public morals have! We have been accustomed to see in American newspapers, and especially in journals proceeding from the rankest slaveholding regions, how nasty an aspect every social act may assume, and how base a construction may be put upon the most innocent or virtuous proceedings; but some things have been seen in our newspapers within a few days which the lowest scribe in the most barbarous Secessionist village would stare to hear of. There are writers among us who have seized the opportunity of President Lincoln's Proclamation[114] to write sensation articles, evolving their images of horror from the depths of their own consciousness of the passions of the white towards the negro, of the oppressor towards the wronged, and we may add, of the vindictive towards the generous. These moral teachers have also turned aside from the records of history, to take their materials from romances and melodramas, in which the action of negro slaves is about as nearly like reality as an operatic hero is like Garibaldi, or the peasants in a ballet are like Lincolnshire labourers at a harvest home. We trust that our British public, which has emancipated a good many slaves in a way particularly trying to the negroes, will not now be scared by sensation articles, prophetic of burnings and ravishings, and all conceivable horrors, as sure to follow upon emancipation in America. As for the intimation that President Lincoln foresees and desires such an exhibition of hell upon earth, to gratify his hatred of the South, it can do no harm to anybody but the fanatics who issue the slander. Every man of sense, and of the good feeling which is an invariable requisite of good sense, will have seen from the beginning that the risk of rebellion and massacre on the plantations lay in the slaves being baulked of emancipation, and not in their being gratified in their desire for freedom. Every man of sense has for some time perceived that the Washington Government was incurring a fearful risk by playing fast and loose with the interests and passions of the servile population of the South; and that whoever, in any country, was aiming at thrusting the four millions of slaves out of sight, in treating of the American quarrel, was making himself answerable for anything the negroes might do in their despair from the world's neglect of their misery. Of all conceivable rashness, none could be so great as that of supposing that slavery would go on as usual after the events of the last two years; and the next great rashness has been that of the American Government, which has tolerated a diversity of treatment of various commanders of the fugitives who have sought refuge within the Federal lines. Over the whole length and breadth of the Slave States, the negroes understand that the war has arisen out of their slavery; they know that many thousands of their number have escaped to the Free States, while other thousands have been slain by Confederate hands to prevent their escape; they know that for thirty years the Republic has been warned of this conflict, if the bondage of the negroes, with its political consequences to the whites, were persevered in; they looked for the day of deliverance after the election of 1856; and when it did not arrive, they waited for 1860. After all this, to expect that they could settle down again, as if nothing has happened, is such madness as would scarcely be excusable in the most blind and brutalised slaveholder, whose only faith is in the power of the cowhide. In an Englishman the folly is hardly credible; and in fact the thorough-going partisans of the slaveholders are everywhere credited with hypocrisy, as well as ignorance. As for the other rashness, that of the Washington government in permitting a return of fugitives to bondage by two or three commanders, while other generals were receiving all who came as free, in virtue of their escape; it is evident that the Government was rendering itself responsible for the consequences of disappointment and discouragement on the part of the slaves. It is known that vast numbers have gone into the wilds, on hearing how uncertain their fate would be if they confided in the Federal whom they had supposed to be their deliverers. The forest, and the swamps, and the hills, are peopled by refugees from the plantations; and if there is to be any ravaging of the plantations, it will be by these perplexed and disappointed men. It may be hoped that the Proclamation has appeared in time to guide them aright. It is an invitation in which they may confide to leave Slaveland till the terms of freedom can be settled; and the only drawback on the peaceable secession from the South of as many negroes as can get away is the part of the Proclamation which treats of their deportation as a practicable plan and a real intention. White people and free coloured people know that the colonizing scheme is nought; but the raw slave may naturally suppose that it is really designed to send him away somewhere. This is an apprehension which it would have been more prudent not to excite; but it is so much milder an evil than continuance in slavery that it may not interfere much with the approaching emancipation.

When people try to raise an alarm about a servile war, they should have in their own minds, and should express, a clear meaning of the term, to which meaning they should adhere. But two separate things are, on this occasion, written about under one name, for purposes of convenient mystification. The common idea of a servile war is of an enslaved race or class rising in revolt against their tyrants of their own accord, and on their own resources. This description does not answer for the American case. The negroes there have not revolted, nor, as far as can be learned, have ever intended to revolt; they have taken no measures of their own accord but simple flight as individuals, and they have no resources for the out-break or the support of a revolt. Their doctrine and practice are, in fact, of a directly opposite tendency. They have always looked to whites to deliver them; and their universal belief is that they are to keep quiet till the Yankees arrive or summon them to free soil. If such have been their doctrine and practice through all the uncertainties of the last eighteen months, it is pretty clear what they will do now that their confidence is at last beginning to be justified. They have nothing to gain now and everything to lose by such violence as the friends of their guilty masters apprehend; and it is not the negroes who will incur the world's disgust, but those of their enemies who are peeping out of their closets and asking when the ravishing is going to begin.

If this ordinary sense of the term "servile war" does not apply, what shall we make of the other?

The released slaves are brought under an organization which is fitting them for one of three departments of service. Some are organized as free labourers on deserted plantations; some are trained to the labours of the camp, the fort, and the field; and some are drilled for service in the army. English secessionists are actually trying to give the name of "servile war" to this last function. The trick needs only a simple mention. From the time these dark-faced recruits are uniformed and drilled, and marched to the rendezvous by white officers, or by any officers in the national pay, they are United States troops, and not revolted slaves. They march under Federal orders, and fight according to Federal methods. What passions may burn in their breasts when they find themselves face to face, as freemen, with men who have always trodden them down as slaves, no one will undertake to answer for; but it is not any such passion which has brought them into the field; and in their presence there every attribute of "servile war" is wanting.

Though this perversion of the term is convenient, the other and ordinary sense is in fact the one intended by the revilers of the new emancipation. They will be wise to take a hint from the long and wide experience of their friends, the slaveholders. It is well understood that the horrors now suggested are always the consequence of direct injury of the same nature inflicted on the slave. We need not explain ourselves more fully. Our readers will see how, in such a case, any ravage on the plantations will be an evidence of what has been going on there under the rule of the owners of human chattels. We hope and believe that nothing of the sort needs be apprehended in a general way; but it is as well that the partisans of the slaveholders should be made aware how they are dealing with the reputation of their friends and their pet institution when they assume that the retaliation of the negroes will take the form which they suggest.

When the best organs of public opinion of the North bless President Lincoln for what he has at length done, they are expressing their sense of relief that the servile war which might become possible through the vacillation of the Government is now precluded. Such danger as there was has passed away—always supposing that there is no more playing fast and loose with the negro and his destiny.

"William Lloyd Garrison and the *Liberator*"
9 January 1866

While the American newspapers show us that good citizens feel the present Christmas and New Year the happiest they have ever known, as the first which have risen upon a nation of free men, it is fitting that the world should remember those to whom these seasons must be the happiest of all. Among the newspapers brought by the last mail is the *Liberator,* which closes its existence with the year that is gone; and in it we read, "With our own hands we have put in type the unspeakably 'cheering announcement' of the abolition of slavery in the whole territory of the United States." The man who has lived to do this is the same who with his own hands put into type, above thirty years ago, the first call upon his country and nation to put away their great sin and avoid the retribution to come. The career of William Lloyd Garrison is one of deep and instructive interest in itself; but it is also so implicated with the great events and influences of his time, that some understanding of it is necessary to any true appreciation of the great issue of the civil war.

Five-and-thirty years ago the main anxiety of the Southern slaveholders, anxiously kept from the knowledge of the world outside, was that the great increase of mulattoes endangered the political operations and the social condition of the Slave States. The white fathers of that race favoured their own offspring, and when the slaves on the estate became too numerous, the light-complexioned ones were emancipated instead of sold. To remedy this increase of freed people of colour, laws were passed compelling the sale of slaves and punishing their liberation. The consequence was the formation of the notorious *Colonization Society*—the hopeless device of the slaveholders for the deportation of their surplus "hands," and especially of those most troublesome from either ability or stupidity. The scheme naturally took hold of the ignorant sympathies of humane people, as well as relieved the perplexities of the more conscientious slaveholders. We need not relate the story of its failure. What concerns us now is, that Garrison was among the humane persons at first deceived, and that he was the first true man who saw through and exposed it. It was in 1829 that, while a poor student at a country college in New England, he heard of the Colonization Society, and supposed, as he was told, that a way had been found for the blacks out of slavery. With his characteristic integrity, he chose to investigate the scheme for himself; and with his characteristic sagacity, he saw through it as soon as he went to the slaveholding city of Baltimore. The inevitable consequence was that he became an abolitionist, at a time when there was no sympathy and no help to be had in a course so mischievous and so heretical. In a little while he was in gaol for having expressed in a newspaper his view of a slave-trading transaction by a New England merchant. His fine for the libel was paid by an entire stranger, Mr. Arthur Tappan, of New York, who thereby showed that a second abolitionist had risen up already. Presently there were four, sitting in a garret with their feet upon a wood pile, engaging with each other that slavery should be abolished in their country. Then was issued the first number of the *Liberator*, the last number of which will arrive by the next mail. Garrison and a friend lived in a garret on bread and water, spending their earnings as printers and their spare time on this newspaper; and when it sold unusually well, they treated themselves to a bowl of milk, as the friend told us afterwards. In the first number of that newspaper was uttered the oracle which we have seen fulfilled. "I am in earnest," said Garrison, on New Year's Day of 1831—"I will not equivocate—I will not excuse—I will not retreat a single inch—AND I WILL BE HEARD." "The apathy of the people," of which he complained, occasioned this language, and the event has justified it.

One of the most fortunate circumstances in the case has been, from first to last, that Garrison holds the Quaker principle of non-resistance, and that this was a conspicuous feature of his conduct throughout his long conflict. It was sure to be said that he wanted to rouse the slaves to insurrection; and for many years this was said: but the slaves knew better. The Southampton massacre, which happened before his voice could reach the South, was the last negro rising in the United States. Up to that time, there had been on an average one every year; but from the hour when it was known on the plantations that somebody was astir on their behalf in the Free States, there were no more insurrections, because there was no more despair. Thus was Garrison counselling peace and patience on the part of the slaves, and securing life and property to the owners, while these latter gentry were crying out upon him as an incendiary, and setting a price upon his head. He never knew the sense of personal safety for many years from this time. Every door was closed against him, except those of comrades who were in almost equal danger; and our elder generation remembers the time when, in the autumn of 1835, he was dragged through the streets of Boston with a halter round his neck, and the tar-kettle heating at the end of the march. A stout arm thrust him into the gaol, and saved him then; but nothing could save him and the few who gathered round him from the utmost contumely and injury that social rancour could inflict. As none of these things moved his noble and serene temper, and as they could not touch him in his happy home, in which poverty itself was scarcely an evil, his work prospered. By degrees his doctrine won its way, and his conscience has at length converted that of his nation. He moulded those who came near him to his own likeness, and his early coadjutors were worthy of him.

It need scarcely be pointed out that he must have failed in a political task so arduous—so apparently impossible—as that of regenerating the idolised constitution of his country, in such a matter as the institution of Slavery, if he had brought to the work no better qualifications than the "one-idea'd fanaticism" which was ascribed to him, against all evidence, for thirty years. In any future historical review of the case, the most striking feature of his mind and his course will probably be his political sagacity. He has been so constantly right in his anticipations, and so successful in his counsels, that few will now question that if his countrymen had had courage and conscience enough to follow his lead at an earlier time, the inevitable revolution might have been wrought without warfare and without ruin to any section of the country. Of those who had his sagacity too few had the courage or conscience to put their hand to the work in time. We now see also that some who had the courage and conscience, but had not the sagacity, have failed in the last stage of the conflict, and are now rather a hindrance than a help to the settlement of society, and the prospects of the negroes in whose rescue they have been as devoted as Garrison himself—the Moses of the coloured race, to whom they looked, in reasonable trust, to bring them out of bondage.

The crowning glory of this man's career must be doubtless in what some, who really are the fanatics that he never was, regard as its eclipse. His unerring sense, untouched by any self-regards, perceived the right moment for exchanging rebuke for encouragement—antagonism for fellowship—the intrepidity of the martyr for the sympathy of the comrade. It was no pleasure to him to be before his nation and his time; and therefore when his nation and his time had come up with him and the right, he fell into their ranks, and thought no more of any personal distinction that belonged to him. Thus he has saved himself from being left behind, as some more ambitious men now find themselves. When slavery was at an end, he saw that Abolition Societies should come to an end. When the liberation of the negroes was effected, he saw that the *Liberator* should stop. When the Government and the people showed their willingness to do right, he saw that the need for invective, reproach, and avowed suspicion was gone by, and that the hour had come for helping the authorities, instead of rendering their great task impracticable. Because he saw this earlier than some others, he was scorned by them as a backslider; and now, when he devotes himself to the welfare of the freed people, and would bring them into harmony with their white neighbours, and unite the two races in a common citizenship and mutual interest, he is regarded as a trimmer by zealots who, if they were not a small minority, would end by driving the President and his government into the arms of the South, and kindling a war of races as a sequel to the civil war. The difference between the two sorts of abolitionists evidently is that the one takes a narrow view and the other a wide one. Garrison has always looked further ahead and abroad than either his friends or his enemies; and it seems that he does so now. We need not institute any moral comparison. It is enough for us to recognise the hero and the patriot as worthy of the highest honour at the moment when he quietly becomes one with his neighbours, and when he ceases to preach simply because his preaching has wrought out its purpose, and the time for working in common has come. This great hour finds him with congenial work before him in the case of the freed negroes. We may not hear much of him henceforth. He said he would be heard; he was heard effectually; and now he proposes to be silent. It is to be hoped that we shall not for such a reason forget him. History certainly will not; and if she relates that before the second American revolution the nation had so sunk that the world taunted it with having no great men, she will add that this was a mistake, for there was one great man—the second printer's journeyman who did a great work for his country—William Lloyd Garrison.

❖ ❖ ❖

THE *SPECTATOR*

1858

Described as "politically Liberal, but moderate," the *Spectator* (1828–1925) pub-lished both news and reviews (Mackenzie 1988, 593). Perhaps it was this unusual combination of liberalism and conservatism that prompted Martineau's critique of the periodical even as she admired certain of its features. Her approximately twenty-five year affiliation with the *Spectator* includes the journal's reviews of her books, occasional letters to the editor, and her series of articles on America's civil conflict. In its review of Martineau's *Illustrations of Political Economy* (1832–1834), the *Spectator* hailed her as the "benefactor of her species" (Webb 1960, 121). But after her return from America, an 1837 *Spectator* article critical of abolitionism prompted Martineau to write a series of letters to the editor in protest, heralding the ideological differences between journal and writer that eventually culminated in a complete break.

Martineau's American-themed articles for the *Spectator*, published between April and December 1858, ceased when control of the journal shifted to editors who were "not only pro-slavery but disreputable."[115] Writing to Fanny Wedgwood that the *Spectator* had been transferred to "the *only* pro-slavery journalist in England,— Thornton Hunt," she disassociated herself entirely from the publication: "I believe and hope it was *all but* unknown that I have written for it at all. If you should ever hear it, please contradict it from this time forward" (Arbuckle, 1983, 177). She later complained, "I am getting as tired of it as some other people are. Its smartness is degenerating into impertinence very fast; and its insolence is so absurd in partner-ship with its incredible ignorance of the world and of social matters!" (286).[116] She was quick to clarify her position with her American friends as well; to Wendell Phillips, she wrote that the new editor was "a man of bad repute, whose family property, while he had any, was in the West Indies. He is a man with whom it is not possible for decent people to have anything to do: . . . we have lost an organ while the enemy have got one."[117]

The *Spectator* selections provide a revealing comparison with the *National Anti-Slavery Standard* (*NASS*) articles (later in this section) in that the former were writ-ten for a British audience while the latter address the American abolitionists. Yet there are striking similarities between the two: both the *Spectator* and the *NASS* articles are sharp, satiric, and undiplomatic—and therefore controversial—in their politically insightful observations. In contrast, dispassionate authority characterizes her *Daily News* leaders (except when she was attacking the "meddling" *Times*).

Martineau's aggressive and uncompromising tone in the *Spectator* series anticipates that demonstrated in the *NASS,* an engagement that began shortly after she
ceased writing for the *Spectator.* In the *Spectator,* for example, Martineau equates
American domestic policy with economics—"in other words, the great natural laws
of society" in which materialism takes precedence over human rights. Similarly,
"The American Difficulty" addresses the international economic concerns generated
by the "mere report and anticipation of war" while indicating that strained relations
between America and Britain during this period clearly predate the 1861 *Trent* incident. "State Rights in America" continues this theme, charging—undiplomatically,
she admits—that states' rights issues, like the conflicts between Massachusetts' Personal Liberty Laws and the federal Fugitive Slave Act, are often obscured behind a
smoke screen of conflicted international relations, resulting in "our ticklish relations
in Washington." The vicious beating of Charles Sumner by Preston Brooks in the
Senate ("What Is the South?"), the vigilante code of lynch law ranging from New
Orleans to New York, the corrupt partisanship characterizing Buchanan's presidency
("American Domestic Policy")—these and other examples come under Martineau's
scrutiny as evidence of America's deterioration as a republic accumulates. "How remarkably the fortunes of the civilised world have suddenly become dependent on
the great question of free and slave labour," she wrote in 1858; "the success of the
antislavery cause . . . in America now would do more for human peace, progress,
welfare and happiness, than any other thing that could happen."[118]

Her stridency during this period indicates that, although her passion for her
"beloved Americans" is stronger than ever, the events preceding the outbreak of
civil war caused her to despair of witnessing a happy outcome for the African
American population during her lifetime. The best encouragement of which she is
capable at this period is this: "[T]he deepest darkness is just before dawn,—the
dreariest discouragement just before success."

. . .

"American Domestic Policy at the Centre and Circumference"
15 May 1858

There was a time when it was excusable for politicians and their newspapers to speak with less reprobation of negro-slavery in America than of the
same institution elsewhere. Besides the old plea that the British established it
in that region, there was the new complaint of the disproportion of land and
labour in the scantily-peopled agricultural States. Twenty years ago there really was some semblance of the question being one with two sides. It was
plain to sound thinkers, however,—as plain then as it is now,—that time
must dissolve the pro-slavery plea, that a few years would probably suffice to
do it. It has turned out so; and we now see the question lodged in a conjunc-
ture of time and circumstance which needs but to be noted to be understood.
The two or three last mails from the United States have brought news in the
highest degree instructive in regard to the future of the American Union.

First, as to the old pleas. It is true, the British introduced negro slavery into their American colonies: but this was no reason for the institution outlasting other despotisms which the republicans cast out, if they had really desired to be rid of it. A stronger point is, however, that the Americans adopted the institution, deliberately and avowedly, when they decreed the Missouri Compromise; and again when they dissolved that Compromise. They made slavery an American institution then, in the face of the world. The excuse of a deficiency of labour in proportion to the land was, in like manner, thrown up by them when they founded their Colonization Society, with the avowed object of settling American negroes, (emancipated slaves,) on the coast of Africa. This is not the moment for exposing the real aim and operation of the scheme. It is a curious story; but we have not room for it here. Our business with it now is merely as a proof, if its founders were sincere, that labour could not be so deficient as to compel the slavery of the labourers, if colonies of those very labourers could be spared for so remote and improbable an achievement as civilizing Africa. A long course of events has wrought out the same proof into perfect clearness. The influx of free labour into the northern States, rendered their lands so productive that, (as appears from the unquestionable authority of Mr. Helper, a North Carolina man, reared in the heart of slave institutions,) the mere hay-crop of the Free States is more valuable than all the cotton, tobacco, and other southern products of the Slave States.[119] If the southern men really desired and sought a sufficiency of labour concentrated on their lands, the means were open to them as to their brethren in the north. Whether it be true or not that whites cannot cultivate and prepare sugar-crops, they can cotton and tobacco, and the ordinary agricultural products of the Slave States. So well was this known on the spot, and so much was the presence of free European labourers dreaded instead of desired, that the Know-nothing party was created in the south, and carefully propagated northwards, under Protestant pretences, but in reality to stop the influx of free-labour with which slavery could not co-exist.[120] While the plea of economical necessity was wearing out before the world's eyes, the slave-holders published their jealousy of the prosperous Free States in a manner which appears more extraordinary from year to year. They have for several years held an annual Convention of Delegates in some southern city, in order to vent their uneasiness at the unprosperous condition of their section of the Union, and to consult on the means of rendering themselves independent of the north. Their annual lamentation over their dependence on their rich and busy fellow citizens of New England and New York for capital with which to cultivate their fields, for shipping with which to carry the produce to a market, for railways and vehicles, for colleges and literature, for everything indeed but mere land and slaves, makes all the world ask why they do not take the same measures to get rich which have made the Free States prosperous. Year by year at these Conventions there are proposals made, which none but slave-holders who live only in a world of their own, could bring forward seriously. They will subscribe (though they complain of mortgaged estates and insolvency,) to set up a line of steamers from their own ports direct to Europe, to cut off the commerce of New York, Philadelphia, and Boston. They try, and raise only money enough to buy coal for five miles of steaming,—if the vessel were given them. They appoint a Committee to prepare school-books for all southern schools, as they have hitherto depended wholly on the north for such literature; and the avowals of the Declaration of Independence, and the principles and laws of human rights and liberties are found more or less in them all. The issue of this measure is not yet known. They advocate the establishment of colleges enough in the south to prevent the race of future slaveholders being sent to see the prosperity of the north, and to form connexions in the land of free labour; but there is little encouragement to build new colleges while those which exist are in a depressed condition, and the young men of Virginia and the Carolinas will go for education where the best is to be had. Thus it is throughout the whole range of efforts to rise, as the organs of the slaveholders themselves explain to us. Nobody but themselves could doubt for a moment that the issue must be the succumbing of slavery to free labour in the south, as happened long ago in the other section.

A series of efforts in a different direction remained, however, to be made. It is assumed by slaveholders that their method of cultivation is supremely profitable on virgin soils, however soon and certainly it impoverishes the land. Now that eastern Virginia is lapsing into swamp and forest, and North Carolina is a dreary wilderness, and even Alabama, (a new state a quarter of a century since,) has degenerated to the point of desolation described in local publications, it is natural that the landed proprietors of the south should desire new areas for the application of the labour which forms the bulk of their capital. Hence the struggles for ascendancy in the Federal Government: hence the cry of "manifest destiny," extorted from an observation of President Monroe: hence the annexation of Texas, and the demand for the acquisition of Cuba, and the filibustering expeditions thither and to Nicaragua:[121] hence the Dred Scott decision, and the Kansas conflict, and the accession of the three last Presidents, and the defection, humiliation, and ruin of the Websters, Clays,[122] and other leading men who ought to have been Presidents: hence the sudden rise and certain fall of a score of political parties, each of which has hoped to rule by avoiding, instead of dealing directly with, the great vice and perplexity which imperils the Republic: hence the present split in the President's party, and the discomfiture of his plans and policy; and hence, finally, the phenomenon which we spoke of at the outset as worthy the fixed attention of the whole civilized world. Political action, in the form of antagonism between the two great sections of the Union would never, (or not for any assignable length of time,) extinguish slavery, even as a national institution. Whether moral action would do it, and how soon, is not a practical question, as other forces are, and ever must be, at work with it. The sure and certain agent which must override political strife, and which is ever on the side of sound morality in the long run is economical experience, or, in other words, the great natural laws of society. Their operation just now in the political field of the American Union is the phenomenon which the world must mark.

It is admitted on all hands now that Kansas must be a Free State. Why? Because a strong and permanent influx of free labour from the eastern States has rendered slavery impossible in the new territory. Thus the game of the southern faction is up throughout the vast north-west area; and the people of Missouri itself have seen enough to be half converted, and to have returned an Anti-Slavery candidate at a contested election. While the conflict was at its height in Kansas, it became known that on the south-west frontier slavery was brought to a stop. Olmsted's account of Texas shows how the thing has happened. A line of German settlers, backed by an impassable desert "where no water is," have established so prosperous a cotton-cultivation before the eyes of the negroes and their masters, that "the peculiar institution" is daily receding, and can never advance. The hint has been taken in the north by those who sent Free labour to Kansas. They poured some into eastern Virginia, well aware that the farming population of western Virginia had long desired the abolition of slavery in their State. This was a false move, as sage observers foretold. European and Yankee immigrants cannot live under the laws, usages, discouragements, and inconveniences of a slaveholding society; and the settlers are pouring out again. Their experiment has produced some good consequences, one of which is that Delaware has protested against being a frontier Slave State in such times; and others are preparing to follow, finding slave property too evaporable, and all other acquisition obviated by its presence. Of all the new areas for immigration, Nicaragua seems to promise the best. The project was welcomed with joy by the inhabitants; and one of the first results was the disappearance of Walker and his company of filibusters. It seems to be proved that Europeans can live and work in Nicaragua; and working and trading whites will be supremely welcome to the inhabitants in comparison with, and as a defence against, freebooters who avow an intention of introducing slavery there, where it is abhorred by government and people alike.

While the world is waiting for President Buchanan's fulfilment of his programme of annexation, he pauses, though his term of office is slipping away. We knew long ago that the sugar-growing portion of his special constituency dreaded the annexation of Cuba, as fatal to their fortunes, unless they removed thither at great sacrifice. Now there is more behind;—the same project which has scared Walker from Nicaragua. The active friends of the emigrant have surveyed the ground there too; and the unburdened immigrant, who has done all when he has paid for his land, will always have the advantage over the purchaser whose capital is locked up in slaves. There is a scarcity of ordinary agricultural products in Cuba; and, the very hour that the South and the President acquire the island in defiance of the Free States, the free settlers will pour in, and slavery will recede before them as it recedes before the Germans in Texas. These truths, which cannot but be known to Mr. Cass, supply a remarkable elucidation of his correspondence with Lord Napier.[123] It is vexatious that Lord Napier's replies are suppressed, because it is of importance to us to know how far our representative at Washington is aware of the discrepancies between the facts of American history, and the assumptions of Mr. Cass's letters. If occasion should require, we are prepared to analyze the latter. Meantime, and till we can learn what Lord Napier has said about slavery and the slave-trade, we may well be satisfied with the wise and peacable citizen-policy of drawing a cordon of free and virtuous industry round the slave territory of the great republic, at once amending its fearful anomaly and rebuking its radical vice. Mr. Cass says truly that while there are slave-markets there will be a slave-trade. It is equally true that as long as there is slavery there will be slave-markets. The way to deal with the whole group of evils is to swamp slave labour by free industry,—of which, as the Americans very well know, the negro is as capable as the white.

"What Is the South?"

28 August 1858

The latest American newspapers tell us that a monument of considerable pretensions, just completed at Charleston, is about to be erected to the memory of the Honourable Preston S. Brooks, member of Congress. Our readers will recognize the name as that of the assailant of Mr. Sumner, who inflicted blows to an unlimited extent on a man unarmed, unwarned, seated, and prevented by his desk from rising to defend himself. This is the act by which Mr. Brooks acquired his fame.[124] One of the inscriptions on the monumental obelisk (of which there are four) is this.

"Ever able, manly, just, and heroic, illustrating true patriotism by his devotion to his country: the whole South unite with his bereaved family in deploring his untimely end."

We need not waste space on any criticism of the terms of this eulogium, as applied to a man who committed a deadly, premeditated assault in the Senate-chamber, on an unconscious antagonist who, for purposes of self-defence might as well have been asleep. There is no difference of opinion among us as to the application of such epithets as "manly, just, and heroic." Our business with the inscription is with the latter part of it; with the declaration that "the whole South" deplores the loss of Mr. Brooks.

Most of us may be conscious of an occasional self-reproach for the wide sweep of our censures,—and particularly of our political censures. In regard to the sectional conflicts in the United States, we may too often adopt, without qualification, the broad statements made by the parties concerned, without sufficient care to distinguish the aggressive from the passive, and the responsible from the unrepresented. It *is* something of an excuse that we are merely following the lead of the parties themselves, and adopting their own classification. But when some incident occurs which impresses us with the injustice of their random estimates, it is useful and right to take the lesson home to ourselves.

This inscription is a case in point. It is a rank libel on hundreds of thousands,—on probably many millions of southern residents, to say, deliberately, and in the permanent form of a monumental marble that "the whole South" deplores the loss of a man who was known as Preston Brooks was known. We well remember his triumphs after his dastardly act; the ovations wherever he went, the banquet and hustings speeches; and the testimonials—the silver-headed canes without end, the pieces of plate, and other rich gifts. We believe, moreover, that many persons who would not subscribe to such tributes, nor come forward at public meetings in his praise, subjected themselves by silence to be regarded as his admirers. Such men declined the responsibility of creating or exhibiting a schism at the South at a very critical period; and they swallowed their disgust and mortification, because they thought that dissent could do no good, and that mischief might come of the deposition of the supposed idol of the hour. But making all allowance for these silent members, thus classed among the assenting, there was always a very large portion of Southern society which felt very much like the rest of the world about the assault on Mr. Sumner; and the number has doubtless been increasing, as time and thought worked their national effect in calming passion. Those who had the opportunity of observing Mr. Brooks were certain that *he* was aware of this. His anxious expression of countenance, his obvious uncertainty and solicitude about his reception wherever he went in private society, and the failure of his health under the wear and tear of his position, showed that being vociferously called "the conquering hero," every day and all day long did not satisfy his own mind as to his reputation for bravery. It is certain that if he could have visited unseen the general run of southern habitations, he would have heard himself denounced as the worst enemy the South ever had,—as a disgrace to the whole caste to which he belonged,—as a mockery on the southern profession of Christian chivalry. How is it, then, it may be asked, that his monument declares him [his death] to be deplored by "the whole South?"

It happens chiefly through the self-importance of a small portion of the great southern section of the American nation. A handful of the aristocracy of the Slave states have so long accustomed themselves to speak as if they were all and their neighbours nothing, that they have really learned to think so. They deceive themselves first, and us afterwards. They are "the Slave power"; the Slave power has by degrees got ahead of all other power in the Federal Union; and its members have acquired the habit of assuming to be half the nation at home, and the whole nation abroad. If our knowledge on any one point—such as that of the impossibility that Preston Brooks's act can be sanctioned by half a great nation—checks our tendency to adopt the view and language of a braggart minority on any one occasion, we may as well extend the admonition a little further, and become careful to impute the blame of an iniquitous policy only to the real advocates of it.

What, then, is the Slave power which calls itself the South?

By the census and other records of analysis, we learn that out of the total population of the American Union, amounting now to above 27,000,000, the owners of slaves are no more than 350,000; and we need not explain that no man who is not a slave-holder counts for anything in southern society. The entire slave-holding caste, including the wives, children, relatives, and white dependants of slave-holders, amount to no more than 2,000,000 at the utmost; while it is doubtful whether so many as 1000 are earnestly and diligently wedded to the institution of slavery. One thousand! Two millions! Out of a population of twenty-seven millions! Is this really what constitutes the South?—"the whole South," which deplores the loss of Preston Brooks? This group of slave-holders is indeed the whole nucleus of the Slave power. It is inferior in numbers even to the free people of colour, who now amount to at least half a million. It is less than a ninth part of the number of the slaves. It is sustained by broad supports, no doubt, in the hopes of the North and the fears of the South, in the commercial interests of the Free states, and the social depression of the non-slave-holding whites in the Slave states: but these supports would disappear at once with the overthrow of the Slave power; and the nucleus is therefore what commonly goes by the name of the South, and that which overbears the President and his Government, and which overrules the national principle and true policy, and makes the republic a spectacle to the world for the exhibition of licence, and the absence of that liberty which is to the life of humanity what daily bread and vital air are to the life of man.

Who, then, are the others? What is the real population of the South?

Of the ten millions, or thereabouts, of the Slave-states, nearly four millions are slaves. The free blacks are not more than 200,000. Of the whites, seven-tenths are not slave-holders. It is only recently that this portentous fact has become known in Europe; and it was before appreciated by very few in the Free states of the Union. Every conceivable effort was made by the dominant class to conceal the numbers of their degraded neighbours, whose existence was never unnecessarily recognized in the presence of strangers. These "mean-whites," "trash,"—locally "sandhillers," "clay-eaters," and so forth,—are intensely hated, as well as despised by their aristocratic neighbours, who, when questioned about them by foreigners, represent them as mere thievish hangers-on, who tempt the negroes to pilfer, and conduct an illicit trade with them, or who mope themselves to death with drink and laziness. Mrs. Stowe, by her "Dred," has saved all necessity for describing this class, as it has hitherto existed. It is now becoming widely understood, however, that the mean-whites are altering fast. It is certain that the upper class are more and more in dread of "rebellion" through the ballot boxes; of an electoral power which will enter into collision with their own, and be therefore in alliance with the North. That this apprehension is reasonable will be admitted by all who have watched the course of events since the Kansas struggle began, and especially by those who have read a remarkable book by one of the class, *The Impending Crisis of the South,* by Mr. Helper of North Carolina. When a man who could write and publish that book declares himself a member of the despised class, it is pretty clear that the class is ceasing to be despicable. Mr. Helper was knocked down in the House of

Representatives at Washington for his book, as Mr. Summer was in the Senate for his speech: and men, book, and speech, have been made very important thereby: but the social brethren of Mr. Helper were rousing themselves before the fist and the bludgeon gave them fame. Some of them were sent to Kansas to fight for "the South." Too many sold their arms and their bibles (the parting gift of the proud men who shuffled them away) and drank themselves to death; and others disappeared; but a considerable number fell in love with free-labour as soon as they saw it in operation, and are now thriving farmers on free-soil. These seven-tenths of Southern whites ought to be exempted from our censures of the pro-slavery policy and tactics, and temper and manners; for they are not "the South." Ignorant, depressed, vitiated, they may be; but they are not answerable for a pro-slavery policy. They are awakening to a sense of the cruel injury they have sustained from that policy; and as soon as they know their own strength, they will reverse it at the polls. Mr. Helper is their pledge and their prophet to this effect.

We have no hesitation in further eliminating a very large element from the pro-slavery section;—almost the entire female sex. The ladies who make the most noisy defence of the institution and its resultant policy are from a distance,—converts, brought over by love, or interest, or imagination. When they talk nonsense, or perpetrate cruelty, let them come under our censure, with those who have tempted them into such a position. But they must not make us forget the far greater number of their mourning sisters, who pass a long life-time of fear and grief, or who die early of heart-sickness, on account of the guilt and sorrow amidst which they live. The wife who would fain honour her husband, the mother who suffers in every taint which corrupts her sons, the sister whose glory in her brothers sinks into hopelessness and shame as she sees the hardness of despotism, and the mould of indolence, and the insolence of high caste, and the poison of licentiousness destroying their manhood,—these are not "the South" in the sense claimed by the South and supposed by the world at large. They are no part of "the whole South" which deplores the loss of a Brooks. Their grief is that many an one who promised better grows up a Brooks, and thinks it chivalrous to insult a Sumner. In a little while, the phrase will need restriction and description. Meantime, we avow that when we use it we do not mean the population of the Slave-states, but the small oligarchy who first inflict dumbness on all the rest, and then assume to speak for all. When the majority have recovered their tongues, we shall hear another tale.

"The Hour of Proof"

9 October 1858

There has been, within the last two or three weeks, a rush of facts about the prosecution of the slave-trade, and a discussion of the practice by various powers which leaves no doubt of the moment being at hand which will test the convictions and the resolution of the nations allied against the traffic.

The hurry and bustle dismay some people: the arrival of what appear to be evil tidings from various parts of both hemispheres disheartens many who suppose the whole affair settled long years ago; and the strange course taken by the *Times,* three or four months since, "perplexing monarchs" and confounding the calculations of the best part of their subjects, has helped to give the aspect of a losing cause to one which may, in our opinion, be more truly regarded as on the point of a final triumph. It was always certain that this, like every other iniquitous traffic, would not be surrendered without a struggle; and that the more desperate the game became, the fiercer would be the struggle. A glance over the whole area of conflict must, we think, convince anybody that the chances of the slave-trade are in no respect better than they were a few years ago; while influences are at work which doom it to speedy extinction, while meantime rousing it to put forth its strength in one last effort.

Three Powers are now prosecuting the slave-trade, under more or less disguise, but all with vigour and pertinacity, in order to get the upper hand of those governments which would keep them to their treaty engagements. Those three Powers have now all others against them: and the respective forces are in course of rapid ascertainment. Those three are France, the United States, and Spain. . . . [Here she discusses Spain and France.]

As for the United States, a mass of grave facts may be conveyed in few words. It will not have been already forgotten that the Washington Government requested our Government to send our cruisers to the Gulf, and that we did so; to recall our cruisers from the African coast, and that we did so; to leave to American vessels the guardianship of the honour of the American flag, and that we did so. The capture of the *Echo* slaver presently followed. A more straightforward case never occurred. The negro victims are already returned to Africa; the pirate captain has confessed the whole transaction, leaving no doubt whatever of his having committed a capital crime, according to the clear and undisputed laws of his country; and, finally, the citizens of the Northern States generally, and many of those of the South, declare that the case does not admit of two interpretations, nor the duty of the authorities of any option. And yet, amidst all this clearness and decision, preparations are making for a contest which is regarded by some as the final struggle which is to determine the character and fortunes, if not the very existence of the Union. This first effort towards protecting the honour of the American flag is found very expensive; but that is the smallest consideration. It is found very perplexing; and in its embarrassments the Government has done an unjustifiable act in consigning the victims to the Colonization Society, with a sum of money for their maintenance, instead of sending them home. They will be landed in Liberia, and kept there—practically as far from home as if the Carolina planters had been allowed to detain them. But the worst of the new task is that it at once brings on the conflict between the free and the slave states which it is Mr. Buchanan's great object to ward off. Elsewhere it is a straightforward affair enough to take a slaver, restore the victims, and deal with the ship and its crew. In America it is so far otherwise that a good watch must be kept over the carrying out of the process, in time to come. At present, the forces are marshalling for conflict. Maryland declares that the "stampedes" of slaves through her territories can be endured no longer, and that something must be done to free her from her difficulties as a frontier state. Missouri is welcoming free labour so heartily that the slave-holders are removing in large numbers, to Arkansas and other slave states, their places being immediately occupied by free settlers. The pro-slavery in-habitants of Kansas are retiring in like manner, giving up the scheme of spreading their institution over fresh territory for the immediate duty of con-centrating the pro-slavery forces in their strongholds. In those strongholds there is strife. The South Carolina newspapers are in virulent opposition to each other on the question of reopening the African slave-trade. And how is it at the center? What is the aspect of things at Washington? The case of the captured slaver *Echo* begins to loom up in all its bearings in the minds of members of the Government. Cabinet officers do not hesitate to say that, as a political and international question—as a question for the next session of Congress—and in its bearings on treaties and laws relating to piracy when tested by the constitution of the United States, "it is of the greatest impor-tance; and we have not yet, by a long way, seen the end of it." Such is the ac-count from head-quarters transmitted to State journals. At the same time grave disclosures are made of the extent to which the slave-trade is carried on from American ports, while the citizens are calling to each other to be ready to defend their Republic from becoming a pirate state.

During this agitation, Denmark has decided the abolition of slavery; and Russia of serfdom. Spain awaits the approaching settlement of the question of the traffic; and such impunity as she permits to her pirates can last no longer than the suspense of the catastrophe. When other and greater powers have come to an agreement, she can no longer evade her treaties. On the whole, it seems to be clear that the fate of the slave-trade is on the point of being determined. We should say that the conditions are as favourable as could rationally be expected; and we have certainly no doubt whatever that the decision will be favourable to the African race, if the people of England sustain the spirit of their government as they ought. It would make the mat-ter easier if we had the French people with us. We know what they would do with their government if they understood their own case. As we cannot make them hear, we will act for them, and enforce their voluntary policy in its last expression, by extinguishing the African slave-trade, according to the letter and the spirit of treaties.

"The World's Interest in the West"

27 November 1858

It is a somewhat strange thing to see our leading newspaper [the *Times*] staring about, and asking how it can be that the new elections in America have issued as they have done, and then going to sleep again on the notion that it is only that the four years have come round again in which, according to its theory of the moment, the Americans regularly attain to a hatred of the ruler they had adored. The mere fact that several Presidents have been re-elected overthrows the theory, which is untenable in every view. We need not dwell on it; nor on the truer view which follows,—of the evil of the four years' term of office, which compels the nation to put up with the sins of the man of their choice, whatever he may do in the way of bad policy, till he must legally vacate the White House. If we find it an intolerable grievance that our Foreign Minister can commit the national honour to an unknown policy during the parliamentary recess, without check or remonstrance from us, what must it be to a republican people to see the mighty powers of their government (powers greater than sovereign and ministers have here) in the hands of a ruler who must have his own way for months or years to come!

The *Times* may safely and easily demonstrate this mischief; but when it stops there, and supposes that the present unparalleled aspects of political affairs in the United States have been sufficiently treated of, or accounted for by criticisms on the Presidential term of four years, it can hardly be aware of the way in which its levity will be regarded in America as at home.

In ordinary years, we English, who have plenty of affairs of our own and our nearest neighbours to attend to, are hardly aware of the connection which exists between the Federal policy of the United States and the interests of the rest of the world; but in this particular year it is only by a truly censurable and disgraceful carelessness or ignorance that that connection can be overlooked, and the recent demonstrations and disclosures regarded as of American interest alone. Even the *Times* asks how the elections can have issued as they have done; and while giving a random answer, thus admits that the phenomenon is remarkable. It does, indeed, seem impossible that any rational person should become acquainted with even the bare outline of recent incidents without feeling convinced that a radical change is taking place in those points of American policy in which the rest of the world has the deepest and closest interest.

One of the chief Southern leaders,—perhaps now the nearest successor to Mr. Calhoun, is Mr. Hammond of South Carolina, a senator at Washington, and formerly Governor of his own State. He has been delivering a speech which, impressive to mere English readers, must be truly revolutionary in its influence on his hearers. Speaking as the organ of southern policy, Senator Hammond avows that the game thus far played by the South is fairly lost; the game of parallel numbers in the Senate. The South can no longer create new States, to answer to those of the North: the free States must have an increasing majority in the Senate; and the new elections prove that the southern minority in the other House will be much smaller than ever. This avowal of defeat is not followed by threats of disunion, of filibustering, or of a new African slave-trade, as in the speeches of meaner men. Governor Hammond assumes the necessity of yielding after a fair struggle, (as he considers it,) and declares that all that can be done now is to protect the rights of the South under the Constitution, under the supremacy of the South. As to how this is to be done, it is enough for our purpose now to notice that Douglas will evidently be the Southern candidate, although he is the deadly enemy at present of Mr. Buchanan and his policy. Mr. Douglas is the least like a Northern Republican and free-soiler that can be accepted, with any chance of carrying the election; and it seems to be anticipated thus far that the entire South will join a portion of the North to carry Mr. Douglas over the head of any genuine anti-slavery candidate. The policy of aggression, annexation, quarrel abroad and repression at home, will be reversed by any successor of Mr. Buchanan. Public opinion has pronounced against it in the elections, and complications with allies have reached such a pass as must be a warning to the next President; and this prospect is not only cheering to all friends of free institutions, but in the highest degree important in relation to the politics of Europe.

At the latest dates, the political excitement of the community was exceeding all ordinary limits. It was known in all the large cities that ships of war of various nations were assembling in the Gulf of Mexico and the Caribbean Sea, and beginning to exhibit themselves off both shores of the Central American Isthmus; and the question was in every mouth whether this assemblage was on account of Mexican troubles, or for the defence of Cuba, or for the protection of Nicaragua? Whether it were one or all of these it was the policy of the Washington Cabinet that took them there. The troubles in Mexico are ascribed, truly or otherwise, to the policy by which the attention of the American people is attracted from the north-west, where they can honestly occupy the land, to a country which would be more convenient to the South, and would bring more glory in the conquest. So say the Americans; adding that the British and French ships in western waters are guarding Cuba while Spain goes to Mexico, to settle her quarrel there. It is owing to the Washington policy that Cuba needs such defence. And if Nicaragua requires the support of her European allies against outrageous demands, the conflicts of rival speculators, and invasion by America freebooters, it is again the Washington Cabinet that is answerable for the disturbance. The recent expression of national opinion through the ballot-boxes has wrought upon the Administration so far as to elicit from the President a proclamation against filibusters and their schemes, and a declaration that all he asks from Central America is the fulfilment of covenants with American contractors, and the perfect freedom of the transit route. These declarations are a great gain. It is true, they command no faith at Washington. Whether it be the fault of Government, bad faith, or popular distrust, there was, in the first week of this month, a vehement suspicion in the native mind—and, we are told, in the Foreign Ambassadorial mind also—that some mighty filibustering scheme of Mr. Buchanan's own was on the point of disclosure. This fact deserves notice, not because anybody on this side the water can be qualified to pronounce on the reasonableness or the vicious quality of the suspicion, but because it supplies one of the answers to the question with which we set out—how it is that the elections have so completely turned the tables on the Administration? Such distrust and disesteem as are disclosed by the present suspicion at Washington may go far to account for the vast majority who have voted their condemnation of Mr. Buchanan's policy.

"What does it mean?" asks the *Times*. It means that the President's Kansas policy has been too flagrant for the moral sense of the nation. It means that the revelations of American slave-trading, caused by the diplomatic conflict of last spring, have appealed to the national conscience. It means that the commercial revulsion of last year has wrought the good effects of adversity in sobering men's minds, and also in snapping the golden chains which fettered the free mind of the north to the overbearing spirit of the south. It means that the ordinary course of American affairs has been protracted to extremity—that process by which evils grow to a disgraceful and insufferable height before the axe is laid to the root: and then a cure instituted, more radical than any reforms elsewhere. This, on the grounds of former parallels, may reasonably be our hope. It means, apparently, that the virtual revolution in which the Republic has been seen from afar to have been engaged for some years, is now becoming recognized by the parties most nearly concerned in it. Mr. Buchanan conveyed very clearly, on taking his lofty seat, that after him would come the deluge. A deluge may not be requisite, we may hope; but that the southern policy will expire with him seems now to be the opinion of all parties. The meaning of this issue of the elections, therefore, is that American politics are about to assume a new phase. We had reason before to anticipate the extinction of the slave-trade within a short time; and now, the American constituencies bid us expect a reversal of their pro-slavery policy altogether. This involves so many points of international collision, such a range of difficulties in all directions, that there is scarcely a people on the globe that has not an interest in the overthrow of a pro-slavery policy in the greatest republic in the world. These recent elections exhibit the entire group of free states united against the Administration which is the very type of southern policy: they therefore promise a reversal of that policy which has marred the peace and the morals of the whole civilized world; and now the *Times* asks what is the meaning of such an event; and gives its own reply—that the people weary of their idol every four years, and that four years make a bad presidential term. When the Americans read this account of their recent action, they will hardly go on to suppose the *Times* the organ of public opinion in England. It is true a southern journal tells us that our two great newspapers, the *London Cotton-Plant* and the *Times*, prove that we are becoming converts to negro slavery; but we may trust the great states of the north to see that we are in sympathy with them, and to believe that every attempt to recover their old liberties and honours will ever endear them to us as allies, more and more.

‹ ‹ ‹

THE *NATIONAL*
ANTI-SLAVERY
STANDARD

1859–1862

In 1835, Martineau wrote to American John G. Palfrey expressing interest in promoting "literary intercourse, and intellectual exchanges" between Britain and America:

> I much desire to occupy . . . some position in your periodical literature which may enable me, possibly, to make some of our European experience useful to your new world. I believe that such a literary companionship . . . might prevent you from innocently copying some of our legislative and philosophical errors, and refresh us with some of the healthy influences which arise from your youth and freedom.[125]

Nearly twenty-five years passed before her wish was granted by the offer of a regular column in the *National Anti-Slavery Standard.* Between 9 April 1859 and 12 March 1862, Harriet Martineau wrote a series of letters (approximately sixty-two) to the editor of the *Standard (NASS),* printed as a column entitled "From Our European Correspondent."[126] Published in New York by the American Anti-Slavery Society, the *Standard,* whose motto was "Without Concealment—Without Compromise," consisted principally of reprinted excerpts from American and sometimes European newspaper articles pertaining to slavery. The *Standard* also reported on abolitionist activities by groups all over the country, including speeches by famous abolitionists of the day—William Lloyd Garrison, Wendell Phillips, and others—and various political and social events related to the cause. Despite the limited circulation of the periodical, Martineau regarded this assignment as an "opportunity to teach the Americans to distrust acting on impulse and to ground their proceedings on some sort of principle" (Webb 1960, 331). Her work for the *NASS,* which offers a revealing illustration of the significance of American slavery politics in the larger context of world events, is distinguished from all her other writing in that it was written with the intention of addressing an exclusively American audience.[127]

As was the case with her association with the *Daily News* and the *Spectator,* Martineau's tenure with the *NASS* coincided with the intensification of the American situation: by 1859, wrote Chapman, "[t]he work of well-nigh thirty years began to tell, and to require additional processes in aid of old principles" (1877, 367). As "one of the earliest abolitionists . . . [who] knew the ground and the subject thoroughly in all its bearings," Martineau was invited to contribute semimonthly letters to the *Standard*. Her sense of mission is made clear in her acceptance letter: "It has long appeared to me that a link was wanting by which much benefit to your cause was lost; namely, a comparison of the doings of the two continents, as they affect the destinies of the oppressed, and of the negro race in particular. . . . I have long endeavored to make your case understood here; and I am most heartily disposed to try what I can do on the converse side" (Chapman 1877, 368).

Martineau's aim to forge international understanding was based on an uncompromising adherence to honesty—to a degree some Americans found more irritating than enlightening. But having by this time invested twenty-five years in producing anti-slavery writing, Martineau found her ideological principles tested by a historical moment aptly symbolized as much by the steady pacifism of Garrison as by the violent activism of John Brown. No doubt the stunning spectacle presented by Brown's insurrection and execution afforded vicarious, though painful, relief for Martineau and others who were tired of words and ready for action.

Garrison scholar Henry Mayer notes that in 1842, soon after the split in the abolitionist movement, women activists like Chapman and Lydia Maria Child urged that "more fiery editorials" be printed in the *NASS* in order to accelerate the cause's progress (1998, 315). Garrison rejected the idea in favor of a more temperate approach—although, notes Mayer, the *Standard* "successfully maintained itself as a national voice of immediate abolitionism" (357). This early indication of editorial dissension at the *Standard* anticipates the increasingly vituperative exchanges in its pages throughout the Civil War.

In between these two periods, another series of explosive exchanges occurred, this time involving Harriet Martineau, who was proposed for the position of European correspondent by Chapman—perhaps as the "fiery" voice she and Child had been denied. But as this remarkably prickly literary relationship unfolded, Martineau's adherence to truthfulness and plain speaking had the effect of highlighting the ideological fragmentation within the abolitionist movement, which ranged from "no Union with slaveholders" to "the Union, love it or leave it." This was not the first time in her life that she held up a mirror in which Americans did not like what they saw. Given the *Standard*'s history of conflict—before and after Martineau—the tradition of blaming her break with the paper on her "hysteria" is one based on the erroneous assumption that she—rather than the *Standard* editors—was the aggressor. It is more accurate to say that she was the scapegoat in a situation not entirely of her making.

Martineau's letters to the *NASS* frequently address the same topics as her *Daily News* leaders, but the similarity ends there. The letters display a far more uncompromising, some thought virulent, attitude than her other writings on slavery, although their tone is clearly of a piece with the *Spectator* articles produced throughout 1858 for a British audience. Employing what defensive readers might interpret as an accusatory "you," the letters imply that England, like an estranged parent, chastises the renegade American colony for its failure to deal with slavery in a timely manner. She defends her approach in a letter to Fanny Wedgwood:

They print all I send over there, but groan over it. . . . I am sure it is not the way to secure peace to flatter the Americans to their faces when they are doing unendurable
things. It is safer to tell them that, as a self-governing people, they are bound to be better informed, and to show more sobriety than at present. Rights carry duties, always:
and it is their duty to qualify themselves for political relations, if they choose to manage their political affairs themselves. (Arbuckle, 1983, 215)

And groan they did: "The trouble about Miss M is . . . that she differs from us
widely," grumbled Samuel May. Hers are "untenable opinions . . . written to us in a
strain of domineering and lecturing and censuring really quite unbearable."[128]

As the impending civil confrontation promised to focus more on party politics
than on the abolition of slavery, Martineau was dumbfounded by the spectacle of political posturing supplanting the anti-slavery agenda—a development supported by
some abolitionists. "The Union will be insisted on, they say; but the Negro matter
will be compromised," she wrote to Charles Sumner, adding, "the war is not for the
abolition of slavery; . . . it is fully intended not to abolish it."[129] As subsequent events
proved, she refused to purchase wholesale the North's actions in the name of the
Union; republican values, as she well knew, did not necessarily dovetail with abolitionist ideology. Like Chapman's first letter to her, Martineau's NASS articles feature a
brand of criticism designed to sting the country out of its ennui and into definitive action on behalf of the slaves. Earlier, following the publication of Society in America,
she regretted those critics "who were too hasty to do me justice . . . and mistook my
real love and interest for their country for a traveller's carpings."[130] Her relationship
with the NASS, which terminated in 1862, reified Americans' sensitivity to foreign
criticism, even from one sharing, and writing in support of, their ideological values.

Among the issues highlighted by the following NASS selections is the electrical
effect produced by John Brown's 1859 uprising in Harper's Ferry, Virginia, and his
consequent execution. The Brown affair galvanized pro- and anti-abolitionists on
both sides of the Atlantic in its potent demonstration that, whereas many decades of
talk, print, and legislation had failed to bring the slavery issue to resolution, the martyrdom of one man garnered the attention of the international community. Although
she initially condemned Brown's radicalism as too incendiary, she quickly recognized Brown as a genuine martyr whose commitment to moral truth far eclipsed the
terms she herself had outlined in 1839's The Martyr Age of the United States.

Martineau's letters objecting to the Morrill Tariff, a tax levied by the protectionists (she was a fierce defender of free-trade policies) to help finance the war by in-
hibiting international trade, hints at strained relations between the journalist and
the NASS, which soon culminated in their final break over the Trent affair. In November 1861, a British ship, the Trent, boarded southerners James Mason and John
Slidell, emissaries to Britain and France seeking official political recognition of the
seceded Confederate states. Union officer Captain Wilkes ordered shots fired at the
Trent, then arrested and imprisoned Mason and Slidell, generating British outrage
against northern aggression and nearly sparking an international incident. When
British troops sailed for Canada in anticipation of a confrontation, Lincoln—now
faced with both a civil and an international war—was forced to placate England by
releasing Mason and Slidell to the British. The episode quickly declined in signifi-

cance, although it vividly demonstrates national and international political tensions just before the Civil War. Her letters, according to Chapman, "had strongly urged the abandonment of the protective policy as the highest expediency and the truest morality: 'The sin of the North is "protection," as the sin of the South is slavery.' If the letters had said the guilt of the two sections on these different grounds was equal, the indignation could hardly have been greater . . . and although the [editorial] committee had given the letters *carte blanche,* it was loudly affirmed that they were 'off the platform'" (1877, 381). These events provoked Martineau's sharpest criticisms of American policy because they displayed political factionalism that sublimated what was for her the real issue—the emancipation of slaves.[131]

Martineau's relationship with the *NASS* illustrates the high idealism informing her attitude toward America, which persisted (sometimes impatiently) through the decades of political and social posturing preceding emancipation. Her sense of urgency is often reiterated:

> [A]ny apathy, any delay, any abeyance of the controversy for a single day is incomprehensible. Therefore are we waiting in wonder . . . for the restoration of your ancient citizen liberties, and the casting out of the curse which is impairing your national character, and destroying your reputation as a people. . . . You know how confidently we look for your self-redemption from the disgrace and peril. (4 April 1860)

Their very lack of diplomacy renders the *Standard* letters essential to a comprehensive picture of Martineau's abolitionism: they demonstrate her great passion for the American "experiment" uninhibited by considerations of sociological objectivity or journalistic credibility. As secession escalated in 1861, Martineau wrote: "I am anything but unhappy about America. It is the resurrection of conscience among them,—the renewal of the soul of the genuine nation. . . . It has come exactly when and as all expected who had a right to an opinion." But her enthusiasm shifted dramatically as events unfolded. Less than a year later, she lamented: "The hideous levity shocks me the most. . . . [W]as there ever such mad and wicked finance! And what corruption everywhere in official life! and what senselessness about England! . . . I see no ground for anticipating self-recovery among the Northern people. No statesman! no reliable politician even! . . . All their behaviour that of novices, and all their temper that of children."[132] Aside from such explosive venting in private, none of her writing more clearly demonstrates the intensity of Anglo-American relations over slavery issues—an involvement that so profoundly defined her life and work—than her letters to the *National Anti-Slavery Standard.*

. . .

"John Brown"

17 December 1859

Sir: I need hardly say that our prominent interest in American affairs is at this moment about the strange disturbance at Harper's Ferry. The Newspapers which have arrived to-day will settle a good many points, and, I hope, stop

John Brown (Boston Athenaeum)

the mischief caused by this wild outbreak. Of course, such an incident brings out the old commonplaces of the newspapers—the fanaticism of Abolitionists, the wickedness of their means to a (granted) good end; in short, pity and allowance for the slaveholders, and severity towards the friends of the negro. All this old twaddle may be let pass, together with demands, renewed at every awkward pause in the argument, that the Abolitionists should instruct the slave-owners how to release their slaves, and should make it easy for them to do so. These old grounds are not worth reverting to for a moment; but it may be right to say, on behalf of English opinion and sentiment, that we hold a different view from the ordinary American one about the duty and the pardonableness of insurrection; that is, about the cases in which insurrection is a duty, and is pardonable. I am aware that the *Liberator* has a perfect right to say what it does about its uniform disapproval of "war and bloodshed, in the best of causes"; and few of us in this country go so far as that; but, on the other hand, we cannot applaud insurrection as something noble and heroic in itself, irrespective of its reasonable chances of success. . . .

And now, on your part, you have unhappily an illustration to deplore in this enterprise at Harper's Ferry, which, we fear, will cause you a great deal of trouble. I will not intrude upon you with speculations about what you will fully know before this can reach you; but the case will be unlike every other on record if the oppressed and their friends are not the worse for a light and ignorant use of the right of rebellion. I say this on the supposition that Brown and his comrades did, as we are told, collect arms, break the peace, use violence and destroy life. If this is untrue, and they merely intended to run off slaves, then the question is merely one of prudence and discretion. I have no doubt that we shall agree on the principle of these cases, though we may differ about individual rebels and heroes. I have had in view, in these remarks, not Abolitionists, nor any body of persons whatever, but the number (great or small, as may be) of your excellent countrymen and countrywomen whom I have heard speak of resistance to law as, on the whole, a virtue in itself, and insurrection as something noble, whatever might be its chances, and whoever might be its victims. It is a natural result of so noble an insurrection as that which made you a nation that the method should be a favorite one for some generations. I don't know that you Abolitionists have rendered a greater service in any directions than by your example of patient pertinacity in your civil action in pursuit of reform, while the more giddy and impulsive of your countrymen are apt to break through law and the peace which it guards, when their wills are crossed, or to admire those who do it. We trust that all who can be called Abolitionists to the extent to which Joshua R. Giddings[133] and Gerrit Smith are will be completely vindicated from all implication in the movement at Harper's Ferry. We do not doubt this; but we are sorry to see their names made free with on the occasion.

"John Brown; South's Political Posturing"

24 December 1859

Sir: Amidst the strong excitement of European politics, which so largely involve the liberties of the whole civilized world, we feel as much interest in *your* great topic as if all Europe were in a state of calm. The only clear thing to us about the Harper's Ferry business is the moral greatness of John Brown. Putting aside the question of the act which brought him into his position, there can be nothing finer than the way in which he holds that position. I doubt whether there is in history anything nobler than the calm devotedness of his temper, and the heroic moderation of his demeanor. If the Irish rebels had been of his stamp, in 1798 and in O'Connell's and John Mitchell's time, Ireland would not have waited so long for deliverance as she did. It was the passion, frenzy and selfish vanity of the agitators which injured the cause more than the prejudices of toryism and the fears of tyrants. There is not a trace in John Brown of the popular agitator; but as entire an absence of self-seeking, of every kind of self-regard, as can be conceived. His act is, to us, a mystery; and a painful one. If he had no intention beyond running off slaves, why the collection of arms? But it would be useless to go into the particulars of a case which you must understand so much better than we can. I will therefore say only that we can see but two ways of accounting for the course of events: that John Brown was insane, or that he was cheated of some expected support. Of his being insane there is not the slightest trace in any part of his subsequent conduct or speech; and if he had promises of support in a scheme so wild and hopeless, the difficulty is not diminished. If the scheme was *not* wild and hopeless, then we on this side the water are too ignorant to form any judgment of the case at all; and this is very possible. In such a case, there will soon be consequences which will make all plain.

There can scarcely be a mistake, however, in regard to the lesson which this rising will teach. Your Southern journals say that the sons and daughters of Virginia are ashamed of the sheepish behavior of the citizens in the presence of the rebels; but to us it appears that there is something more to be ashamed of in the structure of society which generates such cowardice. How any men on earth can so value and stick to any form of property as to undergo for it such terrors as they avow is a perfect marvel to us. We wonder at the miser who, from love of property, lives on mouldy crusts in a garret without fire or candle; but his privations are a less terrible evil than the apprehensions in which your slaveholding countrymen live. There is no torment comparable to that of fear; and that any community should undergo the torment (too strong to be concealed) for the sake of any sort of property is the most astounding evidence of rapacity and worldliness perhaps on record. I take this low view of their "peculiar institution" because it is the one they themselves put forward. "We have our slaves, and we mean to keep them," said some to me, assuring me that they would be destitute of property if they had not slaves. If they quit the property ground of defence for the poetical or the biblical, or any other, of course it makes no difference to us, who are ready, from our experience, to meet them at all points. At present, we take their own point of view, and wonder unboundedly at the value that Christian men (as they claim to be) can attach to property, so as to undergo a martyrdom of terror for its sake. I suppose *Consuelo* is read in the slave States, as I do not remember that there is anything about negroes in it. What does a Southern reader think of the happiness of Consuelo and Joseph Haydn on the bridge, after their conversation with the deserter's wife, when they find themselves without a farthing in the world, and enjoy it immensely? The slaveholders can hardly try the experiment, for they would be instantly richer for emancipation; but if they cannot believe this beforehand, what a blessing it would be to try, and see what it would be to have no property, and a mind free as air and bright as sunshine!

And now, what will be the effect of this rising on your great controversy, and the persons involved in it? Can the slaveholding communities ever get over the exposure now made, and never to be retrieved, of the hollowness of the social state in which slavery is an element? Can slavery ever be again what it has been—in Virginia at least—while the spectre of Old Brown walks in the midst of it, as it always will from this time forward? Henceforth there will be a new thought in common between master and slave which must surely alter their relation—the image of Old Brown, always present to both. In case of such a ripening of events as that the frontier States must take part with either North or South, will not the choice be largely influenced by what has happened? On the other hand, will the lot of the negro (slave and free) be aggravated by the recent alarm? There is nothing in the way of cowardly cruelty which may not be expected from people who would hurry on the trial of wounded men, and fail to consider, in the first place, the rights and needs of the accused in regard to counsel, the appearance of witnesses, &c. It is true, the plea for haste is the danger from suspense—the necessity for getting the old man put out of sight, but things may return to their usual course, and terrified hearts cease to flutter. Such a plea seems to us to have the victory with Old Brown. His is the conquering mind in the case, whatever becomes of the life. We are full of interest and curiosity to know what will happen on a scene where things can never again be as they were. Of Brown's life we have never had any hope—if, indeed, we may speak of hope in a case where life is probably not desired, and where death may be more useful to the cause for which life was imperilled. The old man's terrible bereavements and sufferings no doubt reconcile him to death; and, as to the mode of it, it depends on the victim whether the death degrades him or he ennobles the death. The cross was the deepest of the disgraces before eighteen centuries ago; and the gallows may become honorable if slaveholders do but condemn a few disinterested and wise friends of the negro to die upon it. The halter cannot disgrace Old Brown. The doubt as to whether he will ennoble it hangs on the indefensible character of his enterprise—as far as we can yet see. At all events, I think any one of us had rather die on Brown's gallows than sit on the Bench to sentence him to it, or survive him to bring up children to hate and dread the negro because Brown would have freed him. . . .

"Death of John Brown; Bias in the *Times*"

28 January 1860

Sir: The interest of the news from the United States has never before, in my time, been so great as now. The awakening which your best friends have so long desired seems to have really happened now; and though the method is not exactly what we could have wished, the fact is a thing to be devoutly thankful for. I doubt whether there is on record a finer death than that of

John Brown.[134] Among an aspiring, youthful people like your nation, the tendency is, as in the youth of an individual, to indulgence in fervent talk, in metaphysics and sentiment, in high-flown feelings abundantly expressed. I do not know that any greater blessing could happen to you, under the circumstances, than the uprising and the self-sacrifice of such a man as John Brown, to command the reverence and win the enthusiasm of society. The brave and tender old confessor and martyr, with plainness of manner and paucity of speech, with honest self-assertion and no egotism, with everything about him the reverse of fantastical and sentimental, is precisely the most soul-saving saint your community could be blessed with. The world will be anxious now to see how you express your homage—what you will do, now that all must see that something must be done. You will, as a community, take care of Brown's family. We see that you consider that as a matter of course. That is an affair of private solace. Your public procedure, for the redemption of your national soul, character and reputation, we shall follow with the deepest interest. Meantime, we can perceive that, amidst all your grief and horror about Brown and his comrades, you are all happier than you have been for many a day. The thrill of awakened conviction and resolution is evidently passing through society, and that is bliss, in comparison with the previous thraldom belonging to acquiescence in wrong. The Abolitionists, who have kept their liberty, must be happy to see others entering into it. We hope and believe that better times are before you than you have ever seen, and a truer life than, as a community, you have yet led.

Nothing worse can have been said on your side the water than something that has been published here. The *Times* newspaper of the 28th of December had a "leader" on your present affairs which might have been written by a South Carolina politician. You have no doubt seen it; and if you had not, I would not spend time on what you hear every day from slaveholders. I refer to the fact merely to say that in that article the writer speaks for himself alone. I doubt whether any other Englishman (unless it be some old West India planter) would agree more or less in the statements and feelings of the writer. We are surprised that anything so grossly pro-slavery could appear in this country, where public sentiment has long outgrown such barbarism. You would probably see that the *Daily News* protested, the next day, against the doctrine and facts of the *Times* article, and repudiated it on the part of the people of England.

Where our people are deficient in this matter is not in conviction, nor yet in feeling, when once fairly interested; but perhaps we yield too readily to the weariness and disgust with which the upholding of slave institutions inspires us. It is blindness, too, not even to see how we, as a nation, are interested in your rescue from your fatal curse. Not only are we interested in the welfare of free institutions, and the virtue and happiness of those who live under them, in any part of the earth, but your slavery directly injures us, in a most sensible manner. The territorial cupidity, the quarrelsomeness, and the low official tone and character which are natural consequences of the institution of slavery, occasion great injury and insult to your allies, and especially to ourselves.

Has Mr. Grattan's book, on Civilised America, been read among you? I have not read it; but I have seen the exposure it contains of the transactions at Washington about the Boundary question, which are an illustration of what I refer to. We had before heard the story of the suppressed map, and the opinions of some of your worthier citizens on Mr. Webster's conduct in the case; but we were scarcely able to credit it till the facts were detailed as they are by Mr. Grattan. I need not explain the effect of such a disclosure on public sentiment towards your government. And now, again, in the San Juan business, we see the effects of slavery, and the predominance of its influence in such a man as General Harney being able to imperil the alliance of our two nations. Since I wrote you last, one of your best friends in this country, Mr. W. E. Foster, has exposed the character of Gen. Harney, in a letter to the *Leeds Mercury*—his statements being derived from the *Anti-Slavery Standard* of November 3, 1855. I need not tell you what a story there is there of this Harney (Major Harney as he was then); nor need I tell you what we think of being insulted and assaulted as a nation by a fellow who ought to have been punished as a murderer, instead of promoted to a poet of authority, and to a high rank in the army. We observe that he was duly unpopular in his post, and that nobody undertakes to defend him; but that has nothing to do with the policy of putting such a man into any honorable and responsible position. While such things are done, we are utterly unable to repose any trust in the good faith and good will of your government, and such things will continue to be done as long as the oligarchy of slaveholders keeps its foot on the neck of the majority of your people. The truth is, we sigh for the day when you will have a government with which we can enjoy genuine friendly intercourse, such as ought to exist between two free nations. At present, there is an interchange of occasional flattering speeches, such as cordial friends never think of uttering; with occasional discoveries of such sly tricks as Mr. Webster's with the map; and yet more frequent bickers, arising when the Washington Cabinet is perplexed by home politics, and passing away when the domestic difficulty is got over. It is a regular thing with us to expect some foul imputation, or some unreasonable rage, when the Presidential election is impending, or the South urges some new demand. The effect on the mutual respect of the two nations is bad, and the Washington game is so well understood in Europe that the sympathy is all on one side. Thus it is indispensable for the repute of free government, and for the preservation (or reconquest) of the respect and friendship of foreign nations, that your government should throw off the yoke of the slaveholders, and enter frankly on a new and honest course of foreign policy. I trust we are not mistaken in believing that with slavery the lust of territorial extension would die out; the braggart and bullying manners of sectional officials would subside; and there would be no further need or temptation to insult and quarrel with the nearest ally, to stave off insults and quarrels at home. Thus our interest in the abolition of American slavery is sufficiently apparent for those who desire any such plea to account for their feelings of sympathy with such of your countrymen as are worthy of their theory of government. It is sufficiently apparent to render it a public offence in the *Times* newspaper to pretend that, as a people, the English have any sympathy with your slaveholders. . . .

"The Morrill Tariff"

1 June 1861

Sir: . . . At such a time, what is said by sensible Americans from the free States is eagerly attended to. It is with great satisfaction that we hear from them, in print and in private, that Congress, when it meets on the 4th of July, will not lose an hour in repealing the Morrill tariff.[135] Of its speedy repeal there never has been any doubt on this side, both because it cannot work, and because a republican society, brought back to its principles as yours now is, will not long submit to a class legislation which the old countries of Europe, with all their antique training and feudal prejudices, can no longer tolerate. They inherited a polity formed before the great natural laws of society were understood, or known to exist. A protective trade policy was natural to them: and, once instituted, it had, in the force of habit, a great advantage against the new lights of science; and especially where class legislation existed in other departments. But the mistake is now nearly outgrown, in countries where there is no republican pretension of equal justice to all citizens. In England, the reform took less than a generation to effect; and not one penny of protective duty remains. The blessed effects of a perfectly free trade have shown themselves so rapidly and clearly, in the general welfare, and especially in the prosperity of the working classes, and also of the interests which formerly clung to protection, that France, the very paradise of protectionists, is following as fast as she can. . . . In countries like the United States, where society professes to set out from an advanced point of freedom and knowledge, there is no excuse for class legislation, by which commerce and the whole number of consumers are injured for the supposed benefit of this or that class of producers. While we have been extricating ourselves from the natural mistakes of remote generations, you, of the free States, have been plunging into them, with such violence and extravagance as to preclude the notion of the fault being one of simple ignorance. Much ignorance there must be among the constituencies, if they allow such a violation of the commonest principles of justice; but the parties concerned could not all have been unaware of either the aristocratic principle or the ruinous tendencies of a protective policy. We may hope that, among other good effects of this war, in bringing the citizens from all parts better acquainted, a fuller understanding on this matter may arise. As the citizen soldiers talk for long hours over their camp fires, let us hope that the topics of the rights of industry and the true principles of taxation may come up, in practical shape, so that the commerce of the republic may have fair play, and the honest workers may become too clear-sighted to allow certain orders of manufacturers to help themselves to a large per centage of every man's earnings. Meantime, your countrymen here express their undoubting confidence that the vicious new tariff will be repealed in a few weeks from this time. It nearly concerns the political repute of your republic, and its social credit, especially at a time like this, that it should not adopt a proved injustice, and emulate the sins of the South in oppressing the working man. If it is no practical excuse for slaveholders that they know no better, and have no conception of any other system, much less will it be taken as a justification of the North that it is ignorant of the vice and folly of the protective system. It ought not to be ignorant of what has long been so widely exposed and so thoroughly proved. That the first act of the Republican party should have been to enact such a tariff as this, could not but shake the general confidence in either its ability or its virtue, to an extent which it will take some time to repair. . . .

"The Morrill Tariff"

7 September 1861

. . . The great interest of the case has always been the question whether the anomaly of slavery would and could be cut out of a democratic republic without destroying the organization it had so long infested. But now every effort is used by your countrymen to annihilate that source of interest. Every mail brings a bushel of letters assuring everybody that the contention has nothing whatever to do with slavery; that, in any event, nothing will be done about slavery; and that the silence of the President's message on the subject is a type of the popular mind and the national expression in the whole case. I need not tell you that your Abolitionist friends are not misled by these assurances. There are many others who believe slavery to be virtually abolished; but merely because we are henceforth to get cotton from other countries. But you must perceive that the eager and anxious assurance that slavery will remain unaffected by your civil war has deprived that war of the greater part of its interest to Englishmen. In such circumstances, you may conceive the amusement caused by the imputation that we are hypocritical about slavery, because we do not rush into partisanship with a warfare which has "nothing whatever to do with slavery."

We have a stronger expectation that slavery will be abolished by this war than that the Republic will be preserved by it. The wisest students of politics, philosophy and of history have the most confirmed doubts whether a democratic republic can resume its former condition after a civil war; and there are incidents in your case which aggravate the doubt very seriously.

. . . I need hardly say that the credit of the United States abroad is once more lowered by the omission to repeal the Morrill tariff. The apprehensions from this cause are threefold. International commerce will be checked, and the position of the United states lowered in proportion; your nation is subjected to the calamity of class-hardship, which will introduce among you the worst social grievances of the Old World; and the adoption of a Protectionist policy is an infidelity to republican principle which precludes all practical reliance on republican professions. You will have seen in the city articles of the leading English newspapers how the continued toleration by Congress of the Morrill tariff affects the credit and the prospects of any loan to the Federal government, in the view of business men. You and we shall agree that if, in an age of free and world-wide intercourses, you choose to wall in your Commerce with a *chevaux-de-frise* [portable obstacle for defense] of protection, you ought to raise your own loans at home. If you isolate yourselves in the creation of wealth, you should borrow of that wealth, and not from abroad. The capitalists will settle this matter; and we shall all be best satisfied with that method which shall most rapidly prove the pauperising operation of a protective system.

While writing, I receive my American letters and newspapers. The most extraordinary news they bring is of the continuance of the delusion (as we consider it) that England has any thoughts of acknowledging the Southern Confederacy. We have been wondering how such a notion could be entertained for an hour in the face of the established practice of our country, as well as of the absence of any such idea here; but now I see that somebody must have been hoaxing, or dreaming, or trying to be mischievous. It seems that there is a notion afloat among you that if the Confederates can maintain an army near Washington for a certain time, they will be acknowledged here. If this means recognized as a political power, and an independent State, I will venture to say that no such notion has entered anybody's head in England; and it seems incredible that it should have been gravely received across the water. Our method of recognizing any *de facto* State is plain and clear enough. We have nothing to do with it till it *is* established—that is, organized and accepted and worked by the people who constitute it. Then, when they have settled their affairs, and made their State a Power among the Powers of the world, we accept their decision; in other words, acquiesce in a proved fact. How far the Confederacy is from this I need not point out; nor how irrelevant is the consideration of its maintaining a military stand for any number of weeks or months. We see no evidence that the people of the Southern States are the authors of the Confederation, or that they desire the change of rulers. It is no affair of ours at all; and our sympathies are as little in their favor as our political practice on such occasions. If it is true, as your journals seem to convey, that the blockade[136] is not strictly enforced by the Washington government—that is surely a great folly. Every foreign country respects it while it is strictly kept, but, avowedly, no longer. As for the incessant harping on our supposed passion for cotton, and bias from that passion, I can only say that my experience and opinion are precisely those of Mr. Webb (whose letters appear to me admirable).[137] I do not believe that anybody has acted differently, from first to last, from considerations of cotton. Your countrymen made up their minds that we should, and have all along viewed matters under that view. But I believe it to be a total mistake;

and your countrymen will see this whenever they learn what has already been done towards supplying us with cotton from other fields.

If you wish for further and stronger evidence, you have only to propose the abolition of slavery as an aim of your enterprise, no less essential than the maintenance of the Union. Whenever you do that, you will see what the English do think, and feel, and care about. Whenever you do that, our people will be with the North to a man. While, instead of doing this, your citizens insist that nothing will be done about slavery, you cannot wonder that Europe is content to leave America to settle her own affairs. I believe that slavery is virtually at an end; but how can one satisfy others, in the face of your own assurances? H. M.

"Mason and Slidell: The *Trent* Affair"

28 December 1861

Sir: From month to month the mood in which your friends here have had to address you has been more and more sad; but anything like the dreariness of this day we none of us, I believe, anticipated. Till now, there has been something to be hopeful about, and even to rejoice in, in the midst of your military reverses, your political difficulties, your sufferings of every kind, for you had abjured your complicity with the South; and no shame and grief could compare with that of such guilty complicity. Though you and we, your friends, had to bear the disappointment of finding that there was no statesmanship apparent in the republic—no high quality, political or moral, visible in your Administration, yet there remained the great fact that the free States were in antagonism with the slave States, and that slavery must go down when the people of the North had gained strength and wisdom by suffering. It was too plain that we were to be disappointed of the hoped-for friendship between your countrymen and mine. The temper and manners of the Northern people towards England, and the irrationality of the anger on your side the water did, it is true, overthrow forever (the "ever" of our generation) the *confidence* of your European well-wishers, because it was plain that the bullying spirit and intolerable manners of former governments were not simply ascribable to Southern breeding, as we had believed and trusted. Still, if our hopes of pleasant and confiding intercourse were shaken, we could still rejoice that your day of virtuous struggle had arrived, and hope for a good issue. But now, all is over! Your unhappy country has a more terrible retribution for past unfaithfulness to go through than the most timid of your friends apprehended. Your successive governments plunge you more and more deeply in difficulty, and disgrace, and peril; and now—if this last stroke is indeed the work of the government—your own chosen rulers are giving victory to the South, as wickedly as Mr. Buchanan's ministers did in delivering over to the secessionists the treasure and arms of the republic. When Commander Wilkes fired his shotted guns across the bows of the Trent,[138] he did more for the Confederate cause than giving them half-a-dozen victories;

and when he ordered the seizure of the Southern gentlemen on board the Trent, he simply ruined his country. It is still possible that his act may be disavowed by your government. The next mail may bring the news that he is punished, the Southern gentlemen released, and an apology, and all due reparation offered to the British government; but even then, no power on earth can restore the state of things which existed before. If there can be an officer in the American navy who could perpetrate such an act in such a way, out of his own heart, there can be no confidence on our side that law and civility will be observed on the seas. But it seems inconceivable that such an act should not have been authorized. Not only would the piratical audacity be incredible in any naval service, but it is understood that the Americans on board the Nashville Confederate vessel were in expectation of the event—aware of an intention to intercept and seize Messrs. Slidell and Mason. If this is true—if the movement was planned or known at Washington, there is no hope of peace but in immediate retraction and apology from Washington. There can be no question about the necessity. After a long course of forbearance, allowance and forgiveness, on the part of England in consideration of the peculiar quality and circumstances of a government of slaveholders, the people of England are offered an outrage too gross to be endured; and, grieved, shocked and ashamed, as we shall be to war upon you at the same time as the Southern States, we shall have no option. When we think of the madness of such a risk, it seems incredible that even Mr. Seward, with his purblind policy of trick and bullying, can have incurred it.[139] The first image which presents itself to all minds is of your territory invaded by the Confederates at the South, and by Canada at the North, and blockaded at sea by the British navy. No rational person can for a moment doubt the issue of such a struggle as that; and what is it for? Why are we made enemies of, when we are your only stay and defence? During these latter months, our government has strained its influence to the utmost to prevent the blockade being broken—and not the less though a temper of jealousy and insult prevailed at Washington and in your press generally. And now, your government has outraged your best friend, and rendered it impossible to restrain any further the disgust of the English people at the temper and manners under which they have suffered. Still, we recur to the hope that the next mail may bring the requisite disavowal and reparation. Nothing can replace the two nations on their former footing; but we may again hope for the triumph of the right on your soil.

It is not for me to speak of the legal aspects of the question of this attack on the Trent. Our leading newspapers show what is the opinion of the law-officers of the Crown, on whose authority, of course, all discussion will on this side proceed. There is, I clearly see, every desire on all hands to be just, and even liberal; every intention to admit, to the fullest extent, the right of visit and search, as exercised by ourselves in former times, even though the America law is more in our favor. But there seems to be no doubt that, over and above that question, there has been an amount of illegality, as well as brutality of behavior, which admits of no accommodation at all. Retraction is the only alternative to war, we are assured by those who should know.

The folly seems the more incredible from the fact that boarding the Trent and seizing the American passengers is an irrevocable recognition of those Confederate gentlemen as belligerents and not rebels.[140] If they are rebels, they cannot be seized on board a neutral vessel. As belligerents, there are circumstances under which they might be taken—though those circumstances are not present in this case; but by this act the die is cast. Your government has treated Messrs. Slidell and Mason as belligerents, and they and their Confederates rejoice accordingly. If there were room for hope that the whole transaction was planned in the South, and executed by traitors to the North, it would be the greatest possible relief. As a stroke of policy on behalf of the South, it might be so; but there seems to be no doubt of the San Jacinto and its officers being really under the orders of the United States government.

On the continent, and by some people in England, it is imagined that Mr. Seward and his colleagues have resorted to aggression as a method of drawing off from their conflict with the South—of receding from their scheme of subduing the Confederate States, under the demands and the popularity of a foreign war. I do not believe this; but it is impossible not to see that such a war will be the salvation of the south—as far as the present struggle is concerned. The blockade will be dispersed at once, and trade opened between the South and the rest of the world. I need not go further in detailing what must happen; and every view leads to the shocking truth that all this is for no cause whatever but an act of outrage, unprovoked and intolerable, inflicted on a long-suffering, honorable, placable, and magnanimous ally!

I write in the full sense of the rectitude and reasonableness of those whom I address. I am well aware that you feel as we do about any act of bad faith and violence—any act of piracy committed by any power on an ally. But what renders the case so supremely painful is that, in a self-governing nation, every citizen bears the blame and the shame of the misconduct of the Administration. Not of a single mistake, however great; but of any unprincipled and aggressive act done by the agents of the government. Those who know you and your aims will never for an instant confound you and your brethren with Mr. Seward; but it is a question which must be answered, how a Seward can be in the administration of a self-governing nation? Will such a minister find himself able to plunge you into a war with your best friend, at the most critical moment of your national existence? And if so, why? And what is despotism, if this is the liberty you live under?

If this transaction is imputable to your government, I suppose Mr. Everett and Mr. Beecher, and the other proposed explainers of the Northern case will hardly come here.[141] Strong as is the feeling everywhere on this occurrence, there seems to be a general disposition to exercise self-restraint, and to listen to the instructions of law and authority. Thus, circumstances will be favorable if disavowal should arrive from Washington; but we are only too ready for war, if war it must be. I was surprised to see, some months since, in a leading American journal, a doubt expressed as to whether the English would be withheld from breaking the blockade by "such a shadowy consideration as that of international law." Of all substantial considerations we esteem law, national and international, to be the most solid and stable; and we should as soon expect to hear a clergyman doubting whether men could be kept from theft, murder and adultery, by such "shadowy considerations" as the Ten Commandments, as doubt the habit and tendency of our countrymen to abide by the law. If the same attachment can be trusted on your side, we may yet escape this fearful peril, though not the moral consequences of its having been risked. It is not the thought of war, dreadful as it is—neither the loss of life, nor the other losses, nor the disturbance of intercourse, friendly and commercial, nor even the shame of warfare between peoples of the same blood and language, that causes the keenest pang in the prospect of what is coming. It is the grief of the failure of free government in your country—the discouragement of your disgrace, if your republic from which wise and good men of three generations have hoped so much, should now be an outlaw among the nations. To be an outlaw among the nations is one of the only three possible issues, if reparation for this outrage is now refused. If success in a war with Europe and America were possible for your country (which all sane persons must know it is not), your nation will be isolated by its incapacity of sustaining international relations. The other alternatives are rescue and ruin. You will depose an Administration which has betrayed the country, or you will suffer wreck. Such is the crisis in which you stand. If you, the worthy citizens of a republic founded by such men as your political forefathers, cannot save the republic from such a fate as now impends, you thereby admit that the experiment of popular self-government has failed. If you can save the State, you will. But there is not a moment to be lost.

I had intended to write of Russian affairs, and French, and Italian; but you will be no more disposed to read than I am to write on any other subject than this handiwork of your domestic enemies. Will you cast them out?—or, will you let them extinguish the republic? H. M.

"The *Trent* Affair; War with England Averted"

15 February 1862

Sir: It was welcome news last week that there is to be no war on the Slidell and Mason case. One does not expect that bright news should ever be without some shadow; and one should not, therefore, too much regret the admixture of evil with the good in this case, as in others. It is a blessing to be very thankful for that your government has done what is right without dispute. The next greatest blessing is, that the people have made no opposition to the decision of the government—thus allowing the enemies of free institutions the mistake they committed in supposing that the Administration would be over-awed or constrained by "the mob." It has been a hearty satisfaction to many of us that so many evil anticipations have been discredited by the event—such as the notion of a government plot to divert the war, or a scheme of invading Canada—apprehensions of the people refusing the deliver up Capt. Wilkes's prisoners, etc. On the other hand, there are some unhappy incidents involved which destroy all sense of security in regard to peace, and impede that reflux of English good feeling towards the North which had been supposed a necessary consequence of a satisfactory atonement for Capt. Wilkes's outrage.

Mr. Seward's strange dispatch is full of mischief. We have been in the habit of admiring the State papers issued from Washington; but here is one which is a sad disgrace. It must come into discussion soon, and the best hope is that American lawyers will be prepared by a thorough study of it to speak wisely upon it, and prevent the evil consequences which it must produce if not honestly dealt with. One does not need to be a lawyer to see that it is untenable, because it proceeds on diverse and incompatible grounds. It plays fast and loose with the main point of the recent case—in one part assuming Slidell and Mason to be rebels, and in others belligerents. While the public here find it difficult to account for such a production from any Minister of State, some of us keenly feel the insult to the Americans inflicted by that dispatch. It is inconceivable that Mr. Seward can have believed that England or France could be cajoled by it: and the only supposition is that he hoped to please his own countrymen. According to some American newspapers Mr. Seward's course is guided by his ambition for the Presidentship. If so, certainly nobody else has so insulted the people of the United States. If he can imagine that he is winning their favor by writing State papers which are either dishonest or silly, he is satirizing the people more bitterly than any bystander has ever done. Of the spirit and temper of angry newspapers I need not speak. They condemn themselves sufficiently.

Neither shall I say much of the discontent with myself, which I observe in the letter of S.M., and elsewhere, in the *Standard*.[142] I do not wish to occupy your space with defence of myself; and every practical purpose will be answered by a brief explanation of my point of view. My course has always been—to fight your battles on this side the water, to the utmost extent that truth will allow; and to speak the plain truth on the other side on all matters which relate to the principle and conduct of the cause of human freedom. This is not the way to gain popularity. It is the way to ensure much displeasure on both sides; but that is a small matter in comparison with the least good that may be done in either country. I certainly think that it is the course most conducive to peace and a clear understanding between the two nations. I shall go on, as long as I live, with the part of the work which lies here. As for the other half, it rests with you, as you are aware, whether I continue it. You know that I wait upon your pleasure in regard to corresponding with the *Standard,* as I have always done. A word from you, at any time, will bring my farewell, as I have repeatedly reminded you and the Committee.

It can hardly be necessary to say much about the unfortunate series of mistakes to which the recent painful feelings on your side the water have been owing; for time must already have made them manifest. To indicate them will probably suffice. If we were to go back to the outset, we must notice first the flagrant error, common to North and South, and singularly insulting to England and France—that the policy of the European powers would be determined by their need or greed of cotton. There never was any warrant for this assumption, and there has never been any evidence to confirm it. Mr. Adams came over with his mind full of it (as appears by his published dispatches), and his son went to Manchester to assure himself of it. We see Mr. Adams the elder assuring Mr. Seward, after some weeks' residence, that he is unable to perceive that England has any idea of recognizing the South, while Mr. Adams the younger is astonished at finding that, in Manchester itself, the view of the American case is not affected by considerations of cotton. To the South this rash and injurious assumption has been most disastrous; and the Confederates now see us diligently growing cotton in half a hundred places (literally more than that), and so providing for a supply that we shall never more, under any circumstances, be dependent on American cotton culture. I mention this now for two reasons; that the mistake may be pointed out which has done incalculable mischief for months past; and that Northern men may take warning from the South, and not fall into the same mistake about corn, or any other commodity. We constantly see in America newspapers that England cannot go to war with the United States, because she cannot dispense with these commodities. This is a grave mistake. If we had been so dependent at all it would have been for cotton; and we have braved that inconvenience—employing all the influence of England, as I have already told you, to prevent France and Spain breaking the blockade. Our free trade policy gives us the command of all commodities that are raised anywhere; and we can get any amount of grain from Russia, and the Danube, and various other regions by paying a shilling, or two shillings, per quarter more for it, while the rapid improvement in our tillage brings us nearer every year to an adequate home supply. The loss and inconvenience of a stoppage of trade with America would be very serious; but there is no sort of vital dependence in the case. No voice was heard, from any quarter of the empire, in deprecation of war on this ground, on the recent occasion; and it will be a fatal error to imagine, hereafter, that England will endure insult and injury because she cannot or will not go to war. She would suffer to any extremity sooner than submit further than a principled forbearance justifies; but in fact, no such extremity is within the horizon. She can command the resources of the world, if any one province of it should refuse intercourse with her.

This reminds us of the opposite mistake—altogether incompatible with the above, though I have seen them side by side in the same newspaper. The charge that England wants to pick a quarrel—is bent on war with America—has even appeared in comments on the case of the Trent; so that it really appears as if the writers forgot that, in this case, England is the injured party. If one man unexpectedly knocks another down, is he, when called to account, to accuse his victim of wanting to pick a quarrel? Not a word more can now be needed on this mistake—prevalent as it was when you issued the last *Standard* that has arrived here. The case is, no doubt, better understood now, and I need only say, in reference to the letter of S.M. that I certainly do consider the conduct of our government faultless in this affair. Calm, courteous, clear and brief in purpose and speech, moderate in temper, and unoffending to manner, the ministers have been approved, as far as is known, by everybody in England and out of it. I wish the entire nation had been like its government—and I believe that nearly all have been so in the main—but there are two disgraces on this side which give us much concern. The one is the course pursued by the *Times* newspaper, and some which follow in its track; and the other is the mischievous and delusive procedure of the peace party—or of some very few of its members. They can do no harm here, where their shallowness is gauged very accurately; but they create a false impression abroad, as they did when they misled the ignorant Czar Nicholas into the war which has impoverished his empire. That we have no objection to arbitration in cases which come under certain conditions, our government and people have clearly shown, and repeatedly shown. But the recent case was one in which arbitration was altogether inapplicable; and any proposal of it was ignorant on this side, and could be only misleading on the other. The law was clear and unquestionable; and national honor is not a subject for arbitration. Still worse is the spirit and whole course of the *Times*, emulating as it does the rabid newspapers which respectable Americans disclaim as any expression of their minds and feelings. We, in the same way, disclaim the *Times*, which misleads, I fear, a great multitude, but pleases only a small class which supposes itself more important than it is.

Among the mistakes doubtless cleared up ere this are some which I find in the *Standard* as well as elsewhere. You will have remembered, before this time, that England is in no way answerable for your late peril. She did not make the occasion, nor choose the time for a quarrel. You will have found that the matter in question was, as Mr. Webb said, our Right of Asylum, or of Hospitality. It is on this ground that Capt. Wilkes's offence was against every other people, as well as the British. He infringed the right of free entrance and passage under the English flag, which is a right in possession of all nations. Messrs. Slidell and Mason were, as a matter of fact, private individuals to whom a passage could on no ground be refused (a fact which invalidates Mr. Gerrit Smith's letter, which I see in the *Liberator*). If they were rebels, or if they were belligerents, they could not legally have been taken, but to us they were private individuals, coming from no known government, civilians, and passing from one neutral port to another. No commander could have refused them a passage; and no government could refuse to protect them from violence when once passengers. In this connection have occurred the mistakes of S.M. and others, in supposing that the recent case was of the same class as those in which England showed herself overbearing in old days (I may mention that English captains have *not* fired shotted guns to bring-to unarmed ships). It would have been well for Americans to remember that England has risked the wrath of both the Napoleons, and twice dared the danger of invasion by France rather than permit the smallest encroachment on her right of hospitality. After the Orsini conspiracy, the threats and wrath of certain French colonels and Paris newspapers were as violent as anything we have heard from America. As for the notions that Ireland is discontented, and that the Canadians are disposed for a union with your republic—no words can now be needed to show that they are mere hallucinations. The spirit of Canada has had occasion to show itself; and the general prosperity and contentedness of Ireland are shown by its rapidly-improving industry, and the remarkable diminution both of crime and of pauperism. We rank the nonsense we read about both countries with the assurances of "undying hate," "future revenge," etc., menaced by some of your journalists, who seem to forget that England was forced by a rash American to demand reparation for an injury. Such ravings do not stand in the list of genuine mistakes.

But how melancholy are those mistakes! Nowhere else could popular error be of so much consequence, because nowhere else do the people bear the responsibility of rule. Rights carry their corresponding duties everywhere, and a people who have the right of self-government are bound to be above such vital mistakes as those which have marked this last passage in your history. While they do not inform themselves sufficiently to avoid such faults and embarrassments, they have no right to quarrel with the impression widely entertained in Europe that democratic governments are not qualified for permanent international relations. Practically speaking, the events of the last two months have done more, I believe, to discredit republican government than anything that the advocates of despotism are able to do or say. The more thankful may we be that your government unhesitatingly did its duty by us; and that the American people have acquiesced; not only abstaining from all resistance, but generally approving the decision. They have thus effectually put their enemies in the wrong.

As to the probable effect on the anti-slavery cause—there has never been any fear that an alliance with the Confederates must inevitably ensue from Capt. Wilkes's act. He forced us to be the protectors and champions of four Southern gentlemen whose names would otherwise have never been heard of by 99 out of 100 Englishmen; but this is altogether a different matter from sympathizing with a slaveholding society. There is no doubt of the disinclination of our government, and the nation generally to recognize the Confederates; but the recent levity and passion of the North have given new power to a clique which may soon prove to be stronger, in Parliament and in the Clubs, than they would otherwise have ever been. It is supposed that this clique will urge a recognition of the South on condition of the entire cessation of the slave trade—of the emancipation of all American slaves—and of a treaty of free trade. They urge that this will free the negroes sooner than any other method—as the North seems clearly incapable of compassing her own objects. How far it is true that there is such a clique, and that it meditates such proposals, we shall see when Parliament meets. I need not say that we shall not easily believe in the terms of the compact.

Meantime, there can be no doubt of the daily increasing difficulty of maintaining here the ground of the North. It appears to the experienced of communities of Europe that the Federalists are unaware of the desperate character of their position and prospects. The lapse into national insolvency, which we hear of by the last mails, the division of counsels among the authorities, military and civil, and the absence of all effectual achievement amidst so vast an expenditure of all kinds, seem very fearful. But far worse than all is the feature which most disheartens those who are most friendly— the barbaric character of the warfare. This strikes us dumb, however incessant our advocacy may otherwise be. That the destruction of harbors will bring down all the maritime powers upon the government which perpetrates it seems to be a matter of course. I do trust it may yet be time to stop this insufferable act. We are glad to read of a deep channel left open at Charleston; and this, if true, will save the city; but the injury to people at sea remains. Taking a view of the whole field, it is manifestly impossible to ignore forever, or for very long, a seceding community which its former or proper government cannot bring into reunion; and, in the present case, the testing period is much shortened by the low character of the Northern military policy. That policy relies (as probably the South does, too) on damaging and annoying rather than on conduct and valor in the field; and in Europe there is no sympathy for such a policy. Among military nations, warfare respects men and property more and more, and inflicts no injury which is not essential to a valorous stand-up fight. Unless the North can effect its aims speedily, and by genuine and high-spirited warfare, it will be impossible for its friends in Europe to uphold it.

Dark as the future is, there is, for Abolitionists, the bright conviction that the aim of their labors is near its fulfilment. The one thing that seems certain is that slavery can in no case be maintained. That you will witness emancipation, in one way or another, I cannot doubt. That you may see it accomplished in safety, order, and peace is the hearty hope, I am sure, of all who know what the Northern Abolitionists have done and suffered in the case. H. M.

(Although, for reasons heretofore given,[143] we do not deem it best to print Mrs. Martineau's previous letter entire, we have concluded to give place to the concluding portion thereof, as follows.—[NASS] Editor.)

The President's absurd proposal to remove the four million of negroes to some new territory shows that your time has come. The champions of the enslaved must be supposed ready with a scheme of emancipation; and the rest of society will be only too glad to be led. It is not to be supposed that, after a quarter of a century of subservience to the Slave Power, the signing portion of Northern society can become in an hour such true patriots as the occasion requires; but, if the PEOPLE on whom we are bidden to rely are trustworthy, you have the very opportunity you have prayed for so long, and may now lead the way to deliverance. I am glad to see that our *Daily News* yesterday (Saturday, Dec. 28th) pronounced for a policy of Emancipation as the only possible good issue from your troubles. I trust the same truth will soon become evident to your countrymen throughout the free States. Any other proposal can lead only to disaster. The prospect is grave enough at best, from the singular helplessness in military matters which is fast bringing you to national bankruptcy, and has impaired the prestige of the nation almost past retrieval. Nobody can now suppose any reunion under the old Constitution possible; nor any permanent subjugation of the South. The one chance seems to be the offer of a policy of emancipation, by which the permanent cause of quarrel will be got rid of—the slaveholders put in the way of a more profitable tillage of their lands than they have ever yet tried; and their laboring class rendered safe neighbors for them for the future. There are, no doubt, plenty of difficulties in the way, and an arduous task is in store in organizing the new method of industry; but difficulty must be met when there is no alternative but impossibility. Unless this is done, it is plain that there will be, not two parties to the national break up, but three or four; or, in other words, total wreck. It will not mend the matter to plunge into a foreign war; for the South will be incalculably strengthened by it, however anxious we may be to avoid all alliance with the Confederates; and if, as some of your sagacious countrymen intimate, a foreign war should unite your two sections, all will be over for the negroes for this time. They will be the sacrifice; and we do not believe you Abolitionists will permit that. This memorable year in your history is closing very darkly for you. It has been a year of noble interest on your part, vast sacrifices, high hope, and exulting confidence; and it closes with nothing left but the unaccomplished enterprise. That enterprise is a great blessing; and so is the clear indication of the right way to pursue it; but not the less heavy is the pain of bereavement, disappointment, and mortification; and not the less dreary the prospect of further strife among yourselves, insupportable debt, and the continued desperate hatred between the two sections. The slaves will be freed, evidently; and may this be the blessing of the coming year! If ever men deserved the blessing of release from a national curse it is the American Abolitionists. . . . H. M.

"The Final Break"

1 March 1862

Sir: The communications which I have lately seen in the *Standard* on the affair of the Trent show me what I ought now to do. I have to request space in your columns for a few words—not, certainly, by way of reply to anything that has been said, but as a key to my own letters on that and other topics. It is a subject of strong regret to me, and to other friends of the Cause, that any key should be needed at all.

For a quarter of a century the American Abolitionists have appealed to the world, and particularly to English Abolitionists, against the sins of their own government and people. By that lofty patriotism they secured our sympathy and service. In this sympathy my service, such as it is, has been rendered for five and twenty years; and in that spirit and confidence I have written to you, up to this hour. It now appears that you have descended from that lofty patriotism, to fall behind even your own non-Abolitionist government, by defending or excusing an outrage condemned by all Christendom; and this leaves me no choice but to withdraw from the *Standard.* It never could have entered the imagination of your friends here that Abolitionists, who were once so superior to pseudo-patriotism as to take for their motto, "Our country is the World, and our countrymen are all mankind," could, in the very crisis of their nation's virtue and hope, condescend to say, practically, "Our country, right or wrong"; but, as you have so chosen your stand-point, and consequently misapprehended my correspondence, that correspondence must cease.

I shall be careful not to impute any such change to others than those who have avowed it. I know that some hold the old position, and are in sympathy with English Abolitionists accordingly; and I trust that there are many. While, however, you, sir, and some of your contributors, occupy a different stand-point from them and me, my letters would be, not only useless, but misleading, for they must appear as untrue to you as your recent articles and communications on the Trent affair do to us.

Happily, the larger part of my work for the anti-slavery cause lies here. In that, I hope to labor while I live; and I am sure that that Cause and its promoters will always have my heartfelt good wishes, as they have had my faithful service. It is in the spirit of that service that I now bid you farewell. Harriet Martineau.[144]

Remarks by the Editor: While we must explicitly repel the imputation upon ourselves and "some of our contributors" which Mrs. Martineau puts forward as her reason for the act, we nevertheless think she does well to discontinue her correspondence with the *Standard.* Her recent letters, it is not to be denied, have given serious offence to American Abolitionists, and we should be sorry to think that they have truly reflected the spirit of our British coadjutors. Our belief is that she is entitled to speak not for them, but only for herself.

We are not aware that, in anything we have said in relation to the Trent affair, we have descended by so much as a hair's breadth from "that lofty patriotism" which has ever characterized the American anti-slavery movement. That Capt. Wilkes, misled by British authority and example, committed a breach of international law, we readily grant; but we do not therefore admit that he acted the part of a ruffian and a pirate, nor that the people of the North, in their exultation over the capture of the rebel ambassadors, while yet the legal questions raised by the act had not been tried, proved themselves a "mob," and unfitted for self-government. Capt. Wilkes, we have every reason to believe, thought his course justified by international law, and his purpose was not to insult Great Britain, but to protect the rights of his own government. If, in presenting the case in this light, we have even sunk ourselves so far in Mrs. Martineau's esteem that she can no longer co-operate with us, we do not see how it can be helped. That it has "entered the imagination" of anybody besides herself to charge us with "saying, practically, 'Our country, right or wrong,'" we cannot for a moment believe. If our constant attitude toward the government of our country is not a sufficient refutation of this charge, we must bear the impeachment as patiently as we can. We must be excused for expressing the opinion, that if Mrs. Martineau had kept herself as clear of blind partisanship and "pseudo patriotism" in behalf of the Palmerston ministry as we have from a similar infirmity in respect to the Administration of President Lincoln, she would have had better ground for self-complacency than any she can now find. Whether we have forfeited our claims to "sympathy and service" from the Abolitionists of England by any abatement of fidelity in rebuking "the sins of our own government and people," let those who read our columns decide. We certainly "shall be careful not to impute" such an opinion to British Abolitionists generally until they "avow" it for themselves, or we have unmistakable evidence that Mrs. Martineau is authorized to speak for them.[145]

❖ ❖ ❖

O N C E   A   W E E K

1861–1862

Once a Week: An Illustrated Miscellany of Literature, Art, Science, and Popular Information, edited by Samuel Lucas and published by Bradbury & Evans (1859–1880), published articles designed to inform, instruct, and entertain working-class audiences, an orientation prominent in Martineau's writing since the *Illustrations* period. Martineau's conversational tone and descriptive language in these articles aim at a less politically savvy class of reader by vividly dramatizing the events unfolding across the ocean. According to R. K. Webb, Martineau disliked "writing about America in *Once a Week* . . . because Lucas, the editor, was too much of a *Times* man, but any ground rescued from the enemy" provided sufficient motivation to continue (1960, 327). Given her lifelong animosity toward the *Times*—the sentiment was mutual—writing for such an editor no doubt had a subversive appeal.

Martineau's article "The Slave Difficulty in America," which discusses Lincoln's pivotal role as the "Great Emancipator," notes that his original platform was not an abolitionist one; like many abolitionists, she insisted on complete and immediate emancipation, without compromise. Initially, at least, Lincoln sought to placate both pro- and anti-slavery factions by permitting slavery where it already existed and forbidding slavery in free states and newly annexed territories—a bid for diplomacy that satisfied neither side. At the time she wrote this article, Lincoln had much to overcome as an American president—an office long associated with corruption, ineffectuality, and pandering to the Southern oligarchy—and much to prove to the world in order to redeem the long-tainted ideology of the American Republic. Lincoln had won the 1860 presidential election vowing to preserve the Union but with only a moderate platform on emancipation. Therefore, Martineau's hopes for the abolition of slavery under Lincoln were as yet wary and carefully measured. But by 1864, she had changed her mind: "We judge it best to avow on all reasonable occasions our wish for Mr. Lincoln's re-election, and our respect for the patriotism and wisdom of abolitionists who are forebearing with *his* human frailties, for the sake of the national welfare. . . . I say as much as circumstances permit in honour of Mr. Lincoln. . . ."[146]

Martineau's contributions to *Once a Week* feature one of two signatures: "Harriet Martineau" or "From the Mountain," the latter employed to distinguish her political and social critiques from more generic articles. In the articles signed "From the Mountain," Martineau refers to herself as "the Hermit," no doubt alluding to her reclusive lifestyle at "The Knoll," her home in the Lake District mountains.

Much of this later work serves to bring the entire body of Martineau's anti-slavery writing full circle in a historically satisfying way. It is both retrospective and contemporary in its aim to present a continually unfolding history with a profoundly complex past and, from her positivist perspective, a progressive future. Martineau, as always, is keenly aware of the significance of the history she records and of which she is a part.

. . .

"New Phase of the American Strife"

30 November 1861

The war in America has not been standing still, though "the great battle on the Potomac" has not yet been fought. It has been obvious from the first that deliberation was advantageous for the North, and mischievous for the South, though there is a sense in which the reverse has been supposed to be true. It is set forth that the Northern army is composed of citizens who cannot leave their farms and their shops for many weeks at a time; whereas the work is, in the South, all done by slaves; so that the masters are at liberty for military duty. To this the reply is that the Northern volunteer army is now composed of men who have pledged their services for three years. How their business goes on at home is their affair: but their arrangements are such as enable them to serve for three years. By the glimpses which are opened to us we see something of what life in New England is at present. Everybody is more busy than ever before; and everybody who is not mourning some slain relative or friend is in a higher mood of mind and spirits than ever before. Taking the lowest consideration first,—trade is brisk; mills and shops are full of activity; money comes in plentifully, and goes out lavishly "for the cause." The married men with young families are not taken for the army while bachelors and childless men can be had; and it is astonishing how much those left at home find that they can do. The farm, the shop, the saw-mill and the fishing-boat, are all attended to somehow,—by boys, old men, women, or neighbours: and it is known to be for a three years' term. The women are all knitting at every spare moment. Over whole States the knitting-needles are plied; and hundreds of pairs of warm stockings go off to the camps every day. The force which has thus three years before it may take time (an option existing) for training; and it is well understood that the generals in command anxiously insist that there must be much training before the fate of the Republic is committed to the chances of the battle-field.

With the Southern army the case is different. The elite of the force consists of the landed gentry and the merchants of the cities. The bulk of the troops are the landless and poor whites, of whom we have heard so much of late years. Both these orders of citizens have been handling arms all their lives. Indeed, the only thing the "poor whites" can do, generally speaking, is fighting: and they consider that this war is Fortune's *amende* to them for her harshness hitherto. They get their living, and a great deal of consideration and amusement, in an occupation to which they are adequate. But discontents are yet running high in the Confederate camps at the slow progress of the war. The planters are restless about their homes and property, as winter approaches. The slaves have been left quite long enough to the care of women and old men and boys; and every week adds to the alarms about negro-risings, as more of them disappear from the estates, and as newspapers vanish from the tables of country houses, and tidings from the seat of war spread through the negro quarter almost before they are known in the mansion. In the expectation of a great day coming, numbers of the negroes have secretly learned to read. There were always some who picked up the knowledge,—from the children of the family, from signboards and handbills: and the number has prodigiously increased of late. Such people will require the master's eye and hand when winter comes on; and they have been kept in daily expectation of his return. The masters fully expected that their President would have been in the White House, and their congress in the Capitol and their army quartered in New York and Philadelphia, before this time so that the small proportion who are planters and merchants might have been at home. While they are counting the days of suspense, the lower order of the soldiery are calling out for the plunder which was promised them. They are chafing while the Northern men are drilling and marching; and every week of inaction reduces the one force, while it augments the other. In both sections men are marching southwards; but in the one case it is from, and in the other towards the army they belong to. Sickness and suffering have thinned the Confederate force severely; but many thousands have also gone southwards to defend their own line of coast, or to secure their homes. They had hoped to gain a great battle first, and possess themselves of a northern city or two by a rush: but they can wait no longer.

The Richmond and other Virginia newspapers tell us this much; and the unpopularity of the Confederate government and commanders is declared to be very great, because the troops are undergoing hardships in a stripped country, instead of gaining victories in a rich one. It would not have been so if the authorities could have helped it. The inexperience of the Federalists, and the bad quality of their officers, have afforded ample opportunities to their enemy; but the Confederates have been unable to use any one of the occasions. Thus, while the antagonists have been standing face to face, as it were, on the Potomac, and running about after one another in the West, the world cries out for some result; and the loudest cry of all is from the Southern part of the country itself.

Yet a great deal has happened; and a very great deal has been disclosed of what must happen. It even seems doubtful whether the war will bring about the issue, after all. When experienced observers watch adventures, national or individual, they expect to see the chief aim disappear, and some collateral object rise up. They expect to witness failure in the leading hope, and the gratification of some subordinate or unconscious desire. Thus, it seems that neither of the opposed parties in America will get what it has proposed, while something quite different (whether better or worse in their view), will come about.

It has become plain to the world (what old observers were always aware of), that there is nothing approaching to unanimity on either side. There is not only much difference,—much dissension,—there is an actual split, however anxiously the fact may be concealed to the last moment.

In the Slave States there never was any unanimity at all, great as has been the boast of it up to the present time. It should be remembered, that on the last occasion on which the people of the South were permitted to declare their will as to remaining in the Union, or seceding, the majority in favour of continued union was nearly 200,000. No doubt, a large number of these Unionists became Secessionists, when Secession had actually taken place: but no rational person would suppose that all had so changed, even if we had no evidence of their present state of mind. We may assume that those of that majority who dreaded the annexation of Cuba, the re-opening of the slave trade, the competition of the mean whites with slave-holders, and the continuance of slavery under perilous conditions, still desire the protection of the Union, and would vote for it again, if they could.

There are many more,—immigrants, reduced white families, and merchants, and even political men,—whose declarations on behalf of the Union are kept down only by intimidation. For thirty years past, the abolitionists of the North have been incessantly addressed by unknown correspondents in the Slave States, who have implored them to "go on, for God's sake." They were the only hope, they were told, of sufferers under the system which is now made the basis of the proposed new republic. As might be expected, there have been many fugitives, from the planter and merchant, as well as the negro class, since the last hope of free-voting and free-speaking was lost; and, as every intelligent slave tells of the preparations making by his late comrades to join the Federal army as soon it appears, so every disguised planter or merchant who effects his escape, has tales of horror to tell of the ways in which loyalty to the Union is repressed or punished. I might fill several columns with narratives of the deeds done upon old men, upon honourable gentlemen, upon ladies,—whether long-established residents, or recent guests,—merely for their attachment, or suspected attachment, to the Union;—but it would be painful and could hardly do good. It is enough to say,—what nobody disputes,—that the fury of persecution against attachment to the Union indicates the presence of a good deal of that attachment; though the same fact precludes any estimate of the extent of that loyalty which was so lately extolled as a virtue.

One interesting fact under this head is the adventurous act of the citizens of Hyde County, North Carolina, in sending a memorial to the President, avowing their unchanged attachment to the Union, and desiring a supply of arms, to defend themselves after such a defiance of the Confederate authorities. If, on the first appearance of a Federal force on the coast, the men of a whole county made haste to speak out, it must be supposed that there are others who would be glad to do the same. We can have no doubt of it now, when we see, that of the six Slave States which have had any opportunity of declaring themselves, all have yielded a large Union party. Virginia has actually split; and so has North Carolina,—the loyalists in each freed portion being aware that in the intimidated remnant there are many more waiting an opportunity to declare themselves. How far the other four,—Delaware, Maryland, Kentucky, and Missouri,—are from being sound members of the Confederacy, needs no telling.

Through newspapers, and some accidental upliftings of the weighted curtain suspended in front of the Southern stage, we have lately learnt some very interesting things about the financial condition of the Confederacy, and the discontents caused by it. The bankers are, as a class, thoroughly discontented. The government throws on them a task which they cannot fulfil, in requiring them to provide accommodation for domestic buying and selling, under the total stoppage of the foreign trade, which is the very life-blood of the southern economy. The discontents, political, economical and military, have grown strong enough now to support a split; and Georgia, reluctant to enter the Confederacy, is ready to lead the way out of it. The governor is in open opposition to the Southern President; and there have been some important defections from the Montgomery-clique in favour of the politics of Georgia and its adherents. Whether the common danger, and the remoteness of the Federal force keep up for a longer or a shorter time the appearance of harmony in the Slave States, the fact of their discordance is not the less certain. Some of the citizens are waiting for a great battle, believing that one Federal victory would explode the Confederate cause at once: and others expect to have to wait till the Union army appears, uncovering opinions as it goes. The one thing that no well-informed citizen believes, from the Potomac to the Gulf, is that the South is unanimous, or anything like it, in its desire of independence. It never was so, while the unrest and unpractical habit of mind of its citizens assumed that England and France would speedily interfere on behalf of the cotton states; and, now that it is becoming known that no aid is to be looked for from England and France, the preparation for secession from the secessionists will go on rapidly. Meantime, visitors from Europe, or other privileged guests who have seen the army or the country under the guidance of the authorities, political or military, should be aware that while all that they see is enthusiasm, or looks like it, they are sure not to see the other side. It is certain that, while the "enthusiasts" are waving their flag wherever the stranger turns, there are dauntless people, men or women, as the case may be, who are upholding the Union flag on church tower or domestic roof in defiance of street mobs, incendiary torches, and the simmering of the tar-kettle before the door. Whenever the presence of genuine strength removes the gag imposed by illicit force, it will appear how southern opinion divides itself between the two opposite theories of republic. At present, the fact that opinion is provided is all that we can depend on.

The position of the North is, in many particulars, and on the whole, very like that of the South. There is no more real freedom of opinion on the engrossing subject of the hour in one section than in the other, though the penalties of thinking as people do in the South are less brutal and barbarous. To be sure, we do hear of a citizen here and there being ridden on a rail; but the gutting of printing-offices, and public threats and insults to men of pro-slavery tendencies are what we usually hear of, in the place of the dreadful inflictions on clergymen, governesses, commercial travellers and tradesmen, which are still going on in the Slave States.

Of personal discontent, there is evidently much less. The resources of the North are great; and the armies are well supplied with food, clothes, quarters and pay. The political discontent is, on the other hand, becoming very serious. Without paying any attention at all to the current rumours of disagreements between different departments of the government, and political representatives, we may consider it certain that the President is generally regarded as slow to a degree which gives rise to many explanations, and some unfavourable constructions. Mr. Seward is a minister for any ruler and any people to be ashamed of; and the people are, no doubt, ashamed of him; and, remembering his proposal of a coaxing-policy towards the South, they charge him with delays, for coaxing purposes which may be justified by military reasons. Meantime, a man who is *not* slow—a man keen to perceive an object, and practised in finding a way to it—has said and done, on his own responsibility, what he and the people generally are well aware will have to be said and done. The people have named him the Pathfinder; and the issue of the whole struggle now seems to depend on whether the President and Government will follow his trail, or fumble about in one which will lead them back into the slough.

General Fremont, charged with one division of the war, goes beyond the enlarged declaration of Congress last July, and declares all slaves free by the presence of the United States' army,—adopting in this step the interpretation of the second President Adams, in regard to the operation of "the war-power." My neighbours are asking the meaning of "the war-power," from which so much is expected. It means the scope of that martial law which in certain exigencies necessarily supersedes the orders of the legislature, in regard to slavery as to other arrangements. President J. Q. Adams fully explained his view: General Fremont has fully adopted it, and it remains to be seen whether the nation will uphold him and the doctrine in question, or the Washington Government and the narrower proposal of Congress of last July. This is the Northern split: and it is serious to the last degree.

When General Fremont issued his proclamation, a new spirit thrilled through the northern people: the army was rapidly reinforced with volunteers and the hesitation which before hung like a fog round each centre of action was at once dispelled. Slavery, the cause of the war, was virtually abolished. Then, after some delay, came the President's direction to Fremont to draw back, and Fremont's request, in reply, that the President would himself take the responsibility of the retreat. Then recruiting stopped, wherever the news arrived; a new regiment disbanded, and the fogs drove up again. While there was uncertainty whether the President would remove Fremont from his command, the people remained in ostentatious suspense. Now that he has been superseded, there is a split of the gravest character;—or there will be unless the Government, the creature of the people, comes round in good time to the people's stand-point. And here arise the questions,—who are, in this case, the people? and what is their stand-point?

The people on whom the direction of the policy of the republic depends are a different set from those who have, for thirty years, sold the liberties of their country to the slave-holders. The slave-traders of New York, Philadelphia, and Baltimore, the manufacturers dependent on Southern cotton, the merchants who carry Southern produce, and the host of underlings, from head clerks to warehouse-sweepers and Irish labourers hanging about the docks,—these are the people (reinforced by a timid clergy and the vanity which has been mistaken for patriotism), who have hitherto personated the North generally, and spoken as the whole North at Washington. Their day is over; or, if it be not, another revolution has to be gone through: for the true republicans of the North will not henceforth permit themselves to be represented by this great pro-slavery party. Many of the party are banished, or self-banished as traitors: many are silenced by public opinion or by public intolerance; many are at work to obtain a compromise; many will profess anything to preserve the form and pretentions of the Union: and a daily increasing number are sincerely penitent for past dereliction of principle, and anxious to support a virtuous course of action at last. Against this fluctuating, confused, embarrassed and humbled party, is now ranged the honest and resolute country population of the North: and nearly the whole population of the North-west. These last furnished the President of the time: they are resolute to claim their share of action and influence: they abhor slavery, on every account. After having seen it abolished in their own region by General Fremont, they are not disposed to let it be re-established by their own President, under the compulsion of the time-serving gentry and mob of the ports. These being the people condemned, the inquiry follows,—what is the stand-point which has to be taken or defended?

All parties join in desiring to support the Union; but hitherto the Washington government and the unregenerate North have assumed this to mean the same thing as upholding the constitution as it stood when Mr. Lincoln was elected. But that constitution is, in the main point of present importance, a corruption of the original scheme. Under it the slave power has stressed supremacy, and to overthrow the liberties of the Free States. But that constitution is not only unworthy and unsuitable: it is impracticable. The war has rendered it impossible to observe the engagements of the constitution in regard to fugitive slaves. Therefore the western and the rural populations demand that there shall be an amended constitution, purified of all complicity with slavery; so that the very cause of the disruption of the

Union may be got rid of: and with this view those large, staunch, single-minded populations range themselves with Fremont and his policy, and are not likely to quit their stand-point. The next disclosure will be whether the upholders of the existing constitution will enter upon a struggle with them for the sake of the bare chance of a reconciliation with the South, or in the dread of losing the Border States. To persons outside of the struggle it does not appear likely that the Border States can seriously expect to hold slaves while forming a part of the Northern Union. In bidding farewell to the other slave states, and joining a region of free labour, they must know that they are bidding farewell to slavery: and if not, the few Border States cannot be allowed to spoil the policy of the whole North. As for the government at Washington, it will act according to the will of the strongest party, as it ought to do, and cannot but do. At present it is in an untenable position. It professes to support the constitution, but is duly compelled to violate its conditions. It could not but be aware that it was bringing on the real revolutionary crisis by either countenancing or disavowing General Fremont's policy. After long hesitation it disavowed the policy; and after another interval superseded the man. It will probably never be settled whether the President would have gained most support by upholding the anti-slavery or the constitutional and pro-slavery party: but it is clear that his actual procedure fixes the moment when the real revolution must begin. Mr. Sumner's address at Worcester, Massachusetts, indicates this state of affairs; and the hostility with which it was received by the city people and by Washington politicians shows how significant were its contents.

Thus it appears that there may be issues which the war will not decide. The business of the war will be to ascertain what proportion of the American nation are willing to enter on the question, whether a corrupted and unworkable constitution shall be attempted to be sustained, or whether a new one, consisting of the principles of the original one, purified of its fatal compromises, shall be adopted.

The barbarous character of the warfare is a subject too painful to be needlessly dwelt upon. It arises partly from the unmilitary character of the American nation; and partly from unprecedented conditions of the struggle as a civil war. There are "traitors" in all the departments of a public service which has suddenly changed hands at the most critical moment of the republic. What was patriotism a year ago has become treason. The friendships of a year ago have become snares: the commercial partnerships of the two sections have become embarrassments; the family ties have generated hatreds; sectional grudges have grown into fierce revenges. The brigands of the whole country have come to the front; and the worthiest citizens retire into the darkness to grieve unseen. The sacking and burning of homesteads; the undermining of railway bridges; the infliction of torture and murder for supposed opinions; the suspension of law and rights,—these scandals and miseries are of a nature and extent never required or imagined in international wars. To escape from the disgrace of them it is a poor device to pick quarrels with foreign nations; but foreign nations should understand it too well to be tempted to return railing for railing. Bad temper and uncivil manners must be far more blameable in us than in the struggling and suffering nation who are of our kin.

The woe brings with it a blessed consolation in the heroic patriotism which is conspicuous in both sections; and eminently in the North. There is no sacrifice which has not been made by men of all classes, and by women, and even children. Our hearts warm most towards the virtue which is manifested on behalf of the good cause, rather than the indefensible one: but we gladly, I hope, recognise patriotic self-sacrifice wherever it exists.

A new prospect is opening which demands a word of notice. The planters are called upon by the whole South to cease growing their staple products, in order to grow grain, and keep up the market value of cotton, tobacco, and sugar. Slavery does not answer for growing cereals and root-crops; and this conversion of tillage, if it takes place, will be the doom of slavery. Slavery is doomed, on any supposition; and the Confederate authorities are already saying publicly that the power of emancipation is one which rests in their hands; and that they will use it in the last resort. This is a disclosure full of interest, and full of hope.

England has now received the broadest hint that she must provide herself with cotton where she can. Not only is the war likely to be a long one, but, when it is over, it is probable that this will prove to be the last year's crop of cotton under the slave system. England must provide for the interval till the growth of American cotton by free labour shall open a new period in the intercourse of the two nations.—*From the Mountain*

"Much Right and Much Wrong"

25 January 1862

While we are all thinking more of America than of anything else, it is most natural for the Hermit, as well as the man of the world, to speak of it. There is no reason why I should not; for we are now in possession of facts enough to enable us to form a sort of judicial estimate of the experience of the last few weeks; and I happen to have known so many of the leading Americans, as well as English, of the last and present generations of statesmen, that my view of what has happened and is happening will be at least original—that is, a real judgment of an individual and not an imagination derived from newspapers, or from the notions of a number of people, all equally unacquainted with America, and prejudiced in proportion to their ignorance.

Though we have but just escaped a similarly painful kind of war, we may possibly and reasonably be as calm and as capable of a judicial review of the circumstances as if we had been mere witnesses of a similar adventure in the case of another nation; for we have been in the right throughout, in regard to the merits of the question between the two governments. We sustained an outrage, as unprovoked as indisputable; and, taking the government to represent the nation, we sustained it with all possible temper and dignity.[147] Here we have an advantage which enables us to look back over the field of recent action with a serene eye and a dispassionate spirit. If we had done or invited any wrong, we could hardly have been trusted to see things as they are, or to admit with entire freedom the good and the evil on both sides. As it is, we are free to see and admit that there have been great merits and grave faults of judgment and temper in both countries, though not in the parties immediately charged with the conduct of affairs. If this is true, the danger must have left behind some admirable materials for building up future safety.

As far as is known, our Government acted as well as possible. It ascertained its ground, made its demand, and showed as much firmness and readiness in its preparation for any event as moderation and courtesy in the tone of its correspondence with Washington. On the other hand, it also appears that the American Government behaved thoroughly well. As soon as Captain Wilkes's news was received, the American Secretary of State wrote to Mr. Adams, for communication to our Government in case of need, that Captain Wilkes acted without authority, and that the American Government had none but friendly wishes and feelings on the occasion. When the British demand was received, it was held in silence for five days, and then frankly granted, three days before the expiration of the term assigned for a decision.

Meantime, the conduct of a part of the American people had been as foolish and wrong as Captain Wilkes himself had been. It was not only the newspapers that sinned unpardonably: one expects more or less of that in every country in which there is a free press; and we have but just seen too much of it at home. Not only were many of the American journals dishonest, impudent, ignorant, conceited, bent on mischief, and insufferable in coarseness, levity, and passion, but a considerable number of the citizens lost their heads. There are always unworthy leaders of popular passion in America. It is the great curse of the Republic; and on this occasion old Massachusetts behaved like a raw territory beyond the Mississippi, rather than the foremost State of New England. Boston conceit is thought, over there, to transcend the conceit of any other local society in the country; and Boston conceit has now received a check which will never be forgotten. Mr. Everett and Mr. George (not Charles) Sumner assured Captain Wilkes at a banquet that his act was legal, and falsified history to prove it. Whether they knew better or not, they were guilty of crime in so misleading public opinion while undertaking to guide it. The Governor of the State disgraced himself no less; and a Judge adventured the extraordinary proposal to postpone law to feeling in a case of such interest. Thus misled, the ostensible public of many cities made fools of themselves, and were shockingly offensive to the rest of the world. They gave the freedom of their cities to Captain Wilkes, triumphed over his prisoners, and manifested a levity which, if not grossly ignorant, was hopelessly profligate. This levity was the most disgusting feature throughout, as it appeared in the journals. Writers and public speakers seemed totally unaware of the gravity of the occasion. They spoke of Captain Wilkes's act of snatching unarmed men from an unarmed mail-packet as a deed of pluck, dash, gallantry, and so forth. They fancied England vexed and mortified, but not disposed to make a fatal quarrel of it: some proposed to baffle her by protracted negotiations, while others assured their readers that England would never actually go to war with them, because she could not dispense with American commodities. There was no impertinence, no insolence, no effort at irritation, no perilous jesting, no stupid misapprehension of English conditions and feelings, no profligate instigations, no convenient lies, which were not found in the American newspapers of November and part of December. This is one clear and definite department of the whole case.

If, on the one hand, there were leading citizens—I do not mean the Everett, Andrews, and Phillips order of political self-seekers, but wiser and better men—who were more or less influenced by the ignorant journalism of the hour, there were, on the other hand, some few newspapers, and not a few sensible citizens, who were steadier and more patriotic. There were journals in Philadelphia which throughout admitted arguments that the seizure of the *Trent* was illegal, and that the prisoners would have to be yielded up. There were many sensible men who held their judgment in suspense, and insisted only that right should be done in any event. Certain military leaders were so impressed with the seriousness of the case, that they urged upon the Government the necessity of preparing to undo Captain Wilkes's deed.

We ought not to forget the influences under which all these demonstrations were made. The Americans, one and all, resent the former acts of search and seizure by England, when seamen were carried off from American ships as British subjects, the vessels being left short-handed, and the commanders eating their hearts with rage.

The Americans generally have been, for months past, and still are, perplexed by our recognition of the Confederates as belligerents, and yet not recognising the Confederate Government. They have been led to suppose us inclined to side with the South; and some of the orators, who ought to know better, have been talking for months of our rendering secret aid and comfort to the Confederates. It is known that some British vessels have actually run the blockade, and supplied arms and comforts to Southern purchasers.

It was industriously taught that the passage of Messrs. Slidell and Mason in the *Trent* was a breach of the Queen's proclamation. The recent publication of some of Mr. Adams's correspondence with his own Government, discloses to us some incidents of American feeling which are very valuable. When Mr. Adams arrived, nobody here was giving a thought to taking part in the civil war; whereas, Mr. Adams was supposing us to be longing to join the South. As soon as this was perceived by us, we exerted ourselves to show him his mistake; and now it comes out that he mistook his own process of enlightenment for change in us. At first, he proceeded on the supposition that we favoured the Confederates. Then he wrote to his Government that he had failed to satisfy himself that we had any purpose of alliance with the enemy; and now we find he has been writing of the great change he observes in us in regard to genuine neutrality. If he so believed, living in London, his countrymen across the sea were sure to be suspicious and jealous in a high degree, on very insufficient evidence. If the Confederates believed that we must interpose in their favour, because we must have their cotton, much more must the North believe it. From the outset, they had proceeded on the assumption that cotton must rule the British mind and feelings. On this point it is the young Mr. Adams who enlightens us. He seems to have the same simple cast of character as his father; and he has published in an American newspaper a portion of his diary, which shows his astonishment at finding Manchester itself too liberal to entertain the predilections which his countrymen had attributed to all England.

Besides these prejudices about us, the Americans had some strong feelings about the Commissioners whom they held as prisoners,—and especially about Mr. Mason. The reason why has already been told in *Once a Week*,— that Mr. Mason is the author of the Fugitive Slave Law. It is also to be remembered that he was active in Virginia against the survivors of John Brown's raid. He cross-examined John Brown himself, as he lay bloody and exhausted in his prison, to learn how far he was backed by invisible forces. On the anniversary of John Brown's execution last month, Frederick Douglass was lecturing at Boston—as it happened, on Photography. Neither he nor his audience cared much for photography at the moment; and by a sudden impulse they threw themselves into subjects that they did care for. The black orator came to the front of the platform, and, when he had told how Mason had teased the old puritan champion in his chains, he leaned over and asked, in a low tone which thrilled upon every ear,—"And where is Mason now?" Mason was close by, in Fort Warren,—almost within hearing of the roar of triumph which seemed likely to explode the great hall where the words were spoken.

Of Mr. Slidell it is not necessary to say anything here. Mason's case is enough to show us what it must have been to hold those dangerous envoys and detested traitors as prisoners; and what it must have been to let them go. Yet the American people lost no time in saying, after their Government, "if we have no right to hold them, let them go."

It may help our understanding of the American state of mind to look back for a moment on our own prejudices and mistakes during the weeks of suspense about the war.

At first, we almost unanimously believed that Captain Wilkes had acted under the orders of his Government, or under some strong assurance of its approbation. This was natural; for it was scarcely possible to suppose that a naval commander would perpetrate such an act in such a way on his own responsibility. We were mistaken, however. Out of this mistake others grew, no less naturally. It was pointed out that the time had no doubt been chosen with a view to invading Canada at a season the most disadvantageous to us. We now know that there was no idea of invading Canada at all. We fancied that there was a settled purpose to go to war with us; and that the moment would be chosen so as to shift the burden of the civil war, and make a peace at home, on pretence of the exigencies of a foreign war. This was all a mistake too. The Government at Washington openly alleges the impossibility of a foreign war at present; and the people throughout the country are so resolute to prosecute their quarrel with the South, that we are calling them fanatics. Again; we made the mistake of regarding the American army as the same sort of thing as a European army, and told one another that such a force would never be satisfied without over-running their continent, or the world; and that we should see an invasion of Canada for that reason. But the Northern army is composed almost entirely of a citizen soldiery;—of men who have made a mighty effort to save their polity in an hour of crisis, but who are anxious to get back to their affairs of business and pleasure. There is nothing to be got in Canada or elsewhere which can satisfy these men for being kept away from their farms, and their shops, and their mills, and the fishery, or the law courts, or their round of patients. It is in the South that the filibustering order of soldiers is to be seen;—the landless, listless, uncultivated, idle, or desperate class, who take to arms for a subsistence and a position, and will lose everything by peace and quiet. The Federal soldiery have not been among the blusterers on the affair of the *Trent.* When they have spoken, it has been on behalf of law and right, and in warning to the Government. Our mistake in judging of them as of the French colonels, and the slaves of "glory" in the military service of France, might be natural: but it was a mistake. The Americans are not a military people: almost every man in the Federal army has a home where he is longed for, and to which he longs to return. Washington found this his grand difficulty in the revolutionary war; and it will be the difficulty of every American general while the material prosperity of the country suffices to enrich every man through the arts of peace.

A yet graver mistake was caused here by a kind and degree of ignorance which we ought to have outgrown before this time. We did not all, nor nearly all fall into it: but too many did. Some of us ignorantly fancied, and rashly said, that the American Government would not dare to do right, for fear of the mob,—or, in more civil phrase, in opposition to public opinion. It is not enough to let this pass as a mistake. It is highly necessary to make out where the mistake lies, that we may not fall into it again.

If we had known the American constitution better, we should have been aware that the President and his ministers are precisely the persons who do not, and need not, fear the mob, or unreasoning public opinion. The slaves of the mob are the rising, not the risen men. If the President chooses to abase himself again,—to lapse into the candidate state,—in order to obtain a second presidential term, he may be in fear of the mob during his fourth year: but in his first year, the President is nearly the most powerful of rulers. We ought to know and to remember that his ministers are irremovable except by himself,—unless they commit acts worthy of impeachment. He and his ministers can do what they please within very wide limits indeed; and it would astonish many plain Englishmen to learn to what lengths the Washington

Government may go in despotism, without fear of check, or dread of responsibility. They may, as we see, conduct their transactions in silence and secrecy. It rests with them, as we see, to decide on points of the most critical importance; and they have only to acquiesce in the decision of the Executive, as they can neither preclude it, silence it, nor reverse it.

Again; we anticipated attempts, sly or audacious, at obtaining delay, for purposes of evasion: and in this we were mistaken. Some of the most corrupt and impudent of the American newspapers suggested such delay as a convenient expedient in case of need; but the vulgar ignorance and stupidity of the proposal should have prevented its reception here. As the event proves, no meditation, no arbitration, no "protracted negotiation," is among the ideas of the Washington Government on the case. They disclaimed the outrage before they could hear from us; they frankly admit the law; and they make complete and unhesitating reparation.

Such have been our mistakes of judgment and opinion,—caused by insufficient knowledge. I wish there had been nothing worse: but we are not morally blameless. A portion of our press has been as malignant and as false as any journalism in America.

The sound head of Old England understands that, in all societies, the passion and prejudice, the levity and captiousness of men appear on the surface of the time, while rational convictions and pure sensibilities are running deep below. The sound heart of Old England is not dismayed by the malicious clamour or the irritating contempt with which a small number of the citizens of each country have been endeavouring to provoke each other. The generous temper of Old England dwells rather on the public virtue which the events of the time have brought to light in the great mass of society on each side the Atlantic.

Of our own citizens I need say nothing. Their conduct under the infliction of injury, and in prospect of war, has been precisely what the proudest and heartiest of Englishmen would wish. They let the Americans bully, and the peace coterie at home vapour and fidget, while they themselves made ready to forgive or to fight,—"equal to either fortune." As for the Americans, we must look for their true quality in their own special war. If their case was at all understood here, it would be universally felt that the world has never seen anything finer than the devotedness of the citizens who are now awaiting and working out the redemption of the republic. There are two generations of them,—the elders who have sinned through their idolatry of the Union, surrendering for its sake the virtue, power, and prospects of the republic;—and the younger generation, on whom the task of retrieval is laid. They have begun, conscious of the deterioration of the national character, through dishonest complicity with the slave-holding oligarchy; and only too well aware that it must take time, and require no little adversity, to make clear the right aim of the Federal States, and unite them in the pursuit of it. They have devoted themselves to hasten the time, and to sustain the adversity. While the elder generation have been manifesting their repentance by the largest sacrifices, the younger have been sacrificing themselves;—not as soldiers always do in going out to the wars; but in a way most rare and memorable. They are known to have believed that a large number of them,—some think not less than ten thousand,—must fall for no visible result at all before the hour of apparent achievement could arrive. There are two reasons for this conviction; that the army is badly officered and led; and that all warfare which precedes an avowed policy of emancipation is simply thrown away. So they have believed; and the belief has not discouraged, but stimulated them. Since the morning when the early sun shone into the pass of Thermopylae on the young men who were combing their long hair, and addressing themselves to death, there can have been nothing finer than the spectacle of the New England youths,—many times three hundred,—who have posted themselves where they must fall, in order to secure victory afterwards to the republic. The young Greeks in Thermopylae did not see their fate more plainly, nor meet it more gaily. These Americans have told their mothers what must happen; and their mothers have received back their bodies for burial, and wear no mourning for sons who have so departed. Such is the spirit of the war; and it needs no gift of prophecy to tell what the result must be. The doom of Slavery is fixed; and everybody on that continent knows it. Meantime, there ought to be a fellow-feeling between Englishmen and such patriots as that young generation who are expiating the laches of their fathers.

Both they and we shall have learned a lesson from our recent peril of strife. We see that there is nothing in the spirit or forms of American government which renders the authorities subservient to the mob, or the so-called mob insubordinate to law, or to the decisions of the authorities. We shall henceforth be more rigid and vigilant in our self-defence against encroachment, perhaps; but we shall also be prepared to expect higher conduct from the Americans than we gave them credit for this time.

They, for their part, will draw their own lesson from their present mortification. They must see that they need self-knowledge and self-proof. They must see that Canada is not for them, nor anything that is their neighbour's.[148] We, however, ought to remember that, some few years since a large proportion of the Canadians were actually willing and anxious to join the United States. For years after reforms were nominally established in Canada, the people found no benefit from them, and felt themselves slighted. The effect of free-trade upon them, before the Navigation Laws were repealed, was to place them at a disadvantage in the European markets, as the protective duties of the United States did in the American: and, thus excluded on both sides, the commercial classes might well hanker after the prosperity they saw growing beyond the frontier. The Reciprocity Treaty, however, the repeal of the Navigation Laws, and genuine self-government, have scattered all such discontents, and the Canadians have pretty well shown their neighbours that the subject of annexing Canada had better be dropped.

The Americans must have learned, also, that there is a limit to international forbearance, and that they have now compelled us to indicate that limit in our own case. Whenever they shall have freed themselves from all connection with slavery, there will be no ever-open source of danger to our amity. Meantime, they now see that we have been in earnest in our purpose of self-defence. They certainly respect our course, and the temper of our government and people, with the exception of the war-party, and bullies of the press; and we certainly respect the honourable readiness with which the American Government has offered reparation, and the people have acquiesced in it. Care, caution, and courtesy on both sides may make this the last of our strifes. They must be vigilant and unremitting; and under them there must be a moral sympathy, such as kindred should feel, and such as the closest kindred must cherish, through the whole course of their life, if they would not "fall out by the way."—*From the Mountain*

"The Slave Difficulty in America"

1 February 1862

In a single line, in the smallest type, used in obscure corners of American newspapers, there is now conveyed to us one of the most significant and portentous incidents of our time. Probably not one reader in a thousand of the few English readers of American journals will have taken any particular notice of that single line which will be immortal as history, however carelessly passed over to-day as news. "*We pray for the slave.*" In order to understand its full significance, we must cast a brief glance backwards, to certain incidents of a quarter of a century ago.

In 1835, Mr. Calhoun, the honest fanatic—not to say monomaniac—on behalf of Slavery, was telling European visitors, and New England citizens whom he chanced to meet, that the subject of Slavery would never be introduced in Congress. He was told that he might as well undertake to hedge in Orion and the Pleiades as to lock up from popular use any topic of essential interest. He was positive, however; and no man's words went further with his generation. Slavery was a fundamentally necessary institution; republican liberties depended upon it; yet (or therefore), the subject would never be discussed in Congress. Within two years the roof of the Capitol rang with the shouts and cries of those who chose to speak on slavery and those who did not choose to hear. Ex-president Adams (father of the American Minister now in London), spoke upon it day after day, presenting petitions from the Abolitionists, and refusing to be put down, but with the right of petition itself. That right was put down: but it could not be for long: and before Mr. Calhoun died there was no day of the session on which something was not said about Slavery; and no subject was introduced, however remote, which did not issue in a discussion of the dreaded topic. In dying, Mr. Calhoun declared his country lost. He had failed to preclude dangerous discussion; slavery was doomed, and the Republic with it.

While he was confident that the subject would never be mentioned in the Capitol, the clergy of the Free States were certain that it would never be spoken of from the pulpit. A New England clergyman, however, even at that day, made the unheard of venture of praying for the slaves. It should be understood that all religious denominations there enter into a fuller detail of the kinds and conditions of men for whom they pray than is usual here; and the slaves have been the only class omitted. The Reverend Samuel J. May, then of Massachusetts, was supposed to be the first who supplied the omission; and his name will be preserved for the act. Next, a man of very high quality did the same brave deed;—Dr. Follen, the learned Professor, the accomplished scholar, the nearest friend of Dr. Channing, the man known as a patriot in his native Germany, as a Christian divine in England, and in America from that moment as an abolitionist. One winter night he preached in Boston, and his prayer that night thrilled through the city, and overthrew the prospects of his life. After intercession for all orders of public men, and for sufferers under various woes, the words occurred, "We pray for the miserable, degraded, insulted slave, in chains of iron and chains of gold." From that hour the pulpits of Boston were closed to him; and Dr. Channing suffered keenly from the refusal of his flock to allow his friend to preach in his church. The scandalised clergy taught, and the public accepted the teaching, that they had Scripture for their guide, because they were "if possible, as much as lay in them, to live peaceably with all men"; and silence was the only way to peace and quiet where slavery was in question.—Things had so far changed in twenty years (which was a mere span in the great spaces of history), that, when the long-free negro, Anthony Burns, was awaiting his fate in Boston, and was to know next day whether he was to be returned into slavery, and craved the prayers of all Christians, his request was, in some pulpits, noticed and allowed. Some of the Boston clergy did, and some did not, invite the prayers of their congregation for him. That was seven years ago; and the progress of opinion and feeling must have been much more rapid since; for we now see,—what it would have killed Mr. Calhoun outright to have foreknown,—that intercession for the slave has found a place in the prayers of Congress.

On the opening of the present session in the House of Representatives, there was solemn and special prayer, as at the opening of each session; and the specifications were as numerous as they ever are. Among them may be seen for the first time the words, *"We pray for the slave."* The abolitionists who have laboured in faith that this hour must come, when the slave should be openly admitted into fellowship with men and citizens, must read these few words with strong emotion. They understand the full import of this conversion of a chattel into a man who needs special payers; and they see, more clearly than we can do, how all important the question of the destiny of the slaves must have become at the head-quarters of the Government.

To Europeans, who went through their task of emancipating their negroes long ago, the incident may seem to show a wonderful slowness, rather than a wonderful advance. We should remember, however, that, when we were just emancipating ours, in islands far away, the Americans were considering it a duty to be silent about negroes, because there was no intention of freeing them, while they were not far away in sugar islands, but on all the plantations, and in all the houses of the Southern States, to which the Northern States were in political subjection. As our position and theirs were opposite then, our sensations about this new incident cannot be identical now. It is like the case of the travellers on the Andes when those who were coming down, and those who were going up had opposite sensations at the same point,—the one party complaining of the cold, while the other exulted in the genial heat. Even we Europeans, however, ought to be able to see the importance of the first act of implication of the Government with the question of emancipation. These words, *"We pray for the slave,"* are the first act of implication of the American Congress with the cause of the negro. Some were present who must have wondered whether Calhoun turned in his grave when the prayer was uttered.

The President's Message shows, without disguise, that Mr. Lincoln means to act in the matter of slavery as the people choose him to act. He never was an Abolitionist. He was always willing that Slavery should continue to exist where it existed already; but he objected to its spreading over new territory. He was ready to afford it the protection provided in the Constitution; but he objected to any further efforts in its favour. Such was his view when he became President. He did not see that Slavery was the whole cause of the rupture of the Union; and he believed he saw that the Constitution must be preserved exactly as it stood, and that therefore fugitives must be returned to their owners, according to law. By marking the point he has arrived at now, we may perceive how the question is advancing. The President will go only as far, and as fast, as he is pushed. The resolution of Congress in July, which confiscated the slaves of rebel citizens, troubled Mr. Lincoln exceedingly; and it was only by extreme urging, and under pressure of time, that he agreed to it. It was a long step forward; but he has taken a longer now.

In the interval he showed doubt and hesitation about General Fremont's proclamation, that all slaves became free where the Government was present by its civil or military authorities. After some delay he discountenanced the act, and restored the terms to what Congress had made them. Yet it appeared that he expected General Fremont to be pressed upon him again by the people; and he recalled him in a way which need not prevent his future restoration to a high command. The falling off of popular support from the moment when he disavowed the emancipation act of Fremont was a strong hint; and it appears that the President has taken it.

It was an irksome necessity to him that he must say something on the subject in his Message to Congress. He must do it, however; and in a very strange way indeed he has done it. He had been hearing from all quarters of the perplexities of the commanders by land and sea about what to do with the negroes. One general was returning fugitives to their masters: another was receiving all who came, giving them work, and paying them wages; while a third tried to steer a course between the two, taking no notice of fugitives beyond forbidding them to enter the camp. Such inconsistencies could not go on: the soldiers would not permit it, if we may judge by their discontent at all orders which made them oppress the slaves.

By way of experiment, the negroes on the coasts where the Federal forces have established a footing, in South Carolina and Georgia, have been organised as a free labour force. The men work well; they now come in by thousands instead of hundreds; and the case is already so far clear to Mr. Lincoln himself, that, in his Message to Congress, he assumes the necessity of emancipation by proposing a scheme for disposing of the negroes when freed.

It is true, he proposes a plan which is absurd, and which he, and every man who heard his Message, must know to be impracticable. He proposes, by way of introduction, to recognise the independence of Hayti and Liberia. This is a significant proposal, because it means that men of colour may hereafter come to Washington, and be received as envoys. But there is another word to be said first about this proposal.

Hayti is a free republic, which has won its independence by arms. It is now well governed and prosperous; and a considerable number of American blacks have settled, and are daily settling in Hayti, to grow cotton for the Northern States and for Europe. Mr. Lincoln evidently wishes to encourage the emigration of as many of his black fellow-citizens as possible: and therefore he is trying whether society will bear the presence of a Haytian envoy at Washington, as the price of getting rid of some hundreds or thousands of its dark-skinned members. The origin and condition of Liberia are different. That settlement was formed, half a century ago, by slave-holders, for the purpose (avowed in the Southern States) of sustaining slavery by deporting thither undesirable negroes, free and slave, and keeping the control of the numbers, and therefore of the value of slaves, by having an outlet in the shape of an African colony. As the scheme was not honest, it was not successful; and for forty years the free negroes of the United States have been resisting bribes and threats, and refusing the expatriate themselves to Africa. They were Americans, they said; they had formed friendships at home, and accumulated property, obtained equality for their children in the common schools, and educated them to form an intelligent society: and they would not go into a land of barbarism, to war with savages, and see the slave trade carried on along the coast, and slaves held in the settlement itself. That hungry and somewhat disreputable settlement was acknowledged by England as a free republic many years ago. The circumstances of the cotton trade for some time past have loosened the grasp of the slaveholders upon it: it seems to have been allowed of late to make its own growth, free from the burden of shiploads of helpless negroes, deported from Southern plantations. The President could hardly have proposed at any former time to recognise the existence of a State formed out of the dregs of Southern plantations, in whose representative some member of Congress might chance to meet a former slave of his own—got rid of for being dangerously clever or hopelessly stupid: but the state of opinion at Washington is now such as to induce Mr. Lincoln to propose to acknowledge the Republic of Liberia at the same time with the more advanced, hopeful, dignified Republic of Hayti.

Both, however, are made to usher in the necessary but perplexing question— What is to be done with the slaves in the Confederate States?

The question itself shows that Mr. Lincoln regards emancipation as certain. This is good: but all the rest is so wrong and foolish that we might safely assume that Mr. Lincoln proposed something that would not do, in order to throw upon others the responsibility of whatever will have to be done. He tries to accommodate himself to the vulgar prejudice of colour by taking for granted that the negroes must all go away somewhere. He openly declares that he hopes the free blacks will go away with the slaves; and he holds this out as the great recommendation of the plan to the citizens of the North.

The people are, by Congress, to give money to buy a territory somewhere, outside of their own country; and there the four millions of slaves are to be transported, with as many free blacks as can be induced or compelled to go with them. There they are to be colonised, at the expense, and by the care, of the people of the United States. Such is Mr. Lincoln's pretended scheme.

Thus, the land of the Southern States would be left without labourers. The owners would be left without servants, or any means of tilling their cotton-fields, or raising food, or keeping their live stock, or having their dinners cooked and their houses swept. The plantations would be left to run to waste. The four millions of negroes would be carried away from shelter and food, to be set down in a wilderness to starve. It is such nonsense to talk of separating the capitalists, the land, and the labourers, so as to render all the three helpless and desolate, that no further words are needed. Mr. Lincoln is perfectly well aware that the planters want the negroes, and that the negroes want the land and wages; and he has no apprehension that he will be taken at his word. The proposal is a safe way of making the admission that emancipation has become a necessity which cannot be deferred much longer.

What, then, is to be done with the negroes?

The only serious difficulty is in the state of feeling of slave owners towards their negroes. The simple way of settling the matter is to fix a day, near at hand, when the labourers will receive wages instead of supplies in kind, on their agreeing to certain terms. By those terms, the hours and conditions of labour will be agreed upon, and the rent of their dwellings, and the amount of wages. If the owners were living at home, in peace and quiet, the change would be practicable and easy for all just-minded and kind-hearted men; and they would find it very profitable. So it was with the Northern States, and wherever the process has been well managed. But slave-holders are not, generally speaking, just-minded men, where their labourers are concerned; and not all of them are kind-hearted: and thus difficulties have arisen in emancipation cases, and complaints have been made that the negro is idle;—to which the negro replies that he cannot get his pay, and is badly used besides. In the present case, there is the serious embarrassment that the planters are not at home, in peace and quiet. Some are in the army; some have repaired to the cities for safety; some have armed their negroes against an enemy who is described to the slave as having a particular appetite for negro meat; and all are in more or less dread of what may happen under their "peculiar insti-tution." Last month is not the first time that a great part of Charleston has been burnt; and the negroes knew how to burn cotton before they saw their masters doing it now, all along the coast and the rivers where the Yankees (understood to be a sort of gorillas) can by any means get it. In short, eman-cipation is necessary now to preclude that worst of horrors, a servile insur-rection. It is this pressing need which makes Mr. Lincoln speak of schemes which are an admission of the crisis; and instead of crying out, as some of our journals are doing, against emancipation as setting the slaves to murder their masters, everybody ought to see that in emancipation is the only secu-rity for the slave-holders. It is when freedom is denied, and not when it is conferred, that slaves take their case into their own hands. Thus far, Ameri-can negroes have shown themselves, not murderous but thievish,—not sav-age but sly. Like our West India negroes, they work to accumulate property; are vain in displaying it; are fond of putting it to pious uses; are ambitious of education for their children; are social, imitative, gregarious,—everything which prevents their running into the wilds to squat, or lurking as banditti, as ignorant people suppose. They are fugitive, and not freed slaves, who in-fest the swamps. The Abolitionists know the negroes well; and the Abolition-ists have proposed what the President is probably aware that he will have to carry out. As in former wars in the same States, the presence of the military and civil officers will free the slaves, and appoint the conditions of that free-dom. Those conditions will secure the tillage of the soil, and the carrying on of the regular work of the plantations, under the management of the owners, when they are loyal, and of Government agents when the owner is hostile. Such is the provisional method which will preclude an outbreak at the be-ginning, and afford time and opportunity for such regulations as may be requisite for the negro, on his ceasing to be a slave, and before he is qualified to become a citizen. Beside such a feasible and simple proposal as this, the President's notion of carrying off four millions of people who do not want to go, from half a million of gentry who do not want to part with them, and from land which their departure will turn into a wilderness, to starve in a present wilderness, looks like insanity. It is all meditated, however. The ap-parent leap in the dark is, in fact, crossing a bridge; and the President and all his train are coming over to the Abolitionists.

There is nothing visionary, or even new, in such a scheme as is proposed. There is always some plantation, here or there, where the negroes are, by some accident, living like free labourers. This reminds me of what happened in North Carolina, when I was over there. A widow lady was called away from her estate for a permanence, by some obligation or other; and it be-came a question what to do about the negroes. They were sorely afraid of be-ing "sold South"; and they were delighted at the proposal that they should choose an overseer out of their own number, and manage for themselves.

They were to make themselves comfortable, and earn what they could for their mistress. They chose the ablest negro on the plantation to superintend, and went to work.

Some months later, a great noise and shouting was heard on the estate, and the neighbours said, when the report of insurrection was spread, that they always knew what would become of such a venture. It was only holiday mirth, however. The negroes had gone to work on a general holiday, some time before, because the crop was in a critical state, and would not bear delay: and they were taking their holiday now;—and that was all. The crop was a good one, and their mistress had a larger income than usual from her estate. It would be a pity to send four millions of these people into the wilderness, if it were ever so practicable. But such is not to be their fate.

Already, the destiny of the "the miserable, degraded, insulted" class may be heard told in that voice of supplication in the Capitol, "We pray for the slave."

"Abolition of Slavery in the District of Columbia"
24 May 1862

The District of Columbia is the reserve of land, ten miles square, which is appropriated to Federal occupation, and is under Federal government exclusively. Slavery there once *was* a national institution; whereas everywhere else it *is* a State institution. While it existed there, the whole power and influence of the general government was at the service of the slaveholding portion of the nation; and now that it is extinguished there, the slaveholders must take charge of their own "domestic institution," as they are fond of calling it. There are no two opinions anywhere, I believe, as to the inability of slavery to sustain itself in the hands of only a quarter of a million of proprietors, who have no longer the support of the national government, but must sustain themselves against the jealousy of four times their own number of their own non-slaveholding neighbours, and the public opinion of the rest of the nation. Time will show whether the attempt will be made to preserve the institution against such odds. Meanwhile its foundation is rooted up; there is no longer any controversy on this subject involved in the international relations of the Republic; and the African race has turned the corner of its fate. American statesmen have for many years looked forward to this event as that which would be the doom of Cuban slavery. When their government should at length be at liberty to join ours in inducing Spain to unite with the rest of Christendom to repudiating slavery, there could be no doubt of its speedy disappearance from the black list of national crimes. These statesmen have been so ready to avail themselves of their new freedom and their long desired credit, that they entered upon negotiations with our minister at Washington to stop the slave-trade before the act of their own government was completed.

The first overt act of promise was the incident which I noticed four months ago,—the prayer for the slave offered by the chaplain at the opening of the session of Congress in December last. Though all understood the portent, few perhaps expected that within four months the prayer would be exchanged for the rejoicing words, "We thank thee that our soil is now free from slavery, and that this air is now free air, and so shall remain for ever." Yet this was the thanksgiving uttered in the Capitol on the 17th of April. The next portent was the execution of Captain Gordon, the slave-trader, on whom the President allowed the law to take its course, in spite of the most vehement remonstrances from the pro-slavery interest. The man was as fit a subject for the halter as society could produce,—a ruffian notoriously guilty of a long course of murders: but he would not have suffered death under the rule of any President but one resolved to put down the crime. We all knew what must be coming then: but we were hardly prepared for an intermediate step.

It appears that it must have been in March that Mr. Lincoln commissioned his Secretary of State to propose to our Minister a new Treaty for the repression of the Slave-trade; in which all terms should be granted which were necessary to the effectual accomplishment of the object. Mr. Seward made the proposal to Lord Lyons, who "responded warmly." None of the old difficulties were revived; no obstacles arose; and the treaty was signed by the two ministers on the 7th of April. There is an end now to the shabby evasions and the quarrelsomeness of which we have had so much reason to complain from pro-slavery administrations at Washington. There is an end to the blocking-up of the shallows and river mouths of the African coast by large American ships which caught no slaves, and allowed no smaller vessels to enter for the purpose. There is an end to the holiday-making of the American officers at the Azores for many months of the year, during which they claimed a right of watching long reaches of the coast which they left open to the slave-traders. Moreover, the Right of Search is allowed, and in consequence there is an end at once to the impunity of traffic in negroes under the American flag, and to the danger of international quarrels which has perpetually arisen from the denial of the Right of Search in a cause in which it was indispensable to the prosecution of the objects of the treaty. By the new treaty, the world was given a share in the great boon before it was legally assured to the American people themselves. Not many days, however, had the nation to wait.

It had been supposed that the Emancipation Bill would become law on the anniversary of the attack on Fort Sumpter; but the Senate did not sit on Saturday the 12th. On the Sunday morning, the whole coloured population of the District appeared in the streets and roads, dressed in their best, wearing different countenances from those they were known by; for they were in high excitement, quiet as was their demeanour. They repaired to their churches, of which they have seventeen in the District, served by clergymen of their own colour. The churches were thronged; and the scene was one never to be forgotten by the white people who were present. The prayers and sermons were special, and Moses was, naturally, the patron saint of the celebration. There is no knowing or conjecturing what proportion of the people had any misgivings about what might happen between that hour and the moment of complete deliverance. Throughout the day, everything seemed bright and joyful. But it was a night of woe. The kidnappers had everything ready; and as soon as the whites were safe in bed, they began their devilish work. They seized the strongest and best-looking of the men and women, and carried them by force into Maryland, parting parents and children, husbands and wives, with the ruthlessness which is an attribute of the slave-trader. Cries, groans and tears sounded through the whole District: and we may hope that the members of the Senate will feel bound to search out and restore the poor wretches who were disappointed of liberty by their failure to sit on the Saturday, as was expected of them. It is to be hoped that the new bondage will soon be at an end; for Maryland must follow the example already set by Delaware, of preparing to abolish slavery as a State institution. The kidnapping was done for the mere difference between the 300 dollars per head voted by Congress and the price which might be got in the Maryland market. The choicest were carried off; but, in the present state of the slave-markets, it cannot be long before the new owners will be glad to set them free. I need not say that, if all but the old, sickly, and stupid had been carried off, the event would still have been a call upon all human society to rejoice; for the continued slavery of a few hundred negroes is not for a moment to be weighed against the blessing of the territory being free ground for ever, and the national government released from the sin and disgrace of sanctioning slaveholding.

In a few hours more, the emancipation was secured, as far as Congress was concerned. It only remained for the pro-slavery party to work upon the President, to induce him to veto the Bill. The pressure was very great; so great that many believed that no elective magistrate could withstand it; but Mr. Lincoln is a man of strong determination. On the one hand, heavy bets were offered that he would veto the Bill: on the other, the citizens remembered some remarkable words of his, recently uttered, and believed that he would remain unshaken. The words were: "I am entirely satisfied that no slave who becomes for the time free within the American lines will ever be re-enslaved. Rather than have it so, I would give up and abdicate." To remand the slaves in the District to the yoke after Congress had removed it, would be as cruel as to send Carolina slaves back to their bondage; and the man who uttered those words would not do such an act. This was true; and on the 16th, the President's signature made the Emancipation Bill law.

Throughout the Free States, there was an anxious watching for the news; and as soon as the telegrams were given out from the offices, such rejoicings began as had never before been witnessed, because no such cause of rejoicing had occurred within living memory. Among the New England homesteads there are thousands of families who cannot celebrate with joy a bloody victory; and in the towns and villages, consideration for the mourners who abound in them checks, more or less, every kind of noisy demonstration. At that time, it was told everywhere that all Illinois was in mourning, after the battle of Pittsburg Landing; and multitudes had refused to celebrate the victory, which was then supposed to be much greater than it was. But the event of the 16th of April was not only harmless, but, in the eyes of all good citizens, a national blessing without drawback: and the echoes of the northern hills were roused by salutes of a hundred guns: all along the valleys the inhabitants were brought out into the roads by the clang of all the church-bells within hearing. Presently, all work was thrown over for the day; and the people, in their Sunday best, were thronging to their churches and public halls, to hold meetings, pass resolutions, hear congratulatory speeches, or join in thanksgiving, and shout their most joyful psalms. The old people shed happy tears that they had lived to see the day; and the children, if they live a hundred years, will never forget it. There must have been a rush of thoughts in the minds of the middle-aged people. When they were young, the right of petition to Congress had been lost for a time through the attempt to obtain this very enactment. It had always been clear enough to everybody that the abolition of slavery in the District was the turning point of the destiny of the institution, and of the fate of the Republic which it imperilled; and, like innocent people, who supposed their government to be the popular system which it professed to be, the citizens of a quarter of a century ago applied themselves to government, by petition to Congress, to get rid of slavery in the District. They were put off, ridiculed, rebuked, insulted, and especially in the person of the representative who had courage to present their petitions,—the venerable ex-President Adams. One way in which they were put off must have been recalled to the minds of the survivors by a repetition of the same attempt on Mr. Lincoln, at the last moment. It was proposed to refer the matter to the inhabitants of the District. The northern citizens did not destroy their chance of success by a refusal, but insisted that, if the will of the inhabitants of the District was to decide the case, every adult inhabitant, black and white, must have a vote upon it. If it was a question whether one portion of society should or should not buy and sell the other, the vote of one party was not to the point. In 1836, the proposal was dropped, and the petitioners were silenced. In April, 1862, the proposal is overridden by the President's contempt, after Congress had put the requisite power into his hands. He signed the Bill, and the matter is settled.

It is satisfactory to perceive how great and evident the relief is to some of the slaveholders of the District. Several refused to take any measures for selling their negroes while there was yet time, saying that they preferred taking any price for them that government might fix, and then knowing that they were free, to receiving a larger sum with the consciousness that they were still in slavery. There can be no doubt that the same feeling would be found everywhere in the Slave States, where a large proportion of the proprietors would make any reasonable sacrifice to be rid of their share in the institution which involves so much loss and disgrace. The State laws render emancipation impracticable; and a way out of the position of man-owner is all that is wanted by many thousands who, even if they were not in debt, could not rid themselves of their burden by selling their servants to any chance trader who travels to supply the markets. These metropolitan proprietors, willing and pleased to cease to be slave-owners, open a cheering prospect in other quarters.

The number of negroes released will become known, no doubt, when the Commissioners report. At present, it is mere guesswork how many have been removed in anticipation of the act. I see that 4,000 freed by the act is somebody's estimate; but I do not know what it is worth.

We can form a better judgment of what they will be like as free men and women; for we are in possession, not only of the returns of the Census of 1860, as to the condition of the free blacks in the District, but of a schedule of their property, furnished at so late a date as the 17th of last March.

Though the slavish condition of any considerable proportion of any race or class in society is incalculably depressing to the free members of that race or class, the rise in numbers and position of the free negroes of America between the Census of 1850 and that of 1860 is so great as to be pregnant with significance. In that interval, the increase of numbers was 52,454. Yet more remarkable is the improvement in their position, though any such elevation might have been thought impossible.

For many years there had been colleges in various parts of the Free States where students of that race, and of both sexes, could obtain a capital education. No doubt, the constant issue from those institutions of professional men, and of women trained as governesses and schoolmistresses, must have long operated in raising the spirit of their class; but it was after the Census of 1850 that the most impressive evidences appeared. One demonstration, which is even more important now than it was ten years ago, was against all plans for deporting the people of colour. At annual conventions of their class, strong resolutions were passed against leaving their country on any pretence whatever. They were Americans, and in America they would remain. They did not choose either to impair the chances of their enslaved brethren by leaving them without champions of their own colour, or to be carried to a barbarous country like Africa after being brought up Americans. At the same time, the strongest exhortations were addressed to their free brethren to resist all pressure which should confine them to a low order of occupations, and to qualify themselves for every calling which the law allowed them. While such was the turn their judgment and feelings were taking, the common schools of Massachusetts were thrown open to them,— about seven years ago. It was a terrible doubt with them whether to break up their own schools or hold by what they possessed; but, under due encouragement, they made the venture; and they have had every reason to rejoice that they did so. From that day to this their children have grown up with white men's children, equal in all respects within the school enclosure, and of course in a much improved position beyond it. In the first University in the Republic, Harvard University, near Boston, students of all complexions pursue their education on equal terms; and the black and mulatto gentry issue forth to occupy the pulpit, to practise medicine and law, and to become school-masters, engineers, merchants, or whatever suits them, while the immigrant Irish are digging the canals and making the railways, and Germans and Dutch fill the menial offices and low employments which were once supposed the only field for the free blacks. If the schedule of the property holders of other districts than the metropolitan one were published, it would show how negro owners of hundreds of thousands of dollars obtain and employ their wealth, under legal disabilities which would discourage most of us. They remind one strongly of the Jews of the middle ages in their ambitious use of such means as they have. If deprived of political privileges by law in one State, and custom in another, they obtain power by association and *esprit de corps*. If obstructed in holding land, they lend capital to landholders. If they may not command merchantmen, they own shipping. If confined to their own race for society, they provide dwellings for the proud whites. It does not appear that they either make a secret of their material successes, like the Jews of old, or brag of them, as the vanity of the debased portion of their own race would lead observers to expect. They buy handsome furniture and good pictures, and cultivate music, for their own pleasure, and from a regard to the opinion of their own people: and again, they give a plain answer when interrogated, for government purposes, about their possessions. The latest published inquiry of this kind bears date the 17th of last March. It relates to the District of Columbia, and it is therefore no rule whatever for the condition of the free people of colour anywhere north of the frontier of slavery. The lowest and poorest of the class are found in the presence of slavery, for obvious reasons; for the intelligent, respectable, and refined, while refusing to abandon their enslaved brethren by leaving the country, remove as far as possible from the spectacle of a bondage which they cannot endure to see, because they can do nothing to relieve it. Yet, under the most discouraging circumstances, and in a district where no staple industry exists, there were, last March, 508 owners of real property, averaging 1205 dollars each. There were 1175 owners of property,—the number of males over twenty years of age being 2487. Their possessions ranged from 500 dollars to over 7000. If such are the fruits of the industry of these people in their lowest position, it is easy to believe that the wealth existing among them in the Atlantic ports is what we are told. In Philadelphia there are several black citizens who are worth several hundred thousands dollars each. As for their total numbers, they were (before this Act of Emancipation) 222,745 in the Free States, and 259,078 in the Slave States. As I have already said, their increase between the last Census and the preceding was returned as 52,454, but it was in fact much greater. We all remember the persecution of their class in 1859, when they were driven out by wholesale from most of the Slave States; or rather, the old and young were driven out, and too many of the able-bodied were seized on various pretences, and sold in the market. If those who fled to Canada and elsewhere, because they were utterly adrift, could be reckoned with the increase which remained, the sum would be much larger. We must add to it, also, the considerable emigration to Hayti, under the protection of the agency organised in concert with President Geffrard, and in prospect of the new demand for cotton, which the free coloured people have long foreseen. All these facts indicate a vigorous condition for a race so depressed, and an ascertained capability to take care of themselves.

Those who know them best are least afraid of their being a burden on the North, whenever the whole five millions become free. They will not emigrate to any considerable extent; and they will not settle in the North while there is an opening for them in the South,—which there always will be. In the South they are at present indispensable; and there is every prospect of their continuing to be so: and they love the climate. I have not space to describe the various free settlements now already prospering under the superintendence of white guardians, commissioners, and teachers; nor the military training which large numbers are receiving for garrison duty in the South. It must suffice at present that there is plenty for everybody to do; and that there is a general understanding that the schemes of deportation talked of are mere tubs to occupy the pro-slavery whale for a time. If the Colonisation Society has not deported in half a century the increase of one single year, though founded and sustained by the whole power of the slaveholders, it needs no proving that five millions cannot be removed. If they would go (which they will not), the Southern gentry could not spare them. The whole project, whether discussed by whites or blacks, is a mere convenience for gaining time, while the citizens are tending towards an agreement. Meanwhile, the national institution of slavery is at an end; Delaware, Missouri, and Western Virginia are in full preparation for a similar deliverance; and General Hunter has effected complete emancipation over a portion of Georgia.

If it should be asked how the event of the 16th of April can be greater than that of serf emancipation in Russia (supposing the latter completed), the answer is plain. Russian serfage is not nearly so low an order of bondage as negro-slavery: it involves no slave trade, with the barbaric wars which feed that trade in Africa: and, above all, it is not an anomaly, like chattel-slavery in a democratic republic. However necessary its abolition may be to the social progress of the Russians, it has not undermined any existing liberties, nor corrupted a once high national character, as American slavery has done. There has been more mischief in five millions of American slaves than in fifty millions of Russian serfs: and, when the end of each bondage shall have arrived, the Russian people will have only to advance in their civilisation, while the Americans have to recover a fearful extent of lost ground.

The great step is taken: and they and we are now side by side as Christian nations, instead of having a bottomless gulf between us. It was a great day which closed that gulf.—*From the Mountain*

❖ ❖ ❖

Part Three

JOURNAL ARTICLES

❖ ❖ ❖

INTERPRETING THE SECTIONAL DIVIDE

1854–1857

Martineau's flexibility as a writer and her ability to adapt her style to a variety of genres and formats is perhaps best seen in her longer pieces written for journals. The following selections highlight her capacity to envision the significance of contemporary events through a broader vision—the "big picture" of world events and, especially, of history. One of Martineau's strongest gifts is that of history writing, a tendency evident in even the shortest newspaper leaders. "Interpreting the Sectional Divide, 1854–1857" offers in-depth analyses of three key political issues shaping the pre–Civil War debates: states' rights versus federal law ("Free-dom, or Slavery?"); legislative compromises aimed at placating all sides of the slavery debates but, in fact, satisfying no one ("A History of the American Com-promises"); and territorial expansionism ("'Manifest Destiny' of the American Union"). Implicit in these presentations is the view Martineau shared with the Garrisonians: that nothing less than immediate and universal emancipation would resolve America's social conflicts, as she might say, "let the pieces fall where they may."

"Freedom, or Slavery?"
Household Words, 1854

Given the journalistic tendencies both writers shared, it was inevitable that the paths of Harriet Martineau and Charles Dickens (1812–1870) would cross repeat-edly throughout their careers. Although Dickens declined Martineau's offer to write him letters of introduction for his 1842 American tour and rejected her "meddling" travel advice to Mrs. Dickens, he did prepare himself by reading her American travel books, which he pronounced "the best."[149] Anticipating their later relationship as editor and writer, Dickens became the first editor of London's *Daily News* (1846), for which Martineau began writing in 1852. His *Household Words* enjoyed the distinction of being a mass-distributed periodical that was affordable to lower-class readers yet able to maintain an aura of respectability attractive to the middle-class reading audience. Martineau wrote articles on various topics for the family-oriented *Household Words* between 1850 and 1855, when she resigned after a series of ideological disagreements with the editors, Dickens and William Henry Wills.[150]

As a working woman, Martineau resented Dickens's attitude toward women: "he ignored the fact that nineteen-twentieths of the women of England earn their bread . . .[claiming] the function of Women . . .[is] to dress well and look pretty, as an adornment to the homes of men" (1983, 2:419). Martineau also disagreed with Dickens's stand on the factory controversy in *Hard Times* (published serially in *Household Words*, 1854); her challenge to him in *The Factory Controversy* (1855)—which he termed her "vomit of conceit"—fueled the fire of their already contentious relationship. Finally, although she was herself no champion of organized religion, Martineau found Dickens's anti-Catholic bias offensive enough—as well as inappropriate for a family magazine—to resign her post.

According to Anne Lohrli, Dickens critiqued Martineau's grim determination to effect nothing less than "the enlightenment of mankind" (358); she, in turn, believed "the proprietors of *Household Words* grievously inadequate to their function, philosophically and morally; and they, no doubt, regard me as extravagant, presumptuous and impertinent" (1983, 2:418). She was right about this, although Dickens's actual words were: "there never was such a wrong-headed woman born—such a vain one—or such a Humbug."[151] Comically, Martineau's charge that Dickens was a "humanity monger" like his own character Mrs. Jellyby (*Bleak House*, 1852–1853) was countered by the rumor that this symbolic meddler, who is too absorbed with others' affairs to notice the chaos in her own life, is in fact modeled after Martineau herself.

"Freedom, or Slavery?" the only one of her *Household Words* articles to address the American situation, discusses the controversial Fugitive Slave Act (1850) through examining the 1854 case of Anthony Burns, who sought political asylum in Boston, Massachusetts. The act required all states to arrest and return runaway slaves to their masters, making it illegal to harbor blacks even in the free states and turning abolitionists who aided fugitives into federal outlaws. In its demonstration of the southern oligarchy's power to enforce its ideology even in a free state by forcing it to comply with a pro-slavery federal law, the Burns case drew international attention through the resulting stand-off between abolitionist activists and federal officers in the streets of Boston. The incident dramatized for many the fallacy behind the "patriotic" argument that the Union was sacred and the Constitution inviolable, despite the fact that its wording permits slavery. The Burns episode, which highlighted the conflict between states' rights—like the personal liberty law of Massachusetts—and federal laws like the Fugitive Slave Act, brought into sharp focus the matrix of issues steering the country inevitably toward war. The tone of "Freedom, or Slavery?" aims at a less educated audience in its vivid illustrations and dialogue, while its narrative unfolds by drawing parallels between America's first revolution and its impending "second revolution."

Writing of her sleeplessness over the Burns debacle, Martineau noted despairingly: "I am unable to cheer my American friends much about their country. . . . As a republican experiment it will prove a failure: but we may help to make some salvage out of the wreck. That is all I hope for, and if I have to give up that hope before I die, I will [continue to] work on the cause as long as I am able."[152]

. . .

[Martineau begins by outlining the events culminating in America's first revolution.]

. . . A great and memorable revolution was that, ushered in by these incidents. Incidents more solemn and more striking seem now, in this summer of eighteen hundred and fifty-four, to indicate that a change not less weighty is at hand. Massachusetts is now a sovereign State, and Boston is a metropolis. The inhabitants have now been trained in political action for eighty years; and that action has made them so proud of their nationality, such devout worshippers of their Federal Union, that any great and general commotion, political or social, must proceed from some prodigious cause, and involve vast consequences. What has just been, and is still, happening at Boston, does indeed deserve the most earnest attention of all who are interested in human welfare and social wisdom.

After Massachusetts became a sovereign State, her people abolished negro slavery—chiefly, it may be observed, through the sensible, persevering, and most virtuous efforts of a negro woman, called Mum Bet, to obtain her own freedom. She got it; and that of all her race followed. Many years after, Massachusetts made a law like that of England, whereby every slave that touches her soil becomes free. Other of the New England States made a similar law; and the inhabitants fondly believed that they had done with negro slavery for ever. But alas! They were in federal union with slave States, which have found means through the apathy or timidity, or worse, of the free States, to control the action of the whole in regard to slaves or free blacks, whom any fellow may choose to call slaves. For many years, the slaves have run away, by hundreds and thousands, to Canada; and the slave-catchers, who are paid according to the number they capture, have for some time been kidnapping more and more free persons of colour, and running them down to places whence it is difficult to recover them, and where many have been hidden for a long course of miserable years. This is an evil and crime which the Boston people could withstand without much difficulty before the passing of the Fugitive Slave Bill, but that measure is now driving the matter fast to an issue. It is enough to say in this place (where our business is with the social aspects of politics), that the Fugitive Slave Law is considered by the vast majority of the inhabitants of Massachusetts an unconstitutional act. It overbears the constitution of the state, and requires of the citizens—or may require of them at any moment—acts which are illegal according to the constitution under which they live. By that constitution, there can be no slave within their bounds; whereas, by the new law, they are punishable for treating a negro fugitive otherwise than as a slave, and for not delivering him up to his owner. Such a contrariety cannot go on; and the hour for decision—the hour for a choice between the two contradictory constitutions—is obviously approaching. How it has been hastened within a few weeks we will now see.

Ever since the bill passed which compels the giving up of every fugitive who is claimed unless he can prove his freedom on the spot, it has been known that the kidnappers sent by the owners, use very little scruple about identifying the persons sought. A letter, addressed to a kidnapper under arrest, and intercepted by that accident, explains the matter very fully. It avows that the loss occasioned by the running away of slaves is so serious that the owners must make up for it by catching any negroes they can get hold of; and this is done so often that no man, woman, or child with a dark skin feels safe, although legally as free as our readers and ourselves. The kidnappers get into the confidence of the negro shopman, waiter, or mechanic, who has no suspicion of their quality. They learn their personal marks, and the leading points of their history; they draw out their affidavits and descriptions; they arrest the man or woman at some helpless moment, and too often carry him or her away before the abolitionists and lawyers of the place know of the circumstances. One result of this outrageous abuse is, that the populations of the towns and villages are become more awake and ready, and more excitable when an arrest takes place. Every newspaper from the northern states now contains paragraphs, pointing out districts where kidnappers are supposed to be prowling; and the capture is becoming more difficult every season.

This state of things can no more be borne for a continuance than the neighbourhood of hostile Indians. Another result of the abuse is, that the negroes are becoming cautious; and more than cautious—cunning. There is a man named Jones, a market-gardener, at Pittsburg, in Pennsylvania, whose cunning wits have been much sharpened by the persecution of his race. Not long ago, two gentlemen (for these infamous dogs hunt in couples) made acquaintance with Jones, and were so very polite and kind as to lead him to suspect what sort of gentry they were. Following their lead, he let them know of some scar or mole or something under his clothes—your real fugitive is known by the weals of the whip—and looked mysteriously and talked evasively when they wanted to hear his story. Without having said so, he left them in the belief that he had come from Old Virginny within a year. As he expected, he was arrested that night by his new friends; and a very strong case they made of it next morning. Nothing could be more complete than their story and their proofs; and there were many in that crowded court—for in this case secresy was out of the question—who believed that the poor fellow before them would never be his own man again. . . . [Here follow details of Jones's trial, in which he is proven to be a free black; the kidnappers are arrested instead.]

Escaped slaves, however, have not often the cunning of Jones; and it is not to be wished that they should. Or, if cunning be, as it is, the vice of slaves (of all complexions and in all latitudes), it is less able in the ignorant slave than in the man who has tilled his own ground, and managed his own trade for thirty years.

ANTHONY BURNS,—the sufferer who has unconsciously brought old Massachusetts to its present pass,—has ruined himself by a step which has no cunning in it at all. He had run away from Virginia last winter, it is believed. It is proved that he was earning his living in Boston, on the first of last March. Wishing to let his family know of his safety, he wrote, or got written (for many slaves cannot read or write)—an account of himself and his whereabouts, and got the letter sent round by Canada. In his simplicity he supposed that was security enough; but all communications addressed to slaves are intercepted, and his master learned where he was. The master's name, be it known and remembered, is Suttle,—Charles F. Suttle; and his comrade in his heroic enterprise is called William Brent. Charles Suttle and William Brent set out immediately, and clapped Anthony Burns on the shoulder when he was cleaning clothes for his employer in Brattle Street, Boston, on the morning of Friday, the twenty-sixth of May last. Knowing that by the law of the state they could not, without inconvenient controversy, claim him as a slave, they charged him with pretended felony—an accusation which was dropped as soon as an offer was made to purchase his freedom.

He was taken to the court-house, where he remained all day, knowing nothing of what was doing outside. It was a busy day in Boston,—some of the citizens providing for the federal law being observed, and others for the older Massachusetts constitution not being infringed. Messrs. Suttle and Brent were arrested for attempted abduction; but, foreseeing this move, they were provided with bail, and were at once released. The largest building but one, we believe, in Boston (the exception being the Melodean, where Theodore Parker, a man of great reputation, preaches) is Faneuil Hall, wherein the revolutionary meeting and councils were held, and which is therefore called the cradle of Liberty. In that place, a meeting was held that night, and such speaking was heard as is hardly heard twice in a century by any nation. It was as if the trumpet of their memorable war hung by the gate, and some bold hand had raised it, and made it sound among all the hills of the old granite state. But the citizens were not prepared with any practical measure. Some were for fighting at once. Others were for a different kind of struggle; some for one thing—some for another, and none for submission to an infringement—and such an infringement as was threatened—of their state laws. In the midst the cry arose that the coloured people were breaking into the court house and off went the meeting to see. It was so; the black citizens were battering away at the court house door with a beam, which they used as a battering-ram. Several whites rushed to get hold of the beam, and wrought well with the negroes, till the door gave way. A pistol shot had been heard from within the hall; it was followed by more in the streets; and a shower of brickbats brought down the court house windows in shivers. Amid the rattle of glass, the roar of the crowd, and the popping of pistols, the heavy bang of the beam was heard till the door crashed down, and yet louder was the steady cry, repeated every minute by a group of leaders, "Rescue him!" Above all, just at half-past nine of that May night was heard the clang of the alarm bell.

The first who entered the court house were received with shots, and a waving of clubs from a posse of city officers, who were mustered on the stairs. Rushing back for the moment, the leaders were intercepted by a body of police who gained the steps, and successfully held the place. A special constable named Batchelder was killed in the entry by a pistol-shot. For want of a plan, and some sort of organization, and because many of Burn's best friends were averse to violence when they believed law to be on their side, nothing more was done that night. The police made some arrests; and, by midnight, the military were posted in the square. The affrighted slave-owner now offered to sell his slave—aided in his resolution, probably, by finding that there was a serious mistake in his affidavit. He had sworn that Burns ran away on the twenty-fourth of March, whereas there was abundant evidence of his being at work at Boston on the first of March. The money was instantly raised: but when it was brought to Suttle, he had changed his mind, and refused to sell his man for any price. There is no doubt that this was in consequence of directions from Washington; for the President sent letters under his own hand, desiring that no expense should be spared in carrying out the law of the United States. Thus the revolutionary character of the transaction was avowed by the President of the Republic itself.

On the Saturday the court-house was found to be guarded, within and without, by the whole military force of the district—even the soldiers from the fort, the cadets, and the marines from the Navy-yard, had been summoned in the night. The poor slave was handcuffed and strongly guarded. His countenance was wistful and sad in the extreme. He no doubt knew that the last fugitive who had been carried back had been flogged every day with the greatest number of lashes that human patience could endure without death, for an example to runaways. Alas! It may too probably be so with himself, even now.

His counsel obtained a delay until Monday to prepare his defence; and the rest of Saturday was occupied with the coroner's inquest on Batchelder, and the committal of the ringleaders.

On Sunday, that largest place in Boston, mentioned above, was crowded—clustered with people wherever they could hang on; and if we ever did copy sermons into this publication, we would give Mr. Parker's discourse of that day, with the past and coming week for his text. It reads like a Lutheran denunciation of the times of the Reformation; and if we could say anything stronger in description of it, we would. Among the audience were two leading abolitionists, whom their townsmen were glad to see in safety. Their houses, and that of Mr. Parker, were saved, by a strong police muster, from destruction by the partisans of the kidnappers. In every pulpit in Boston that day lay a slip of paper, requesting, in the name of Burns, the prayers of the congregation on behalf of one in sore distress. This was done at Burns's special request, in his tribulation. On this day, too, the people of colour held a secret meeting, and afterwards put out a handbill, imploring that nobody would believe the report that Burns would be purchased; and entreating that his release might not be prevented by belief in such a lie. They were but too right. All that day handbills were circulating in the furthest part of the state, requesting all who loved the liberties of Massachusetts to come into Boston, armed only with the arms that God gave them, to see what was doing there; and on Monday they came pouring in, these sons of the pilgrims, and sons of the declarers of independence. Some were there already from a distance of eighty miles. The summons reads like a solemn call to vigilance over national liberties; and as such, we have no doubt, it will stand in history hereafter; and a future generation will emphasize the last line: "Come,—but, this time, with only such arms as God gave you." The yeomanry who did not come, staid to hold meetings in all the townships; and the excitement immediately rose to a pitch never before witnessed since the grave closed over Washington.

The pleadings were protracted by every possible device till Wednesday evening; when the commissioner promised judgment on the Friday morning. Every one knew but too well what that decision would be; for the misstatement of date was slurred over as an incident of no consequence. A steamer stole up, and was refused a place at one wharf after another, when it was whispered that this was the vessel that was getting up its steam to carry away Burns. A wharfinger at last let a wharf without communicating the knowledge thereof to the owners, who immediately discharged him; but he was soon snugly harboured in a good post in the Custom House.

Other preparations for the verdict were made. The court square was cleared, and cannon were planted. The military lined the way to the harbour, and gathered about the door, to receive the slave within their hollow square.

Other preparations were also made. Twenty thousand people filled the side-pavements, besides those who thronged every wharf but one, and the multitude who clustered to the very topmasts of every ship in the harbour.

When the doom was pronounced, down dropped the flags of the Union and of the State, hung with black. The shops were shut. The balconies and windows were filled with women dressed in mourning. One of the hardest things for the citizens to bear was the volunteer offer of an artillery troop of seventy-five Irishmen to come into the city and control the inhabitants by force of arms. For our part we are not very sorry that our ex-patriots have thus shown to all sympathisers how they carry their practice of making bulls into their social conduct. Throughout the townships of the interior, the bells were tolled as for a great public calamity.

The moment came. Burns appeared on the steps, a slave. Not often has the dignity of that misfortune been so blazoned. Before him went dragoons, marines, guards, artillery, the gun of the latter being the only carriage in the streets; and the ear-piercing hiss, and the wary execration, went on rising and redoubling from street to street. Nowhere was it louder than at the Exchange, where the great merchants of the city stood. That this book of Wrong and Infamy will end here, we think no one can believe who has studied the incidents of the first American Revolution, or the character of the

Sons of the Pilgrims; a character which lies deep and firm under all such ac-
cretions of a less noble quality as have concealed it for a time. It is well that
for one while the oppressor had his own way—a complete enjoyment of law
and order, as he calls it. Can there be a doubt that, next time, Massachusetts
will be ready; every man convinced to his own mind what law he is living
under; every citizen prepared to sustain that law; and all good men agreed as
to the action to be taken? Meanwhile, the free blacks are flying to Canada,
feeling that there is no safety for them in Massachusetts, free-born citizens
of that so-called free state though they be!

But let them take courage, and be of good heart. If there were men, once,
who refused to harbour King George's stamped paper, and who emptied the
India Company's tea into the dock, and who supported those acts at Lexington and Bunker's Hill, there are descendants of those men, now who will
refuse to be made the slave-catchers of the planters, and will insist on the
practical working of their own noble law, that every slave who touches the
soil of Massachusetts becomes free.

A History of the American Compromises

London: John Chapman, 1856

Originally published in the *Daily News* and reprinted as a pamphlet by John
Chapman, *A History of the American Compromises* aimed to clarify what was to
British readers a confusing array of legislative bills governing American slavery politics. As its title indicates, this article presents the history of relevant policies from
the inception of the Republic through 1856, when the intensification of social and
political events pointed to the inevitability of civil war. The first document under
consideration is the Constitution which, as Garrison and others made clear, is so
worded as to permit individual states to sanction slavery; it was on this crucial
point that pro-slavers defended slavery, abolitionists demanded emancipation, and
republicans insisted on preservation of the Union at all costs. Martineau notes that
one of the great ironies of this document is that, of the eighty-two articles in the
Constitution, only two deal with slavery. This suggests that the issue was comparatively insignificant yet, given the number of policies necessary to regulate the institution, the reverse was clearly the case.

Among the topics Martineau discusses in this brief *History* are: southern slaveholders' collective power in Congress which, because of the nonvoting numbers of
blacks they represented, tipped the balance of power away from northern policy
makers; the Fugitive Slave Law; the annexation of states that might later decide to
adopt slavery; the Missouri Compromise and the Texas "question"; the destruction of
family values by prohibiting marriage among slaves and separating families through
slave auctions; the Seminole War, which effectually put Union soldiers "in the service of the South"; and the necessity for abolishing slavery in Washington, D.C., the
seat of the federal government. This last event Martineau believed was crucial for
bringing the slavery issue to resolution. In her view, the "Idolatry of the Union,"
causing some to seek solidarity over secession at any cost—or, as her title indicates,

compromise—and "Mammon-worship" or economic greed, obstructed the abolition of slavery as surely as the southern "planter interest" itself. Providing a revelatory contrast between Martineau's travel writing and newspaper leaders, this extended article aptly displays her strongest literary gifts—politics and history writing.[153]

. . .

The existing condition of affairs in the United States naturally sets people inquiring of one another about the meaning of the prominent terms of the great domestic controversy; and there are few who can give a precise answer. "What is the "MISSOURI COMPROMISE?" "What is the NEBRASKA Bill?" "Why is the settlement of KANSAS so critical?" These are the questions about which everybody has some idea, but which require an accurate answer before the interior politics of the AMERICAN UNION can be so clearly understood as they ought now to be by every Englishman. A brief statement of the historical antecedents of the controversy which has at present assumed the character of civil war, may supply a want; and I therefore propose to sketch the history of "the Difficulty" of the great Republic, from the time when the founders of the Constitution brooded over it till now.

It has been truly said that America is the country of two ideas, and that those ideas are—SLAVERY and ANTI-SLAVERY. My short narrative will show how the leading points of American government and policy have been determined by those ideas, from the first days of the Republic till now; and a more detailed history would exhibit the same truth in regard to the minutest ramifications of the political action of the United States. It was by an early recognition of this truth that the Abolitionists were rendered at once confident in their own ground, hateful to idolators of the Union, and formidable to rulers who dreaded change. The Abolitionists knew that the great modifying anomaly of their social structure must come into question some day; and they were feared and hated for saying so. The day has arrived, and the entire nation is openly divided into two sections,—pro-slavery and anti-slavery.

These ideas were in the minds of the founders of the Republic, scarcely less prominently, perhaps, than they are now in the minds of President Pierce and of every public man in the Union. The difference was, that the first set of men used no disguise about their difficulty, while the efforts to conceal it have been redoubled in the most recent times, and the more eagerly in proportion to the growth of political danger. Franklin made the broadest abolition speeches in the Pennsylvania Legislature, without apparently exciting either surprise or wrath. Washington declared that the possession of slaves was a heavy weight on his mind; and he made testamentary dispositions designed to secure their emancipation. Jefferson's avowal on this subject is perhaps the most celebrated of his sayings:—"God has no attribute which can take part with the American slaveholder." Franklin was President of the Abolition Society of Pennsylvania, and Washington and Jefferson were members. This society has existed ever since; and the present Secretary is the Quaker Confessor, Passmore Williamson, whose imprisonment made so much noise last year. The danger of the position has much increased since Franklin's time. When the Republic was founded, Slavery existed over nearly the whole territory. Its effects were so mischievous, even in those days of small things, that there could be no doubt of future trouble, first bringing on and then determining the alternative whether to abolish or continue it, amidst fears and perils on either hand. On this account the Constitution was arranged with the best skill available at the time. The Constitution took the least possible notice of Slavery, and gave powers to the separate States, and balanced those powers in the Central Government, in a manner which might enable it to evade the future difficulty, and to throw the settlement of it on the separate States.

Thus there were, in the original Constitution, only two clauses which had any relation whatever to Slavery. This is a point so important to the understanding of the subsequent history, that I cannot too strongly draw attention to these two clauses, and to the fact that there were no more. "We," says the preamble of the American Constitution, "the People of the United States, in order to form a more perfect union, establish justice, ensure domestic tranquillity, provide for the common defence, promote the general welfare, and secure the blessings of liberty to ourselves and our posterity, do ordain and establish this Constitution for the United States of America." The Constitution of 1787 consists of seven Articles, each divided into *Sections;* and the sections again into clauses; and of this last minute division, consisting of eighty-two, only two have any reference to Slavery. The reason is not the insignificance of the subject, but its difficulty. The first of the clauses I shall quote is obviously of extreme political importance. It was in the hope that the separate States would manage the difficulty, each for itself,—that it was so concisely dealt with in the fundamental document of the Republic. The significant clause I refer to is in the second Section of the first Article. The clause decrees the proportion of representatives to population; viz., not less than one for every thirty thousand; and then ensues the remarkable provision for reckoning slaves among the constituency. After giving the suffrage to "free persons," excluding Indians, this clause enacts that there shall be added "to the whole number of free persons, three-fifths of all other persons," that is, of slaves. A free white population does not flourish in the presence of Slavery; and, therefore, slave territory was to be endowed with a fictitious constituency of no less than three-fifths of the slave population. The obvious difficulty was in prospect that, sooner or later, somebody would insist on knowing whether the slaves were or were not men, with social capacities. If they were, they had a right to citizenship in a democratic Republic; and if they were not, they could be only a sham constituency. The further difficulty arose long ago, and is yearly on the increase; that the Northern citizens find the Southern representation to be out of all proportion to the population; while, on the other hand, the South, exasperated at the rapid growth of Northern populations, and at the danger of being swamped in Congress, is driven to territorial aggression and to encroachment on the Constitution, to keep up its numbers in the Senate at Washington. Liable to these dangers, however, the clause was established; and three-fifths of the slaves are reckoned as free men in the particular of supplying representatives to Congress. That such a provision should have been submitted to by the Northern citizens would be inexplicable if we did not remember that Slavery was nearly universal when the Constitution was framed. That it should be still submitted to is wonderful enough; but it will not be for long, judging by recent applications to Congress for a rectification of this basis of the Southern suffrage. . . . Such as the clause was, however, in 1787, it is now, though the slaveholders are only 350,000 in a population of 27,000,000. It is by this clause alone that they have been enabled to balance the representation of the free states in Congress. That they have been permitted to overbalance it is due to the idolatry of the Constitution, which has lowered the republican spirit, and sapped the political virtue of the North.

The other clause bearing on Slavery is the third clause of Section 2, Article IV, and is thus worded:—"No person held to service or labour in one State under the laws thereof, escaping into another, shall, in consequence of any law or regulation therein, be discharged from such service or labour, but shall be delivered up on claim of the party to whom such service or labour may be due." This is the Fugitive Slave Law of 1787. It must be again remembered, that when it was made, the States were all slave States, and that there was no likeness between their mutual relation and that of existing States which have opposite interests, from some leaving abolished, while others have eagerly and pertinaciously retained, the "institution" which has become "peculiar." Such was, in regard to slavery, the Constitution signed by Washington as President, and by all the most eminent of his political comrades, as representatives of their respective States.

Each State, it must be remembered, sends two members to the Senate. The largest and the smallest have the same representation in the Senate; while the members of the other House nearly correspond in proportion with the population. As the Northern States abolished Slavery one after the other, the South became alarmed lest the slave States should fall into a minority in the Senate, as it was too clear that they must sooner or later in the other House. As long as the slave States can preserve a majority in the Senate, or a mere equality, together with a President whose veto on any troublesome law, or repeal of a law, can be depended on, the House of Representatives is powerless. For a quarter of a century there has not been a President who was not actually or virtually pledged to veto any law unacceptable to the South; and the key to the entire policy of the United States, domestic and foreign, for that course of years, is the effort of the South to maintain a majority in the Senate at Washington. This is the explanation of the MISSOURI COMPROMISE, and of its repeal; of the political failure of every eminent man in the United States since the close of the first series of Presidents; and of the origin of every American war of late years; and of the formation and breaking-up of every political party; and of the ill-success of the free-soil representatives, headed by Mr. Sumner; and, finally, of the Kansas controversy, and its exasperation into civil war.

The distribution, appropriation, and administration of the Public Lands, which happen to be the ground on which the battle of republican principle is going forward, was a serious prospective difficulty when the Constitution was framed. Geographical ignorance has been, and still is, the cause of many wars, and an obstacle to arrangements for peace, as the Commissioners of the Allies in Bessarabia seem to be finding now. Never was there a more unmanageable case of geographical ignorance than that of our old English Government, when it gave to its colony of Virginia a patent for lands extending to—there is no saying where, as similar wild grants to other colonies clashed with that to Virginia. All that could be ascertained was, that the Virginia patent claim extended to the Northern Lakes, and away northwest of the Ohio, "to the Pacific." The States began to quarrel about their lands after the Revolution; and as there was no standard of reference by which their claims might be divided, Washington advised that each State should fix its own boundaries, and then throw the residue into a common stock, to be explored, surveyed, and used as the nation expanded. Virginia led the way in this sensible and honourable procedure. She fixed her own boundary, and the General Government made terms with the people resident on the excluded lands which lay northwest of the Ohio. The residents and General Washington were entirely agreed as to the evil of Slavery; and the terms were, that it should never be established on that territory, and that, when the due population was attained, the territory should be divided into States, which were not to be less than three nor more than five. This compact was made in 1787; and the power of the Federal Government to preclude and prohibit Slavery on new territory was not called in question.

It is scarcely known, or not at all remembered, in England, while Americans are glad to forget it, that a struggle took place twenty years ago between the General Government and the State of Michigan, which foreshadowed that of Kansas of the present day. The Michigan difficulty, ostensibly relating to the distribution of lands in 1787, really arose, like the Missouri and Kansas conflicts, out of the ambition and jealousy of preponderance in the Senate. Ohio, anxious for admission into the Union, found the frontier line between her territory and that of Michigan "not convenient"; and, Michigan being in no condition to insist on the guaranteed boundary, was compelled to yield a portion of her domain. Ohio was admitted as a sovereign State in 1803, and the boundary she desired was ratified by Congress. Within a dozen years, Indiana followed the example of Ohio, found the guaranteed boundary inconvenient, and obtained a ratification by Congress of a boundary laid down by herself. On this occasion, however, some compensation was offered to Michigan, a slice of territory from Wisconsin being placed at her disposal. But this slice was on the further shore of Lake Michigan, which is the natural boundary of the State of that name; and there was little doubt that, from this real and indisputable "inconvenience," the residents on that section of land would prefer belonging to Wisconsin, whenever Wisconsin became a State. The decision of this kind of dispute belongs to the Supreme Court of the United States; and to that tribunal the business would have been left, but for the ever-present jealousy of the slave States about preponderance in the Senate. While awaiting the time when the Supreme Court could hear the cause (that is, on the admission of all the parties into the Union,) Michigan was borne down on every side. Ohio and Indiana wished to keep the territory they had acquired, and did not want the question to be stirred,—whether the original allotment had been constitutionally ignored by Congress: and the whole body of slave States desired to give a piece of Wisconsin to Michigan, in order to render the Wisconsin territory too small to be divided into two States, as it might be by a *proviso* in the original allotment, and was likely to be, if the Southern States pursued, on their part, a course of annexation of territory, for the manufacture of States, and for senatorial representation. When Michigan became qualified by a sufficient population to request admission to the Union, in 1834, she declared her discontent with the boundaries prescribed by Congress, and her intention of claiming, in the Supreme Court, the restitution of the original lines. She organized her State Government, and sent her senators to Washington for the session of 1835–1836. Her senators were allowed to witness the proceedings of Congress, but not to vote: and the next proceeding was one which fixed the attention of the whole Union on the dispute, and which should have precluded, by rousing a due indignation, the vital conflicts which must sooner or later follow political pusillanimity in such a case. Congress, moved by Southern influence, actually usurped the judicial functions of the Supreme Court, and undertook to decide the controversy, by proposing to admit Michigan into the Union, on condition of her surrendering all claim to the disputed lands. This was usurping the judicial function, deciding without evidence, and requiring a candidate State to lay down her rights on the threshold of Congress, as a fine on a benefit to which she had an unrestricted right. Two characteristic speeches of that date which came under my own knowledge laid open the real bearings of the dispute to the mind of a stranger. Ex-President Adams declared that Michigan had a stronger reason for retiring from the Union than South Carolina had ever had; and a South Carolina leader declared, in conversation, that he believed the claims of Michigan to be sound, but that he would rather strive against her admission as long as he lived, than give her opportunity to summon another sovereign State before the Supreme Court. There was, probably, an *arriere pensee* [hidden motive] in his mind about the convenience of so reducing the area of Wisconsin, as to disqualify it for division into two States.

The opportunity was a noble one for the young State. Her right course was to remain sovereign at home, but outside the Union. But some of her citizens lusted after the portion of surplus revenue which would fall to her share if she was a member of the Federation; others feared for the fortunes of the new canal; and others were nervous about war, though there was no necessity for war, when the dispute lay within the province of the Supreme Court. In 1836, Michigan bore her testimony honestly. She refused to enter the Union on unconstitutional terms. But the struggle was too unequal. A tumultuous minority, aided by trickery at Washington, made concessions in the name of the people at large, and Michigan became a member of the Union a few months after; throwing in her lot with the rest for future glory or shame, instead of standing out for the glory all alone. While she was still too young to protest or resist under the aggressions of her neighbours (that is, four years after she was robbed by Indiana,) the Missouri Compromise was passed; and it was regarded as immutable and eternal, when Michigan became one of the United States.

By 1820, there was a balance of free and slave States; and here we meet again the struggle for the majority in the Senate. Northern men desired that the inhabitants of any new territory should choose their institutions for themselves; but it was the resolute purpose of the South, either to secure the establishment of Slavery in the candidate State, or to get a new slave State admitted for every free one. On the first alternative they were beaten; the second appeared to be the only feasible one. It seemed probable that new States would be admitted in pairs for an indefinite time; but circumstances compelled a coming to the point in the case of the admission of Missouri. The Missouri Compromise was believed by all but the most far-sighted of the citizens of the Union to have settled "the Difficulty" for ever.

In 1803, Bonaparte sold to the United States the whole territory which belonged to the French in America, and which was called Louisiana, though the State which now bears that name was a very small part of it. Bonaparte despaired of defending the Mississippi from the British, and was delighted to sell the territory for 80,000,000 francs. The southernmost portion of this territory was presently erected into the State of Louisiana. In 1819, another portion, not contiguous to Louisiana, but bordering on the Missouri as well as the Mississippi, applied for admission into the Union, when duly peopled; and the question of the terms of admission of the State of Missouri was debated in 1819.

By that time the free and slave States were, as I have said, equal; and desperate was the struggle to establish Slavery in Missouri, or to exclude it by the terms of admission. There was nothing in the climate and productions of Missouri to justify a special resort to negro labour; but it was otherwise with the new acquisition of Florida, and with the territory of Arkansas, a portion of the French lands lying between Louisiana and Missouri. Arkansas and Florida were only waiting for the admission of Missouri to qualify and apply for their own admission; and the South was determined to have them all on the side of her policy, and thus to obtain a majority of six in the Senate. The North, and the leading statesmen of the time, contended that the Constitution conferred a power to make conditions, on matters of fundamental republican principle, with candidate States; and that such principle now required that the extension of Slavery to a new soil should be prohibited. The prohibition of Slavery on the distribution of the Virginia lands in 1787 proves, as I remarked before, that the power was no matter of doubt at that time; yet it was now contested, in the teeth of as many as survived of the very men who had made the Constitution and distributed the lands. The conflict was fierce; and it embittered the latter days of the patriots who yet survived—Jefferson, Jay, Adams, Marshall, and indeed all the old political heroes. "From the Battle of Bunker's Hill to the Treaty of Paris"[154] says Jefferson[155] to Adams, "we never had so ominous a question. I thank God I shall not live to witness its issue." Again, after the compromise:[156] "This momentous question, like a fire-bell in the night, awakened and filled me with terror. I considered it at once as the knell of the Union. It is hushed, indeed, for the moment. But this is a reprieve only, not a final sentence. A geographical line, coinciding with a marked principle, moral or political, once conceived and held up to the angry passions of men, will never be obliterated; and every new irritation will mark it deeper and deeper." Jay wrote, "I concur in the opinion that Slavery ought not to be introduced nor permitted in any new States; and that it ought to be gradually diminished, and finally abolished in all of them." The most cautious of politicians, Judge Story, never threw himself into any great public question but once; and this was the occasion.[157] He spoke in public on behalf of the absolute prohibition of Slavery, by express act of Congress, in all the Territories, and against the admission of any new slave-holding State, except on the unalterable condition of the abolition of Slavery. He grounded his argument on the Declaration of Independence, and on the Constitution of the United States, as well as on the radical principle of Republicanism. When the result was trembling in the balance, and the issue seemed to depend on the votes of six waverers, Judge Story predicted a settlement by compromise—a present yielding to the South on condition that it should be for the last time; this "last time," however, involving the admission of the two waiting States, whose climate and productions afforded an excuse for Slavery to which Missouri could not pretend. A short and pregnant sentence, in a letter of Judge Story's, shows that a new light had begun to break in upon him at Washington, which might make him glad of such a compromise, as a means of gaining time for the preservation of the Union. After relating the extraordinary pretensions of the South, he concludes thus:[158] "But of this say but little; I will talk about it on my return: but our friends in general are not ripe for a disclosure of the great truths respecting Virginia policy." Republican citizens ought to be always "ripe" for all possible "disclosures"; and if Judge Story and others had had due faith in their countrymen, a timely exposition of the truth might have saved a long course of guilt and misery, and have precluded the civil war which seems likely to solve the question after all. When the compromise was effected, he wrote to Mr. Everett,[159] "We have foolishly suffered ourselves to be wheedled by Southern politicians until we have almost forgotten that the honours and the Constitution of the Union are as much our birthright and our protection as of the rest of the United States. . . . I trust that the Missouri question will arouse all the spirit of New England. All the

South and West stood in solid column, while the Eastern States were thinned by desertion, and disgraced by the want of (military) commanders." Judge Story wrote to Lord Stowell, and sent him materials for a judgment, requesting his opinion in regard to the powers of Congress to impose a condition upon the admission of Missouri into the Union. But there was no real doubt of the existence of such a power; and when this became more and more apparent from day to day, the deficiency in argument was made up for by excess of passion; and almost every statesman in the country believed the Union to be on the verge of dissolution. At this moment Mr. Clay proposed such a compromise as Judge Story had anticipated.

Up to this time the slaveholders had pleaded that Slavery was an inherited institution; that it was imposed upon them—a necessary evil which they had no choice but to endure. This was Mr. Clay's usual plea; and yet it was well known that it was Mr. Clay who prevented his own State, Kentucky, from abolishing Slavery when the condition of her population would have enabled her to do it. And now, there was not the smallest pretence for introducing Slavery into Missouri. The inhabitants saw how well their opposite neighbours of Indiana and Illinois prospered under that prohibition of Slavery which was involved in the terms of cession of their land; and they would have acquiesced in a restriction which imposed no sort of hardship or disappointment at the moment; but Mr. Clay imposed slave institutions on them to please the South, and destroyed for ever the old plea, that Slavery was an inherited mischief, and not a cherished vice. He proposed an enactment that, on condition of Missouri being now admitted on Southern terms, Slavery should be henceforth prohibited for ever on all the territory recently acquired from France, lying north of 36′ 30′ north latitude—that is, of the southern boundary of Missouri. These are the terms:—"And be it further enacted, that in all that territory ceded by France to the United States, under the name of Louisiana, which lies north of 36′ 30′ north latitude, not included within the limits of the State contemplated by this act, Slavery and involuntary servitude, otherwise than in the punishment of crime whereof the parties shall have been duly convicted, shall be, and hereby is, prohibited for ever."

This is the celebrated Missouri Compromise, passed early in 1820. It needs no showing that the prohibition of Slavery, north of a certain line, determined its existence in new States south of that line; and Florida and Arkansas were soon admitted as slave Territories, and then as slave States. Among the first fruits of the arrangement was the Seminole War. The truth of that war, when disencumbered of the patriotic cant which invested it is this: By the law of all the slave States, where there is no legal marriage among the negroes, the children "follow the fortunes of the mother"—are the property of the owner of the mother. Many slaves escaped into Florida, and lived there among the swamps, and intermarried with the Seminole Indians. As soon as Florida entered the Union as a Territory the Southern slaveholders alleged that they were at war with the Seminoles, and demanded and obtained the aid of the Federal forces. Many fine young men were there among those troops who died in the swamps without knowing that they were used by the slaveholders for the purpose of recovering runaway slaves; and, yet more, of seizing the half-caste children of negro women married to Indians, on the legal plea that the children of slaves "follow the fortunes of the mother." This incident is only one in the long series which exhibit the free and prosperous North as the tool and the servant of the slaveholding and declining South. I could detail enough to fill volumes.

The experience of Michigan has shown how little reliance could be placed on compromises between the National Government and the separate States, when it was the interest of a strong party to violate them; and in the course of a dozen years from the passage of the Missouri Compromise, the General Government found how difficult it was to deal with the separate States when they, on their side, had a mind to "nullify" the decisions of Congress and the provisions of the Constitution. It must suffice here to say, that in 1829, the President found himself in the awkward predicament of having, in the first instance, encouraged Georgia to disobey a federal arrangement about the lands of the Cherokee Indians, and then finding other States follow the example. South Carolina "nullified" the acts of Congress about the tariff; and Virginia claimed the right, for every State, of interpreting the Constitution for itself, instead of deferring to the interpretation of the Supreme Court. If this were allowed, the Federal Government could not be secure for a day; and the President saw this when, in 1829, three States were on the point of seceding from the Union. I relate this now merely to account for Mr. Clay's second great Compromise, which was one of the most important political acts of its time, though its importance was merely temporary, and not of the vast significance of the Missouri Compromise.

At the close of 1832, all the preparations for civil war were complete. The United States' forces were marching down upon Charleston, and a sloop of war was in the harbour to protect the federal officers in the discharge of their duties. The South Carolinians, on the other hand, had collected their militia, levied funds for war, and put forth proclamations in defiance of those of the President. The real quarrel was about the rights of the General and State Governments; but South Carolina found it convenient to assume the stronger ground of free trade,—the immediate occasion of the dispute being the tariff. When the dissolution of the Union appeared inevitable, Mr. Clay, himself a Protectionist, proposed terms which all were glad to accept,—a regulation of the tariff, spread over a long course of years, which gave the victory to South Carolina, in regard to the lowering of duties, while it secured time to the General Government to provide against the recurrence of such dangerous conflicts. After that date (February, 1833) Mr. Clay was called the Saviour of the Union, his two Compromises having deferred the crisis which has come up again more than once since. Neither he nor his admirers seem thus far to have perceived that, in a federal republic, such compromises can never be more than postponements of difficulty. Before he died, he had learned the lesson.

The South Carolina Compromise had no further connexion with the vital Land and Labour controversy than this:—That South Carolina, harassed and mortified by the decline of her strength and importance, chose to attribute her adversity to the prosperity of the North, instead of to its real cause—the bad quality of slave labour. In her advocacy of free trade she was doubtless right, but not in taking for granted that free trade would render her prosperous without free labour. She gained her point of the ultimate reduction of the tariff, and has not found her affairs retrieved thereby. Her consequent irritation against the North, and resort to new enterprises of an unconstitutional kind, lead us back to the Missouri Compromise and the great Land Question, which it was to have settled for ever.

After the Missouri Compromise, the state of affairs was this:—The oldest slave States were becoming impoverished under the natural and invariable operation of "the peculiar institution." Virginia was yearly lapsing into wilderness, and depending more and more on slave-breeding for existence. North Carolina was sunk past retrieval, and others were declining; new territory was wanted for products and population, as well as for keeping up numbers in the Senate; the North could no longer be looked to; beyond the Ohio, the land was pledged to free institutions; there remained only the Far West, beyond Arkansas, and south of 36 deg. 30 min. north latitude, of American territory; but to the south-west there was Texas, and beyond Texas, Mexico. The first American settlers in Texas were farmers, who had gone thither to escape from the curse of slave institutions, and who tilled their lands with their own hands, rejoicing that Slavery had been abolished in Texas and Mexico. Southern adventurers followed them; and by the "peculiar methods" now so familiar to the observers of American, as also of Russian, aggression, they first stirred up mischief, then interposed to put it down, then offered protection, and at length proceeded to the act of annexation. I need not relate the story of the annexation of Texas; everybody knows the facts, though few are aware of the origin and bearings of the enterprise.

As soon as it was known that the South proposed to divide Texas into five states, sending ten Senators to Congress, the inhabitants of the less sophisticated and most rural Northern States determined to be even with their rival. Natural as is the ambition to belong to a large new State, with a view to its future importance, the settlers in the North-western territories resolved rather to cut up their free lands into five or more States than to allow the thinly-peopled South a preponderance in the Senate. An equality there, with a pro-slavery President, was bad enough, since it enabled the South to throw out every measure which did not suit her institutions. A decisive majority in the Senate would overawe the House of Representatives, so as to leave no choice to the North but to be chained to the wheels of the triumphal car, of which the slave-driver would be the charioteer. It may thus be seen how the vital American controversy is determined to the new lands, within and beyond the frontier—honestly American, or Mexican, Costa Rican, or other.

There was, however, another center of action. The Congressional District of which Washington is the capital, is wholly and absolutely under congressional government. It is a territory of sixteen miles square, ceded by Maryland and Virginia for federal purposes. In the great struggle for supremacy, the struggle, as Sumner puts it, *whether Liberty shall be sectional and Slavery national, or the reverse,* the political position of this District of Columbia must be of high importance. If there could be an exact balance in the two Houses, and perfect impartiality in the President, Slavery would still be a national institution while it existed in the District, and particularly if the sale of slaves went on within its boundaries. The Abolitionists, who rose into notice (as a moral sect, not a political party) in 1832, began their enterprise by pertinacious petitioning for the abolition of Slavery in the District of Columbia. The consequence was, as my readers can scarcely need to be reminded, that the right of petition itself was suspended. After this, no man in the whole Union could pretend to consider "the Difficulty" as anything less than all important. The defence of the right of petition by ex-President Adams, on the floor of the House of Representatives, in 1837, is a fine passage of history. In 1835, Mr. Clay, Mr. Calhoun, and other Southern leaders, were, or pretended to be, confident that the subject of Slavery would never be discussed in Congress: and they thought they had secured the fulfilment of their own prophecy when they had obtained the suppression of the right of petition. But they merely changed the course of action of the Abolitionists, and strengthened their hands by furnishing them with the argument that the whites were now made slaves by the deprivation of their constitutional liberties in Congress. In ten years from the suppression of the right of petition, not only had the right been restored, but the Southern policy received its first decided check by the rejection of a proposal to extend the line of the Missouri Compromise to the Pacific Ocean; that is, to establish Slavery everywhere south of that line. It now appears probable that before the second ten years are over, the South will either have succumbed to the true republican policy, or have been repudiated by the North,—so rapid has been the progress of the question which was never to be mentioned in Congress.

In January, 1842, the first petition for the dissolution of the Union was presented to Congress by ex-President Adams, the ground assigned being the tyrannous supremacy of the South, which involved the whole Union in the disgrace and mischief of slave institutions. This was from a town in Massachusetts. In 1844, the legislature of Massachusetts sent to Congress resolutions in favour of an amendment of the Constitution, by which the element of slave representation should be removed, and the electoral basis of the Southern States made the same with that of the Northern. These moves excited the Southern legislatures to extreme insolence, such as that of returning the copy of the resolutions sent. The annexation of Texas was next carried with a high hand, after a delay of some years, caused by the noble resistance and exposure made by Dr. Channing, in his celebrated Letter to Mr. Clay. During this time the Abolitionists were suffering to extremity: now the burning of their houses or public halls; now the destruction of their commerce, or the professional prospects of their children; and now, public whippings, or tarring and feathering; and, in more than one case, death by assassination. The original group, however, steadily declined political action, not only from a deep sense and long observation of the uncertainties of political issues in their country, but because they could not qualify for Congress by taking an oath of complete fidelity to the Constitution, which it was their object to annul, in preparation for a better. Those Abolitionists who did not feel themselves so restricted became the Free-soil Party; and some of their leaders, with Mr. Sumner at their head, entered Congress. It will be seen at once, that their object is not the abolition of Slavery, as incompatible with democratic republicanism, but its limitation within present bounds. They will be satisfied if Slavery is only sectional, instead of national. They contended for the Wilmot proviso, which prohibited Slavery in all territories acquired from Mexico;[160] and they have found plenty of occupation during the more recent struggles to plant down Slavery in all new States; but they never have been, and never can be a powerful party, for want of a sounder and broader basis than they profess. They have been defeated in Congress in every instance, except that of California; and their success in that case was merely nominal. Mr. Brooks has at length tried knocking the party on the head in the Person of its representative, Mr. Sumner; but it was scarcely worth his while, now that there is in the other House a majority of representatives who go for more than the preservation of things as they are. But description or discussion of Political parties does not fall within my province. I am writing of certain Compromises, and not of those who framed and enacted them.

The next first-class Compromise was that of 1850. Before that date, the signs of pressure on pro-slavery champions became visible. Mr. Clay proposed a scheme (impracticable, of course) for gradual emancipation in Kentucky, which, but for him, would have been as free as Ohio for thirty years past. Col. Benton, of Missouri, opposed the introduction of slavery into new territories. California, with Col. Fremont for her champion and spokesman, was allowed to legislate for herself on the great question, and decided against Slavery. Lastly, the slave market was removed from the District of Columbia. Sanguine people at a distance believed that all was now going on well; but in fact, the crash of ruin was actually visiting statesmen and their parties. We need but name the Fugitive Slave Law, to show that the South would yield nothing without a large consideration. In fact it was the North which yielded everything. Southern citizens have carried their slaves into California without hindrance: and as for the slave-trade in the District, it is simply removed beyond the frontier (which cannot be more than eight miles distant in any direction), and it is rather an evil than a good that the scandal is removed from under the eyes of Northern men. In the other scale, there was the Fugitive Slave Bill, which was carried over the heads of the Free States, whose constitutions are wholly irreconcilable with this law. Its unconstitutional character, from its encroachments on state rights, is, we believe, uncontested. Its results are seen in the affrays produced wherever slave-catchers have appeared; in the imprisonment of Quakers, clergymen, and magistrates; in Boston being in a state of siege for the first time since the revolutionary war; in the assertion of *Habeas Corpus* against the new law; in the sending of thirty pieces of silver to the commissioner who delivered up Burns; and finally, in the passage and re-affirmation of the Personal Liberty Bill of Massachusetts first, and then of Ohio, by which the two States are placed virtually outside the pale of the Union. Meantime, the escape of slaves to Canada, prodigious before, has been on the increase ever since; and this loss has reacted on the mind of the South, stimulating the desire for a fresh and more remote territory, where the "peculiar institution" may have another chance.

The last of Mr. Clay's compromises should be stated with some precision, as it is that about which Englishmen are the most anxious,—regarding it as the first stage of the troubles which now threaten the speedy dissolution of the Union in earnest. The causes of trouble were, in fact, all in existence; and the attempt to compromise them simply made them more manifest. There was sufficient evidence by this time that Mr. Clay's method was mere quackery; but in the stress of difficulty, when the South was declining and discontented, in spite of her predominance at Washington, and her aggressions on neighbouring territories, the great Western leader was applied to once more for his nostrum. With all confidence and complacency he set to work to prepare it in January, 1850. These were the terms—

California was to be admitted into the Union with her anti-slavery constitution; and the slave market in the District of Columbia was to be removed beyond the frontier. The worth of this last so-called concession I have indicated. As to the former, Colonel Fremont (the present candidate for the Presidentship) had taken care that California should remain, as far as her laws were concerned, free soil; while there was no interdict upon the residence of slaveholders and their negroes in the new State. This was all on the one side. On the other, there were the following provisions—Two other candidate States—New Mexico and Utah—were to be admitted without any prohibition of Slavery; the south-western boundary of Texas was to be extended to Rio Grande; and a portion of the debt of Texas was to be paid on condition of her ceasing to claim a region of New Mexico. The maintenance of Slavery in the District of Columbia was to be guaranteed to the inhabitants as long as they desired to keep it; and the interstate slave-trade was to be sanctioned till the respective States should themselves forbid it. These last stipulations were made malignant by the addition of a stringent Fugitive Slave Law, which made the citizens of the northern States slave-catchers, and their magistrates kidnappers, in the service of the South. The first Fugitive Slave Law was mischievous enough, from the time when the northern States ceased to hold slaves; but this aggravation of it was sure to be found intolerable. When negroes were universally the working class, living in every house in the country, and transferred whenever convenient, it was natural that an arrangement should be made for their restoration when they ran from one service to another. But the case was altered when all the citizens north of a certain line abjured Slavery, and rendered it illegal. From that time, runaway negroes escaped, not from one service to another, but from slavery to freedom. Mr. Clay himself had said long before that "no *gentleman* would deliver up a slave seeking his freedom." Yet, under this Compromise, a system of law and office was devised which subjected every citizen to penalties who failed to deliver up a fugitive slave. The special judges appointed for the hearing of the cases on the arrest of negroes, were to be paid a large fee if they sent back the negro to the South, and a small fee if they decreed him a freeman. There were other provisions which no upright and humane citizen has found himself able to obey. It was in the apprehension of this, while aware that the South would not be satisfied with less, that Mr. Clay clubbed together provisions which seemed to have nothing to do with each other, and which procured for the whole measure the nickname of the Omnibus Bill. The violence with which the measure was argued is probably remembered by everybody; and especially that Mr. Foote, a senator from Mississippi, presented a pistol at the aged Colonel Benton, of Missouri, a slaveholder, but an unwilling convert by this time to free-soil doctrine. The course and conclusion of the debate were further rendered memorable by the extinction of some eminent political reputation. Mr. Webster had long been distrusted and despised by the best men of his own and other States; but he was still the pride of Massachusetts, and regarded as an eminent statesman by the Union generally. He now committed political suicide by supporting Clay's last Compromise. A great public meeting in Faneuil Hall, Boston, was held, on the ground that the citizens of all parties "had read with surprise, alarm, and deep regret, Mr. Webster's late speech on the subject of Slavery." Mr. Webster avoided meeting his constituents by taking office, and resigning his seat in the Senate; but he never held up his head again. When he permitted himself to be nominated for President, two years later, his last remaining hope was, that he had gained the favour of the South by his sacrifice of the rights and dignities of the North; and when the paucity of votes for him in the Convention showed that all was lost, he sank at once, and died brokenhearted, in October, 1852. Mr. Clay had preceded him, dying in June of the same year, and having failed also in the aims of his life—disappointed of the Presidentship, seeing his compromises unavailing, obscure and incompetent men raised over his head by the very spirit of compromise which he had fostered, and his country left exposed to all the old perils—perils aggravated by delay, and the long chafing of passions and sectional strifes. The third great leader, Mr. Calhoun, had died during the first discussion of Mr. Clay's new Compromise. Mr. Calhoun had never compromised. He was the champion (and a very sanguine one) of Slavery; yet he, with his dying breath, declared himself broken-hearted at the prospects of his State and of the whole South. Slavery was doomed, he said; and nothing but ruin, he was unhappily persuaded, could follow on the extinction of the "peculiar institution."

The Omnibus Bill did not pass when first proposed. It was thrown out by a great effort; but each of its provisions was afterwards carried by hook or by crook. For a year or two, the conflicts of the new law and the "higher law" of republican principle became more fierce, close, and portentous. More slaves ran away, and fewer citizens were willing to deliver them up. The southern claimants became exasperated, and they employed agents (or men claimed to be their agents) who kidnapped any negroes who came conveniently to hand. The South complained of being pillaged of their human property; and the North of being coerced to Southern interests. Clear-sighted men in all countries had said from the beginning that the Fugitive Slave Law would not work. The South was exasperated because it did not; and the North was resolved that it should not. Every public man who advocated it sank under the rising tide of popular indignation, and reappeared no more.

The same was the case after the passage of the Nebraska Bill—the last great outrage. The three leaders above mentioned were all dead before 1853, when the Nebraska Bill passed. Mr. Everett had never been relied on for strength of principle, nor for any degree of political courage. When the time of crisis came—the vote on the Nebraska Bill—he absented himself. His retirement was a natural consequence of the disgust of his constituents; and his political life was closed. While these well-known men were dropping out of sight, Mr. Sumner, and a very few companions of the Free-Soil Party were making an unavailing stand against the encroachments of the slave power in Congress. At the beginning of his second session in the Senate Mr. Summer and two comrades were excluded from all congressional committees, on the assigned ground that they were "outside of any healthy organization in the country." When the Kansas and Nebraska measures came on, their influence was found to be increased rather than diminished by this proscription by the slave power.

While the Fugitive Slave Law was working ill for the South, the other portions of the last Clay Compromise were more satisfactory in their operation. New Mexico and Utah were officered with Southern men in the interests of the slave power; and some slaves had been successfully carried into California. There was even a hope that California might be divided, and the southern half made into a slave State. Yet the South regarded with apprehension the stretch of northwestern territory which was protected from Slavery by the Missouri Compromise. Immigrants from Europe were traversing the Northern States by tens of thousands; and free labour was likely to flourish, and form States, and send new senators to Congress. The South, therefore, formed the audacious project of repealing the Missouri Compromise, of breaking down the barrier which the whole nation was sworn to maintain, to save the whole expanse of north-western territory from being inundated by Slavery.

When the Nebraska Bill was introduced for this concealed purpose, it appeared harmless enough. The proposal was, to establish a territorial government in Nebraska—the region which extends west and north-west of Missouri. Nothing was said about Slavery; and everybody but those in the plot supposed that there was no question of Slavery, as the entire region lay beyond the line appointed under the Missouri Compromise. By a sudden device the Bill was delayed on the last day of the session; and by the beginning of the next, the slave power had its policy ready. Mr. Douglas, a fitting tool for such instigators as are believed to have employed him, pleaded that New Mexico and Utah had been allowed to please themselves about admitting or rejecting Slavery; and that all other new States—and Kansas and Nebraska first—should have the same liberty of choice. To effect this, he moved that the Compromise of 1850 should be regarded as final and conclusive, and that the Missouri Compromise should be repealed. It was in January, 1854, that Mr. Douglas brought forward his proposal. It will be best to cite the words of both enactments, though that of 1820 has been already quoted. The Missouri Compromise provided thus:—

"And be it further enacted, that in all that territory ceded by France to the United States, under the name of Louisiana, which lies north of 36 deg. 30 min. north latitude, not included within the limits of the State contemplated by this Act, Slavery and involuntary servitude, otherwise than in the punishment of crime whereof the parties shall have been duly convicted, *shall be, and hereby is, prohibited for ever.*"

Mr. Douglas's amendment was this, (in the Bill for the Territorial organization of Nebraska):—

"And when admitted *as a State or States,* the said Territory, or any portion of the same, shall be received into the Union, *with or without Slavery, as their Constitutions may prescribe at the time of their admission.*"

The reader will at once observe that provision is here made for a plurality of States, in case of the admission of Slavery being carried; and he will foresee that, if the Bill was carried, there must be a race run for the settlement of the Territory, to decide whether it should be pro-slavery or anti-slavery, when the time came for its admission into the Union. It was even so. As soon as the measure was (by highly disgraceful means) rendered secure, the territory was divided, and we began to hear of Kansas: and what the struggle for possession has been, the existing plight of Kansas makes manifest to all eyes. The South believed that, by Senator Douglas's audacity, their party in the Senate would be reinforced by four votes which the Missouri Compromise had prospectively assigned to the free states; and great was their triumph. But they had now touched the summit of their power, and decline seems to be in store for them. The choice appears to be simply between their submission to have Slavery made sectional and Liberty national, and—the dissolution of the Union. Already the prominent men on that occasion are disgraced. Their constituents have rejected them; and Mr. Everett is only the first of a long line of public men whom the infamous Nebraska Bill has driven into retirement. It has closed the career of President Pierce; and there is hope that the ravage which it has wrought may prove an opening to a just, faithful, and constitutional policy. The precise date of this iniquitous Bill ought to be recorded. It was passed at 5 A.M. of the fourth of March, 1854, by a vote in the Senate of twenty-three to fourteen. One fact which casts a curious light on the affair is that, of the majority of twenty-three, fourteen votes were given by senators from the free States, while two of the minority were given by senators from slave States (Texas and Tennessee). Six from the free States, and three from the slave States absented themselves, Mr. Everett being one of the six.

All was not lost; though this throwing open of the wide, free North-west to slave institutions, and the political thraldom which always accompanies them, was enough to make the stoutest heart "despair of the Republic." All was not lost while the land lay open for settlement. There must now be a race for possession, between the slaveholders of the South and the labourers (supported by the capitalists) of the North.

The northern youth, always ready for "fresh fields and pastures anew," were not slow to people Kansas. Fertile lands, well drained by parallel rivers, cutting ravines in the rich soil, were to be found over a large proportion of the territory. On the great rivers, there were facilities for an almost boundless trade; while the game and fish of the remoter districts were tempting to the hunter and sportsman. Some recent allegations of Southern newspapers have brought out the fact that the free State settlers of Kansas were, as far as the New England immigrants were concerned, of the true old sort,—hardy, laborious, temperate, earnest,—as anxious to carry their bibles with them as their brides. A great number more appear to be European immigrants, especially Germans.

The enterprise of settling Kansas took form, as other enterprises do, in the United States. An Emigrant Aid Association was formed, partly, it seems, for the purpose of securing free-labour institutions in Kansas by facilitating and regulating the settlement of the land; partly for the purpose of shifting European immigration from the east, where it was not wanted, to the west, where it is; and partly, of course, to make money. A very large hotel was erected at the town of Lawrence in Kansas for the reception of the new comers, and proper arrangements were made for their distribution and settlement on the land. Thus was it managed by the free States. Every body meantime was wondering how the slave states could at all compete with the North. The whole number of slaveholders was, at the time of the last census, under 350,000, of the 27,000,000 of inhabitants of the United States: and the removal to Kansas of any considerable number of planters, with their slaves, would be ruinous to the States they left. So thought the world in general— the world in general being scarcely aware of the existence of that wretched and degraded race, the "mean-whites" of the slave States, and scarcely anybody being fully aware of the numbers included under that local term.

Wherever Slavery exists, labour becomes, of course, a badge of degradation. In America, no class,—not even the slaves, are so utterly degraded as the whites who, in slave States, have no property, and must live by work or theft. The planters are always trying to get rid of them, as dangerous and vexatious neighbours; and these poor wretches—the descendants, for the most part, of the proud colonists of two centuries ago,—are reduced to sell their last foot of land, and be driven forth to live where they can. They are receivers of stolen goods from plantations, and traffickers in bad whiskey, doing no honest work that they can avoid, and being employed by nobody who can get work done by any abler hands. Few of them can read; most of them drink; and the missionaries report of them as savage to an unparalleled degree,—many having never heard of God or of Jesus Christ. Of this class are the "Sand-hillers," the "Clay-eaters," and other fearful abnormal classes of residents in the slave States. Strangers hear, in visits to plantations, of these "mean-whites" as the supreme nuisance of the South, but are led to suppose that they are a mere handful of people, able to do a good deal of mischief by tampering with and corrupting the slaves. The last census, however, reveals the tremendous fact that these "mean-whites" are seven-tenths of the whole white populations of the slave States. Members of Congress never allude to these people; and in all notices of Southern affairs the population is assumed to consist of planters and their slaves. Everything is done in the name of the slaveholders, as if the other seven-tenths of the white population did not exist. These are the immigrants whom the slave-power is sending into Kansas. These are, with a very few exceptions, the only possible settlers from the South, where the slaveholders are few, and, if they desire to move, would go Southwards. They have raised bodies of "mean-whites," clothed and armed them, and sent them to Kansas to uphold slave institutions. But these people are not to be depended on for upholding Slavery, after they have once witnessed the privileges of free labour. In the free States on the Ohio, they have occasionally exhibited a curious spectacle of conversion. In Kansas, they appear to be, thus far, a mere banditti. Of one company from Alabama, of which great boast was made, many deserted on the way, others absconded with the cash-box, and the rest are ravaging Kansas as marauders,—burning farmsteads, stealing horses, clothes, and money, and compelling the women to fly to the thickets, or across the frontier.

Of course, if left to themselves, the rival settlers would decide their own case; the sober and industrious and well-organized free labourers would presently obtain the ascendancy, and determine that Kansas should be free soil, as it would have been under the Missouri Compromise. But the intervention which has postponed, if not ruined, this prospect—the intervention of the Border Ruffians from Missouri,—is sufficiently well known to the reader. To baffle the free-settlers, who had made their arrangements and elected their officers in an orderly and constitutional way, in pursuance of leave from Federal Government, an armed banditti from Missouri crossed the frontier, voted without any qualification of residence, and finally undermined the house where the votes were taken, seized the ballot-boxes, put the free settlers to flight, removed the Governor, and set up another, and murdered several citizens. The President upheld these intruders in the first instance, sanctioned their appointment, sent United States' troops, arms, and ammunition to their support, and obstructed to the utmost of his power the appointment of a Congressional Committee of Inquiry. The Commission deputed by Congress has sat, has transmitted a Report, by smuggling devices, to Washington, and escaped without loss of life; and the publication of their Report has just disclosed the horrors they witnessed in Kansas. Lawrence, the capital, is burnt, and almost every village and farmstead is sacked and destroyed. The free-state settlers have sent their wives and children over the frontier, and retired to the south-western portion of the territory, hoping to subsist on wild game and fish till reinforced from the free states. They are hemmed in by the Border Ruffians and Southern whites in hope of starving them into surrender; and forces are posted on the river and along the frontier to disarm all comers, and seize ammunition and supplies of every kind. Large bodies of free State settlers are marching down through Iowa, Wisconsin and Indiana; the Northern States are sending men, money, and supplies; and, in fact, the civil war has begun, which it was the object of so many Compromises to evade. It has begun, too, on the soil of Kansas, which the great Missouri Compromise was broken to deprive of its guaranteed freedom.

The first question—I might say, the inexhaustible wonder—caused by this state of affairs is, why the free States have permitted all this ravage? With the numbers, the industry, the wealth in their own hands, why have they allowed the slave-power to override all other interests, and determine the entire policy of the United States for so long a course of years? One cannot read a Southern newspaper without meeting with peevish complaints that the Northern States engross all the commerce, the manufactures, the wealth, the science, arts, and improvements, which benefit society, leaving the South poor and half-peopled, the estates mortgaged, the harbours empty, the roads and bridges decayed, and the rising generation without prospect, unless by seeking their fortunes in a new region. This is all true; and yet this is the section of the Union which has overborne all the rest. It has impressed a retrograde character on the whole policy and government of the nation; lowered the *prestige* of its Presidents; bullied its allies; made light of international good faith; warred upon weak neighbours; created intense sectional hatred at home; annulled the constitutional rights of the citizens; broken the hearts of ambitious statesmen; and jeopardized free institutions all over the world, as far as corruption, leading to failure, can do so. It has, as we have seen, invented Compromises to evade danger, and broken them when advantage invited. I had rather leave the North to explain why it has permitted all this mischief, and made itself a party to all this disgrace. It is a sad story; and all I need say of it now is, that Idolatry of the Union is one chief cause of the apparent pusillanimity and complicity in guilt; and Mammon-worship is another. Dr. Channing explained the case up to his time; and history will reveal the rest when the issue has become manifest. The Abolitionists—the Old Organization—have been right from first to last, it now appears;—right in their interpretation of events, in their principles, in their conduct, in their insight and foresight, and now, especially, in their persistent repudiation of political entanglement of every sort. They will save their country (if it is to be saved) by refusing to commit its chief cause to the uncertain issues of political party movement of any kind. They will still keep the citadel of Republican principle while other forces go down into the field of politics to fight for the lesser matter—not whether every man in the Republic shall be free, but whether Slavery shall be national and Freedom sectional, or the reverse.

Taking the lower political view merely—the nearness of the presidential election, and the characters of the two candidates between whom the choice really lies, are of extreme importance. President Pierce is out of the question—a necessary consequence of his having sacrificed all other interests to those of the slave power, while, at the same time, he has alienated the South by incurring the danger of foreign war, of which the South has, very reasonably, an extreme dread. If it were not a great mistake to look to any political choice for redemption in such a crisis as the present, the probable return of Colonel Fremont as President, and Mr. Dayton as Vice-President, would seem to open a bright prospect. Colonel Fremont would almost seem to have been created for the difficulty. He is a Southern man by birth,—was educated in South Carolina, where, and in Virginia, he passed a youth and early manhood of vigorous study first, and then of humble and heroic labour (as a teacher of mathematics), for the sake of his widowed mother and her children. He is a classical scholar of no ordinary attainments;—his surveying achievements attest his mathematical accomplishments. His virtuous life and refined manners have attached everybody to him wherever he went. Thus he is—what the South professes to make a point of—a gentleman. His professional occupations and his travels and adventures have kept him out of the field of politics and the entanglements of party; while his relations with the Indians, and his connexion with California, have proved his administrative ability to be very great. His wide experience has made him a thorough-going Free-soiler; and to him the Union owes free California, while to him California owes her being free. Like most military officials, he is more pacifically inclined than civilians often are, and than President Pierce has shown himself to be. On this ground also the South may probably incline to him. The North is enthusiastic even beyond its wont in this contest; and grave men declare that since the time of Washington no such demonstration has been witnessed in the Eastern States as the Convention at Philadelphia for the nomination of Fremont and Dayton. The latter candidate is also a well and favourably-known man. He consistently opposed all the retrograde measures of the last two Presidential terms, and sacrificed his political position to his principles, in days when the minority of men like himself was exceedingly small.

Of Mr. Buchanan, the rival of Colonel Fremont, it is only necessary to say what he himself and his supporters say for him. By the *Richmond Enquirer*, of June 20th (a leading newspaper in the South), I see that Mr. Buchanan supported the restrictions of the post-office, the press, and the right of petition, twenty years ago; and between that time and this, the slave-trade in the District of Columbia, the annexation of Texas, the admission of Arkansas, the encouragement of Slavery in new territories, the extension of the Missouri Compromise to the Pacific, and then the abolition of that Compromise; the Fugitive Slave law, the Nebraska Bill; and, finally, "the Monroe doctrine" of aggression, in order to the absorption of neighbouring States. The Ostend Circular is the die which he cast for his acceptance or rejection as President. By this he will stand or fall. As the South has recently manifested an indisputable disinclination to war, and, in some portions, to the annexation of even Cuba, it may be concluded that the Ostend Circular will not be so serviceable to Mr. Buchanan as he expected. No one who is at all familiar with American politics will venture upon prophecy with regard to the presidential election, or any other future event. All that is certain is, first, the respective programmes (in American language, "platforms") of the Democratic and Republican Parties; and, next, that some new and decisive issue will be found from the present crisis. As for "platforms,"—that of the supporters of Buchanan, the Democratic Convention, shaped by the pressure of the time, is this:—

1st. Congress not to preclude Slavery in candidate territories.

2nd. Kansas to be a slave State.

3rd. War, for acquisition of territory.

That of Fremont's supporters, the Republican Convention, is this:—

1st. Congress to preclude Slavery in candidate territories, as in the first days of the Republic.

2nd. Kansas to be a free State, as resolved by three-fourths of its resident population.

3rd. Peace abroad, in order to development at home.

As for the issue to be looked for from the present crisis, it is not likely to be by compromise of any sort. Not only have the failures of compromise been too many and too great, but the case has gone too far for any but a radical settlement,—whether it be immediate or of slow operation,—whether by concession on either hand, or by a dissolution of the Union. Further compromise would be but another name for retrogression and ruin; and every friend of free institutions will, therefore, hope that the time is indeed past for compromise.

I have endeavoured to meet an expressed want by explaining the terms of the great American Controversy, and thus furnishing a key to the existing crisis. For the rest, events are likely henceforth to speak very plainly for themselves.

"'Manifest Destiny' of the American Union"

Westminster Review, 1857

The *Westminster Review* (founded 1824), a monthly periodical devoted to philosophical radicalism, was established by utilitarian social thinker Jeremy Bentham as a counterpoint to the Whig *Edinburgh Review* and Tory *Quarterly Review*. The *Westminster Review* drew such names as John Stuart Mill and George Eliot (both as writers and editors), James Mill, G. H. Lewes, Thomas Huxley, J. A.

Froude, and John Tyndall to its editorial ranks and enjoyed a solid reputation as a publication of critical and literary authority. Like the *Monthly Repository* in which Martineau first published in the 1820s, the *Westminster* also supported "Woman's Cause" by calling for radical reforms. Published monthly rather than quarterly, periodicals like the *Westminster* gradually acquired greater influence than such "high" journals as the *Edinburgh Review.*

Originally published in the *Westminster Review* in July 1857, "'Manifest Destiny' of the American Union" was reprinted by New York's American Anti-Slavery Society later that same year. Like *The Martyr Age of the United States* (published first in the *Westminster Review* in 1838, then separately in 1839), Martineau's article provides an overview of the American situation—this time through an analysis of contemporary writings on the topic, including her own *History of the American Compromises.* The American editor's appendix notes that the typical journalistic habit of writing from event to event results in a loss of the broad perspective necessary for comprehensive cultural understanding; in contrast, the ability to perceive "the big picture" through an impartial spirit, philosophical viewpoint, and sympathetic nature enables the foreigner Harriet Martineau to "see more clearly and appreciate more justly . . . than a native" (67). "'Manifest Destiny'" exemplifies such cross-cultural insight "with a rare power of rapid generalization and correct deduction," which the editor declares it is his "duty to circulate as widely as possible."

The appendix concludes by offering a novel alternative to the threat of southern secession—*northern* secession:

> One thing is certain: the relations which the North sustains to the slave system of the South, under the Constitution, involves her in all its guilt, and much of its danger— from which she can extricate herself only by dissolving the Union, and organizing a free Northern republic. To this result events are rapidly tending, as indicated by the masterly article from the *Westminster Review.* (72)

Threats by the slaveholding southern states to secede from the Union—later fully acted on with Lincoln's assumption of the presidency and the Emancipation Proclamation—were common. But as Martineau's title suggests, an equally viable alternative, a movement promoting northern secession as a protest against slavery, is the impetus behind "'Manifest Destiny' of the American Union." By appropriating the catchphrase "manifest destiny" to urge the North to adopt more assertive tactics toward the South, Martineau implicitly criticizes the expansionist ambitions of certain policy makers (like James Buchanan) that aimed to avoid, rather than confront and resolve, the slavery issue. This article further establishes that the conditions necessary for a revolution sufficient to eradicate slavery had long been accumulating and were now in place. As the American editor recognizes and as Martineau repeatedly proves, her best work is that which displays both her profound understanding of history as a continuum linking the past with the future and her keen awareness of the significance of contemporary events in that continually unfolding process.

The threatened collision of a comet headed toward Earth in 1857 appropriately inspired Martineau's organizing metaphor: the impending American revolution promises to be no less explosive or have less cultural "impact" than this potentially catastrophic "cometary" event.[161]

. . .

Art. VI.—"Manifest Destiny" of the American Union.
1. *American Slavery and Colour.* By William Chambers, author of "Things as they are in America." London: W. and R. Chambers. 1857.
2. *A Journey in the Seaboard Slave States; with remarks on their economy.* By Fred. Law Olmsted. London: Sampson Low and Co. New York: Dix and Edwards. 1856.
3. *A Journey through Texas: or, a Saddletrip on the South-western Frontier; with a Statistical Appendix.* By Fred. Law Olmsted. 1857.
4. *A History of the American Compromises.* Reprinted, with additions, from the *Daily News.* By Harriet Martineau. London: John Chapman. 1856.

The Empress of the French amused herself a few months since with pretending to represent the alarms of the ladies of Europe about the comet which was to strike the earth in the course of June, 1857. She played off a man of science at one of her evening receptions, by an affectation of panic about the comet, trying to make him ridiculous between his eagerness to show how absurd her idea was and his deference for the person to whom he was speaking. What he endeavored to convey was the same comfort that has been administered to timid Englishwomen—that, in the first place, the comet would not come near us; and, in the next, that if it did "strike the earth," we should not find it out, but simply complain of misty weather. Americans and their revolutions are illustrated by such cometary facts and fancies. An American, like an Englishman or a German, starts at the word revolution, deprecates it, prays to Heaven against it, disavows and denies it when it begins to envelope him, and, while he is in the very midst of it, insists that, however gloomy the political times are, he sees nothing like chaos and destruction, and cannot therefore be passing through a revolution. . . . [Here Martineau discusses America's first revolution resulting in independence from Britain.]

Our readers are by this time making comparisons, no doubt, between the incidents and feelings belonging to the first American revolution and those which have for some time past, and with perpetual increasing force, and clearness, indicated a second. We believe we have the means of showing that a second great revolution is not only approaching, but actually far advanced, and that some of the wisest and best of American citizens have so far profited by the lessons of their fathers as to be fully aware of their real position, though a vast majority still insist, as the new president did in his inauguration address, that "all is calm" because his party has carried the election. During the fifteen years preceding the separation of the American colonies, almost everybody supposed, as often as there was a lull, that matters were settled; and in like manner, the president and all commonplace people among the millions whom he addressed in March last, are satisfied that the declaration of the poll was sufficient to annul all the controversies and colli-sions which had lately caused the Union to ring with threats and promises of dissolution on either hand. When observers stroke their chins, and re-mark that the state of things looks very like revolution, the old reply comes up, "Revolution! O dear no! nothing of the sort! The Union is so dear to the American people that no lapse of ages will dissolve it." And the laugh raised against such observers is at least as contemptuous as any ridicule directed against trembling inquirers after the comet of June, 1857. . . .

To the Abolitionists proper belongs the honour of all the ameliorations in the condition of the slaves of the South, and of the free blacks of the North for the last quarter of a century. They fixed the attention of the world on the treatment of the slaves, and thereby improved that treatment,—the slave-holders being at least as sensitive to the world's opinion as other classes of their countrymen. In the North, so far from deserving the reproach which Mr. Chambers directs against them, of inhuman and practical aversion to the coloured race, they have earned the opprobrious title of "amalgamationists" from the South by their success in opening to the free blacks the colleges, the pulpits, and the common schools of their communities, as well as the steam-boat and the omnibus, the concert-room and church-sittings, with collateral benefits in proportion. By their stout warfare with the prejudice of colour, they have brought on themselves a long series of fearful persecutions. Their houses have been laid in ruins, their public halls burnt, their children excom-municated, their lives threatened and embittered with insult. They have watched with increasing vigilance over such liberties as were provided by the Constitution, and have so analyzed that Constitution as to prove to all minds that it must be amended before the Republic can ever again be tran-quillized. By this small band of devoted and enlightened men and women the conscience of the nation has been kept alive, and the country has been revolutionized, thus far without violence and bloodshed, and by the force of reason and conscience. The revolutionary crisis being (as is agreed on all hands) inevitable, its being accomplished by other means than a servile war will be due to the Abolitionists, if that fearful catastrophe should be indeed escaped. Superficial observers, and strangers indoctrinated by the slavehold-ers and their creatures, the Colonization Society, have been apt till lately to despise the Abolitionists on account of the smallness of their numbers, and their severance from all political parties; but a deeper sagacity and the most ordinary impartiality will discern that these two particulars are the very se-cret of their influence. It is because they know that political factions can never regenerate the public that they keep aloof from parties, and thus main-tain their ground and their power through all political changes; and it is through their abstinence from intrigue on the one hand, and violence on the other, that their numbers must ever be small. To obtain any great accession of numbers they must lower their standard, which they are not likely to do after a quarter of a century of severer temptation than can beset them again, and after achieving an amount of success which renders their principle and procedure unquestionable by all rational persons who understand the case. The range of their services has been wide and various. The condition of the slaves, in regard to material treatment, has been greatly equalized and improved by the attention of the world being fixed upon their case; the false pretences of all dishonest parties have been continuously exposed: the Church, the judiciary, the legislatures, and all leading men in each department, have been tested, and their true quality exhibited. The worldliness of the commercial North has been rebuked as effectually as the despotism of the slaveholding South: the whole country has been roused to a sense of the approaching crisis; and, while the field has been cleared for the conflict, the slave population has been deterred from insurrection. Before 1832, when the first Abolitionist spoke his first word, the slave insurrections averaged twelve in a year; whereas, from 1832 to 1856, there was no insurrection whatever. The slaves were aware that their cause was in better hands than their own, and they waited patiently, till, in the course of the election of last year, Southern men themselves imprudently identified the success of Fremont with the abolition of slavery, and thus, according to their own confession, made themselves answerable for a partial rising. Even so bare a recapitulation as we have given of the services of the Abolitionists may be welcome to the readers of Mr. Chambers's latest work, as opening some prospect of a good and happy issue where to him all appears perplexing and desperate. The ten righteous men, having wrought for so long, may save the city yet.

Before we survey the recent transactions of the respective sections and States of the Union, it may be well to denote the various parties concerned in the existing struggle and its issue. We do not mean to waste any space in describing the political parties whose very denominations are a ludicrous puzzle to strangers. Such parties rise and disappear like bubbles on a turbulent stream; so that they are hardly worth a stranger's attention in ordinary times. But, at present, scarcely any of them appear to exist. The current of events is too strong for them; the times are too grave for political skirmishing; and the whole people are massed in sections characterized by distinctions which cannot be admitted and discussed in a day.

The leading sections are the North and the South, of course: but it is a mistake to suppose that the division of the men is as clear as the distinction of the policy. The South has a policy; and, as it is a slaveholding policy, the very small body of slaveholders usurps the title of the Southern section. Of the 27,000,000 of inhabitants of the United States, less than 350,000 are slaveholders in any sense; and it is computed that of these not more than 1,000 are indoctrinated and zealous slaveholders. Of whom, then, does the so-called "South" really consist? There are, as we have said, 350,000 slaveholders; and if their connexions of every sort are included, the entire oligarchy cannot consist of more than 2,000,000. Then there are, at least, 4,000,000 slaves. The slaves being double the number of the ruling class is a formidable circumstance in itself; and it becomes of proportionate importance to learn what the remaining element is. That element it has been the policy of the South to keep out of view; and till lately it has succeeded: but the last census revealed the fact that the "mean-white" population of the South—the non-slave-holding whites—constitute no less than seven-tenths of the whole free population of the slave states. . . . [Here Martineau discusses "mean-whites."]

Here, then, we have the three classes which constitute the population of the South:—1st. The owners of property and their families, composed of a small caste of 2,000,000 of persons; 2nd. Their slaves, now more than double the number of the oligarchy; and, 3rd, the poor whites, who have neither property nor power to labour, and who outnumber the other two classes together. Till very recently these were literally all: for free negroes are excluded from slave States by law and usage, and in fact; and white labour cannot co-exist with black. But the eagerness of the Southern oligarchy to extend the area of slave States has led to the unexpected issue of slavery being stopped in its spread to the south-west by the intervention of a substantial industrial body of immigrants. . . . [Here she quotes Olmsted on German immigrant population in Texas.]

Here, then, is a fourth element of Southern population, small at present, but steadily increasing, and admirably placed for driving back slavery from the south-western frontier. The planters fear and hate this element; the negroes love it, as far as they recognise it; and the "mean-whites" hardly know what to make of it. The Germans, meantime, have no liking for any of the three classes of neighbours.

How are the 17,000,000 of the North massed in regard to political questions? Their numbers alone would seem to give them power to carry any point in which they believed the welfare of the Republic to be involved; and when it is considered that the suffrage is *bona fide* in the Northern states, while in the South three-fifths of the slaves count as voters by a constitutional fiction, strangers may well wonder how it is that the freemen of the North, being much more than double the number of those of the other section, permit any conflict which can endanger their country. Hitherto, it seems to have been the business of the slave-holding aristocracy to govern the Republic for their own purposes, in virtue of their compact organization, their strong and united will, and their accomplishments as men of letters and leisure; whereas the freemen of the North have had only a negative policy with regard to the great subject on which the South has a positive one; and the next great question, that of protection and free-trade, is one which is supposed to render the commercial and manufacturing portion of the Republic dependent on the producing section,—the merchants and manufacturers on the cotton-growers. Hence, mainly, it is that the vast body of free, industrious and prosperous inhabitants of the Union are regarded only as a party, and a subordinate party, in the political history of the country. It is obvious that whenever the *prestige* of the governing party is shaken, and the bulk of the free population is fairly roused to honest political exertion, the constitution of the United States may become whatever they choose to make it, by means peaceable in proportion to the preponderant force of numbers. But they are not roused to honest political exertion; and hence it is that, though the Southern Oligarchy are deteriorated in ability, degraded in morals, and brutalized in manners, as a necessary consequence of a protraction of slave institutions into an age too advanced for them, their abler and more civilized fellow-countrymen of the North are involved in a revolutionary struggle, instead of carrying their Government up to the head of the free governments of the world. This immense population, which lives in subservience to half a million of fellow-citizens, consists of hundreds of thousands of merchants, millions of land-owners, innumerable clergy of all denominations, multitudes of other professional men, large corporate bodies of manufacturers, and crowds of individual producers in all crafts. The only part of the 17,000,000 of the North not included in this mass of freemen are the two classes of immigrants and free coloured people. The latter are few, though more numerous than the slaveholders. They are somewhat under half a million, and they have no political weight at present, except in an indirect way, by their political competency and rights being one of the questions of the controversy. Till quite recently, the full importance of the immigrant element of the population was not recognised, though the slave states have manifested a growing jealousy of the labour-power by which the superiority of the North in wealth and prosperity has been created. The formation of the Know-Nothing party—a southern device—was the first great recognition of the vital importance of the foreign industrial element,—being neither more nor less than an admission that slavery and immigration could not co-exist in the Republic. A similar testimony was afforded when, on the disappearance of the Know-Nothing party, some Southern governors and legislatures opened the fresh project of a renewal of the African slave trade. The northern states have borne the same testimony by the formation of their Emigrant Aid Societies; the object of which is not so much the keeping up of the supply of labourers in the old States, as the settlement of fresh territory,—at once preventing the extension of slavery over new soil, and giving the benefit of the increase of production to the commercial North, instead of the agricultural South. This important body of citizens—the European element—consists chiefly at present of Germans, whom we have just seen actually turning back the tide of slavery on its remotest frontier, and who afford a good rampart on the northern frontier,—in Illinois, Indiana, and the back of Pennsylvania and New York. The distinctive and highly useful characteristic of the Germans is, that they are commonly capitalists and labourers in one. So are the Hungarians, Belgians, Dutch and Swedes, while the Irish afford an element more resembling the slave labour of the South than any other that can be found in the free States. The whole body is, in combination, one of vast and growing consequence.

Lastly, there is the very small body of Abolitionists, properly so called. In number probably much under one in a thousand of the citizens, standing outside of political life and action altogether, and combined by no other bond than that of hostility to an institution which everybody about them ostensibly condemns, they make no show to account for their importance. We do not include under the term any political party which assumes any convenient portion of their doctrine; because it is clear to all impartial persons that the great problem now harassing the Republic cannot be solved by the ascendancy of any political party. We are, therefore, classing the free-soil party, and every other transient embodiment of the great difficulty, with the general mass of the Northern population; and when we speak of the Abolitionists, we mean the permanent, small, active, agitating anti-slavery body to which the South attributes all its woes, and which really is answerable for the critical condition of the question at this day. There is no truth in the Southern accusations that the Abolitionists tamper with the slaves, or countenance violence in any form, or under any pretence. The great majority of them are non-resistants, and moral means are their only weapons; but they are, as the slave power says, the antagonistic power by which the destinies of the Republic have been pledged to a principle, as in the days of their fathers, and at whose instigation the conflict must be carried through, and the fate of the nation decided. They are the actual revolutionizers of the Republic, while, for the most part, peacemen in the doctrinal sense of the term. The difference between them and the amateur peacemen of some European societies is that they do not consider the shedding of blood the greatest of evils, but simply an inexpedient method of prosecuting their aim; and thus they are not bound to "cry peace where there is no peace," but will not cease to agitate while the wrong is unrectified; and, at the same time, their mode of procedure is of incalculable value where the solution to be apprehended is that of servile war on the one hand, and a military despotism on the other.

These, then, are the sections of the population, North and South, among and by whom the second great American revolution is to be wrought out. What has been done up to this time? What is doing now? By what phenomena are we justified in speaking of American affairs as in a revolutionary state at this moment? We will cast a glance round that great circle of grouped sovereignties, and see what social symptoms are exhibited from point to point within the frontier. . . .

The survivors of the founders of the Republic believed—we now see how wisely—that the first move in the second revolution was made in 1820. Thoughtless persons wondered at the solemnity of their language; but time is fully justifying it. In 1787, when there was a distribution of lands belonging to Virginia, the establishment of slavery on new territory was prohibited; and nobody called in question the power of the National Congress of that day to impose such a prohibition. During the thirty following years there was no dispute on the point; and it was with dread and surprise that in 1819, the venerable statesmen of the Revolution began to apprehend the course which the South is following out at this moment. It was on the occasion of the Missouri compromise that the doubt was insinuated whether Congress could impose conditions on the admission of new States into the Union. . . .

For thirty-seven years the great constitutional question has come up again on all marked occasions, and under many phases, till the present year, when all the conditions of revolution are fulfilled, and there appears to be no escape from the alternative of an overthrow of the original constitution of the Republic, or its preservation by means of a separation of the States. To this issue the recent decision of the Supreme Court in the case of Dred Scott seems to have brought the great controversy, which may be briefly thus described.

In the original draft of the Declaration of Independence, there is a paragraph which was struck out as unnecessary. It charged George III with the crime of the slave trade, among the other offences there set forth in solemn order. Mr. Chambers saw this document in the rooms of the American Philosophical Society at Philadelphia; and he naturally considers it "the greatest archaeological curiosity" that he saw in the country. When that paper was drawn up, slavery existed in all the States; but its abolition was so near and certain in many of them, and the universal dislike of it appeared to be so strong, that even the far-sighted Franklin believed that it would soon be got rid of, with other mischiefs imposed by the connexion with England. We have Lafayette's testimony (given in grief at the bad spirit which had grown up between 1776 and 1830), that during the revolutionary war there was no distinction between the blacks and the whites as soldiers and citizens. Soldiers of the two races bivouacked together, eating out of the same dish, as well as fighting side by side: and in the towns, the free coloured men were citizens, in every sense as good as the whites. Even so late as 1814, nearly the same position was held by the black soldiers, as is proved by General Jackson's address to them a few weeks before the battle of New Orleans. "As sons of freedom," the general wrote, "you are called upon to defend our most inestimable blessing. As Americans, your country looks with confidence for a valorous support," &c. In a subsequent address, the recognition of the citizenship of the negroes was as ample as possible. "When on the banks of the Mobile," he says, "I called you to take up arms, inviting you to partake the perils and glories of your white fellow-citizens, I expected much from you," &c. When the Americans began to govern themselves, therefore, and for long after, the condition of the negro race was this: Those who were slaves were rapidly obtaining freedom by the abolition of slavery in State after State; all importation of negroes was forbidden after 1808; and the emancipated slaves became citizens in the fullest sense of the term. While the eradication of slavery was supposed to be thus proceeding in the settled States, the institution was excluded from new territory by express provision, as in the case of the distribution of the Virginian lands, under the compact of 1787. The mischief and disgrace of the institution were charged upon Great Britain, fairly and sincerely; and there was more or less reason for the excuse of inherited crime up to 1820, when the Missouri Compromise destroyed it, by unnecessarily introducing slavery into the new State of Missouri, where it was not justified by circumstance of climate, or any overpowering expediency whatever. Still, it was the practice to speak of slavery as an evil and a disgrace, and to cast the blame of it on England which introduced it, till the repeal of the Missouri Compromise in 1850, by which the institution was adopted as the substantial policy of the Republic, to the support of which every State of the Union should be pledged. American ambassadors in Europe, and the entertainers of European travellers in the United States, were wont to speak plaintively and deprecatingly of the misfortune they had inherited from the mother-country. But for seven years past—we may say for thirty-seven years past—the excuse has been invalid; and now the nation, if judged by the action of the federal government, proclaims to the world that "slavery is the corner-stone of the Republic," as Governor McDuffie of South Carolina declared it to be when few had courage to make such an avowal.

It was in a continental or national Congress—the last—that the prohibition to introduce slavery into new territory was passed in 1787; but acts of that Congress were sanctioned and adopted by the federal Congress, without dispute or demur, for a long course of years. We have seen how great the shock to the surviving statesmen of the revolution when the right of that Congress to rule the conditions of new States was brought into question in 1820. The controversy was suspended by a compromise, which, by excluding slavery from all territory north of a certain line, licensed it in all territory south of that line. Ten years after that compromise, the Abolitionists began to see how fearful were the condition and prospects of their country, if slavery should continue to impoverish the soil of half the States, and to undermine the liberties and corrupt the morals of the whole; and they have worked devotedly, and made the most magnanimous sacrifices, during the intervening quarter of a century, to revolutionize their country by moral agitation, with a steady avoidance of political movement, in order to intercept the last fatal result of a servile war, bringing on a total national overthrow.

Though there were more signs of political disturbance prior to 1850 than we have space to detail—such as the suppression of the right of petition to Congress, the violences inflicted with impunity on the abolitionists, and the prostitution of the mail service,—there was a sufficient external quiet and decorum preserved to cover up the wounds of the Republic from foreign observation, and to excuse timid or indifferent citizens from appearing to see that anything was wrong. The warnings of the Abolitionists were troublesome and vexatious: the rebukes of Dr. Channing were smiled at as coming from a mere divine, who could be no judge of practical affairs. The legislation of 1850 was a thunderclap to many who had been apathetic before; but its portentous character was not estimated till the broad tokens of revolution were displayed in the leading state of the Union. They might not be recognised as revolution, any more than the pouring out of tea and of blood on a former occasion; but they were something so serious as to rouse and prepare the general mind for the yet more critical manifestations of the present day.

When the Fugitive Slave Bill passed, there were about 9000 persons of colour in Massachusetts. Within three days after its passage was known, forty of them were in flight for Canada, though legally protected by the constitution of the sovereign State in which they were living. One day in May, 1854, the old Faneuil Hall in Boston rang with speeches which were as revolutionary as any which had ever been uttered there before, on occasion of the arrest of Burns, a fugitive slave, whose liberty was guaranteed by the laws of the State while annihilated by the new federal law. Nothing can be more revolutionary than a direct collision between a law of the Union and a law of any State; and nothing can be more absolutely opposed than those laws in the present case. . . . [Here follow details of the Anthony Burns episode and Justice Loring's role.]

Chief Justice Taney has immortalized his old age by the judgment in the case of Dred Scott, which, whether recalled or allowed to stand, will, in all probability, be renowned hereafter as the occasion, though not specifically the cause, of the outbreak of the second great American Revolution. . . . [Details of the Dred Scott case follow.] The judges (five out of seven present) went so much further than was necessary in the judgment they pronounced, that it is evident that they seized the occasion for establishing the supremacy of the Southern policy, at the outset of a new presidential term. The decision embraced five points; whereas the first was enough for the case before them. The points are these:—

1st. That negroes and people of colour are not citizens; and that, as a consequence, Dred Scott could not come into court. This, if true, settled Dred Scott's business, and that of four millions of his race, natives of the United States.

2nd. That slaves are property, in the same sense as any kind of chattel: so that a slave-owner may carry his negroes into any State of the Union, and settle them there, as slaves, notwithstanding any State laws to the contrary. If this is true, the whole Union is slave territory, and the sovereign States have no power to deliver themselves from it. It needs no showing that this cuts up by the roots the fundamental liberties of every republic in the Union; and enslaves the federal Union itself under an assumed ordinance of a long-dead generation.

3rd. That Congress has no power over the institutions of the Territories: in other words, that all the provisions of the Settlement of 1787, all the enactments at the time of the Missouri Compromise, all the reversals of those enactments in 1850, all the proceedings of seventy years which suppose the citizenship of the coloured people, the limitations of slavery, and an antagonistic policy between North and South, are mere waste paper.

4th. That Congress cannot delegate a power which it does not possess; and that, therefore, the Territories themselves have no power to exclude slavery from their own borders.

5th (included in the second). That the slaveholder has a right to settle his slaves on any soil within the Union, as a Northern man may establish his cattle and horses wherever he pleases to live.

We need not waste our space in any discussion of this judgment. On the face of it, it makes slavery as perpetually and everywhere present as the atmosphere, over the whole area of the United States; and it overthrows the entire legislation of the Federal Union and of most of the States, for above seventy years, in all that concerns inter-state relations, and the rights of the sovereign States. Thus the rights of the negroes are only one portion, and not the chief portion, of the interests involved. The judgment is of the strongest revolutionary character,—subversive as it is of the whole mass of legislation, and the whole policy of the founders of the Republic and their successors to this day. If it could be acted out, *that* would be revolution. If it is resisted, *that* is also revolution, because the entire organization of the federal government stands or falls with the Supreme Court. . . .

While this was going forward, what was the general aspect of society at Washington? For many years past, the imperious temper and bullying manners of the untraveled Southern members of Congress had so encroached on conventional usages, in regard to the Northern members, that it was clear that some explosion must take place, showing whether or not the two kinds and degrees of civilization could combine for political action. The outrage on Mr. Sumner was the explosion which so many were looking for: and the world in general seems to think that the question is pretty nearly settled. The South at large supported and rewarded the ruffian who assailed an unarmed man at a defenceless moment; and it is not easy to see how two sets of legislators who are of directly opposite opinions as to which was the hero and which the coward of the occasion, can legislate together on matters which involve the very principles of liberty and the civilization which belongs to it. The one set of members are living under a retrograde military *regime,* in a period of despotism and physical force; and the other is living under the advanced period of the commercial *regime,* which supposes and guarantees personal liberty, and sanctions intelligence and self-interest, superseding physical force. Emerson was roused by the occasion of the assault on Mr. Sumner to utter words which were caught up throughout the free States: and public opinion in the world generally seems to corroborate his conclusion. "I do not see," said Emerson, in his address to the citizens of Concord, "how a barbarous community and a civilized community can constitute one State." This is the question in which the continuance of the Union is involved; and it was proposed in its most critical form by Preston Brooks when he half murdered the Massachusetts senator on the floor of Congress. The South, by recognising the deed as an act of patriotism, has sealed the doom of the Union, if the more civilized portion of the States choose to exact the legitimate consequences. About the same time, another member of Congress took occasion to exemplify the Southern view of industrial relations. He shot through the heart an Irish waiter at an hotel, and escaped all punishment but a small fine, imposed by the District Court, as if for the purpose of endorsing the murderer's opinion that "a menial" is not a man,—white labourers reducing themselves, by the very act of labor, to the social position of slaves. The *Charleston Standard* observed on the occasion— "If white men accept the office of menials, it should be expected that they will do so with an apprehension of their relation to society, and the disposition quietly to encounter both the responsibilities and the liabilities which the relation implies." An Alabama paper hoped that "waiters at the North" would take a lesson in prudence, and not expect the security of gentlemen while they did the work of gentlemen's live chattels. Can those who work, and those who thus regard work, "constitute one State?". . .

At Washington, we thus see one-half of the senate is in direct hostility with the other; while the leading men of the great Northern majority, in both houses, live under threats of assault, and carry arms in fear of murder by "southern chivalry," if caught defenceless. The Supreme Court has descended into the dirt of political partisanship, and adventured the overthrow of the principles and policy of the Republic, directly provoking a revolution. No man in the capital of this democratic Republic can safely speak his mind; and even the clergy cannot freely preach the gospel from their own pulpits. As murder skulks in the street, so poison is hidden at the board. The President tells the world in his public addresses, that nothing can be better than the state of the country; and that, in regard to political agitation, in particular, "all is calm": while aware that treason reigns in the courts, violence in the legislative chambers, assassination in the streets and public vehicles, and a most potent spirit of vengeance in the kitchen; while he is himself feeble and suffering from "an accident," which he can perhaps account for better than we can. He is understood to promise "a totally new policy, domestic and foreign," about which he is to explain himself in the summer. Meanwhile, it is for our readers to judge whether Washington is prepared, by a spirit of union, loyalty, and mutual confidence among its residents, to be the citadel of the federal government, in case of revolutionary action among the states.

What is the aspect of the respective States? The two leading sovereignties, according to tradition and *prestige,* are Virginia and Massachusetts; the first leading the "gallant South" and its "peculiar institution"; and the other heading the puritan descended populations and governments of New England. . . . [Here Martineau details the economic decline of Virginia due to slavery.]

Massachusetts, the intellectual and moral leader of the States of the federation, is at this moment actually not in the Union. Its Personal Liberty law is in direct contradiction to the federal law regarding fugitive slaves; and the position of antagonism seems likely to be maintained by the spirit of the people. A fugitive family now in Boston affords an occasion for bringing the discrepancy to a decision; but the slave-power does not seem disposed to try. The slave-mother in this case is as white as any lady in Boston; and this practical testimony to the "amalgamation" prevalent in the South gives force to the case, and makes it a good one for a test. The alternative was fairly placed before the fugitive—whether she would proceed to Canada with her children, or remain under the guardianship of the laws of Massachusetts and of its vigilant citizens. She decided to remain; and visitors have gone from house to house to engage the citizens in a pledge to defend their guests against all hostile comers, at all risks. . . .

An incident which occurred a few months ago reveals a prodigious change in the sentiment of Boston itself, which is about as timid, and aristocratic, and dull-hearted a city, in regard to matters of reality, as any in the Union. Twenty-one years before the date of Mr. Sumner's reception in Boston on his partial recovery, Mr. Garrison had been mobbed in the streets, and in imminent danger of being destroyed as an incendiary; and for many long years he endured ill-usage from almost every class of his neighbours. He was considered a revolutionary agitator of the most dangerous character. When Mr. Sumner returned to his constituents, half-murdered, he was received with the highest honours by as vast a multitude as could find standing room along the route. He was enjoined by his physicians to make no exertion whatever, and, above all things, to keep his head covered. He must not remove his hat on any consideration. In the doorway of a corner house (a well-known Abolitionist house) stood Garrison, on the top step, as it happened. Mr. Sumner saw him, and, for the only time that day, removed his hat. The crowd cheered the act, and, turning to Garrison, cheered him long and loudly. The incident disclosed what seems to be the mind of Massachusetts in the present crisis. Mr. Sumner is re-elected, as the nearest to an abolitionist who will go to Congress.

Several other States have assumed the same attitude towards the decision of the Supreme Court that Massachusetts did before in regard to the Fugitive Slave Act by her Personal Liberty Law. The action of the Legislatures of New York and Pennsylvania has been open and decided. That of New York, reported as early as the 9th of April, denouncing the Washington judgment as unconstitutional and altogether intolerable, and recommending certain resolutions which were passed by large majorities. It will be enough to cite the first:

"*Resolved,* That this State will not allow slavery within its borders, in any form, or under any pretence, for any time, however short, *LET THE CONSEQUENCES BE WHAT THEY MAY.*"

On the 1st of May, the Pennsylvania Legislature pronounced on the decision of the Supreme Court that it was null in law because it was gratuitously offered, wholly uncalled for, and to no purpose, if the judges themselves were right in declaring that Dred Scott was not, because he could not be, before the Court. The judgment was further declared to be "a wanton attack on the sovereignty of the free States, and an impotent attempt to nullify the established laws of the country." The Legislature of Maine passed two Acts, which received the Governor's approval in April, protecting the liberty of all coloured persons touching the soil of the State, and providing them with all possible aid, legal and executive, in case of their being arrested as slaves; and the New England States have all, we believe, declared in one form or another, that they do not intend to yield up their laws and liberties; and there seems to be no doubt of their following the lead of Massachusetts in regard to sound Personal Liberty laws, as in other matters. . . .

Ohio takes the lead of the Western States; and, as a part of the territory dedicated to perpetual freedom by the Ordinance of 1787, she has the strongest interest in the decision of 1857. No time was lost by the Legislature in enacting "that it shall be unlawful to confine in the Penitentiary of this State, or in the jails of any county of this State, any person or persons charged with simply being a fugitive from slavery." Our readers need not be informed that Ohio knows more about fugitive slaves than perhaps any other equal area of civilization. Kidnappers are the local horror there, as Indians are in Oregon, and discontented slaves in Louisiana. It is in Cincinnati that negro mothers slay their own infants with virtuous intentions, to save them from the hell of female slavery.[162] It is there that, on the river frontier, fugitives cross by scores and by hundreds when the ice affords a passage ever so perilous; while on the opposite lake-frontier on the north the bright side of the picture is seen—that of the sailing away of the wanderers for the free soil of Canada. In Ohio, the "Underground Railway" is busiest; unless, indeed, the activity of the other great branch, through Pennsylvania, New York and New England now rivals the western one. We observe, also, that Maryland is fiercely denounced by Southern newspapers as rapidly going over to the free States, and especially as affording the safest path for fugitives to the north. It is through Ohio, however, that the greatest number of successful escapes is supposed to be made: and the noble list of ruined hosts is remarkably long in that State—the list of good men and women who have suffered loss for the sake of speeding the fugitives on their way. It was in Ohio that a constant influx of facts, visible incidents, and strong emotions filled the large heart of Harriet Beecher Stowe, and made it overflow into the general heart of the world. Year by year, petitions are sent up to the Legislature of Ohio, demanding the dissolution of its union with the slave States; and at length some notice is granted to these petitions,—enough to proceed upon if the demand becomes prevalent. Meanwhile, the State is in fact outside the pale of the Union, like Massachusetts, from the incompatibility of its laws relating to personal liberty with those recently enacted at Washington. The only recognition of the new Supreme Court law in any of that group of States seems to be in the way of joke. . . . Ohio, being already in collision with the federal laws, may be confidently reckoned on as one of the revolutionary group, if the slave-power compels such an issue. As for the most westerly States, all north of Missouri have acted decisively in favour of the establishment of free labor in Kansas. Iowa is to vote, next August, for or against the proposition that people of colour are to have the suffrage on precisely equal terms with whites. The mere proposition, whatever may be its fate, is a revolutionary act; and the support it meets with shows that a great number of the citizens are rendering themselves responsible for such a step at such a time. Wisconsin is no less agitated. The action there on personal liberty legislation is too extensive and protracted to be fully cited here. The whole group of north-western States and Territories have opened roads, set up mails, forwarded supplies, furnished armed guards, and bodies of militia,—done, in short, all they could to compensate for the stoppage of the river communication during the struggle in Kansas. They have, if not a larger, a more exclusive stake in the establishment of free labor than any other part of the nation: and they will be well able to prevent the extension of slavery if they give a due welcome to the immigrants from Europe and the Eastern States, who are always pouring in to occupy their fertile plains.

Does such a survey as this convey any idea that the free States will yield obedience to the decision of the Supreme Court, and will invite the benumbing touch of slavery to paralyze their activity—to empty their treasuries—to debase their citizens into the condition of "mean-whites"—to banish literature, gag the press, pervert or silence the clergy, and convert a condition of eminent freedom and commercial prosperity like that of London into a state of depression, distrust, and poverty, worse than that of Jamaica just before the abolition of slavery? Who can believe in such a possibility? And yet, the North has much to do to give the world assurance that the impending revolution will be worthy of a comparison with the former. . . . The Northern States, having all the power in their own hands, might have spared their country all talk of revolution, by simply maintaining their constitutional liberties by constitutional means. They can never be absolved from the crime of having allowed their country to be dragged into the abyss of revolution: but it is inconceivable that, now that a choice is imperative, they will allow a quarter of a million of citizens, who cannot attain prosperity in their private affairs, to rule seventeen millions of active citizens, who, if they have no great public virtue to boast of, can at least buy up the whole South ten times over.

While the Southern and federal leaders and newspapers declare themselves scandalized at the treason and rebellion of the North, what is the condition of the slave States? The North declares it to be one of nullification of all the great principles and laws of the Union, from end to end of the list of States.

It is true; the press is nowhere free in the slave States. So vigilant is the censorship, that the readers of the few newspapers which exist have no more knowledge of their real condition than the citizens of Paris. The best, as well as the largest part of the world's literature is unknown there, because it breathes a freedom unsuited to the climate. There is no freedom of trade in the South: not only may a bookseller sell none but emasculated and permitted books, but a planter or merchant must deal only with firms or individuals supposed to be well inclined towards slavery. The mail service is violated to such an extent, that the contents of the bags are well known to be at the mercy of the postmasters, who are compelled to detain and destroy all documents which seem to them to threaten "the peculiar institution." The citizens have no security of person, property, or residence, being liable to assault on any such mob-incitement as happens somewhere or other every day: incendiarism is a besetting peril wherever slaves are at hand; and if a man sells an obnoxious book, or entertains a mistrusted guest, or speaks his mind where walls have ears, he is ordered off at a few hours' warning—only too happy to get away with his life. These are the ordinary conditions of existence in the slave States; and with us they would be called revolutionary. There is nothing of an organic character in such a mode of life. But the chronic distrust and instability of ordinary times are freedom and security in comparison with the present condition of affairs throughout the slave States.

We have spoken of Virginia. Pursuing the frontier line, Kentucky comes next. So deep is the discontent with slavery there, that nothing short of Henry Clay's great influence could have sustained it for many years past: and now there is a scheme afloat for buying out the inveterate slave-holders, in order to allow to others a choice between free and slave labor. . . .

The recent slave insurrection is a fearful warning. . . . The slaves heard predictions from the wisest men they knew that the success of Fremont would occasion the overthrow of slavery; and there were plenty of "mean-whites" at hand to establish concert among them, and supply them with muskets and ammunition. The chaotic state of society which ensued in a dozen States, where the women and children were gathered into camps, and their husbands and fathers organized into a patrol, while negroes were hung in long rows, or burned alive, or whipped to death from day to day, was a remarkable preparation for such a revolutionary crisis as the Supreme Court has since brought on. Any abnormal condition of the States on the free shore of the great rivers must be at least equalled by that of the slave States opposite. The Kansas question is too large for our bounds at present. We can only observe in passing, that nowhere is the conflict of principles more remarkable than in Missouri. That State is held answerable for the troubles in Kansas; and yet, in the very country of the Border Ruffians, the desire for the blessings of free labor and free speech is so strong, that many people (much better judges than we can be) imagine that Missouri will ere long be purged of the bully element of her population, and allowed to live according to her own convictions. Others fear that the movement is a mere sham, to be carried on only as long as it is the interest of Missouri to keep terms with both parties. However this may be, such a condition of such a territory is a fresh revolutionary element thrown in among the conditions of the time. We observe that the result of recent elections in Missouri—in which "the anti-slavery ticket" was carried by a majority supposed to be due to the votes of white labourers—is regarded as intently by the Northern states as by the excitable and alarmed South. . . . By the latest accounts, this question of the frontier slave States seems to be producing a schism at the South. . . .

There seems to be a sort of general understanding that the turbulence of South Carolina may be taken for granted, and need not be displayed as one of the revolutionary elements of the case. "The gallant little State," as her citizens call her, was never known to be in a quiet condition and amiable mood for any length of time; and her citizens glory in a revolutionary attitude. South Carolina may therefore be left to assert her own claims to disorder and disloyalty; but it is necessary to remind our readers, in the briefest way, that large assemblages, in the chief towns of the State last autumn, ratified with acclamations the proposal to summon the citizens for a march upon Washington, in case of Fremont being elected, to seize the Treasury, burn the archives, and make the Halls of Congress resound with the din of actual war.

Thus did South Carolina take up her position in defence of the recent corruptions of the Federal Constitution, in opposition to the Northern citizens, who proclaim their fidelity to the fundamental principles of the Republic.

No revolution recorded by history has had a more serious cause or complete justification than is afforded by a sectional antagonism like this. Is it to be supposed that a sectional population yielding 2,900,000 votes should grant to a rival numbering 1,100,000 votes (inclusive of the fictitious slave-suffrage), power to bring slavery and slaves among the children of free labor? And, again, to carry off the children of free labor into bondage on a slave soil? Can any one for a moment believe that such a thing can happen?

What, then, will happen? The North has the numbers, the wealth, the good cause, and the sympathy of Christendom. The South (meaning the dominant party in that section) is so poor in numbers that the world abroad will not believe the figures of the census; it is so poor in wealth that its annual convention of planters and merchants sends forth the same complaints, year by year, of want of capital and the high price of labor, on the very same page with threats of setting up steamers, railways, colleges, factories, and a complete new literature, whereby New York will be ruined as a port, and England supplied with cotton without any intervention of Northern capitalists; threats that New England colleges will have no aristocratic youths within their walls, to be corrupted with vulgar notions of constitutional rights and the dignity of work; while a bright day will open on the whole class of pro-slavery authors, whose works are henceforth to supply the place of the literature of all past ages. The business of expurgating books from every other part of the world, and of creating a complete system of school-books suitable to the South, is actually confided to a committee, headed by a bishop, and chiefly composed of university men. . . . "Are such sentiments to be instilled into the minds of our children? If not, then banish Grimshaw's History from our schools and academies. Men will not regard them (the postulates of the Declaration of Independence); but they may warp the more impressible minds of uninformed and unreflecting childhood." This appears to us revolutionary in the highest degree,—that the fundamental principles of the Declaration of Independence should be regarded as warping the mind!

No hindrance has been offered to the Southern scheme of domestic policy; but it does not appear to be yet instituted: and the question recurs why a people so subject to disappointment, failure, and poverty within their own States has thus far over-ridden a rival of ten times its own force. The answer is a sorrowful one. The South has a will, and the North has not. A common average of righteous will on the part of the North, would have preserved the Constitution, and dealt with the great anomaly long ago: but the only righteous will was in the Abolitionists, who are, and always will be, outside the political and the military sphere. If the Northern heart and mind once fairly kindle at the alter-fire of the confessors and martyrs of the cause, everything may be at their disposal as regards federal relations; because *all* the power, except that of will, is on their side: but then the slave States must be regarded as delivered over to the horrors of a servile war. Half a million of the slaveholding class will be at the mercy of their "mean-white" and negro neighbours, from the hour when the North effectually repudiates slavery. The South would doubtless try the experiment of a military despotism in the several States; but the loss of Northern aid, and of the cotton market of Europe, would be fatal from the outset; and they could not compete with the cotton growth of free labor. In short, such a position would be wholly untenable. To the next question—what else?—there is no present answer; and herein lies the unmistakable token of revolution,—not merely impending, but actual. The mist of the comet blurs everything. We can only ask questions,—and the first questions are, whether, if they wished it ever so much, the American people could now wait four years for such a reversal of political parties as a presidential election may effect; and, next, whether the strife about slavery-extension can be suspended for the fifteen years required for the reversal of the preponderance in the Supreme Court. There can, of course, be no such suspension of the vital social interests of daily life: and those who say most about waiting, best know that it is impossible.

As for us, we decline to prophesy amidst so dire a confusion, and under the shadow of so black a thunder-cloud. The one thing we are sure of is, that the old Constitution, laden with new corruptions, cannot serve and sustain the Republic. We believe that if a radical reconstruction is not immediately agreed upon, there must be a dissolution of the Union,—the slave States being subject to the curse of a military despotism, and the perils of a servile war. It hardly appears that there can be a question about this: but of the issue we cannot venture to vaticinate. Our trust is, that the Abolitionists will not abate a jot of that strong will which renders them the real antagonists of the South; that they will press on the more strenuously as the critical moment discloses itself; and that, by upholding in the sight of all men the democratic principles which first gave them a country, they may justify that instinct of the highest minds in the Old World which has recognised them, amidst the depressions and obscurities of a quarter of a century of adversity, as the ten righteous men who should save their city.

❖ ❖ ❖

ON THE EVE OF WAR

1858–1860

Although Britain outlawed the slave trade in 1807, followed by the United States a year later, and the first half of the nineteenth century was marked by various European treaties prohibiting the slave trade, continued trafficking in Africans destined for southern plantations was the period's worst-kept secret. "The Slave-Trade in 1858" foregrounds the direct role played by the unofficial, and extremely lively, slave trade in fueling and perpetuating American slavery. There was much money to be made from these enterprises, prompting Martineau to reiterate her claim that, culpable as America is in its present situation, the country is hardly alone in bearing the guilt. Most of Europe, in fact, was implicated in the trade in human lives that came to rest so profoundly on America's doorstep. But, to Martineau's mind, the American political bureaucracy—official and public as it was—was as direct an affront to American ideals as the most notorious slave-trading pirates on the high seas. Her exposé of President Buchanan ("The United States under the Presidentship of Mr. Buchanan") clarifies the difficult situation inherited by Abraham Lincoln upon his election in 1860, vividly demonstrating the official and unofficial acts culminating in the American Civil War.

"The Slave-Trade in 1858"

Edinburgh Review, 1858

Regarded by some estimates as the most influential periodical of its day, the *Edinburgh Review* (1802–1929) was affiliated with many famous literary names of the period. Founded in 1802 by Lord Jeffrey, Sydney Smith, and Lord Brougham, the quarterly featured such writers as Walter Scott, William Hazlitt, Thomas Carlyle, and Thomas Macaulay and was famous for its negative criticisms of the "Lake Poets," Wordsworth, Coleridge, and Southey. The focus of the *Edinburgh Review* eventually shifted away from literature to political commentary (characterized as "militant" Whig), a move anticipated by the political contentiousness of its literary criticism. As was true of other periodicals of its kind, the *Edinburgh*'s political commentary was presented through book reviews, which served as a basis for the writer's own political arguments. According to R. K. Webb, Martineau had earlier dismissed the "dull imbecility" of the *Edinburgh Review*—until, that is, her cousin Henry Reeve assumed the editorship in 1858. She then published three of her finest articles on slavery in the quarterly.

Before the publication of "The Slave-Trade in 1858," Martineau noted that her niece Maria "thinks it will make a noise" (Arbuckle 1983, 165). The article addresses the Liberian scheme, in which an African colony was established by the American Colonization Society in 1822 for the resettlement of former slaves, and the 1857 *Regina Coeli* incident, in which a French ship was caught transporting African slaves under the guise of paid labor. Initially, Martineau thought the colonization idea—vigorously promoted by Henry Clay—a viable one; when she later learned that it served to mask the illegal international slave trade, she quickly withdrew her support. Although the article was published anonymously, its authorship was quickly detected. Maria Martineau's prediction proved correct when the British and Foreign Anti-Slavery Society threatened a libel suit against the *Edinburgh Review* on behalf of the President of Liberia, who was implicated in the article as a central link in the international slave trade. The threatened suit never materialized.

Officially, both Britain and America had outlawed slave trading in 1807; in 1817, Britain signed a treaty with Portugal prohibiting slave trading north of the equator and another with Spain in the same year, prohibiting slave trading altogether, while France had promised to eliminate the trade by 1820.[163] But the practice continued under all sorts of guises, not the least of which were colonization and missionary schemes; French slave trading continued, illegally, well into the 1860s. Echoing the sort of disgust Martineau expressed over the apparent meaninglessness of such treaties, historian Robin Blackburn observes: "International agreements against the slave trade were so riddled with loopholes, and bedevilled by bad faith, that they completely failed to stem a strong recovery in the cross Atlantic traffic" (322). Martineau's daring in exposing this open international secret demonstrates her continued willingness to court controversy for the sake of truth. To Wendell Phillips she wrote:

> I believe the French Emperor will go on with his slave trade too. The badness of his Frenchmen and of your President's Americans . . . renders it difficult to do anything here. The universal impression of the utter faithlessness and badness of both bars any action based on the supposition of goodness. Was ever anything so bad as the blustering politicians at Washington on the one hand, and the malignant traitors at Paris on the other![164]

"The Slave-Trade in 1858" anticipates a theme more fully developed in 1864's "Negro Race in America" in its refutation of the claim—so devastatingly promoted by the Dred Scott decision—that blacks are chattel and deserve no human or civil rights. Martineau seizes on this justification for slavery by an appeal not to emotions or morals but to logic and economics. By illustrating the impressive self-sufficiency of free African communities, which provided an essential contribution to the international cotton market, she presents an eloquent argument for the idea that the true barbarism of the slave milieu resides in the "civilising" mission of the white, Western capitalists and Christian missionaries.

Finally, while holding America accountable for perpetuating slavery as well as providing the primary market for it, the article's historical analysis of the past and present implications of European involvement in Africa dramatizes the vast complexity of the issues, countries, politicians, and economics involved in the traffic in human beings. Far from being simply an American issue, the conspiracy Martineau unveils is appallingly well entrenched, self-aggrandizing, and international in its scope.[165]

. . .

ART. IX.—1. *The London Cotton Plant: a Journal of Tropical Civilisation.* Published for the Proprietors by C. Mitchell. London: June, 1858.
2. *Report of the Special Committee on the Revival of the African Slave-trade, made to the Southern Convention at Montgomery, Alabama, May 10th, 1858.*
3. *Resolutions passed at a Public Meeting of Free Coloured Men, held at New Bedford, Massachusetts, on the 16th of June, 1858.*

The news of the abolition of the slave-trade reached Sir James Mackintosh when he was residing in India. He wrote from Bombay on the 27th of July of that memorable year 1807, of the impression that Mr. Wilberforce's victory made upon him, in these words:

> Who knows whether the greater part of the benefit that he has conferred on the world (the greatest that any individual has had the means of conferring) may not be the encouraging example that the exertions of virtue may be crowned by such splendid success? We are apt petulantly to express our wonder that so much exertion should be necessary to suppress such flagrant injustice. The more just reflection will be, that a short period of the life of one man is, well and wisely directed, sufficient to remedy the miseries of millions for ages. Benevolence has hitherto been too often disheartened by frequent failures. Hundreds and thousands will be animated by Mr. Wilberforce's example, by his success, and (let me use the word only in the moral sense of preserving his example) by a renown that can only perish with the world, to attack all the forms of corruption and cruelty that scourge mankind.[166]

At the end of half a century from the writing of that letter, when the next generation of the Wilberforces and Mackintoshes had grown old, an alarm arose that the slave-trade was in course of revival by France,—or rather, by the Emperor of the French,—under a thin disguise; and that certain State governors in the United States were openly proposing a reopening of the African trade in negroes. One year more, and we had the French importation of negro labourers into Martinique, Guadaloupe, and Cayenne to be a real trade in slaves; the subject of a revived slave-trade to be the most important of the moment in the United States; and some English newspapers, adopting a tone, and putting forth sentiments, of which many a West India planter of the last generation would have been ashamed.

What then? Where is the change? What will be the result? What is to be done? What is to be expected? Is any conclusion arrived at? And what is it?

There is no change in the grounds on which slavery, and the trade which supplies it, have always been condemned by all good and impartial men.

There is no change in the facts and reasons which condemn slavery as in every sense impolitic; as ruinous alike to the character and the fortunes of all who are implicated in it; and incompatible with political liberty and social welfare of every kind. There is therefore no change in the views and spirit of this Journal in relation to the infamous traffic by which the institution is upheld. We will venture to say that there never will be any change in the decision and energy with which the people of Great Britain will demand of their government all possible vigilance in the prevention of the traffic on the high seas, and all necessary resolution in keeping the Powers of the world to their treaty engagements in regard to the African race. This Journal was able to announce, in 1836,[167] that "every Power of Europe has acknowledged that a solemn obligation is upon them to contribute to the abolition of the cursed traffic in our fellow-creatures." The reasons which brought those Powers into the compact exist unchanged; and the compact must be fulfilled accordingly. What change there is is merely that which ordinarily ensues upon so vast and difficult a reform as the abolitionists inaugurated. It is a form of the reaction which selfish habits of mind and life are always urging, as long as the restoration of bad institutions can be conceived of by the sanguine egotist: and if the reaction seems to have any force at all, it is simply through the unreadiness of a generation which has long ceased to hear the subject discussed, but which has only to listen and to think, in order to see the truth as plainly as their fathers ever saw it, and to take care that the great work of their fathers shall never be reversed.

We are told by the retrogressive party that the subject is old and tiresome; the arguments against slave-labour worn out; the sentiment superannuated; the whole opposition an obsolete affair, which must give way to modern views and fresh interests. By way of presenting us with fresh and interesting matter, the organs of pro-slavery opinion, from Mr. Carlyle's pamphlets to the latest border-ruffian sermon in a far-west newspaper, serve up again conceptions and assumptions far more antique than any anti-slavery publications have to show;—notions of the negro and his fate, of the planter and his prerogative, of the superiority of a life of indolence and debt to one of industry and independence;—assumptions as absurd to the man of business and the economist as they are shocking to the man of principle and feeling;—arguments old as tyranny, tiresome as egotism, silly and worn-out as mediaeval arguments against antipodes, or vindications of the divine right of kings. The latest statements within our knowledge of the arguments on behalf of the slave-system, as it at present exists, are put forth by the new Journal of the American slaveowners, the *London Cotton Plant,* the first number of which appeared in May last. One paragraph of the prospectus is this:—

> Avowing our utter detestation of "slavery" in any form whatever, we hold that negro servitude to the white man is not human slavery, but the normal condition of the inferior race, and his natural relation in life. We hold that the negro is an inferior and specifically different MAN, and can only be christianised

and civilised through daily contact with the superior race; that he must of necessity, by an organised system of labour, take a self-sustaining part in his own progress and improvement, and is utterly incapable as now constituted, of self-government, self-christianity, or self-civilisation. While we shall bring to the illustration of this philosophy the evidences of science and the clear deduction of well-fortified reason, we trust to maintain the argument with dignity and decorum, and a just regard for the prejudices and feelings of others.[168]

Appended to this view of the negro, we do not observe any explanation of the remarkable circumstance that, throughout the Southern States of the Union, the negroes in "servitude" afford a large proportion of the constituency which sends members to Congress. Three-fifths of the slaves count for as many votes; without which the Southern representation at Washington would be something very unlike what it is, and the Southern policy could never have predominated in the Capitol and in the Cabinet. If the negro is not a man, capable of political ideas and an organised social existence, it ought to be explained how he can, in any way, help to send representatives to Congress. . . . [Martineau here discusses reconstruction in the West Indies following emancipation.] The journalist proceeds:—

> The actual state of negro servitude as it exists in America has never been understood in England, nor the theory of the American constitution, the organic law of which consists in the full recognition of the inferiority of the negro, and the natural superiority of the white man. The immediate representatives of the institution of negro servitude as a wise and just system of tropical labour, of course have a conscientious and honest conviction in regard to the matter. The Southern philosophy is this: that negro servitude is not "slavery" at all in the true acceptation of that term; that involuntary servitude to the white man is the normal condition of the negro, his natural relation in life, and is the same measure of freedom to him as what we call "liberty" is to the white man; that in this relation he finds his greatest happiness, makes the greatest progress, and is of the best service; that in no other relation has he ever been found except as a barbarian of the lowest grade, or when sustained in unnatural freedom by a mistaken philanthropy; that the negro must either be in christian servitude or in heathen and barbarian slavery; and that every dictate of wise economy, true charity, and honest intention enforces the necessity of making him take an active and productive part in his own civilisation.[169]

We need not waste our space on any exposure of the amount of nonsense contained in this paragraph of what the authors call "Southern philosophy." We will simply remind our readers that this sort of philosophy is no better in the eyes of twenty-five millions of the inhabitants of the United States than in ours. The largest allowance gives to the slaveholding class in the United States,—the owners, their families and connexions,—the number of two millions, out of the total population of twenty-seven millions at the time of the census of 1850. Of these, only 350,000 at the utmost are actual holders of slaves: and, further, the earnest, determined, deliberate defenders of the "philosophy," and of its concrete form, are believed to be not more than one thousand persons, and probably less. We say this merely to prevent a whole nation being charged with entertaining such notions of matters of fact, and contenting themselves with such logic as we see sprouting from this young *Cotton Plant.*

Its appearance in London, however, and its rapturous references to Mr. Carlyle and quotations from the *Times,* may warn us that one of those occasions has arisen, on which, according to Sir James Mackintosh, "hundreds and thousands will be animated by Mr. Wilberforce's example" to attack all the forms of corruption and cruelty" that can cover a revived slave-trade. It is too true that a vehement effort is made just now to reopen the African slave-trade, for purposes which we propose to exhibit: by means which we hope to expose; and in reliance on the indifference of a new generation, which yet, we are certain, needs only to be warned of the danger to show a spirit as generous, convictions as clear, and a temper as persistent as those of their fathers. Our own belief is very confident; that the slave-trade is approaching its extinction; that the present reactionary effort is a sign of its extreme peril; and that the effort itself, if properly turned to account, will accelerate the certain victory of free over slave labour. . . . Whether there be more or less of the old battle to be fought over again, the thing must be done; and every man ought to qualify himself to take his part in it, at a time when the American slaveholders undertake to teach us, in our own London, who the negro is, what slavery is, and that the "Free-negro theory of Wilberforce, Brougham and Clarkson" ought to be opposed "on the broad ground of civilisation and humanity." There can be no better encouragement to the requisite action than a survey of the plain, clear facts of the two cases,—of free-labour and slaveholding; and we prefer that method of appeal to any other, simply because the zeal which the occasion requires must be kindled through the understanding. We will not give to "Southern philosophers" the advantage of a sneer at our enthusiasm or our prejudices. They will not be able to ridicule us as sentimental philanthropists, or to rouse disgust against us as "nigger-worshippers." We have nothing to say at present in the character of Protector-of-Negroes. We have at least as much tenderness for the white men. We speak in the general interest of civilisation and human progress, in admiration of the part taken by our country in extinguishing the most fatal of barbaric institutions, and in simple fidelity to a policy with which the reputation of Great Britain is bound up. . . .

There has been hitherto no opportunity of understanding and presenting the evidence appropriate to the present time; that of the operation of the slave-trade and slavery on the countries and peoples where it has existed after being got rid of by the rest of the civilised world. The United States stand first in all eyes among the very few countries which still come under this description. Brazil having actually retired from the slave-trade, the United

States and Cuba are generally regarded as the two countries which sustain the traffic. France—or rather the French Government—has recently been ranked with these two, on account of the real, though disguised, slave-trade to her West India colonies; but, as this new crime may be soon repented of (on account of its folly, if not its guilt), we may adhere to the usual classification,—the United States and Cuba against the world. We are bound to take the independent, and self-governing country for examination before the colony, which may plead the nondescript character of the home-government on which it depends. Let us then trace, rapidly but carefully, the relations between the slave-trade and slavery and the political social condition of the North American republic, including the foreign policy of the United States and their place in the world at this hour. This time is suitable, for it is one of crisis in the Republic. All leading men, and all the separate sovereign States agree, if on no other point, in declaring that some sort of revolutionary crisis is at hand, and that the institution of slavery is the cause. There could not be a better time for investigating the real relation between the old element and the new changes; and we believe ourselves to be safe from all reproach as to the worn-out character of our inquiry. As far as we know, it is, as a body of evidence, altogether untouched.

When the Americans of our time complain of their "geographical difficulty" (as they do in London to this hour), declaring that an equal distribution of slaves over their territory would have preserved their Republic in unimpaired moral glory, they should remember two or three particulars which they are apt to overlook. They should remember the diversities in the original settlement of the various States; they should remember that the worn-out plea of diversity of climate is now excluded by the attempt to establish slavery in Kansas; and, in a converse way, by the superior success of free-labour culture of cotton and tobacco, now that the experiment has been fairly tried in Texas, and on estates in Virginia and elsewhere. They should remember that the old and once-true complaint that England introduced slavery into their country related only to the mild form of slavery which existed in the last century, when it was common in all the States; and that when the southern section insisted, in 1819, on the permanent establishment, and in 1854 on the extension, of the institution, it made the Republic answerable, from that time forwards, for American slavery, and for all the aggravations which were sure to accrue after such an adoption. In a very small space we may compare the earlier phase with the later—the British importation of slavery with the present indigenous sort, which is the express choice and demand of the citizens who have risked everything else to perpetuate it. . . .

All the world knows that the compromise was made; but all the world may not know, or may not remember, what the compromise was. It is as well to understand and remember it, as our recent difficulties at Washington, and the present attempts at reviving the African slave-trade, are among the consequences of it. The compromise was this: the Northern States consented to the artifice of reckoning three-fifths of the slaves as whites, and the

South agreed to a taxation proportioned to its nominal constituency. The North permitted an interval of twenty years before the arrest of the African Slave-trade, and the South agreed to an equal representation in the Senate of States of all dimensions, though the small States were Northern ones. The most fatal provision of the series was that which bound the citizens of all the States to deliver up to claimants "persons held to labour and service escaping from another State." The word "slave" does not appear at all in any constitutional document from that date onwards; and the term disappeared till revived by the Abolitionists. The hope was, that the substitution of the words "servant" and "service," for "slave" and "slavery," would assist the corresponding conversion of the things themselves; a strange expectation, while the traffic in human beings went on by sea and land! . . .

One constitutional safeguard after another was surrendered for some brilliant immediate advantage, till the internal slave-trade had become the organic disease of the Republic which it is now admitted to be. In short, the inevitable change was now coming over the American character which, we have a right to suppose, might have been escaped if the labour-market had not been early corrupted. . . . Since the regular establishment of an internal slave-trade, there has always been a bad social element drawn from the North, a floating population of thoughtless and idle young men or broken down elders, who wanted adventure, or fancied they could grow rich in a hurry by extending the area of southern slavery. A more numerous reinforcement, of a far lower character, from the slave States,—fellows of the bully and rowdy sort, such as have figured in the Kansas drama,—have depressed the national character incalculably, and the national reputation almost irreparably, through the factitious demand for new territory on which to employ the slaves who had worn out the old. Hence the whole invention and prosecution of *filibustering;* hence the wars, Mexican and other, and the annexations, Texan and other, which have created a world-wide distrust of the American republic, as the great buccaneering Power of the coming time.

Before considering the history of this phase, however, we must draw the attention of our readers to an incident in the life of the American slave-trade which has not been duly appreciated in England, even where it has been known as a matter of fact. It would have been a great advantage to some of our legislators who spoke on the case of the *Regina Coeli* in June last to have known more of the history and condition of the settlement of Liberia. For want of such information as the American slaveholders or abolitionists could furnish at any time, the opportunity of exposing the new "disguised French slave-trade" was nearly lost. Our information is derived from full communication with the advocates and opponents of the scheme of African Colonisation. We have learned, from the highest office-bearers of the Society, all that was to be said on behalf of it; and the facts on the other side have been so openly placed before the American public by witnesses of character, and so long acted upon by others who had means of knowing the truth, that we offer their statements without any doubt whatever of their substantial truth. We may add that the strongest confirmation that could be obtained is afforded by the recent transactions of French agents in Liberia, and comments on them by residents there. . . . [Here Martineau describes the Colonization Society and its advocate, Elliot Cresson.]

How far had the Society fulfilled its promise of "providing a peaceful exit from slavery?" During the first twenty years, the number carried to both settlements—Liberia and Cape Palmas—was under 3000, though the machinery of transportation was used to get rid of slaves inconvenient from either too much or too little capacity; scarred, stupefied, helpless wretches, as we hear from the African side, and "bright boys," who think and feel too much for the safety of the plantation. In 1853, when the Society was in its thirty-sixth year, it had removed 8500 to Africa. When our readers are reminded that the annual increase of the mere slaves was 60,000 during Mr. Clay's Presidentship of the Society, they will not require us to dwell longer on the proportion of means to ends in the case.

It was enough for all but very thoughtless people that the Southern planters were vehemently jealous of the immigration of Europeans into the Northern States. While the wealthy North was more hated every year for the prosperity which grew out of an adequate supply of labour, it was not credible that the South was really sending any labourers away. American shipping was not in fact passing to and fro across the ocean for the purpose of pouring labourers into the North, and deporting them from the South. The use that *was* made of the scheme, in this view, is now fully understood. No truer information is ever given to the European traveller in America than in the saying that the condition of the cotton crop determines the shipments of negroes to Liberia. Trifling as they always are, the largest deportations take place when cotton is lowest; that being the time when the plantation is weeded of its least valuable slaves. Between 1820 and 1830 a larger number were sent than before, or for some time after,—cotton prices being nearly stationary during that time. Through the next ten years, cotton was nearly doubled in value, and little was heard of Liberia. During the last rise in cotton and slaves, the subject seemed to be dropped. The agency was kept up, however; and the case of the *Regina Coeli* may show us why. . . .

[American] free negroes are assuming a social position which points significantly to an approaching annihilation of the slave-trade, while it settles the fate of Liberia and its adjuncts. For some time past we have observed signs of a determination on the part of leading free negroes to raise their class above that doom of mere menial labour to which their countrymen have hitherto consigned them. They will not henceforth be only barbers and porters, and hotel-waiters, and hack-drivers, and hangers-on where there is dirty work to be done. But the most remarkable demonstration is that of the present year, in which the lead is taken by the free-coloured men of New Bedford, a flourishing commercial city in Massachusetts. If we had space for the whole series of resolutions passed by them at a public meeting on the 16th of June last, our readers would find them interesting; but we must content ourselves with citing those which refer to the colonisation scheme. The preamble declared the grounds on which the meeting believed that the American Government desired three things in regard to their class: its enslavement, its expatriation, and its extirpation as a social element; and the resolutions which followed contemplated the three provisions. In regard to expatriation, they declared that no attempt to banish them, by rendering their grievances permanent, and increasingly intolerable, should make them give up their native land. "We believe," they say, "the design is, now more than ever before, to make our grievances permanent, by greatly multiplying the disabilities under which we labour; nevertheless, we are determined to remain in this country, our right and title being as clear and indisputable as that of any class of people." Such resolutions, following forty-one years' trial of American colonisation in Africa, spares all doubt as to the effect of Liberia in extinguishing slavery and the slave-trade. We must now take a rapid glance at the remaining aspect of the scheme, and see whether the influence of Liberia may not in fact be enlisted on the other side.

The territory chosen for the American settlement was one which flourished well before the slave-traders found it. Along the river St. Paul, and between that and the Mesurado, an agricultural population lived in a succession of villages, extending two miles inward from the river banks. After the appearance of slave-ships off the coast, all became barren. The people were carried off or dispersed, and the hamlets burned. The Colonisation Society chose a strip of coast, about 300 miles long, and of varying extent towards the interior. It has several rivers, but they are rapid, with rocky channels, and apt to form sandbanks at their mouths, where there are no materials for a good anchorage. Monrovia, the capital of Liberia, is ill-placed for ventilation, and therefore health; and it is difficult of access from the sea. It has never had the life-like appearance of a place of business; and the depression caused by the first aspect, on mounting the wretched roads to it, is confirmed by all that is seen elsewhere. At the time that Mr. Cresson was extolling in England the climate, productions, and American population of Liberia (in 1832), Mr. Laird was at Monrovia obtaining that information about the free-negro scheme which he soon after published. He at once discovered that the colony was a mere device for ridding American slaveholders of troublesome negroes, free or slave. The former told him how they had been made wretched by oppression at home, and then betrayed into this hungry wilderness by representations of its being a paradise. The condition of the colony five years later accorded with Mr. Laird's description.

The name of the Bacon family of New England is well known in this country. The Rev. Leonard Bacon is an eminent professor at a New England University; and his brother, Dr. Bacon, is the enlightened and intrepid physician to whom we chiefly owe the exposure of the slave-trading character of the Liberian colony. Dr. Bacon went forth "an enthusiastic promoter" of the enterprise,—misled, like Webster, and like Garrison himself, by the specious pretences of the scheme. He landed in Liberia in 1837, and lived there nearly two years, spending a third year on other parts of the coast. He found the number of Americans to be at the utmost 5000, to 80,000 natives. He found Roberts, now known as the late President of the Republic of Liberia, acting as the agent and factor of the great slave-trader, Pedro Blanco. He found John N. Lewis, Secretary of the Colony, also an agent of Blanco's. He found Payne, known as the Missionary Payne, a regular workman at the slave factory of New Sesters. Roberts was employed in purchasing condemned vessels at Sierra Leone for Blanco's use as slavers; and Lewis stored the goods and merchandise which were to be bartered for slaves. It was known in America that one of the branches of industry on the spot was the forging of shackles for the slave cargoes carried off from the coast. Thousands of dollars were received by these three agents from the slave-traders; and from 1835 to 1840, the colony was one of the chief auxiliaries of the traffic which it pretended to supercede. Dr. Bacon saw as many as six slave-ships anchored at once before Monrovia; and while they were present no other method of industry than stocking them was thought of. We have not space for the details of the scheme by which condemned vessels at Sierra Leone (which could not be legally purchased by the English agent of Pedro Blanco, nor by Spaniards in person,) were bought by Roberts, removed under the American or the Liberian flag, and subsequently transferred, through a third person, to Blanco, at his great establishment at Gallinhas. Dr. Bacon kept his eye on one vessel,— the slave-schooner which Roberts christened the *Monrovia*,—and which, after lying idle till attention was supposed to be diverted from it, was laden with slaves from Gallinhas for Havannah, where she arrived under another name. The whole narrative, with all the objections unavailingly brought against it, may be found in the *New York Day-Book*, of July 11th and 15th, 1848. Dr. Bacon was an eye-witness of the slave-trading at Gallinhas and New Sesters, during two voyages which he took along the coast; the vessels in which he was a passenger having business with the slave-traders in both places. So much for the occupation of the colony. What of its condition?

Dr. Bacon left the colony simply because the deficiency of food rendered his self-sacrifice useless. He was willing to bear hardship himself; but he could not keep his patients alive. His convalescents sank through hunger. Some of the colonists ran through the bush, and overtook him when he was stepping into the boat to depart, imploring him, as they implored every man who was so fortunate as to get away, to take them with him,—anywhere, and in any capacity, if they could only escape from that horrible place. No one took care of the immigrants; and everybody robbed them. The colonists beat the natives, pillaged them, starved them;—these colonists being the "missionaries" who were to evangelise Africa. "Here," said a clergyman on the colonisation platform in America, "they are nuisances: there they will be missionaries."

It may be said that this happened long ago: matters may have mended since. Not so, however. Before us lies a series of published letters from the colony, dated from March to June, 1854, which gives a more appalling representation than even Dr. Bacon's. These letters are understood to be (and the signature leaves no doubt of it) by one of the missionaries sent out by the Colonisation Society,—Mr. Augustus Washington. All considerations induced him to think and say the best he could of the settlement: but the anguish of the spectacle overcame all restrictions and all prudence; and, with much fear and trembling, such as the black agent of white slaveholders was likely to feel, he wrote the truth to the New York *Tribune,* by which it was published to the world. "Ninety-five per cent. of all who come here with nothing," he says, "endure suffering and death to an extent almost incredible." What of those who came with something? The *Morgan Dix* brought 151 immigrants, negroes, "all well" on arrival, and fully supplied with agricultural implements, a saw-mill, &c. It arrived at the close of 1851; and in two years the only question was whether the survivors were nine or fourteen. Other such companies lost only a third of their number, or less: but the mortality is always frightful; and those who fare best do it by the exercise of a fearful tyranny. The immigrants play the slaveholder over the native niggers; they complain that the missionaries make the people insolent and restless; and they "keep the cow-hide handy," for application "in nearly all families, by boys, women, and gentlemen of rank and standing, calling themselves Christians." The starving immigrants are sent up the rivers, out of begging distance. The sick are hidden away in wattle huts when British vessels are looked for; and the dead are thrust underground "in old gun-boxes." It is of importance that the disposition of the immigrant population should be noted. It is this. Those who carry money can grow rich rapidly; they purchase from British ships, and sell their goods at a vast profit, because nothing of the sort is produced in the colony. In regard to the commonest necessaries, they can make the highest profits. The next class is not much larger. It consists of men who can do a little carpentering or other artisan labour, and who are thereby encouraged to settle, to break up a piece of ground for a garden, and to rear poultry. A few more simply squat, and raise rice and cassava enough for themselves, without attempting more. The mass of the immigrants, however, disappear; "bondmen, scarred, worn out, and expatriated"; "poor miserable slaves, that are thrown on their shores nearly all destitute of means to help themselves." These are sent "up the rivers," and when far enough off not to incommode the people on the coast they are dropped into the native huts, or left to shift for themselves. Till very recently it was supposed that this largest class of American immigrants was really lost sight of, and done with. There is now reason for suspicion that it is not so.

It appears that some time before the Emperor of the French made his contract with M. Regis and Co. for carrying free negroes to the French colonies, the President of Liberia (Roberts) delighted the House of Assembly by announcing in his message a gift from the Emperor of the French of 1000 stand of arms. This will appear to our readers very odd till they hear of further transactions. For some distance from Monrovia the shore presents for many miles only one phenomenon besides the villages, and the interminable forests of mangrove and acacia; and that one object is a slave barracoon here and there. Here did the agents of M. Regis repair for their cargo; and here they purchased a number of "labourers" from a notorious slave-dealer. But a difficulty occurred. The ship must clear out from Monrovia, because there was no other port that would serve; and the Liberian laws (the ground of alliance with England and other Powers) prohibit the exportation of *emigrants* without passports. First the French agents were found employing menaces to induce the President (Benson) to grant a general passport to the whole company of negroes they had just obtained by purchase. The tale of the *Regina Coeli* is the next illustration of the case. On the 29th of October last, says the French account, cited by Lord Malmesbury in the House of Lords, Captain Simon, of the *Regina Coeli*, having been urged to fill his vessel from that part of the coast, paid to the authorities the sum of 1564 piastres as passport duty for 400 labourers, who should be supplied to him in the course of forty days. Of these, 271 were on board, and the rest ready to embark, when the scuffle arose on which so much dispute has since hung. The "emigrants" murdered several of the crew, and then took possession of the ship. They would not allow the captain (who was on shore at the time) to approach the vessel, but at length delivered it to the British consul, who sent the *Ethiope* to take charge of the *Regina Coeli*. Captain Simon protested against any claim in regard to his ship; and a French man-of-war appeared on the scene to carry her off.

The "emigrants" meantime attempted to swim ashore, their "manacles" having been removed before the English boarded the ship. Many were drowned, and more escaped up the country. There was some speculation in Parliament, as elsewhere, about these emigrants, as to who they were, and how they came to be manacled, and to rise upon the crew, if they were free and willing to go. Our readers will not be surprised, after what we have shown of the character of Liberia, at the French boast that these men were not debased native Africans, but "free Americans," who would have carried the Christian civilisation of their native land, and the habits and manners of American society, to the French colonies. Our readers will also need little suggestion now as to what becomes of the mass of American "immigrants" who disappear up the rivers after being landed. The puzzle in Parliament was to make out whether Captain Simon's company of passengers came from up the rivers, or from the settlement on the shore. They were Americans (the French say), and yet they did not apparently come from Monrovia or the neighbourhood. Can we not solve the difficulty? And can it be necessary to direct attention to the glimpses we seem now to be obtaining of a system by which American planters philanthropically deport negroes *to* Liberia, and French planters benevolently import negroes *from* Liberia, paying head-money under the name of passport duty, and incurring the risk of mutiny from the free and voluntary labourers who, as soon as released from "manacles," kill the crew and swim off to shore?

While we are writing, the Liberian and American accounts of the transaction arrive. The Judge of the Liberia Court of Probate, Mr. B. B. R. James, writes from New York under the date of the 15th of July. He declares that President Benson did accede to the French captain's proposal to engage labourers on the coast, as, indeed, the President's preceding message informed the Legislature; that Captain Simon did obtain a large number from the chief at Cape Mount; that there was great eagerness on the part of residents to supply such labourers, on account of the extreme poverty of the place; but that the emigrants themselves had no notion of being penned up on board ship, and rose upon the crew accordingly, after several previous unsuccessful attempts; and that 300 of them got to shore. "Not till then," the Judge continues, "did the Government of Liberia know by what means these emigrants had been procured. It appears that the greater number of them had been kidnapped and forced aboard that ship, making it nothing more nor less than the actual slave-trade." From other Liberian authorities, we learn a remarkable fact, in connexion with French patronage of the settlement. The Emperor promised to present the Republic of Liberia with a war-brig; some add, because the schooner given by the British Government had become unseaworthy. A time and place was appointed for the transfer of the war-brig; but the Emperor revoked his promise, and sent the vessel to serve his own colonies, because the Liberian authorities were not sufficiently accommodating in promoting the new French slave-trade. The defence of the Colonisation Society consists mainly of the denial of the particulars of the French defence; denial that the "emigrants" were Americans; denial that 200 of them could, as the French surgeon declares, read; denial that the passport duty could have amounted to the sum alleged. Assuming that the emigrants are natives, they are said to have been terrified at their fetters and confinement on board the *Regina Coeli,* and hence their rebellion; and, again, we are assured that the precautions against the inveigling away of the natives are so express, that the authorities in Liberia could not possibly have been cognisant of the enterprise, as they are alleged by the French to have been. The result, so far, is that the French deny the fetters and the native African character of the emigrants, declaring them to be free Americans, 200 of whom could read; and that the President and other authorities sanctioned the scheme, and took the money. The Colonisation Society, on the other hand, declares that the victims were wild natives, that they were fettered and confined on board; and that there must be some mistake about the money, as the President and his officers could have known nothing of this application of the new French method of slave-trading. Another party now comes forward with its comment,—the American public, which is a disinterested judge, like ourselves, of the whole transaction. The *New York Times* analyses the defence of the Colonisation Society, and finds it open to grave question; and it thus concludes:—

> We state these points, and would urge them upon the Colonisation people, because we believe the entire purgation of the Liberians from this accusation to be highly important. The exculpation will be worthless if partial. Since we

abandoned the traffic in the United States, and since we are suspected the world over of desiring to resume it, the allegation that an American colony on the African coast is actually tampering with the vile business does us infinite mischief. It suggests a doubt whether these anti-slavery settlements were not designed to recruit our slave-markets; and it calls our sincerity in question, when we declare our freedom from all thought of returning to negro-stealing. The entire exoneration of President Benson is therefore of no slight consequence. Let us have it, if practicable.

The French commentary on the case may be presented in brief space. The *Moniteur de la Flotte* tells us that the title of French consular agent has been withdrawn from the British consul at Monrovia, and that a special consul will probably be immediately appointed, "to represent the interests of France on the coast, and which are every day becoming more extensive, to the great but unjust displeasure of England." Meantime, the Emperor has bestowed the Cross of the Legion of Honour on Lieutenant Pointel, the chief of the staff of the Commandant on the African station, and the writer of the report which is impugned by the American and Liberian authorities. Moreover, the surgeon of the *Regina Coeli* is favoured with a pension of 1800 francs.

There is yet another party to the case—ourselves. We have treaties, such as should prevent such a transaction as this with France, the United States, and Liberia. It is our business to see that no conspiracy takes place among our professing coadjutors, by which they carry on a slave-trade under false pretences. Those among our American kindred who are our genuine allies, will assist us (in the spirit of the paragraph we have quoted above) to ascertain the facts of every dubious case, and enforce the provisions of treaties with all the firmness that international good faith requires.

Before concluding our view of the American case, we must here give another illustration of what this French method of supplying negro labour to French colonies is like. We obtain it from our own colonial newspapers. Dominica is naturally the first to become acquainted with the real character of the "immigration," from its position between Martinique and Guadaloupe. It is to be hoped that its press will tell all that it knows, as the French colonial newspapers are not allowed to print anything on the subject. The *Dominican* of June 16, we observe, offers its columns to anybody in Martinique who may wish to explain any transaction reported therein, as the *Outre Mer* of St. Pierre had been "silenced" by the government for having discussed the African emigration scheme.

On the 2d of last May, two negroes landed in Dominica from Martinique, in the capacity of escaped slaves. On the 15th of June, three more appeared alongside the *Mayborough,* in Roseau roadstead, in a canoe, at three o'clock in the morning. One of these named Zaba (or, by the English off Cape Coast, Tom Dick), could speak English; and from him the history of all the five was obtained. Zaba had worked for Bristol and Liverpool vessels trading to Cape Coast for ivory and gold dust, the method being for the captains to make an agreement with the chief of the district, King Peter, for the services of a certain number of "boys" for six months, at a certain rate of wages. These "boys" always came home at the end of the term, with their money; so that no distrust existed when, at the close of 1856, a French captain applied for "boys," "to work same as they did for Englishmen, only they were to go further, would be paid good wages, and would be returned to their country at the end of six moons." Forty "boys" were engaged on these terms, the captain writing their names in two books, one of which he gave to King Peter. The Africans supposed the books to contain the captain's "word" that they should be paid as agreed, and returned at the end of six months. The first surprise was at the great number of "boys" collected on board, and at their diversity of race and tribe,—there being no common language among the different groups. The next surprise (for there was nothing to complain of during the voyage), was their reception in Martinique. After a long "palaver" between the captain and the governor, Zaba, and the four others who escaped to Dominica, and one more, who died, were delivered into a harsh slavery under the immediate control of a M. Jules, the overseer of a planter named Enou, whose estate of L'autrebord lies on the windward side of the island. The thirty-four others were carried off in like manner, in different directions, and nothing more had been heard of them. M. Jules' victims were cruelly overworked, with scant food, many blows, and no pay. One of the party died from the effect of blows on the spine. This made the others eager to return home; but the attempt to claim their rights proved to them that they were "niggers," that is, slaves.[170] At the end of the six months, there was no pay, nor move to send them home. After another half year, Zaba told M. Jules he must go back to his woman and his little boy, and that his five comrades wanted their wages and their liberty. The overseer's reply was that they were "niggers," and would never go back. The only hope now was in the high mountain which rose out of the sea on the horizon—"Englishman's country," as they were told. Two went off on the 1st of May; and at once precautions against further loss were taken on the estate,—the canoes secured every night, and great vigilance observed. Zaba heard, nevertheless, of the safety of the fugitives; and the rest of the party soon followed. Zaba spied out the place where the sail, oars, and paddle of a canoe were secreted; and, when he could not unlock the canoe from the beam to which it was chained, carried off beam and all. Once afloat, the three pushed off quietly to a good distance from the shore, then stepped the mast, and were safe. They needed assurance that they were so, however. When satisfied that they would not be delivered up, but might go to Liverpool, on their way home, as soon as they had earned enough to pay their passage, they were overjoyed. The district from which these poor fellows were carried off was near the French settlement of Grand Bassin, on the Cape Coast. Hence the French captain's knowledge of the English method of hiring labourers; and hence the negroes' knowledge of M. Jules' language. As for the rest, they prefer the English as employers, because "the English have only one mouth" everywhere, whereas the French have two; a pleasant ("sugar") one in Africa, and a less agreeable one in Martinique. Moreover, the "Englishman Queen" has put a letter into the hands of all kings, to say that the black men are not to be made niggers any more. This faith in the great letter and the "one mouth" must be justified, any amount of diplomatic correspondence and clamorous rage, and double-tongued intrigue notwithstanding.

The briefest possible statement of the facts of American legislation, in connexion with slavery, will suffice here, both because those facts are notorious, and because it is more to our purpose to mark the temper which underlies the facts; but some reference to leading acts of Congress is indispensable to the completeness of the case.

The point on which the policy of the Republic has turned, since it involved the anomaly of slavery, is the equal representation of States in the Senate. A majority in the Senate was the same thing as preponderance in the Federal Government; and the faster the free States advanced in population, and in the consequent importance in the House of Representatives, the more essential it was to the Southern section to multiply States below the slave line, and to push up the slave line so as to include more States. Hence the controversies and struggles about Missouri, and the revolutionary abrogation of the old provision, made by the founders of the Republic, for the eternal exclusion of slavery from the new lands north-west of the Ohio. Hence the adoption of a policy corresponding with the Russian, in regard to neighbouring countries: the policy of first introducing harmless cultivators of the soil; sending after them a more stirring order of rovers, who generated discontents among the inhabitants, offered their aid in the struggle they had provoked, made themselves arbiters or protectors, and at length conquerors and masters. Such was the process in the Texas case, with the aggravation that slavery was introduced and re-established where it had been successfully abolished. The story is more painful than it is generally known to be. The first settlers were more innocent, and the next batch more guilty, than is commonly supposed. The experience of two or three English travellers is enough to illustrate the scheme. An English clergyman, who took his wife down the Mississippi to die of consumption, was ensnared by the pretences of the schemers, who took him on the weak side of his benevolence, and not only engaged him to frame a constitution which should be a model of a Christian democracy, but employed him as a decoy to bring in other Britishers, who might induce their Government to sanction emigration to Texas, or to appear to countenance American proceedings there. Carefully concealing the fact of their leader being then in a Mexican prison, and that there was no prospect of the territory being granted to them, they made great offers of land to English travellers of any importance, in return for their counsel in making the new constitution, and for their residence for a term of years. The first inquiry of the English, in such cases, was about the intention in regard to slavery. "Oh, there was to be no slavery. Slavery was to be prohibited by the constitution." Closer inquiry brought out the explanation. There were to be plenty of negroes; but they were all to be "apprentices for 99 years." There were to be no slaves: only apprentices. But even this profession was not true. An extensive slave-trade was carried on at that very time. Companies of slaves were landed at night, from Louisiana, on a spit of sand near Galveston; and the importation from Cuba was even then considerable. The clergyman died ignorant of the frauds which had been practised upon him; ignorant of the promulgation of a "scrip" which represented nothing; of the conspiracies going on in Mexico, and the recruiting in the United States, and the fraud and violence which resulted in the Mexican war, and the annexation of the territory which he trusted was to be a model republic. A fever carried him off the first season, and left his children orphans. The object of his tempters was twofold;—to obtain a territory which would cut up into several States,—five or more, giving to the South ten or more new seats in the Senate; and to open a virgin soil to planters and their slaves, who were fast going down into debt and destitution on the exhausted lands of the old States. Hence the subsequent conflict in regard to the North-western lands beyond the Ohio, which the free States hoped to divide, in like manner, so as to keep up their equality in the Senate. We need not detail the well-known facts of the struggle; the abrogation of the security of the North-western area from slavery; the imposition of the Fugitive Slave Law; the extension of pro-slavery law over the whole Union; and finally the DRED SCOTT decision, by which it is declared of four millions of the inhabitants of the Republic that "the black man has no rights which the white man is bound to respect." This is enough to say of the federal legislation of the Republic.

A quarter of a century ago, the Abolitionists, then a new sect, were petitioning Congress for the extinction of slavery in the Congressional District (of ten miles square) in which Washington stands; the object being to remove the institution from its federal lodgment, and render it a concern of the separate States. The immediate effect was, that the right of petition was suspended. The scandal was so great, that, on the one hand, many eyes were opened to the vital character of the difficulty, and, on the other, the subject was pronounced by the Southern members of Congress, "got rid of for ever" at Washington. This was seen by many to be "the beginning of the end"; and the conflict has proceeded with great activity ever since. In ten years, the Capitol resounded with complaints that, whatever subject was introduced in either House, it always merged in that of slavery; and this was simply a type of the politics of the whole country. The South was always predominant at Washington, and always conscious that its tether was a shortening one; and therefore the South was encroaching, insolent, degenerate in constitutionalism, and insufferable in manners. The Northern men declined in public spirit and republican courage, and showed more and more of the lower sort of mercantile *animus,* while becoming more and more prone to reckless speculation, and to an aggressive foreign policy which might postpone the settlement of troubles at home. It began to be said of the Americans that they had made a mistake in supposing Washington to be the type of their national character; that it had been more like Franklin, but that the nearest resemblance would be found in the worst side of Jefferson's reputation, as his enemies would describe it. Is the world to be afflicted with the spectacle of a further decline?—of Paul Jones being the model founder of the Republic?[171] To arrest the deterioration, the slave-trade must be dealt with speedily and resolutely.

The nation was becoming partially wealthy, but it was growing very sick. It lost the use of its great men. The noble race of Presidents came to an end when a tool of the South was required for the post. No great man commanded suffrages by his merits; and any great man who coveted the post was certain to lose his merits—happily in vain. Webster bowed his splendid head to the yoke of the South, and died broken-hearted at the consequences of the humiliation. Clay sustained repeated disappointments, and left a tainted reputation, as having been the obstacle to the restriction and reduction of slavery in some of the frontier States, and the cause of its establishment in Missouri, Florida, and Arkansas. Calhoun died broken-hearted also;—not on account of any forfeiture of political honour, for he was courageous and consistent as a public man; but because he saw, as he declared on his death-bed, that the interior slave-trade and the Union were incompatible, and that slavery must go down in the struggle. His theory was, that "slavery was the corner-stone of republican liberties," meaning by this the oligarchical privileges of South Carolina; and the extinction of slavery, which he saw to be inevitable, was, in his eyes, equivalent to the downfall of his "gallant little South Carolina." As it is impossible to suppose that the politicians who have ruled the Republic for the last dozen years can be the best statesmen the country can produce, the conclusion is inevitable, that the sectional conflict has delivered over the State to the management of an inferior and perpetually declining order of men; while it is, at the same time, too clear, that the average character of the American people has sunk far below its traditional reputation. Instead of the cultivated aristocracy of the old slave States, who exemplified for the moment the ordinary plea for an oligarchical system—the benefit of a lettered class blessed with leisure—we now see a race of bullies, ignorant of books and of life, and unskilled in all gentle arts and high-bred manners. This is immediately owing to the presence of slavery, not only from the immorality and coarseness which grow out of the institution, but from the necessary restriction of the press, and discouragement of liberal thought and speech. There is scarcely a good book in any language which can now be admitted freely and without emasculation in the slave States (hence our difficulty in obtaining an international copy right law); and when we add, that a Commission is now sitting to prepare a literature suitable to the institutions of the Southern States, the case will be found sufficiently plain. A complete series of school and university books is to be prepared, because the planters will no longer send their sons north for education, nor admit the received morality and political history of the world into their own circle. Yet their schools and colleges languish, and the aristocracy of the

South presents a spectacle of intellectual barbarism as wonderful as it is painful. The much larger class of non-slaveholding whites is, generally speaking, totally ignorant. We need not describe the class, now sufficiently well known through Mrs. Stowe's novels, the descriptions of recent travellers, Mr. Helper's book on "the Impending Crisis of the South," and the war in Kansas, where the "ruffian" class consisted of these people, sent thither by the planters, to fight for the extension of slavery. Some of them, who learned to resent such treatment as plying them with drink and bombast, putting arms and bibles in their hands, and sending them to propagate the institution which had ruined them, soon settled down on the new soil, and are experiencing the blessings of industry in a free atmosphere; and these may yet stimulate their class in the South to that "rebellion" through the ballot-boxes which their slave-holding neighbours supremely dread, and which explains much of their recent action. We need say nothing of the exhausted estates, of the poverty, so ostentatiously deplored in Southern Conventions every year, the hopeless mortgages, the crumbling mansions, the fruitless attempt to raise capital for shipping, roads, and public institutions; and the jealousy of the North, by whose capital and industry the machinery of society goes on. We need only refer to all local newspapers for testimony of the depravation of manners which shows itself by the evidence of personal violence. We will add only two remarks. First, we repeat (and shall be forgiven for doing so), the scarcely credible numbers given by the Census and other local accounts of the population—that the entire slaveholding class is under 350,000 in a total population of 27,000,000; and that in the Slave States themselves, the slaveholding class amounts to no more than three-tenths of the *white* population. Next, we must recall to the reader's memory, that the immunity from insurrection which the South has enjoyed ever since the existence of the Abolitionists became known throughout the negro population, has been broken up by the Southern politicians themselves. By their own account, they made speeches two years ago, within earshot of negro listeners, by which the slaves learned that the first consequence of Fremont's success would be the abolition of slavery. We shall see presently the bearing of these facts on the African slave-trade, and on some highly important interests of our own.

The North has not declined so thoroughly and universally as the South, but there are sad tales to tell there also. The old industry and its pleasant results have gradually merged in a rapacity, sharp dealing, and ostentation of wealth which would never have distinguished such a race as peopled in the northern States if there had not been an uneasy consciousness of a radical mischief, impelling towards intoxication of the mind in business or pleasure. In all the great ports it has always been known that the slave-trade was largely participated in by the American citizens, both at home and abroad. The inter-state slave-trade has usually been carried on by northern speculators; and merchants of reputation and wealth in New York, Baltimore, and even Boston, could tell, quite as well as their acquaintance in Virginia, what has become of the scores of thousands of slaves over and above those acknowledged as received in the importing States. They could tell us a good deal of the amount of American capital invested in the traffic on the African coast. Much of the deterioration in the commercial spirit in the Northern States may be ascribed to this clandestine practice, and much also to the corrupting effect of a close mercantile connexion with the South. But, on the other hand, symptoms are not wanting of increasing public spirit and increasing means to meet the crisis. The practical failure of the Southern policy in regard to Kansas arrests the advance of slavery to the Northwest, and the progress of free labour in the cultivation of cotton and other commodities begins to be felt in the older States.

Virginia leads the frontier States, which will necessarily all act together. As an exhausted country, with little other connexion with slavery than by the business of slave-breeding, Virginia is now a telegraph of public opinion in regard to slave-trade questions. Alarmed at the propositions made by conventions and legislatures at the South to re-open the African slave-trade, the old State has made some strong demonstrations. One party, it is true, has sentenced a merchant captain to forty years in the penitentiary for giving a passage to five fugitive slaves, and has procured from the legislature a prohibition to emancipate slaves by will; but these are acts which show by their excess their insecure character. Nobody believes that Captain Baylis will wear out his forty years; and more negroes are emancipated at once as a consequence of the prohibition to do it by testamentary process. On the other hand, free labourers are encouraged to enter the State, and form settlements on lapsed plantations; the upland farmers west of the mountains are resolved on a plan of gradual emancipation, well-intended though impracticable; the State is becoming rapidly drained of slaves, and the political leaders of Old Virginia are strenuously opposing every attempt to revive the slave-trade in any form or degree whatever. . . .

With Virginia, Maryland and Delaware, Kentucky and Missouri would probably join the Northern federation. The two former are scarcely slave States now, so impossible is it to keep possession of slaves on the frontier, while difficulties are incessantly arising from the passage of fugitives on the one hand, and the aggressions of kidnappers on the other. The abduction of free persons, and especially of children, white as well as coloured, is becoming an evil which renders frontier life intolerable. . . .

This survey of American conditions and symptoms exhibits the operation of the most fatal of institutions on the most flourishing of republics. We need not describe more of the indications of the malady which has already disorganised the most promising social condition in the world. All great men sunk beneath the surface; liberty of speech and of the press everywhere more or less restricted; the churches discredited, divided and enfeebled; the social temper soured and exasperated; the manners of the North rendered artificial or suspicious, and those of the South depraved beyond retrieval, and the two great sections of the Union alienated by a hatred unparalleled (as far as we know) in intensity and in violence of expression by any international hostility on record; a too inflated wealth in one section, a too ruinous poverty in the other; secret pangs of conscience among northern mammon worshippers, and suppressed groans and curses among southern victims of that mammon worship;—these are some of the consequences of that fatal original compromise which buried an explosive anomaly in the foundations of a fair-seeming structure of liberty. So much for the domestic results. . . . [Here Martineau discusses American foreign policy.]

No consideration, however, is more plain than that of the high merit and hopeful greatness of the genuine republicans throughout the Union. There are true-hearted citizens scattered everywhere; and the body of the people in the Free States are probably sound. The blusterers, who undertake to speak for the nation, are no representatives of anybody or of anything but the abuses of the State. How the women of the South are disposed towards slavery, may be understood by its influence on domestic morals. Slavery will not be preserved by the wives and mothers of southern society. The millions of non-slaveholding whites would abolish it at the first election, if they were not sequestrated from books, news, and companionship as they are, partly by the policy of the superior class, and partly by their own depression of mind and fortunes. Elsewhere, the multitudes who can and who will rescue their country from its curse have been kept quiet by an idolatrous worship of the Union, and by an infinity of connexions with the South. Whenever the necessity of a decision for or against the institution is at hand, there can be no doubt what it will be. There are a few political men, and there are many moral and social leaders who will bring up to the front the mighty force of sound opinion which at present terrifies the slave power by the warnings it utters from its retreats. The Republic has suffered in every way. Let us hope that it has suffered enough. The true way out of the mischief and misery is now provided. A faithful alliance with England in carrying out the provisions of anti-slave-trade treaties is the first step. This taken, the institution of slavery must die out, and within a short date.

It is quite natural that so critical a season should be eagerly made use of by the lovers of power and pelf for a last attempt to shake off the restraints of treaties, and to reopen the African slave-trade. Reasonable men must always have known that this would be the way in which the old practice would expire. Some one or two countries would be the last in which slavery would exist in a manner requiring replenishment; when the day came for abolishing slavery there (as a national institution), there must inevitably be a conflict between the slaveholders and the reformers; and the opportunity of the strife would be seized by all piratically-disposed parties to drive a great trade while they could, so as, perhaps, to intimidate England, and dishearten its government and people with the prospect of losing the results of a struggle of half a century. This is precisely what is happening now. Mackintosh's prophecy about the future use of Wilberforce's example becomes apt and cheering. The duty of all parties who care for duty is just what our fathers would have laid down as such, in contemplation of the crisis we have reached. Our duty is to hold to our purpose, and prosecute it with more vigour than ever, rallying to the cause all good allies, and gaining over by prudence and energy all who may be vacillating. As to audacious violators of treaties, and treacherous allies, who cover over perjury with cant, England knows very well how to deal with them. She has authority to overawe the one class, and energy and coolness to spoil the game of the other. The occasion is grave enough, and of sufficient interest. Twenty years ago, when we had spent 15,000,000£ in suppressing the trade alone, besides the sacrifices to procure emancipation in our own colonies, we were full of heart and hope, though slavery existed in such vigour, in so many lands, that the prospect of the extinction of the traffic was obscure and remote. Now, when our sacrifices have been increased, while the slave-trade has sunk to a very manageable amount, through the reduction of the area of slavery, we shall hardly relax in our efforts on account of a temporary flutter in cabinets, and hubbub in the Cuban waters,—designed to alarm us with fears of war, and to conceal from us our real command over the whole case.

The United States and Cuba keep up the slave-trade. If Cuba were alone, such an obstacle would be quickly disposed of, for Spain could not withstand the pressure—"the moral blockade," as Mr. Sumner calls it,—of the whole civilised world. Of all the remonstrants, the Americans would, in that case, be the most vigorous; partly because converts are zealous, and partly through jealousy of what is erroneously considered cheap labour in a rival country. This is just the state of things which may be near at hand, and which may be peaceably accomplished, if England and her true allies are faithful to their duty. We hear a great deal of one side of the question, and nothing of the other, in regard to the American desire for the annexation of Cuba. The existing President is best known in Europe by his part in the Ostend Manifesto; and he has been expected to annex Cuba, from the day of his entrance upon office. No doubt, he intended to win fame from future generations for that act; but the thing is not done yet; and an increasing number of his countrymen are determined that it shall not be done;—that is, not done by him, nor for his purposes. It is not only the virtue of the country that is enlisted against the project. In the sugar-growing districts of the United States, there is a strong repugnance to the acquisition of Cuba, the planters seeing that they must either migrate to Cuba, or leave off producing sugar. There is a wide impression throughout the slave States that their fortunes would sink yet lower if their impoverished estates were brought into direct comparison with those of Cuba. Many of the citizens appear to believe what they tell others,—that the annexation of Cuba would be followed by that of Canada, where 60,000 free negroes are living near the frontier, and would be recoverable as fugitives from the South; and for the sake of this consideration—(so wild in our view!), they advocate the purchase of Cuba, which they would not otherwise consider desirable. Of the nature of the northern objections we need not say much. For a counterpoise to the morbid excitability, vanity, and cupidity of the filibustering element of society, there is the old virtue of honesty which has come down from "forefathers' days"; the patriotism which dreads the deterioration of national character by perpetual acquisition and roving; and an apprehension of having to balance Cuba in the Senate by disturbing the northern frontier again. On the whole, however, public opinion is much less united, less definite, less ascertained on this subject than the speechifiers on "manifest destiny" would have us believe.

In 1840, and perhaps even five years later, 135,000 negroes were annually exported from Africa; whereas only 15,000 have been obtained for Cuba (the only market) within the last three years.[172] The trade to Brazil is extinguished. In former days, there were three Powers notoriously difficult to deal with in regard to their anti-slave-trade treaties,—Spain, Portugal, and the United States. Now Portugal is acting faithfully and vigorously on the right side. From the peace of 1815, abundant legal provision was made for stigmatising and punishing violations of the treaty entered into with England; but practically the traffic did not cease. The profession was good; but the practice was nought, as is now the case with Spain,—and not with Spain alone. In 1847, however, the Portuguese Government compelled the destruction of certain slave-barracoons which existed on the Angola coast, and by subsequent acts controlled the mischievous petty kings within the colonial area of Portugal. In 1855, regulations on behalf of colonial slaves were confirmed, and provision was made for their redemption. Thenceforward, the chief colonial ports were freely opened to foreign commerce, which must drive out traffic in slaves; and when Ambriz, on the Congo coast, was thus opened slavery was declared to be abolished there. In April last, a decree was published which ordained the total abolition of slavery throughout the colonial dominions of Portugal within twenty years. Experienced observers understand that such terms of preparation answer as ill in the case of emancipation as in that of the removal of an impost; and they therefore expect to see all Portuguese slaves freed long before the lapse of twenty years. Meantime, our old ally is faithfully assisting us in the task of naval watch. Besides the small-armed craft employed on colonial objects, there are ships of war,—at present three, and often more,—guarding the African coast, with our cruisers.

Spain has always been the very worst Power to deal with of the whole group of sovereign States. At the Peace, King Ferdinand had the same sensibilities as the other Christian monarchs, and expressed them very solemnly; but it needed a bribe of 400,000£ three years afterwards to induce him to take any steps at all towards the fulfilment of his promises. Then ensued a long series of evasions, followed by decrees which were not obeyed,—disputed, or said to be disputed, in Cuba, and found at last to have been never heard of there. During the nine years ending in 1832, 236 vessels imported 100,000 slaves into Cuba, while eighty-nine other vessels, from Havanna, were captured by our cruisers, or perished with their cargoes of negroes. Lord Clarendon obtained a treaty in 1836, when he was at Madrid, by which vessels equipped for the traffic were made seizable, the officers punishable, the vessels liable to condemnation, and the negroes committed to the care of the British Government. In a trice, nineteen captured vessels, Spanish, were carried into Sierra Leone for adjudication; whereas six in a year was the former average. This was the immediate result of the working of the treaty being lodged in British, instead of Spanish, hands. We hoped then that the Spanish slave-trade had received its death-blow. It is certainly a vast gain that the importation has been so considerably reduced; but we must not relax in vigilance and energy while Spain employs American ships in procuring slaves for Cuba, and while official personages in the colony, and in the capital, and royal personages in the courts of allies, as well as at Madrid, accept a rich revenue from a trade which is publicly admitted to be abominable in the eyes of all Christian people. As long as we allow such a violation of treaty-obligations, we shall be subject to painful remonstrances from the sound republicans of the United States, who declare that the redemption of their own country is delayed by nothing so much as by that state of things in Cuba which Great Britain holds the power of putting an end to. If we could induce Spain to emancipate the slaves in Cuba,—which is the desire of a large proportion of residents,—there would be an end, say these Americans, of the Slave-trade; of the expense of guarding against it, of disputes with other Powers as to the conduct of our cruisers; of buccaneering expeditions from the United States; of threats from Washington of war with Spain; of the overbearing predominance of the slave-power in the Federal Government; and finally, of slavery itself in the United States. Such are the representations of the best men in the Republic; and very earnest is the request they urge that we will use our treaty relations with Spain to the utmost, to induce this change of policy, while that of the American Republic is trembling in the balance.

What does the American slave-trade on behalf of Cuba amount to? When other nations have withdrawn from the traffic, leaving it almost exclusively to the United States and Spain, and when we know how many negroes are imported into Cuba, we have only to divide the amount between Spain and the United States.[173] . . . We read of vessels by the dozen chased by cruisers, obliged to yield, or to run ashore, for the change of the crew's escape, or watched under suspicion, while carrying the American flag, and sometimes escaping, but occasionally caught in the act of embarking or discharging their cargoes. There is a group of seven, gravely suspected, and consigned to firms in New York, connected with the slave-trade; and another group of four, understood to belong to New Orleans; and yet another group of four, captured with cargoes of negroes, bound for the south coast of Cuba. These facts accompanied by the names of the vessels, and of their owners, are, we trust, sufficient to rouse the same deep abhorrence of the slave-trade throughout the free Northern states, which prevailed when the trade was made piracy by law, in 1808, before any other country had gone so far. Relying on the disposition of the American people to protect the honour of their flag from the outrages of piracy, under whatsoever form the British Government have explicitly renounced (what, indeed, they never claimed or possessed), the right of searching in time of peace the merchant vessels of any foreign Power; for as we never had the right of enforcing the municipal laws of any other country, it is admitted that an American slaver *in flagranti delictu* might sail with impunity through a fleet of our cruisers. But in endeavouring to establish the common interest of the civilised world to put down piracy and slave-trade, we have asked for nothing which we have not granted to others, and those powers have been as freely exercised by American cruisers over British ships as over American ships by British cruisers. Some such protection we hold to be indispensable to the safety of the high seas. Were it altogether withdrawn, the banks of the Bahamas and the entrance to the Gulf would again be infested with sea-rovers, and in their anxiety to escape from the vigilance of the British squadron, the Americans have contracted a peremptory obligation to provide for the safety of navigation and the execution of their own laws conjointly with our own authorities in those seas. . . .

This is the moment chosen by the French colonial planters, and their ruler at home, for discomposing the whole train of circumstances, and throwing back the entire policy, by reviving the African slave-trade on their own account. At the out-set of our remarks, we called it a disguised slave-trade that the French Emperor had instituted: but, from evidence which has since arrived in abundance, we must now call it an undisguised traffic of the kind condemned, a quarter of a century ago, by all the Powers of the civilised world. It is enough to say here that we are aware of what is doing, and of what is planned. We shall keep attention fixed on French agents and their doings round the whole circuit of Africa,—emphatically including Algeria: and when a long array of evidence becomes as patent as that which we are now obtaining about the transactions in Liberia, the world will decide between the negro race and an emperor, who, with all his meditativeness of character, seems to forget that he is living in the nineteenth century, and among nations who have risen to a capacity of having principles and a policy. A man of any amount of ability may easily wreck himself upon a rock so reared by time from the depths; but he can no more overthrow our principle and our policy in regard to the negro races than he can pluck up our islands by the roots, and float them as rafts for his convenience on the high seas. His new policy is a troublesome and vexatious accident. It is not only a burden and an interruption in itself, but it acts unfavourably on the evil-minded in all directions. It is the cause and occasion of that wonderful mistake between Mr. Mason and Count Walewski which has been so thoroughly canvassed, and so completely detected in America,—the false declaration that England would not object to this French slave-trade while the Coolie importation into our colonies went on. It is the impulse which has quickened the slave-trade into new life along hundreds of miles of African coast. It has caused a British consul to be insulted and stoned in even a Portuguese colony, by renewing the hopes of sordid traders "of the viler sort." It has brought out the bad side of human nature wherever it has been broached: and the same method of rule keeps the right mind of France ignorant of the facts of the case. But all these misfortunes affect merely the question of time, in regard to the extinction of the slave-trade. The same influences which procured its condemnation first, and its reduction afterwards to its present dimensions, exist in all their original force, and others are added. The trade is as wicked as ever it was, and it is known and felt to be so by a much greater number of persons, of greater experience than our fathers could have possessed when they gained their victory. Since their day a new order of considerations, of unsurpassed significance, has risen up.

The aspect of Africa and its people to European eyes is wholly changed within one generation. The world at large knows Africa better; and Africa is the better for knowing the rest of the world. Perhaps the report of the American Southern Convention for this year presents as fair an account of negro-life, as our fathers regarded it, as could now be obtained. In that report, we meet with quotations from books of travel of various date, including Barth's and Livingstone's,—the extracts being throughout those which describe the worst barbarisms of the most barbarous tribes. These are offered by the American committee as evidence of the incapacity of the negro for social organisation, no notice being taken of any changes which occur in consequence of intercourse with more advanced races. Thus did negro nations appear to Europeans half a century ago. For many years our estimate of the native African has been changing; and now the time has come when argument without premises is seen to be absurd, and we point to the facts of what negro communities *can do*, instead of speculating at random on what they *must be*. The merest glance at accounts of our imports from Africa will show how the suppression of the slave-trade has operated in developing industry and commerce among as primitive a society as can be found in the world.

When living in peace and quiet, the natives bring down palm oil to the markets in earthen pots which they carry on their heads. This one product now sells for above 2,000,000£ a year. The French prefer the oil from ground nuts, of which they can consume any quantity, and this is fortunate, because the cultivation of the ground nut is a step in advance of collecting palm oil. The produce increases rapidly; and to it we now find added an oil from cucumber seeds, on which a good deal of labour is spent, and an assortment of dyes about which the natives have a secret. Cotton culture seems to be spreading all over the country; for travellers who enter it in any direction report of more or less of it in the interior. The exportation of cotton cloths from the west coast has long been considerable; but, as British manufactures penetrate the interior, it becomes more profitable to the natives to exchange their raw cotton for our woven fabrics. The fact that 1250 bales were produced in 1857 for consignment to one trader at Manchester, Mr. Clegg, is enough to show what may be expected if this progressive branch of industry is not destroyed by the introduction of slave-trading. Young natives have been trained in England, and have established the cleaning and dressing of cotton at home; the quantity and quality are improving every year; and the purchase of commodities from abroad is becoming a great benefit and delight to the people; and the idea is intolerable that strangers should come and throw everything into chaos again, on the canting plea that it is for the good of Africa to take away the people and make them work elsewhere. All the way up the frequented rivers, and in many regions of the interior, the people are now picking cotton, and travelling to and fro with it, and with what they get in exchange: the faculties are developed; their hearts are gayer; their habits are purer; their homes are safer: and when all is going well,—when the prospect opens of a variety of other crops being raised, indigo, grain, spices, roots, rice, and fruits, besides a large business in timber, beeswax, gums, dyes, feathers and hides,—the emissaries of M. Regis, or of Spanish traders on the coast, or of firms at New York or Baltimore, burst in upon the scene, and bring back a legion of the devils which had been exorcised with so much pains.[174] Dr. Barth has told us what happens when a stimulus is given to the expiring slave traffic of the interior. He has shown us the desolate villages and the plundered towns; the gangs of captives; the victims not wanted for slaves who are left on the ground bleeding to death,—a leg or arm having been cut off for that purpose. On being applied to, in regard to affording supplies of free labourers for the colonies, for a term of years, African potentates all make pretty much the same answer. The letter from the king of Calabar, which Lord Brougham read in the House of Lords, may serve for the whole order. The people will not go if asked, says the King of Calabar: if they went, they would not be expected back, but, "King Archibury and all Calabar gentlemen all be very glad to do the same;—we shall buy them alsam [sic] we do that time slave tradebin [sic]. . . . We have all agreed to charges four boxes of brass and copper rod for man, woman and children, but shall not be able to supply quantity you mention. I think we shall be able to get four or five hundred for one vessel," &c.

Let the King of Calabar's words have their due weight with other sovereigns when he writes, "Regard to free emigration we man no will go for himself" [sic]. Why should they go, when at home there is food enough for all, and society has just entered on that stage when industry and its blessings are beginning to be understood and relished? If they never had any migratory tendencies, while their attachment to home is eminently strong; if they have no ideas of foreign countries, no knowledge of wages, no desire of accumulation of money; but, on the contrary, fresh hopes and rising desires at home, what a senseless project, or shameless hypocrisy, is that of calling them free labourers, disposing of themselves by contract to go they know not wither, for objects they cannot understand, and with persons whom they regard as slave-traders! This is the scheme which Count Walewski tells the American Minister, and the American Minister tells Congress, that England does not object to, and whence the American newspapers infer that the English people and their Government have changed their minds about the freedom of the negro races—fresh evidence being derived from a capricious journal or two, supposed to represent public opinion in England. England must afford a practical contradiction, emphatic and speedy; and there need be no doubt that such journals will speak loudest, as soon as the good old principles of justice, honour, and humanity are found to be more popular than the worn-out barbarisms and fallacies which cynics and the *London Cotton Plant* have been trying to pass upon us as new and wise.

There are whole classes of commodities in Africa which have scarcely been heard of yet. The Portuguese in certain settlements have sent nearly 1000 miles for lime; and now it turns out that there were several varieties of marble within 100 miles of them. There is coal in some parts; and in Angola, veins have been found, whence the natives have obtained fine copper, and dug out malachite of splendid quality. These ores are now brought to market by a British association to which the King of Portugal has granted the working of the mines, on well secured conditions that no slave labour shall be employed, and that the wages given shall be fair. The rich and abundant produce transmitted to England in a few weeks, before any machinery was sent out, left no doubt of the prospects of the adventurers; and when the road to the coast is finished, no slave-trader need ever pry into that region again. The natives are ready and willing to work; and there can be no doubt of the nearest coast down to Ambriz and Loanda becoming a great center of trade. Thus far, some natural wealth has been discovered wherever the natives are living; and if a returning wave of barbarism (European and American) does not sweep over the African continent, leaving that blossoming world desolate, the whole human race will be the better for the laying open of a new continent to civilisation and the bringing up of whole races to a capacity for industry and general commercial intercourse.

It is the business of all the parties to anti-slave-trade treaties to see to this. England has the further duty of taking care that all the parties are faithful to their pledges. We can rely on Portugal for faithful companionship in the work before us. We can rely on every Power which has extinguished slavery in its own dominions, with the temporary exception of France. If we could obtain the ear of the people of France, all would be well; for a nation which has abolished colonial slavery, as the French did, will certainly refuse to perpetuate the curse under false pretences, as their government is doing at this moment. While unable, through the coercion of the French press, to reach the national mind, we must enforce existing treaties with the same vigour and resolution which our fathers put forth to obtain them.

There remain the Americans. Never were we and they more bound to each other in a common duty and a common sentiment than now. When we speak of the American people, we are thinking, first, of the sons and daughters of the founders of the Republic, and next of European immigrants who have entered the Republic as sons by adoption. For the moment, we put out of view the turbulent classes which have sprung from the one great corruption of the American polity, and which would be closed at once by the mere reappearance of the old spirit which raised a group of colonies into a great nation. To the small band of retrograde slaveholders, and the smaller group of buccaneering guards of slavery, we have nothing to say here. We are thinking of the free millions who regard labour and social organisation in the light of the century in which they live; and human liberties with the love which their great men of a past century bequeathed to them. Will they not agree with us that they and we are standing at a critical point of time, when progress or retrogression, honour or disgrace, is before them and us;— before them as republicans by choice, and before us both as members of the league of Christendom? This is their profession in greeting us for the first time through the electric cable which brings us within speaking distance; and the opportunity and this use of it are alike critical.

They know, and we know, that the decision of this great question rests with ourselves and them. We do not intend to yield it. Cost what it may, England will extinguish the slave-trade, because any yielding of so clear and determinate a policy would cost yet more: but a full, free, cordial companionship in the effort on the part of the United States would save a world of guilt and woe. The citizens can do it if they will. The existence of slavery in their nation is their misery and their shame. It has lowered their reputation, degraded their national character, barred their progress, vitiated their foreign policy, poisoned their domestic peace, divided their hearts and minds; and may ultimately explode their Union. The train has long been laid, and the match is applied; there is probably no escape from the catastrophe: but a vigorous and instant effort may yet avail. If not, there remains a broad future in which to build up a better polity. In any case, the citizens have it now in their power to save the world from a revival of the slave-trade, by abjuring slavery as a national institution. An ignorant and perverse minority may choose to cherish the curse within their own small frontier; but they cannot revive the trade, and must soon adopt free labour in self-defence. The opportunity of regenerating the Republic, and regaining the old place of honour among nations, is now present and pressing. If our American kindred accept and use it, in cordial alliance with England, their best days are yet to come. If they let it pass, the world will grieve, but the work will not the less be done. It is the "manifest destiny" of justice and humanity to lead the world onward; and no retrograde ignorance, no sordid self-interest, no guile, however audacious or refined, can prevail against them.

"The United States under the Presidentship of Mr. Buchanan"
Edinburgh Review, 1860

Reflecting Martineau's enduring interest in American presidential elections and presidencies, this article examines politicians' roles in America's civil conflict. Emphasizing the need to bring the slavery crisis to resolution, Martineau analyzes how American politics was shaped by the powerful economic forces that ultimately controlled Congress and, in turn, the presidency. Martineau's shrewd assessment of census figures and their impact on the outcomes of elections makes clear how the institution of slavery and the power wielded by a comparative minority of slaveholders perpetuated and strengthened the foundations of the South's "peculiar" domestic arrangement at the expense of northern interests and republican values. The article traces Buchanan's political history by outlining his stands on controversial issues—he held, for example, that the Dred Scott decision "settled the slavery question"—including his foreign policy, his support of the pro-slavery perspective, his handling of the John Brown raid at Harper's Ferry, and his determination to annex Cuba and other territories as potential slave states. This article thus continues the analysis begun in "The Slave-Trade in 1858" of Spain's interest in the slave trade, in which Cuba plays a central role, and of Cuba's connection with the American situation; similarly, the proposed annexation of Mexico offers another example of Buchanan's expansionist ambitions. Buchanan's expansionism was designed, Martineau argues, to "amuse the people" while postponing resolution of the slavery issue, to be dealt with by his successor.

Among the dramatic examples Martineau offers illustrating the character of Buchanan's administration is the political partisanship that played havoc with the moral, ethical, and human rights issues motivating the abolitionists. The "flagrant corruption of Mr. Buchanan's electioneering machinery" yielded an equally corrupt administration, prompting the anti-slavery faction to despair of ever realizing the goal of emancipation. Indeed, in Martineau's view, this presidency constituted a "Reign of Terror," complete with political and social martyrdom.[175]

Yet it was precisely the blatant, undisguised political corruption and human rights abuses of the Buchanan administration that created a climate sufficient to secure Abraham Lincoln's election as the next president. Thus, Buchanan's presidency may be seen as the extreme that was necessary to swing the balance of political power and popular opinion to the abolitionists.

. . .

ART. IX.—1. *Compendium of "The Impending Crisis of the South."* By Hinton Rowan Helper, of North Carolina. New York: 1860.

2. *Civilised America.* By Thos. Colley Grattan. London: 1859.

3. *Life of Stephen A. Douglas.* By James W. Sheahan. London: 1860.

4. *The Barbarism of Slavery. A Speech of Hon. Charles Sumner, on the Bill for the Admission of Kansas as a Free State. In the United States Senate, June 4th,* 1860.

5. *Oration of Hon. Edward Everett, at Boston, on the 4th of July,* 1860.

If the question is frankly put to any sensible and instructed man in England, what we ought to care most about of all that is going on in the world outside our own country, he will answer, the conduct and fortunes of the United States. Our interest, however, does not correspond with our sense of the importance of American affairs to the world and to ourselves. A movement in Italy, a word spoken by Switzerland, a sign of mutual confidence among the German Powers, or a change of mood in the French newspapers, excites and occupies more attention in England than events of the greatest moment and indications of the deepest significance in the United States. We need no convincing that the prospects of every civilised nation depend, to an incalculable extent, on the issue of the ostensible experiment of self-government instituted in the great Republic; and that the subsistence of four millions of our people is implicated with the cotton-growing of half the States of the Union; yet we have to overcome a sensation of weariness and distaste before we can throw our minds into the study of American affairs, even during a crisis like the present. There are reasons for this distaste, so obvious as to require only the briefest reference. We are perplexed by the incessant growth of new parties, and by the unintelligible character of most of them. We are disgusted by the virulence of party language throughout the country, and annoyed at the captious temper and bickering tendencies of the Washington Government in its relations with its allies, and especially with ourselves. Again, some among us who might not otherwise dislike an exposure of the faults and sufferings of the republican nation, apprehend disaster to freedom from any calamitous issue of the great enterprise inaugurated by Washington and his peers; and the best friends of civil liberty feel so painfully the shortcomings and transgressions of the Government in the United States, as to desire to evade the subject whenever they can. All this is wrong, however. We are bound by every consideration to inform ourselves of the true state of American affairs: and it is certain that the subject becomes, as is usual, the more interesting the better it is understood: and that it has not, for a long course of years, been so easily intelligible as during the Presidential election of 1860. Much more than the immediate fate of the Republic may hang on the choice of the next President: events of a decisive character must happen during his term of rule, as during that of Mr. Buchanan; and as if the critical nature of the action of the next few months were universally understood, the arbitrary divisions of party have disappeared, and we see the nation massing itself in the two large divisions which must always be found under a system of representative government. It is not our business at the moment to make a study of these parties; much less to venture on any course of prophecy as to the results of the conflict. We refer to the reduction of a crowd of parties to the two called Democratic and Republican,—to which some may think the Union party worthy to be added,—merely to show how the case is simplified to the foreign observer. As for the rest, we shall confine ourselves to a cursory notice of the phenomena of Mr. Buchanan's administration, and of the state of affairs to which the new President will succeed.

Four years ago there seemed reason to hope that the American people were becoming sensible of the evil of choosing for their rulers obscure men, appointed for some special object of convenience, and by the very conditions of their elevation certain to be mere tools of their party. Polk and Pierce would be better forgotten, if that were possible; but Mr. Buchanan was known in statesmanship at home and broad, was practised in political life at European Courts, as well as in Congress at Washington, and was understood to have excited favourable expectations among the allies of the Republic, in spite of the misgivings inspired by his share in the Ostend Manifesto. He was an educated man: he had entered early into political life, having appeared as a representative in his own State (Pennsylvania) at three-and-twenty, and in Congress at thirty years of age. After his mission to Russia, under General Jackson's administration, he became a member of the Senate, conspicuous for his business-like qualities and his accomplishments. His reputation preceded him when he came to England as Minister in 1854; and if some speculations were excited by the appointment, it was among the few only who understood what must be the tendencies of the politician who could be a Secretary of State under Mr. Polk. The annexation of Texas was the final cause of Mr. Polk's presidentship, and no man could be a member of his Cabinet who was not pledged to a policy of territorial aggrandisement, for the sake of the extension of slavery. The Oregon question was under the management of Mr. Buchanan as soon as he entered the Cabinet. . . .

Mr. Buchanan was the eighteenth choice of the Republic for President,—twelve terms having been occupied by Southern slaveholders and six by Northern men,—non-slaveholders, of course, but, in local language, nearly all "Northern men with Southern principles." No Northern man has ever been re-elected; but five slaveholders have served twice. As Mr. Buchanan had no reforms to propose, his policy was marked out by these facts, as much as by the Ostend Manifesto. Five years before, the number of slaveholders in the country was 347,000; and their connexions might swell the number immediately interested in slavery to 2,000,000; while the rest of the population (excluding the slaves) amounted to 22,000,000. Mr. Buchanan was elected in the interest of the minority; and he lost no time in intimating that his policy would be regulated in favour of that interest. If this appears astonishing, we can only remind our readers that the Republican party of the present day was then in its infancy; and that of the 20,000,000 of non-slaveholders, the larger proportion were politically paralyzed by fear;—fear of an explosion of the Union; fear for their commerce; fear of the disgrace of civil war. Again, a large number were as yet unawakened on the vital question of the Republic; and, above all, the three-fifths franchise possessed by the Slave States,—the franchise based on property and not on numbers,—has always conferred a vast proportion of political power on the Southern population. Mr. Buchanan's policy was to take any advantage which might accrue from his Northern birth and connexions, while lending his utmost aid to carry the Southern States over the difficulties which were menacing them with a deposition from power, after their long course of oligarchical government. This was done with so much audacity, and the election was conducted in the manner so singularly corrupt, as to develop, on the instant, the Republican party which now proposes a reversal of the Southern policy. A recent speech of Mr. Sumner's, on the origin, necessity, and permanence of the Republican party, exhibits the mode in which the flagrant corruption of Mr. Buchanan's electioneering machinery created the party in 1854; and how the yet more flagrant corruption of his administration has since wrought to increase the numbers and the influence of the party of reform.

The great controversy of the day, whatever it be, always turns in the United States, on the constitutional question. The fathers of the Republic hoped that a written constitution would make all safe,—as so many have supposed in other cases, before and since, in the Old World and the New; but, when it became necessary to provide for the interpretation of the constitution, it was clear that the security was imaginary. The strife about the limitations of Federal and State rights is never-ending; and never was the struggle more desperate than when Mr. Buchanan came into power. We need not enlarge on the disturbance occasioned by the repeal of the Missouri Compromise, the passage and attempted enforcement of the Fugitive Slave Law, and those demands of the South for the prevalence of slave institutions throughout the Republic, which were agitating the whole country at the time of Mr. Buchanan's inauguration. While, on the other hand, the new laws were regarded as unconstitutional on the very face of them, on the other, stringent demands were made for their vigorous enforcement: there were incessant conflicts in the streets and the courts between kidnappers and the protectors of negroes; in Boston, chains had been drawn round the court-house; cannon had been placed in the streets; a black resident had been yielded up amidst a general mourning that there had been no adequate organisation for resistance; and a clear warning was given to the Southern intruders that this was the last rendition under the Fugitive Slave Law that would ever be made in Massachusetts. A similar turmoil had been witnessed in many states when Mr. Buchanan delivered his Inauguration Address; and the world was not a little curious to see what a President from Pennsylvania would make of such a state of things. All were not aware of the tacit understanding which had existed for some time between him and the Supreme Court.

It has since become known that the decision of the Court on the DRED SCOTT Case had been formed for some months, and communicated to those whom it most concerned. It was suppressed during the election, and the following winter, from the fear of injuring Mr. Buchanan's prospects first, and next, embarrassing his entrance upon the Presidentship. In his Inauguration Address he professed ignorance of the nature of the decision, but so earnestly exhorted the people to reverent acceptance of it as to satisfy his hearers as to what they had to expect. Four days afterwards the celebrated judgment was announced, and the nation was informed that slavery existed everywhere in the Republic but where it was locally repudiated; that it was a Federal institution, without exception or reversal. The Democratic party headed by the President, assumed the controversy between the North and South to be settled by this judgment; while others denied, not only the constitutional character of the decision, but its being a binding decision at all, because it was extra-judicial. The majority of the Court had pronounced at the outset that Scott has no right to bring his case before them; and after this, it was said, their further conclusions were nothing more than the opinions of the judges on a case which was not within their jurisdiction. On Mr. Buchanan's accession to office, therefore, the struggles of many parties had just been converted into a distinct and circumscribed conflict between the two,—the Northern and Southern, or the Anti-slavery and Pro-slavery parties. The Republican party was vigorous, for its age,—only two years and some months. It had failed in carrying the election of Colonel Fremont; but it was Mr. Buchanan's main cause of solicitude in his entrance upon office.

While every man of the multitude who heard him on that portentous 4th of March, 1857, was aware that the sectional antagonism would be concentrated and exasperated by the decision on the DRED SCOTT Case, the President congratulated the nation, in a tone of pious and patriotic satisfaction, on the "calm" that would be spread over the whole era of society by that unrevealed decision. All strifes and troubles would now cease; and henceforth all would be well with everybody. He should have the happiness of conducting the affairs of a united nation, and should retire, at the close of his term, into the state of repose congenial to his years, satisfied that all serious troubles and dangers were surmounted or averted, and that a career of honor and glory lay open before the Republic. Those who best knew the Presidential orator were of opinion that his real hope was to defer the inevitable struggle to the time of his successor; and to amuse the people meanwhile with the acquisition of Cuba, and the turn of his foreign policy, in Central America and Mexico, as well as Europe. However this may be, he assumed that all troublesome questions would be laid to rest at his bidding, and under the authority of the Supreme Court.

What was the actual condition of the strife to be thus suddenly stilled? A glance at the facts is necessary to any true understanding of the new President's views and policy. Unhappily those facts are only too interesting. . . . [Martineau outlines the social chaos throughout the country resulting from Buchanan's election.] A Disunion Convention had been held in Massachusetts, the leading State of New England. Several Southern States had, throughout the presidential election, propounded schemes of marching on Washington, in case of Colonel Fremont's success, seizing the archives, and assuming the government, and bringing the political quarrel to the issue of civil war. When their candidate succeeded, they declared their scheme adjourned over another Presidential term; it would be resumed on the first prospect of the success of an anti-slavery candidate. As to the temper of Congress itself, we need only point to the murderous assault on Mr. Sumner in the Senate, in the preceding May, and the result of his appeal to the laws on that occasion. These are only a few of the social phenomena of the time; but they will suffice to enable any reader to form an opinion of the new President's sincerity or soundness of judgment in promising a great calm as the characteristic of his term of office.

As to foreign affairs, the most conspicuous point was Cuba. The ambition of Mr. Buchanan's life has been to connect his name with the annexation of Cuba to the United States. For this object he underwent the obloquy attaching to the Ostend Manifesto, and for this he ran the risk of avowing his favourite project before he could accurately calculate his chances of success.

He thus set out under the disadvantages of the suspicion of Europe, and the discredit of being the accomplice of the late American Minister in Spain, Mr. Soulé, in his bullying and tricky course. Mr. Soulé was recalled; but the taint of his disgrace hung about Mr. Buchanan. On the same grounds his conduct in regard to the filibuster Walker and his comrades was narrowly watched, and believed to be as friendly to the pirates as events soon proved to be. The Central American question was likely to be a troublesome one, it was evident. As to the European Powers, they were incommoded by the refusal of the Washington Government to sign the declaration of the Treaty of Paris in regard to privateering in time of war; and England had just been annoyed by the dismissal of her Minister and two consuls, on the ground of their having infringed upon the American law relating to foreign enlistment. The Clayton-Bulwer treaty was an instrument always at hand when a wrangle with a foreign State was convenient, and "the Monroe Doctrine" was serving something like the same purpose at Washington as the Immaculate Conception at Rome.[176] A new or revived dogma is a godsend in troubled political times, and one was extracted from a saying of President Monroe's, which he would no more recognise in its new dress than Jefferson or Adams would recognise a modern presidential election as the offspring of the constitution they superintended in its early workings. There was the Dallas-Clarendon treaty, growing out of the other, and relating to the dispute about the Mosquito Territory. There was occasional trouble about the Northwestern boundary, and about the fishery rights; and thus a state of irritation had long existed between our Government and that of Washington. Spain was dissatisfied about both Mexico and Cuba; and American claims against the Spanish Exchequer were urged with great vigour with a view to an ostensible purchase of Cuba.

Such was the condition of affairs in the United States when Mr. Buchanan undertook to carry them on. Next we have to note the course of his policy and the events which marked that course.

I. The strength and activity of the Republican party was one of the earliest phenomena of the term; and its vigour indicated one main feature of Mr. Buchanan's policy,—its method of corruption. That party, says it leading men, was created by the corruption of the Democratic party, which Mr. Buchanan (before he was discarded by it) called "the only national and Conservative party." . . . [Martineau here lists examples of corruption and political favoritism.]

The entire mass of evidence before the Covode Committee (so called from the member who obtained its appointment) went to prove that the country was governed by "bribers and bribees," from the Custom House porters to the Cabinet itself; and it has never since been disputed that corruption is a distinguishing feature of the policy of Mr. Buchanan. The latest disclosure of the sort of traffic to which official men were considered pledged, is afforded by a circular recently posted all over Ohio. This circular reminds all who hold official positions that they are expected to contribute not less than the value of 10£ to the expenses of the election of the Democratic candidate for the Presidentship. The audacity seems to have grown with the corruption.

II. A natural commentary on Mr. Buchanan's declaration that the Dred Scott decision had settled the slavery question was afforded without delay. Instead of "calm," the Southern and Western newspapers soon gave hints that something was wrong in Tennessee, something wrong in Kentucky, in Arkansas, in Missouri, in Louisiana, where gentlemen could not get their proper night's rest, and families did not know whether to go home for winter as usual, or protract their summer absence at watering places. By November the troubles were past concealment; though we are still told that not one half that happened is known, because there is danger in publishing the facts. . . . [Martineau here details the social unrest that followed the Dred Scott decision.]

III. The functionaries of Mr. Buchanan's Government did not promote the "calm" announced by the head of the State. Mr. Cass, Secretary of State, began to refuse passports to persons of colour who wished to travel abroad. . . . The supposed right of preemption of the public lands hitherto enjoyed by persons of colour, was now denied, . . . [and] it was now announced that no man of colour could register a vessel owned by himself, nor command a vessel sailing under United States marine papers. . . . This new exclusion of free negroes from old departments of industry increased the social restlessness of the time. . . . Mr. Buchanan seems to have imagined that by carrying matters with a high hand in Kansas, he might at once gratify the Southern party and subdue the Northern. This part of his policy will perhaps always be regarded as the most characteristic; and it will be the most conspicuous because out of it arose the antagonism which has left him politically stranded.

IV. There is no need to explain that Kansas was, several years ago, pointed out to universal observation as the field on which the conflict between the authors and opponents of the modern pro-slavery policy and legislation would be fought out; nor need we go over again the dreary story of the wrongs inflicted on the settlers in Kansas by the bands of marauders from over the frontier, and the hired "mean whites" engaged in the south by the planters to go and secure a footing for slave establishments in the new territory. We have heard enough of stuffed ballot-boxes, imaginary constituencies, incendiarism, kidnapping, murder, and the hunger and misery which follow civil wars of so barbarous a character. The point was reached at last at Washington that the people of Kansas should have the power of voting for or against a constitution directly submitted to them. Mr. Douglas, who had risen to the position of leader of the Democratic party, avowed that the President, the Legislature, himself and his party, were pledged to this. Mr. Buchanan admitted the pledge, on his own part, by appointing Robert J. Walker to be Governor of Kansas, in spite of the strongest reluctance on the part of Mr. Walker. . . . [Here follows a discussion of Stephen Douglas and Robert Walker.]

At this juncture occurred that split in the Democratic party which is now determining the course of the Presidential Election, the policy of the next four years, and probably the fate of the Union. . . .

Mr. Buchanan failed in his attempt to saddle Kansas with the pseudo-constitution; and now, in the last year of his term of office, the affairs of Kansas remain to be settled, and are as doubtful and dangerous as ever. It was in asserting the right of the people of Kansas to reject slavery and its institutions, that Mr. Sumner was struck down in the Senate in the May before Mr. Buchanan's election; and it is in continuation of the same suspended argument that now, after four years of suffering from the assault, Mr. Sumner, in the June before Mr. Buchanan's retirement, has delivered the noble speech on the Barbarism of Slavery, which will be an event in the history of American politics. As for Mr. Buchanan, in deserting to the South on the subject of Kansas, he forfeited his political reputation, and he lost his best ally. In return, he gained nothing. The South, for whose favour he sacrificed so much, is not benefited by the sacrifice, and would prefer for President a Northern man who should effectually suppress the slave trade, or a man of its own way of thinking, who should be able to cope with the spirit of the North. Mr. Buchanan is neither the one nor the other; and he leaves the country more disturbed than he found it; therefore he is deserted in that quarter as in the North and the West.

V. This brings us to the consideration of Mr. Buchanan's policy, domestic and foreign, in regard to the slave-trade.

Some of the leading newspapers of the Free States have lately been publishing lists of the mercantile houses known to have been engaged in the slave-trade, and of the vessels employed in the traffic, during Mr Buchanan's term of office. . . . Mr. Buchanan's Cabinet insisted that the complaints of the extensive use of the American flag to cover slave-trading were unfounded; that the United States had done all that was possible, and that it was the business of England to control Spain and the Cuban trade, and set up preventive means in Africa. . . .

Such was the view professed in February, 1859, just a year after an exposure had been made on the actual conduct of the United States ships on the African coast. . . . From the Congo River alone 1000 negroes per month were carried off, under cover of the American flag. . . . Such were the disclosures made by Americans on the spot, in 1858. "Five-sixths of the slave ships sail from New York," says this authority; and the statement is followed by sketches of slave trading white society as it exists in Africa. . . . All the world knows now that the cruising of our ships in Cuban waters was a suggestion of Mr. Buchanan's Government; and Americans are not likely to forget that when, taking advantage of the popular wrath about imaginary "British outrages," Mr. Buchanan asked for new powers from Congress, in order to defend or avenge American rights in an emergency, he was refused. Loud as was the temporary clamour, it did not so confound the senses of Congress as to induce them to confer on the President new and unconstitutional powers. As for the rest, two or three cargoes of negroes have been recaptured and carried to the United States, to the great embarrassment of all the parties concerned. One set was sent to Liberia, and found to be a very inconvenient expense.

Another has been recently reported as dying off fast at Key West, while waiting for means to transport to Africa; but it has oozed out that, though many
may have died, the greater number of coffins interred were empty—representing negroes who were not dead or sick, but learning cotton cultivation in the
interior. The novelty of the spectacle of recaptured slaves at once shows what
the inefficiency of American cruising has hitherto been, and opens a new difficulty to the rulers of a Federal union, the members of which are in a state of
violent antagonism on the question whether negro labour shall be slave or
free. At present the professions of the government are in favour of an obser-
vance of the laws at home, and of the treaties abroad. . . .

Between these ways, in the slave states, of disposing of their neighbours
without asking their leave, and the rapid increase of the practice of kidnapping in the Free States, the barbarising influences of the Dred Scott decision
have become manifest in Mr. Buchanan's time to an extent which will char-
acterise his period of rule very unfavourably. . . .

VI. To gratify those, however, who may think they have heard enough of
Mr. Buchanan's relations to slavery, we will turn to his own special topic,—
his intended acquisition of Cuba and other outlying territory. Let us see
what has been done in his own field of ambition.

There was a time when Mr. Buchanan had reason to believe that he could
most effectually obtain the support of the Southern Democracy by proposing the annexation of Cuba as the next great fact in the history of the Republic; but changes may have taken place which have left him stranded on
this, as on other questions. The Cuban enterprise was begun in the same
way as the Texan and Mexican;—that is, by first endeavouring to stir up discontent, and then entering the territory by force of arms on pretext of aiding the malcontents against an oppressive government. Lopez, the leader in
the first serious attempt on Cuba, could not find any malcontents to support
him, and died garroted on the scaffold. By degrees the project has assumed a
commercial character. The alleged grievances are commercial, and "the solution" is to be "by purchase." From year to year Mr. Buchanan has announced
in his Messages that Spain was vexing the Republic, ending his narrative
with an intimation that money would be wanted for the purchase of Cuba;
or, less confidently, that measures must be taken for the acquisition of an island which is now an annoyance, instead of a great blessing, to the United
States; or, more recently, that Cuba will no doubt, sooner or later, belong to
the United States; and that to get it by purchase is the only method worthy
of a great people. Thus has the urgency of the question declined as the Spanish nation has risen in prosperity and importance. The wrath of the authorities in Spain and Cuba, and of the Spanish ambassador at Washington, at
the insult of the President's Messages to Congress about buying what Spain
did not mean to sell, seemed at first to produce no effect on Mr. Buchanan's
serenity: but now that he finds Spain preparing for the defence, and his
southern constituents at feud about the acquisition of Cuba, some deprecat-
ing it more vehemently than others desire it, he pretends to let the question

down gently, and to admit that he will have to leave office with this object also unaccomplished.

VII. The truth appears to be that experience has imposed some check on the passion for territorial aggrandisement in the Slave States, and among the floating population of adventurers which the northern cities are glad to get rid of on any pretence. One consequence of that change is, that the authorities at Washington have undergone some damaging exposures. Members of either House of Congress, in their courses of itinerant oratory, undertaken to rouse the old ambition of the South, have added a final touch of persuasion, which to foreign observers, looks very strange;—a hint, or an open declaration, that the views put forth were those of the President. . . . [Martineau here discusses Cuba, Central America, and Nicaragua.]

We will not enter into the perplexed subject of Mexico. There is no attempt at concealing the general expectation that the whole of Mexico will be absorbed, when convenient, as some of her provinces have already been. On the whole, however, we hear somewhat less of the scheme of aggression on neighbours than for some time past. The tremendous sectional strife at home, and the consequences of a retrograde method of rule, as shown in the troubled state of all the outlying regions of the Republic, are now too grave to be put out of sight by new schemes of glory and plunder: and the next President will have enough upon his hands, without undertaking to conquer more worlds. The unorganised condition of Kansas, the unsettled troubles with the Mormons, the Indian wars throughout the western territories, the chaos of blood and confusion in Texas, the responsibility of the filibustering in Central America, and the incessant bickering about Cuba, are quite enough for any President to have the charge of, without any schemes of further territorial aggrandisement. Meantime, the facts afford a singular commentary on Mr. Buchanan's professions about the "calm" which was to prevail, and a very vivid illustration of the Monroe doctrine which was to govern his rule.

VIII. Our readers will not need to be reminded of some trouble of our own about a boundary; but we shall avoid any mere superficial discussion of it while the controversy remains undecided. . . . [Here Martineau discusses San Juan.]

IX. In following the course of Mr. Buchanan's term of office we next arrive at an event which shows (as some incident always does show in times of crisis) through how narrow a sluice an over-mastering deluge may begin to flow.

Our readers may perhaps have a vague impression that the name of Helper is familiar to their eyes, if not to their minds; for it is a name which has been uttered many millions of times within three years. It is known in this country, where known at all, from the circumstance that the election for Speaker of the House of Representatives at Washington last winter was protracted for weeks and months on some question about Mr. Helper. It was really so; and it was Mr. Helper's book which finally discomfited the advocates of silence on the Slavery question, including Mr. Buchanan. . . . It may be remembered by some of our readers that, among the outrages committed in Congress during Mr. Buchanan's term, one was a stranger named Helper who was knocked down and beaten in the Capitol. It was this Hinton Rowan Helper; and it was on account of this book: and that assault was, if the newspapers have followed his course with any accuracy, far from being his only suffering for his courage in publishing his work. On opening it, a reader would think it impossible that a man could be persecuted for such a book; for it is full of statistical facts and tabular statements: but the same spirit which moved the Brahmin to break the microscope which showed him what he did not wish to see, and which made Galileo's enemies refuse to look at the moon and planets through a telescope, caused the fellow citizens of Mr. Helper to fall into rage with columns of figures, and rail at government returns as at works of heresy or licentiousness. . . . [Martineau discusses Helper's book, which analyses Southern economic decline as a direct result of the slave economy.]

X. The crisis was, indeed, a grave one. The invasion of Virginia by John Brown had taken place; and the character and issue of that invasion justified a strong persuasion that there was more behind them than the whole amount of what had appeared. It is scarcely conceivable that the invaders should have attempted what they did with so few resources as they disclosed; rumors were all abroad of further forces being in ambush every where, which accident had prevented from arriving in time: and the excessive panic to which slaveholding societies are always subject, spread from Maryland to Texas, and from Florida to Arkansas. Among an infinity of portents, two were grave beyond all estimate. The Federal Senate exceeded its constitutional powers in enforcing its pleasure on citizens of various States; and the Slave States threw off all semblance of obedience to law and regard to constitutional rights. . . . [Martineau discusses the role of the federal government in the Harper's Ferry insurrection.]

The condition of the country, in its Northern section, did not by this time bear witness to the calming effects of the Dred Scott decision, or to the success of Mr. Buchanan's policy, avowedly grounded upon it. The affair of Kansas remained unsettled; long trains of pilgrims were seeking the graves of John Brown and his sons; arrangements were making for resisting the aggressions of the Senate; there was plenty of both legislation and action against the new pro-slavery laws, with occasional escapes of good citizens from gaol, a profusion of public meetings, with speeches which quickened the blood of old men, in memory of revolutionary days; and, amidst the excitement, there was a steady and rapid growth of the Republican party, which has now charged itself with the ancient liberties of the Republic. . . . [Martineau discusses the South's "reign of terror" and compares the northern economy with the southern.]

A more interesting group of facts, as regards the prospects of the Republic, is that which relates to education. The two sections were once so nearly equal in their apparatus of college education, that there are now only two more colleges in the Free than in the Slave States,—the number being sixty-one to fifty-nine; but the Slave States are educating 747 ministers of the Gospel, while the Free States educate that number, and nearly 10,000 more, viz. 10,702; and something of the same proportion is shown by the professional schools, where the South shows 3,812 students, to 23,513 in the North. In the free schools of the North there is a larger proportion of the small, despised, free-negro element of the population, than there is in the South of the dominant white population. There are nearly three millions of pupils in the one section, to little more than half a million in the other; and the difference is not compensated for by private schools, which are everywhere inferior to those of the North. As for the press, South Carolina, which leads the march of intelligence in the South, and is five times as large as Massachusetts, had, at the last census, 141 printers, and not one publisher, to the 1,229 printers and fifty-nine publishers of Massachusetts. Of authors, South Carolina had two, and Massachusetts seventeen. *Duyckink's Cyclopedia of American Literature* shows 403 authors in the Free, to 87 in the Slave, States. Patents of invention are seven times as numerous in the Northern as in the Southern section. In the South, with its small white population, there are half a million of adults unable to read, to less than a quarter of a million in the vast and heterogeneous white population of the North. The statistics of migration are very striking, after all we hear of the hosts of Northern men who disperse themselves over the South and West: for it appears that six times as many in proportion to the population pass over from the Slave States to the Free as the reverse.

These facts are enough to show that the alienation of the two sections of the Union is not, as Mr. Buchanan assumes, a passing mood of irritation, nor, as Mr. Everett urges, a disagreeable topic which good breeding would ignore. On the one hand, there is wrath and disgust that the inferior section should overrule the superior in the whole course of the policy of the Republic; and on the other, there is fear, mortification, and envy in the sinking section, at the strength and growth of the rising Free States. We see in Southern newspapers white and black lists of Northern mercantile firms, the members of which are set down by guess as pro or anti-slavery: and some of these firms are known to subsidise the newspapers, in order to preserve their trade. Agents are constantly busy in New York collecting these bribes. The mails are searched for matter of an incendiary (anti-slavery) character. Vigilance Committees are in full activity in scores of towns, watching over trade and professions, and summarily expelling every shopkeeper, teacher, artisan, and even clergyman and physician, whose opinions are suspected. . . . In Texas, thirteen towns and villages have recently been fired in one afternoon. Sixty persons have been summarily hanged without trial. Two of these were charged with having supplied a hundred bottles of strychnine to negroes, wherewith to poison the wells. . . . We will stop here, for tales of horror are not needed. It is enough to say, in accounting for the hostility between the two sections, that in the North there are families and communities mourning the imprisonment of such men as Captain Baylis, who is wearing out his term of forty years in the Penitentiary, for five negro slaves having been found on board his ship in the Delaware: or the disappearance of some relative or fellow-citizen who has been kidnapped, and carried no one knows wither; or some friend, father, or brother, hanged or burned alive under a mistake, in too great a hurry to admit of his explaining who he was. On the other hand, the slaveholders are suffering agonies under the delusions which beset their class. They see in every negro a murderer, in every stranger a spy, and in every move of any State, and in every opposition speech in Congress, a conspiracy to destroy them. The North protests against the pro-slavery legislation of late years, and supplies an organisation to agitate for the dissolution and reconstitution of the Union: and at the same time several Southern States are openly proposing to secede from the Union, and establish a new Federation for themselves. It is not our intention to comment on these facts. We simply present them as features of the society which the new President will have to rule, and as evidences of the ill-success of Mr. Buchanan's policy of favouring the dominant minority, and "crying peace, when there is no peace."

In considering the prospects and the duty of the new President, we must remember two things above all others: and first, that the power of the American President is, if short in duration, very strong in quality; if he rules for only four or eight years, it is ruling in earnest, if he so pleases. Next, we must remember that there is no question in the case of the abolition of slavery. The Central Government has no immediate concern with the institution, except as it exists in the district of ten miles square which is under the jurisdiction of Congress. The separate Sovereign States have their own policy and their own institutions; and the part of the Washington Government is to promote the free action of the whole nation in conducting its collective affairs, and not to interfere with the respective States. . . . [Martineau here analyzes the candidates for the next election.]

It would require so great a man to establish even a working agreement between the warring sections of the nation that it would be unreasonable to anticipate so much as even a temporary accommodation. Washington himself never had so hard a task before him as to govern a group of enlightened and a group of half-barbarous sovereign States at the same moment and by the common policy. The "irrepressible conflict" indicated by Mr. Seward must be encountered and dealt with in one way or another. The Slave States-men persist in supposing this to mean civil war thrust upon the South by a tyrannical majority in the North; while the North always understood the expression to refer to the eternal opposition of the principles of free and despotic institutions. The man who might so preside over the struggle as to bring it to a favourable issue would be the true comrade of Washington. Such a man is nowhere recognised at present. In his absence, a multitude of citizens doing their duty faithfully may in part compensate for the want.

What is that duty, in a special sense? To us it seems very clear. The Republican State was founded on a moral basis. Every one of the great men who put a hand to the work had the hope that long generations of citizens would be better and happier than the men of Europe, because more free. To make the nation better and happier than they could otherwise be was the aim; and the means chosen for the purpose were, in the first place, truths moral and political laid down as the basis of the new polity. The worst symptom of the existing condition of affairs is that very few of the citizens,—or very few of those whose views and actions become known to us,—adhere to this basis at all. If a large number in the South have arrived at approving of slavery, instead of regarding it as the misfortune and disgrace which they once considered it, so also the multitudes of so-called anti-slavery men in the North overlook the moral decline of the national spirit for the sake of glorying in its material prospects. . . . There are bad people in every nation, the boasters say, and not more in their country than in others; every polity has its dark side; and there is no patriotism in making the worst of it. Their nation is the first in the world, in its prospects at least. It will get over its sins and their consequences; and then,—it will carry the whole world before it, and hold the first place in history for ever. If this humour of vanity could ever become universal, all would be over with the Republic. The hope is in there being true patriots enough to keep their country up to the original mark, or to bring it back to the principles of mutual good faith and common liberty which saved it, in its first feebleness, from the scoffs of the proud old world of Europe, and which alone can now reinstate it in the cordial respect of the human race.

❖ ❖ ❖

W A R   A N D

R E C O N S T R U C T I O N

1862–1864

So much of Martineau's adult life and professional career was bound up in the American situation that the final outbreak of the Civil War seemed almost an anticlimax. Writing during an era when many social problems, lacking viable solutions, were framed as questions—"The Irish Question," "The Woman Question," "The India Question"—Martineau's argument in "The Brewing of the American Storm" rejects the idea that the inevitability of civil war was ever in doubt. To her, the solution was obvious: war was unavoidable, she states flatly, and this was clear to many with whom she debated these issues during her 1834–1836 tour. Although she was a thorough Garrisonian and therefore a pacifist, Martineau was not convinced that pacifism would resolve the slavery issue; even Garrison himself was eventually forced to concede this point. On a distinctly positive note that resoundingly heralds the conclusion of Martineau's role as the American affairs expert in Britain's periodical press, "The Negro Race in America" directs readers' attention to the Reconstruction era and beyond—when, she predicts, America will at last begin to manifest the values on which the country was originally founded.

"The Brewing of the American Storm"
Macmillan's, 1862

As one of the new "shilling monthlies," *Macmillan's* (1859–1907) aimed at educated readers of limited means and is credited with sharpening the distinctions between "reviews" and "magazines." Although it printed new fiction, *Macmillan's* was also noted for its serious commentary on religion and politics. In the spring of 1862 Martineau, overwhelmed with an abundance of literary commitments, "refused all other new offers" except for one from Professor David Masson of University College of London, editor of *Macmillan's* (Arbuckle 1983, 222). "Every help is needed on this set of subjects," she explained, "and I *could* not refuse, believing myself able to say something more than a newspaper can give." Initially, Martineau criticized President Lincoln, believing him to be an ineffectual leader at this crisis point in American history. But his subsequent actions gradually won her admiration, a regard enhanced by the abolition of slavery in Washington, D.C. (16 April 1862) and, later, by the Emancipation Proclamation (1 January 1863).

"The Brewing of the American Storm" heralds an episode in American history that Martineau had long believed necessary for the redemption of American ideology, the significance of which she is eager to promote. That the seat of the republic's government had finally taken a definitive stand against slavery by abolishing it in the District of Columbia indicated an optimistic future for the realization of America's founding values through the abolition of slavery. As Martineau's history of American events illustrates, differing analyses of the ideology outlined in the Constitution had failed to be resolved through compromise; now, nothing less than an uncompromising stand against the Southern oligarchy would redeem the American "experiment."

A notable feature of "The Brewing of the American Storm" is the authority evoked by its author, whose anecdotal references to famous Americans she had met thirty years earlier enhance her already strong credibility as an authority on American political affairs. Adams, Madison, Webster, Clay, Calhoun, Chief Justice Marshall, Bishop White, Catharine Sedgwick—Americans representing various ideological perspectives—all had hosted this eclectic literary woman whose passion for America's lofty ideals sustained her through three decades of watching, waiting, and writing about emancipation. In this article, Martineau compares attitudes she witnessed in 1834–1836 to those shaping the events of the Civil War in the 1860s, arguing that it should come as no surprise to anyone concerned that war is and always has been inevitable. Garrison's pacifism, Thoreau's civil disobedience, Emerson's transcendentalism, Clay's compromises—all such attempts by "non-resistants" or "peace-men" to resolve the issues peaceably proved to be futile in retrospect. Although she objected to war as a solution, Martineau was forced to accept, along with many pacifists, that only such an apocalyptic event could settle the question definitively.

. . .

The abolition of slavery in the District of Columbia is the greatest event in the history of the American Republic. It suits the policy of certain parties in this country to conceal the importance of the fact, if they cannot conceal the fact itself; but not the less will wise men now, and all men hereafter, recognise in the event of April 16th, 1862, the closing of a period of guilt and danger, and the entrance upon one of genuine republicanism. In the fewest words, the case is this:—The District of Columbia, a space of ten miles square, is the only portion of territory subject to the Federal Government. All the people of the republic are, to a specified extent, the subjects of the Federal Government; but the inhabited lands are under State rule, with the one exception of this standpoint for the National Legislature and Executive. While slavery existed there, it was a national institution; now that it is abolished there, slavery becomes a State institution, and the national government is as free to denounce and condemn it as the government of any other country. One more, and the greatest, of the few powers of Christendom which have been reckoned as slaveholding nations, has come over from the wrong side to the right. The same sort of people who would have called Luther's Theses a piece of paper with writing on it, and the Ship-money Controversy a question of a few shillings, may now point out that the District of

Columbia is only ten miles square, and that there were not nearly so many slaves in it as formerly; but not the less will one of the great chapters of history close, now and for ever, at the date of April 16th, 1862, because on that day the American republic ceased to be a slaveholding power.

For the same reasons that the magnitude of the event is concealed in England, the tokens of its approach have been denied. We still see it assumed that the civil war in America was something sudden, unexpected, even absurd and revolting in its needlessness. So far from this being true, it would be difficult to point to any great event in history more distinctly and confidently anticipated by all public men in the country, and by all well-informed observers abroad. From George Washington to Abraham Lincoln, every statesman has seen what must happen, and has done his part in bringing on the catastrophe; and, as the time drew near, persons of any political insight knew and said, that the range of uncertainty lay within five years. If the disruption did not take place in 1856, it must in 1860. As it would be a serious falsification of history to say that the civil war was unnecessary, sudden, unexpected, and the like, it may be worth while to record what one person can testify to the contrary.

Of the first generation of the public men of the republic, four (and I believe no more) were living when I was in the United States, and I knew them all, more or less. They were Madison, Gallatin,[177] Chief Justice Marshall, and the venerable Bishop White. Of these four, three were unquestionably aware that the existence of the republic depended on the extinction of negro slavery, in one way or another; and no one of them saw any probability of the thing being done in time. Bishop White—"the Bishop of all the Churches," as he was called—was as sensible as every good clergyman must be of the ravage which the institution of slavery was making in the religion of the country; but I do not know what he supposed would be the result of the fearful and growing hypocrisy. Mr. Gallatin described to me, with the vividness of an eye-witness, the growth of the three great sections of the republic; and, as the introduction of slavery into the north-west was then supposed to be precluded for ever, he had the strongest confidence that, whenever the Southern section might be disposed to try again to dominate the Union by a threat of secession, the accordance of the North and West on the slavery question would overawe the disturbers. At that date—a year after the Nullification struggle—every statesman's mind was impressed with the importunate character of the danger, and aware that it was disguised in every political question of the day.

With the other two venerable survivors of the band of founders of the republic, I had much conversation on the subject which was always uppermost in their minds. They had been, not only friends, but coadjutors, in framing the constitution; though differing on some points, they had carried it through a host of dangers, and had seen it apparently established and prosperous beyond all controversy and all peril. Both had received due honour from their countrymen, and were passing their old age in honour and ease; yet they told me—the one, that he was "in despair," and the other, that he was "almost in despair," about the future of the country; and both on account of slavery. . . . [Martineau discusses Chief Justice Marshall and his distress over the decline of Virginia and former president James Madison, a Colonizationist.]

[Madison] talked more of slavery than of all other subjects together, returning to it morning, noon, and night. He said that the clergy perverted the Bible, because it was altogether against slavery; that the coloured population was increasing faster than the white; and that the state of morals was such as barely permitted society to exist. He did not see any way back to decency, but by removing the lower race. . . .

Such were Mr. Madison's opinions in 1835; and the share he had in bringing on the conflict which he foresaw was, first, permitting a compromise about slavery to be introduced into the constitution; next, inviting confidence to a delusive scheme for getting rid of danger, by getting rid of negroes; and, again, keeping up the traffic in slaves, by sending his own to market. If we desire to find an excuse for such conduct in a man so honoured and beloved, we can only remember that he was "almost in despair" of the fate of a polity which he had mainly created, and had administered during two Presidential terms. . . .] Mr. Madison had seen how the Union was made, and had been so far preserved; viz. by the Southern policy of proposing together an encroachment and a bribe. This method, of introducing measures in pairs, had at first succeeded; and it has succeeded again, since Mr. Madison's death, when the repeal of the Missouri Compromise was coupled with the removal of the Washington slave-market to a spot outside of the District of Columbia: but such a method must be exhausted in time; and the final quarrel could only be exasperated by the preceding insolence of the South, and abjectness of the North. . . .

Of the next generation of statesmen there were many more living; and they were, for the most part, active. I must begin, of course, with General Jackson, then President.

Of President Jackson I need not say much; for nobody ever supposed him a great statesman, or a man of distinguished forecast. He need not come into the account at all, but for two reasons: that the secession movement of his day was put down by him; and that he had practically countenanced the citizenship of negroes, in the war of 1812.

It was a ludicrous idea to those who conversed with General Jackson, that the preservation of the Union could depend on his opinion in a matter perplexing to senators and judges. His was, indeed, a mind not qualified to form opinions at all. He expressed his will, and the people about him supplied him with reasons. With a grave, even melancholy, countenance, and in few and passionate words, the grey-headed and haggard old man declared what could, and what could not, be allowed; and it did not occur to him to reconcile opposite decisions. He had encouraged the State of Georgia to break through Federal decisions in a dispute with the Cherokees about their lands; but, when South Carolina followed suit in the matter of the tariff, he intimated to the leaders at Charleston, that, if they dared to nullify the decisions of the Washington authorities, he should know how to punish them. He ordered the Federal troops to march upon Charleston, sent a sloop of war there to protect the port officers, and issued a proclamation warning South Carolina against rebellion. The Governor of the State issued a counter proclamation; and the crisis of the Union was understood to have arrived. Mr. Clay's Compromise Bill averted the strife for the time; but South Carolina justly claimed the victory of principle in regard to free trade, and remained convinced that she could have seceded if she had thought proper. Almost every leading statesman told me, a year later, that the prospects of the republic were entirely changed. The use and value of the Union had become a question. It was a question which would be stirred again on any occasion of rival pretensions between the General and State Governments; and it would assuredly be decisively contested whenever the settlement of the slavery question could be deferred no longer. From that hour the virtue and independence of the North succumbed. The South would not allow any question of its "peculiar institution"; and the North was, at least, as eager for silence. On that silence depended, as every public man with whom I conversed told me, the continuance of the Union. General Jackson believed it; and for this reason he was supported by the South. . . .

At the close of General Jackson's double term of presidentship, the common sentence on his administration was that it had unsettled every great question, and settled none. . . .

This brings us to Mr. Calhoun—then, and still, the greatest representative of his section of the republic. It was the pleasure of the chief Nullifiers to wear an appearance of mystery. . . . A year after that crisis, when they came about me at Washington, and invited me to their cities and plantations, they were as stern as ever on their special question, but capable of a grim mirth about their recent preparations for secession. They were haughty beyond description to Northerners; but to a stranger they would open out at a word; and I profited largely by that willingness. . . . [Martineau describes John Calhoun's background.] Wherever he went, all his life through, he commanded everybody's belief in his being an irrefragable logician: yet, somehow, he was always ultimately wrong. . . . His speech poured out of him as if it came from some incarnate intelligence or passion, of which he was the mere vehicle. . . . He spoke more or less to the point, but rarely to any practical purpose. . . . This great representative of his section was further removed from the traditional character of the gay, careless, social, winning Southern Cavalier than any Puritan New Englander I ever saw. . . . [H]e had always insisted that the existence of the republic was bound up with slavery; and when he saw that "all was over," he said so, and died. . . .

He told me that the subject of slavery would never be mentioned in Congress. . . . The republic would last for ages; and it would be by slavery being never mentioned in Congress. Southern members would take care that it was not. He did his best to stifle speech. He was responsible for the Gag Bill, by which postmasters were empowered and required to stop all publications and letters about which there was ground of suspicion that they treated unfavourably of slavery, and to burn the documents thus abstracted from the mail-bags. I saw him arrive, with his family, at Charleston; I saw how he strode through the streets, receiving homage as if he were the ruling prince; I saw him in the arsenal, handling the little groups of weapons, and in a barrack-yard, reviewing, and then addressing, ten or eleven recruits (the rest were wanted as sentinels or patrols all over the city); and I wondered what would be the effect on him if he should ever learn what the Free States had to say to his pet institutions and defences. . . . The representative man of the Southern section foresaw the present revolution. His share in bringing it on was larger, perhaps, than that of any other man. He taught the doctrine and introduced the practice of secession, and he led the profession of the South (new at that time in those States), that slavery was the indispensable basis of republican liberty.

The voice which so appalled him, as a voice of doom in Congress, was that of the venerable ex-President, John Quincy Adams. . . . [Martineau discusses Adams's insistence on the right of petition.] The Union must not be questioned: therefore slavery must not be questioned; and petitions must be thrust under the table if people could not be prevented from sending them. I remember a remarkable disclosure—remarkable to me—of the peril of the republic, from the unsoundness of the popular mind about it in that crisis of its political condition. I was walking arm-in-arm with Miss Sedgwick, in the valley of the Housatonic, when conversing about times to come, I spoke of the inevitable rupture of the Union. She snatched her arm from mine, and started back, saying that I could not be aware of the sacredness of the Union, which precluded its dissolution from being even imagined. I asked her if there was not something more sacred still which she herself admitted to be irreconcilable with the existing constitution? "If the will of God is against slavery, and your constitution involves it, which must give way?". . . Our concern with the matter is, that Mr. Adams foresaw what must happen: and that he did his part by vindicating a right which the preceding generation could not have conceived to be, in any circumstances, even threatened.

While speaking of one Northern statesman, I may as well say what I have to say of the rest. It is painful to look back to that time; but it is unavoidable, if I am to show that the present convulsion has not been sudden, unexpected, and unnecessary.

Mr. Webster occurs first to all minds. He won, and deserved, great distinction as the ablest antagonist of the Nullifiers in the crisis of 1832. On constitutional questions he was, I believe, the best authority in the country after the Supreme Court; and his speeches were as beautiful as they were, on those subjects, sound. Here his merits ended. He was the most abject of the whole band of Northern vassals, holding the stirrup for the Southern "chivalry." His ambition for the Presidentship was a chain round his neck; and he taught the Southern leaders how to handle it, and lead him wherever they would. . . .

If the civil war is to be laid to the charge of any one man, that man is assuredly Daniel Webster. No man knew better than he the weakness of the
citizens of the republic—and especially of the Northern section of it—the
idolatry of ability which puts unlimited power into the hands of a man of
genius. He availed himself of that weakness, and of the vanity which the citizens indulge about their public men, for his personal purposes, when he
might have turned his influence to the account of lifting his country out of
its great perplexity. . . . There can never be any question of the power he
might have wielded if he had directed his genius to the preservation of the
liberties of the citizens. Worshipped as he was, he might have led the whole
North to withstand the encroachments of the South, and have guided at will
the genuine republican force, which could have easily controlled the oligarchical pretensions and operations of the slave-holding minority. There
should have been no Gag Law, and no suspension of the right of petition in
Daniel Webster's time. An honest and intrepid course would have led him to
the highest honours. When it was by far too late, he dishonoured himself
for the sake of the Presidentship. He might have had it by early sustaining
and guiding the best public opinion in the North. Instead of this, he discouraged and betrayed it, in order to avert collision, till his own purposes
were served. . . . The Northern pride in him, and the Southern trust in his
gratitude and obedience, might, he believed, join in electing him. So he
courted the South, which he should have long before taught its place and its
duty. He enabled the Missouri Compromise to be repealed, and the Fugitive
Slave Law to be passed; and the immediate retribution broke his heart. . . .

If anything about him was universally agreed upon, it was his devouring
ambition; yet he expected to make me bring home an account of his taste
for retirement and obscurity. "My dear woman," he said, laying a strong fin-
ger on my arm, to emphasize his words, "don't you go and believe me to be
ambitious." . . .

Mr. Everett's career has been a weak imitation of Webster's. . . . The only
part of his story which concerns us is his view of the future, and his share of
preparation for it. That he did foresee, from his first appearance in Congress,
the issue of the public trouble in war, servile or civil, was plain to all consid-
erate eyes. His speech about the alacrity with which he would buckle on his
knapsack to fight side by side with the slaveholders against negroes or negroes' friends was understood at first, and has been always remembered, as a
disclosure of his devotion to the Union, at all costs; and that devotion has
ever since cost him everything. In Congress he has shuffled, to avoid committing himself in any respect against the South. As Governor of Massachusetts, he rebuked and discountenanced the abolitionists on the declared
ground of the danger of offending the South. As a member of the Government at Washington, he bullied England, in order to gratify the South about
the slave-trade and the Monroe doctrine. . . . Mr. Everett did, to my knowledge, foresee the existing struggle at least a quarter of a century ago. Instead
of defending the liberties of the republic, he applied himself to propitiate

the aggressors on those liberties; and now, though he assumes the semblance of patriotism, he can do nothing; for everybody understands that he would sacrifice liberty to purchase any semblance of union. . . .

Judge Story so carefully avoided all implication in politics that I will say no more than that he certainly was fully aware of what must happen. For hours together we have discussed the inevitable issue of accumulating compromises: and he lost all hope—as far as so sanguine a man can lose hope—when he was passed over on the death of Chief Justice Marshall, and Judge Taney was appointed, in contempt of all considerations but the pleasure of the South. Some such act of the Supreme Court as the Dred Scott decision was sure to follow on such a packing of the Supreme Court as began with the slight to Judge Story.[178]

There remains Henry Clay. Of the whole company I knew him best. It was impossible, as he was fully aware, that I could avoid seeing the insincerity to which his position committed him; but he hoped that much might be forgiven to a man so placed. He was interesting from the contrariety between his nature and the requirements of his career. He was a man of impulse, even of passion; and he was the great Professor of Prudence in the State. He was the great mediator; and he learned to grow as proud of his compromises as other men are of being above compromise. It was as a means of postponing revolution that he valued his compromises; and it was as the saviour of his country from revolution that he was idolized in the North and West. . . . He was applauded; but he had no power. He was set up as a candidate, often and often, but others gained the prize. . . . I had occasion, more than once, to show him that he went too far in his attempts to lead me away from it: but his anticipations of the catastrophe were too clear and precise to be concealed. He knew that I understood what the Colonization Society could and could not do; and there we left it.

As for what he did in regard to the catastrophe, he aggravated its guilt and bitterness by buying it off for a time by sacrifices of liberty and honour. He considered it patriotic to defer the crisis by the use of his great powers of persuasion, coming in aid of the national pride in the Union. . . . With Henry Clay, compromise faded and died out; and the South, in the seats of power at Washington, began to fleece, out of the national stores, for the coming revolution.

"All this is very dreary," some will say. "Is this the life of statesmanship in America?" Yes; for the last quarter of a century. It is not the natural life of republican statesmanship; but it is the experience of a generation of political leaders who are one and all burdened with the consciousness of a radical sin and an impending retribution. Throughout the whole period, every man of two generations has known that the turning point of the national fortunes was the fate of slavery in the District of Columbia. While it lasted, the nation was isolated in Christendom as a slaveholding people—a people holding slaves in the very metropolis of the republic. Whenever the offence was done away, the nation would at once join company with other Christian

Till now ye have gone on and filled the time
With all licentious measure, making your wills
The scope of justice: till now, as many such
As slept within the shadow of your power,
Have wandered with their traversed arms, and breathed
Their sufferance vainly. Now the time is flush
When crouching marrow, in the bearer strong,
Cries of itself — NO MORE.

—Shakespeare, *Timon of Athens* (V:iv:3–10)
epigraph to "Demerara," *Illustrations of Political Economy* IV

"AM I NOT A MAN . . ."

peoples, free to reprobate and extinguish a barbarism and a curse. That day
has arrived, and the American people and we are on the same side.

It is needless, after what I have related, to dwell upon the absurdity of
saying and assuming that the American conflict is unexpected, or, as I have
repeatedly read, "undreamed of." It was discussed with me, a quarter of a
century ago, by every man and woman I met in the United States who had
any political knowledge or sense; and, as we have seen, the forecast of it has
clouded the lives of statesmen of all sections and degrees, from the founders
of the republic down to their grandsons. If we English have been thoughtless
about providing a supply of cotton from other territory, let us say so; but let
us not incur the charge of either ignorance or hypocrisy by saying that the

Second American Revolution was not foreseen long ago, and in the very time and manner of its happening.

"The Negro Race in America"
Edinburgh Review, 1864

This article exemplifies Martineau's periodicals writing at its best, and it is particularly satisfying as a mature piece of work virtually marking the conclusion of her thirty-year affiliation with American slavery politics. Of the hundreds of newspaper and periodical articles Martineau produced on various slavery-related topics, "The Negro Race in America" is most fittingly distinguished by its focus on black Americans, rather than on the whites who determined their fates politically, socially, and institutionally. Responding to Henry Bright on "the disposal of the Southern negroes," she asks: "Why dispose of them at all? Why not let them be,— as to where and how they live? . . . They don't choose to go away; . . . and when Congress has said –Hands off!' to the savage mean whites, they will be among the most thriving folk in the country."[179]

Although the status of African Americans is not a new theme, since it is addressed throughout her anti-slavery writings, "The Negro Race in America" reflects the period's social and political reconstruction by shifting focus away from the power imbalances of the slavery years and toward the practical concerns of establishing black Americans as free citizens. In contrast, her earlier writing on the topic, for example, *Society in America* and *Retrospect of Western Travel,* aimed to dramatize the dehumanization created by slavery through depictions of southern blacks as animalized—not through some vague quality inherent to the black race, but through the suffering, violence, and deprivation inflicted on them by whites. As is typical of Martineau's approach, this 1864 article presents an overview of African American history as a means through which to consider blacks' present condition and future prospects. Emancipation, in other words, liberates not just the bodies but the minds and the souls of a people whose future promises to vindicate the institutionalized dehumanization of the past.

"The Negro Race in America" traces blacks' contributions to the building of the republic, including various legal and social triumphs. Martineau admired a race she regarded as remarkable for its ability to endure unthinkable abuse and deprivation and still manage to survive. Turning racists' social Darwinism to a quite different end, Martineau singles out runaway slaves as the most remarkable examples of survival of the fittest; their energy, determination, and drive in the face of impossible odds promise a future of progress marked by what is to her the one quality essential for both individual and communal progress: hope. As she outlines some of the means being employed to help newly freed blacks become economically self-sufficient, Martineau demonstrates yet again her prophetic, anticipatory foresight in her observation that true emancipation will be realized once blacks speak for themselves *and are heard.* That white abolitionists like herself will become redundant as champions for black rights is a future she looks forward to with great anticipation.[180]

. . .

ART. VII.—1. *Instructions to the Commissioners for Emancipation in the District of Columbia:* 1862.

2. *The President's Message to Congress on his Plan of Gradual Emancipation:* July, 1862.

3. *Official Report on the Freedmen of South Carolina to the Secretary of the Treasury.* Washington: 1862.

4. *First Annual Report of the Education Commission for Freedmen.* Boston: May, 1863.

5. *Circulars of the Freedmen's Inquiry Commissioners, appointed by the Government of the United States:* August, 1863.

Two years ago we treated of the condition and prospects of that portion of the negro race[181] which has already past, or is about to pass, through the critical transition from slavery to freedom in the Western hemisphere. The emancipated negroes of the West Indies were our chief subject in that article, not only because we were discussing a book relating to those colonies, but because, in studying the case of our own former slaves, we stood on a solid ground of fact; whereas, in regard to the case of the negroes still enslaved in America, we had no certainty of the accuracy of any expectations we might form, or of the degree of fitness for the duties of freedom which the process of emancipation might disclose among them. The intervening two years have changed the condition and prospects of the race in the United States to an extent which few living men expected to witness with their own eyes; and with the changes have come results which render speculation on the future of the American negro much less wild or vague than it could ever have been before. We propose to consider some of these results, and to look forward a little in the direction in which they point. We shall say nothing on the politics of the white inhabitants of the States, because our topic is the character and probable destiny of the negroes, quite apart from the merits and demerits of the classes or parties by whose strifes they have been brought into their present position. If it is talking politics to assume that slavery is drawing to an end in the United States, then we must be political to that extent; but, as there is probably no one in Europe, and as there are certainly few in America, who believe that "the peculiar institution" can ever be again what it was in the Slave States before the war, we incur no charge of political partisanship in assuming that negro slavery in America has received its death-sentence.

Of the disclosures here referred to, the greatest and most interesting is that of the effective education the negroes have been receiving, for a long course of years, for the new destiny which is opening before them. Where the speculations of their friends or of their enemies are now found to be wide of the mark, it is because they were unaware to what extent the process of training for freedom had already advanced, and that it was becoming accelerated from day to day. By looking over the facts of the life of one or two generations of American slaves, we shall learn how the process went on, and see how easily all the parties concerned might be unconscious of it to the last moment.

So far as it is true that the first emancipation of a slave on the ground of personal or political right is a pledge of ultimate release for all, the doom of American slavery was passed before the Declaration of Independence. A negro woman was born in slavery in 1742 who obtained her own freedom on that ground, and thus brought about the abolition of slavery in Massachusetts first, and afterwards in the other Northern States. This Elizabeth Freeman, better known as Mum Bet, heard, while waiting at table, discussions of the Bill of Rights, and the new Constitution of Massachusetts; and it was clear to her that all but "dumb beasts" had, under those provisions, a claim to personal liberty. She consulted an eminent lawyer—no less a man than Judge Sedgwick: he took up the case seriously, and obtained her freedom, with wages for her services from twenty-one years of age. This happened in 1772; and so many of her class followed her example that it soon became a matter of convenience to abolish slavery in Massachusetts; and drop the subject.

This story discloses a state of society entirely unlike anything that has existed in the Southern States within living memory; but there was less unlikeness between the two sections of the Union in those times than of late years. We know this by the testimony, express or indirect, of several of the highest order of citizens and observers. Washington, in pointing out for special honour the best regiments engaged in the revolutionary war, placed a negro regiment in the first rank. Moreover, he had no idea whatever of regarding them as aliens. He praised their patriotism exactly as he praised the patriotism of the other good soldiers. . . . This kind of fellowship certainly existed, in the very heart of the Slave States, so late as 1814; for, at the close of the war with England of that year, General Jackson, slaveholder as he was, addressed the blacks and mulattoes of the South as patriots. . . .

The doleful middle period of extreme humiliation was, however, drawing on. Events have shown that the easier and the harder period were both preparatory for freedom. The tradition of what the blacks were at the time of the great wars and dangers of the Republic may elevate the educated people of colour, and possibly encourage the general body of them; and how the succeeding time of deep adversity wrought upon them in heart and mind is now becoming known, in proportion as they find means of expressing their experience and their aspirations. . . . [Martineau discusses colonization schemes.]

These proceedings were highly exciting to all negroes who heard of them. The mere notion of a choice of homes, of a special country of their own, of freedom to be given, of enterprise to be recommended, was in itself a new stage of education. One sign of the awakening was the growing frequency of insurrections. There is no knowing what to believe when slaveholders utter the impressions of their terror; but, by the testimony of the residents in the Slave States at that time, risings, great and small, occurred monthly. For some years prior to 1832, there had been on an average twelve in a year. As a natural consequence, the severities of the masters increased; the depression of the slaves deepened; and it is made clear by every kind of evidence that the condition of American slaves was never so low as at the time of the great insurrection of 1831, called the Southampton [Nat Turner] Massacre. It is as important as it is interesting to understand the phase of negro character which presented itself at that time, because it is so far unlike that which has appeared under recent circumstances as to show that the ultimate destiny of the race or class really does depend very largely on the wisdom of the will of the whites among whom they live.

It was during this period that, without any sufficient reason publicly assigned, emancipation was, throughout the Slave States, rendered so difficult as to be almost impracticable. There was a reason, no doubt; and it was no secret to any slaveholder, though little known out of bounds. The mulatto race was increasing very rapidly, so that it was rare to see a plantation, or any slave-quarter, where light-coloured children were not intermixed with the black. The fathers were apt to be less ready to sell, and more ready to liberate, these than their blacker slaves; and it was apprehended that the free mulattoes would in a very few years become a too dangerous element in Southern society. Laws were therefore passed which compelled the white fathers to sell their slave-children, if it was inconvenient to keep them. Though the change in the laws was for a limited reason, the evil to the slaves was unlimited. The chance of release, which had always existed before, was annihilated; and a new desperation took possession of the people whose *insouciance* had always been praised and despised by their proprietors. . . .

The effect on negro character was evident enough. The newspapers exhibited more and more little pictures of a black man running, with a bundle over his shoulder; and the planters had to make larger deductions every year from their profits for losses by runaways. The negroes would not go to Africa; but some buried themselves in inaccessible swamps, and more made their way North, though abolitionism was not yet heard of there. Then there were more bloodhounds, and harder punishments for captured runaways. This was the period of strong passion on the part of slaves; and, as a necessary consequence, fear took possession of the masters also. Negro husbands became more ferocious when their homes were defiled, and murders of whites assumed a shocking character. Whether the practice of burning negroes alive had existed before, there seems to be no evidence; but at this time it became not infrequent; and four instances in the course of thirteen months became accidentally known to persons who were connected with the Southern States. There were still thousands of slaves who kept up the reputation of their race for contentedness, household attachment, and gaiety of spirits; and there were proprietors who sincerely relied on their attachment, and believed that all was well while laughter and singing went on; but there were more, perhaps, who depended on the terrors of their negroes. It was common to show strangers how any slave would, however black, change colour and tremble at a loud tone or angry word from master or mistress, and to ask what was to be feared from such a craven race. Yet the fear was growing daily; and with it, of course, grew the cruelty on the one side, and the desperation on the other. . . . [Here Martineau details the notorious cruelties of a New Orleans slave mistress, Madame Lalaurie.]

On the other side were cruelties also—some sly, some reckless—poisonings by petted house-slaves, murders of infants, and the like; and also that singular form of revenge—men and women maiming themselves, in order to be a mere burden to those who were bound to maintain them for life. Where hope still existed, it was of escape by flight, and of learning meanwhile to read and write, for this purpose. . . .The effect on the negro character of these fears of the owners became more marked as they became more apparent in ordinary life. The negroes perfectly understood why the vigilance of the citizens kept watch over every street and every house; why a few hisses or catcalls at the theatre sent the whole audience home in the middle of a piece; why the whole city got up and dressed—dressed even the little children—at the first cry of fire; and why negroes, however young were hanged for causing a fire, when a "mean white" would have undergone a much slighter punishment.

Here were all the elements for insurrection, and a state of things in which the only hope for the greater number lay in insurrection. Any extended concert was impossible; and the little that was practicable was of a very imperfect kind. Restless negroes found occasional means of making known to each other that they were miserable; and this kept them in constant expectation of some great event—some deliverance from above or from abroad. This then was the fitting season for monthly insurrections, and for the frightful Southampton Massacre. Desperate and fanatical negroes, who believed themselves commissioned to "slay and spare not," butchered in that rising upwards of seventy whites, of both sexes and all ages. This event wrought strongly on both whites and blacks. The masters were aghast at finding that their "attached servants" would not stand by them for a single moment after being summoned on the other side; and the negroes sank into deeper hopelessness on finding the chances of insurrection closed against them. They were henceforth to be more strictly confined; they were to have less liberty of meeting even for religious exercises, fewer suppers and dances, and shorter hours in the evenings. Life was to be graver and sadder henceforth, and they did not yet know that it was to be more secure from ill-treatment. They were soon to be less overworked and less flogged and safer from torture, and more comfortable in their homes; but they could not foresee this, and they bitterly felt the restraints put upon their dancing and feasting, and prayer-meetings in the woods at night.

Here the lowest period of American slavery may be seen to have closed. Dreary and hopeless as it seemed, it was, in its way, preparatory, and even disciplinary, in regard to the changes in reserve for the slaves and their masters. Both the free blacks and the slaves had obtained a firm grasp of the idea that they were Americans and not Africans. A few old people among them, and returned emigrants, could tell something about Africa; and a multitude more could boast of what General Jackson had said of America being their country. Moreover, they had learned that their removal from the soil had been proposed, and that the first men in the States were consulting what to do with them. These ideas were widely spread among them when that happened which put a stop to negro-risings at once and for ever.

Though the Colonization Society was of Southern origin, and formed avowedly in the interests of the slaveholders, it was likely to meet with support in the Free States from the very large proportion of the citizens who were troubled by the presence of free negroes, and uneasy as to the issues of slavery. . . . [Martineau details the rise of abolitionism through Garrison's rejection of colonization.] They [the Colonizationists] prosecuted for libel a Northern citizen who exposed the false pretensions and real tendencies of their scheme, and thus fixed attention on an adversary whose words of those days have become a tradition which will never be lost. When they fined and imprisoned Garrison for saying what was proveably true, they destroyed their own cause to set up his. . . .

The free people of colour were at that time about 400,000 in all the States; and though their social position was low, and could not be much raised while their colour marked them as members of an enslaved race, there were not a few educated and wealthy families among them. . . . Whatever the Southern or the Northern aristocracy might think, the negro owners of houses and ships, the merchants, surgeons, schoolmasters, and clergymen of the despised race, had influence to discredit the Colonization scheme among the people of their own colour, from the capitalist to whom brilliant prospects were held out in the colonies to the stupidest slave whom his owner was anxious to get rid of.

By means of the influence of opinion, white and black, the minds of the slaves were at once turned against the proposed deportation, and inspired with hope of deliverance by some other chance. Through the scattered population of free blacks, knowledge and opinion were certainly transmitted to the remotest corners of the Slave States; and so marked a change came over the temper and manners of the slaves that their owners assumed without any evidence that a secret agitation was carried on by "prowling Abolitionists." . . . It was absurd to marvel how the desire, or the very idea, of freedom should have occurred to the slaves, while liberty was the bribe held out to make them willing to go to Africa. . . . The runaways were a standing evidence, from year to year, that the idea of freedom was active in the negro mind, before Abolition was heard of as well as afterwards. But from the time of Mr. Garrison's imprisonment—from the day when the news spread that a white man had taken up their case—they became a changed people.

Their outward condition improved markedly and steadily, in the first place. From the hour when the attention of the outside world was directed to the condition of the slaves, there was a natural anxiety among all but the most sordid and shameless slaveholders to satisfy the world that the Southern "peasantry" were a highly-favoured class. They had less and less liberty, because of the prevalent terror of "prowling" seducers—the more dreaded for being invisible—who were supposed to want to set them running north-wards. They had less liberty; but they had more comfort and better superin-tendence. In religious observances they were indulged and encouraged, be-cause it was safer to have prayer-meetings within sight and hearing; and the shocking fanaticism which certainly was fostered by the whites was in-tended to divert their thoughts from dangerous aspirations. As it happened, so much reality got mixed up with the visions that the result baffled all an-ticipation. However the prayer-leader might use the imagery of the Book of Revelations ("Come down, O Lord God! On your great white horse, a kickin' and snortin'"), there was a rational allegory connected with it. The captive people had a Moses ready to lead them out of their land of bondage, by whom they were waiting to be led. The mingling of fact and aspiration was to them a real inspiration of faith; and the proof of this appeared in the im-provement of their character and manners. Not only were there no more ris-ings, but the murders and other acts of violence became fewer and fewer. This improvement took place in full view of a reverse process among the whites. The sermons, newspapers, and other chronicles of the South show an increase of homicide within the last quarter of a century which has been appalling to society. Much of this is owing, no doubt, to the panic excited by the mere name of Abolition. The great majority of the murders, duels, flog-gings and burnings of the last thirty years, which have disgraced American society, were caused by disputes connected with slavery. Blacks were killed on the merest suspicion, and whites were lynched or shot: strangers were punished by the roadside and in market-places, neighbours, and even inti-mate friends, were challenged, warned, beaten, banished, or killed in duels, on some supposition of an offence against slavery. While society was thus becoming barbarised, the effect on the negroes was more favourable than mischievous. Many resident whites, who abhorred the system under which they were living, and even slaveholders, saw this, and stimulated the aboli-tion movement to the utmost of their power, sending money to the North, and earnest entreaties to perseverance till the slaves should be converted to free labourers. They dared not speak; they dared not take in Northern news-papers; but they could send money and encouragement, and promises of co-operation when the day of escape from the curse of slavery should come.

When the time arrives for the blacks to write their own history, the world will learn that the millions who seemed to be living so quietly and, as their owners boasted, contentedly, were undergoing a process of education in the expectation of something great which was about to befall them. Their vices grew, as well as their intelligence and their courage. The runaways are always the best and brightest specimens, for obvious reasons; and some of them have told us what their latter years of slavery were like. They were more in-dustrious than before, because they wanted a store of money. They were more cunning and lying, because they had more to conceal and misrepre-sent. The absurdity of the popular notion that the negroes are like children in the matter of ingenuousness has been abundantly shown within the last few months; for it now appears that the body of slaves has been living under a mask for a generation at least. The slaveholders have always assumed that nobody knew anything about negroes but themselves; they have been excessively amused when assured, now and then, that none knew negroes so little as themselves: but at length they are finding this to be the simple truth. Their grandfathers probably did establish a genuine intercourse with their negroes; but, in the present generation, both slaves and owners have changed so essentially that their relation is something new even to their own imaginations. Once placed in antagonism, avowed or secret, the slaveholder is sure to become violent and reckless, and the negro to grow intelligent, cunning, hypocritical, and firm in purpose. Thus is explained the present high position of many negroes who escaped from Southern slavery during this period. It is probable that some of our readers may have heard the public speaking of Frederick Douglass, or of William Wells Brown, or of William Craft; and, if so, they will have seen how inadequate the slaveholders' notion of the capacity of these people is to account for the elevation they actually reach, after their own energy has put them in the way of education.[182]

Year by year the slaves, generally speaking, were growing more reserved and occupied, and less gay. Somehow or other, they always knew what was the tendency of affairs in the Free States. They knew of the establishment of colleges for the instruction of young people of their own colour. They knew of the opening of schools to children of all complexions. They knew when great men were discussing at Washington whether or not to make the whole Union slave territory, as far as Canada; and the dire import of the Fugitive Slave Law; and the chances that remained that good friends might prevent all runaways from being remanded to their old hovels and whipping posts. There was much to occupy them in all this; and other observers besides Mr. Olmsted have expressed surprise at finding, not gaiety and childish mirth, but a silence and sadness among the slaves which they had never heard or dreamed of.

It will be interesting to learn, some future day, how these depressed creatures, watched incessantly and punished for every approach to transgression of bounds, came to know what they did know of affairs in the North. Since their emancipation on the South-east coast, we have learned that it had long been customary for some house-servant to carry off, before the family came down to breakfast, the newspaper left on the table over night. In all neighbourhoods there were negroes who could read, little as their masters suspected it. When there was any particular news, the paper was sure to disappear; but it was seldom asked for. When it was not interesting, it lay in full view. This was one way. Again, these house-servants stole down to the negro quarter at night; and, when it was certain that the overseer was in bed, the fastest runner started for the next plantation, to send on the news of any disclosure made at table, or in the dressing-room, in the hearing of waiters or lady's-maids. The messenger was always at home before the overseer was up.

Another resource was the "underground railway," an institution or enterprise which our readers can hardly need to have described to them. As

passengers could go North by this means, so news could come South. Tidings
of escapes, completed or baffled, almost always reached the old comrades; and
a good deal of other news naturally came to them. . . . [Martineau discusses
the 1856 election.] They learned that their prospects depended on Presidential
elections, and that they must be ready when the hour of deliverance came.
"Contrabands" who now arrive with money in the Federal lines mention six
years as the time during which they have been accumulating their cash.[183]. . .
[Here Martineau discusses the use of religion to control slaves.]

There can hardly be a stronger test, both of the force of the desire of liberty and of the personal heroism of certain negro slaves, than the mode of
escape adventured by some few of them when the Fugitive Slave Law rendered the old methods too hazardous. We can understand how men and
women may have stood in the swamp, up to the chin, for days; and how
they may have borne hunger and fatigue, and have thrown themselves into
the broad Ohio or Potomac, preferring to drown within sight of the free
shore to being caught by the horsemen who are shouting behind. We can
understand the daring of the young mother who, with her babe, was almost
in the grasp of her pursuers, and sprang upon a fragment of ice floating past.
From one swirling fragment to another she leaped, sometimes apparently
without a chance, and then making another spring for dear life and for her
child—her pursuers themselves standing fixed in wonder and admiration at
the heroism of her flight. Such adventures are conceivable enough; but to escape by being coffined in a chest, and thrown about among the cargo of a
steamer or the luggage in a railway-van, requires uncommon courage and
power of endurance. There are several men of colour in the Free States—
some of them now educated persons—who for years laid by money from extra work, prepared by unknown means for a peculiar reception in some
Northern city, trained wife and children to bear the suspense of the adventure, and finally obtained secretly a large chest, bored it with holes for air on
all its sides, put in the money, and the necessary food, and then lay down to
be nailed up in what proved only a living grave. The reception of such fugitives was indeed a peculiar one. Some citizen of colour in Philadelphia, probably, as the nearest safe point, was on the wharf, inquiring for a chest of
goods consigned to him by this steamer; and he had a truck and men of his
own colour waiting to carry it away. There was no use in impatience, but
much risk: so the inquirer must keep calm. When put ashore at last, the
chest might be set on end, or bottom up. Not till it was in the hall at home,
and the door shut, did the host venture the signal, which he had scarcely
strength by this time to make. If his knocks on the lid were answered, the
fugitive was alive. Perhaps the failures have been unreported. We have heard
of none; while there have been several men known in the Free States by the
names of Box Brown, Box Smith, Box Jones, &c., in honour of some such adventure. The hero is found in dreadful condition, of course; sometimes
speechless for hours. The cup of broth is ready, and the warm bath, and the
comfortable bed. In a wonderfully short time, his wife knows the issue of the

experiment; and she is probably aware what the next news will be. It seems to be always the same. He goes to work with intense diligence, buys first his daughter or daughters, then his wife, and afterwards his boys, if they have not been sold away out of reach. Then follows the education of the children: at school first, and, if there is yet time, at college. In one form of expression or another, such families as these are always calling attention to the fact that negroes can use their freedom like other people, when allowed to try.

These successful fugitives are the very best of the slave race, as the plantation field-hands are the worst. The higher sort show that negroes are capable of taking care of themselves; while the lower do not prove that they are not. Some respectable free men of colour in the North were once field-hands; and they look back with amazement on the notions and feelings of their early life. Still, through all the heights and depths of their destiny, one universal tone is always sounding, prophesying of liberty at length to all. Whatever the slaves, old and young, wise or foolish, grave or gay, may say in answer to questions before strangers, the desire of freedom is absolutely universal among them. It has certainly been so for many years; and there is every reason to suppose that it always was so. Some may be too lazy, some too luxurious, some too timid, to make any effort on their own behalf, and all are too cunning to admit that they feel anything that is inconvenient to their owners; but no one fact about them is so well ascertained as that they all regard freedom as the one desirable thing in life, and the crowning blessing which is in store for their race, sooner or later. . . . [Martineau discusses school integration in Boston and the New Bedford Convention of Free Blacks.]

The only point which remains to be noticed, before the date of the civil war, is the avowed and increasing alarm of Southern society at the results disclosed by each census. Small as the negro increase has been, it has borne an ever-increasing proportion to the white element in South Carolina and several other States. There is no evidence that the fact created any special hope among the blacks, but it inspired a strong fear in their proprietors; this fear induced greater severity of control, and greater severity again caused more escapes. In one free State on the Ohio, fifteen hundred fugitives were known to have passed through in a single year; and there was no getting them back again.

A new Presidential Election had now come round. That of 1856 had not brought any good to the slaves; they had heard nothing more of Fremont; and they had heard a great deal of the DRED SCOTT decision, as rendering escape almost impossible. Nowhere short of Canada could they now be any safer than in the Gulf States. Would Fremont come forward again? From the talk at table and in the carriage, and in town and country meetings, the listeners, who never failed to have their ears open, learned that there were other men as hateful in the South as Fremont; and at length it appeared to be Breckinridge who would keep all straight at the South, and Lincoln who was the Fremont of the day.[184] . . . [Here Martineau describes the southern propaganda against "Yankees" used to frighten slaves.]

Here we have reached the ground of the great speculation—what the future of the negro will be in America. The best material for a judgment is, unquestionably, our knowledge of the character of the negro—of his ideas, his capacities, and his moral state and tendencies—under the test of the present crisis of his fate. Of this material there is a great deal at our command, derived from official sources, and vouched for by the direct testimony of the Federal Commissioners for Freedmen. Relying on the accuracy of their statements, the facts they describe are in the highest degree interesting and important.

For some time after the opening of the war, the freed (or escaped) negroes were as miserable in their circumstances as could well be imagined. In their eagerness to escape from bondage they cast themselves upon the mercy of camps and cities, by tens of thousands; and they found, for many weeks and months, little enough of mercy anywhere but among people of their own race. It should be remembered for ever that long before any sort of provision was made for these destitute creatures, and before either the Government or general society in the North took their case into consideration at all, they were fed, clothed, comforted, and assisted to get into work, by the despised free blacks of the Northern cities. In Washington, and Philadelphia in particular, the humblest dwellings were open to all who came from the South. So great was the crowding in the houses, and so reduced was the condition of the fugitives, that fever, cholera, and dysentery soon created alarm wherever the "contrabands," as they were by this time called, had assembled. The state of things was truly appalling at the beginning of 1862. Nothing can be said in justification of the Washington Government for its apathy and its delays in making up its mind what to do with the multitude of negroes who were sure to come into its hands when the war was carried into the South. Up to that time the fugitives who arrived in the Free States were provided with employment without much difficulty—the demands of the war having perceptibly reduced the supply of labour. The negroes who took occasion to quit Virginia and the Border States which were the seat of war were presently in demand, as far north as the wharves of Chicago and the farms of New England. But only a small proportion go so far; for they were in demand in the camps, to relieve soldiers of the coarsest duties, and be the personal servants of officers. The women washed, cooked, and cleaned, the men did everything else required in camp. Even northern citizens were surprised to see how well and diligently they worked under the stimulus of pay. And thus, on the whole, the state of affairs, so far, was not so alarming or vexatious as to rouse the Government to its duty. The able-bodied of both sexes seemed to be taking care of themselves; and the helpless were taken care of by friends of their own colour.

The case was very different when the war was carried down to the South and the Southwest; and the Government must have known that it would be so. There, every negro who escaped being driven into the interior, with the planter's cattle or goods, would be sure to appear in the Federal lines; and some principle of action in regard to them ought to have been decided on and promulgated throughout the United States' armies. The whole matter, however, was left to chance. Negroes came flocking in from the deserted plantations, or plantations that were not yet deserted; they issued from the woods by day and by night; they swam from the main to the islands; they all refused to go back again, and said that their wives and children, and the old people, were all coming as soon as they should get some news which was on the way. On the whole, and in most places, the next state of things was terrible. The commanders had their several opinions as to what ought to be the fate of these people. While one declared that he could have done nothing in this hostile territory without negro guides, scouts, messengers, and channel pilots, others regarded every black as a nuisance, and encouraged all overtures from claimants to come and take them back. The "contrabands" were too often baulked of their pay, or made to work without it; they were kicked and cuffed and sworn at by the soldiers (especially the Irish and Germans); they were robbed, abused, and (worst of all) tempted in every way; so that there was every prospect of the negroes within the influence of the camps sinking to even a lower depth of degradation than they had known in slavery.

Where the commanders refused to open their lines to negroes at all, the poor creatures fled wherever river or rail, or their own feet, would carry them. The worst spectacle of all seems to have been at Cairo, where at the best, residents ought to bear a charmed life to escape the perils of damp and malaria. On that comfortless point of land, at the junction of the Mississippi and Ohio, the fugitives sickened immediately and died very fast. If the able-bodied could have got on to Chicago, their fortunes would have been made: for Chicago was getting rich at only half speed for want of labour. The wages proffered by advertisement were enormous, if these poor people had but been able to read the papers, and to get on the right road to the lake. But the farmers in Illinois wanted hands too; and being from the South, for the most part, they had a mind for negro labour, and for an absolute command of it. They helped themselves first, before allowing the Chicago people any choice, even if the fugitives could have made their way out of the swamps of Cairo. These Illinois settlers threw the fugitives into prison, and then paid the fine to get them out again, on condition of unlimited and unpaid service for a term of years, in consideration of their involuntary debt. Thus did Southern men who were too poor to settle in a slave country find themselves slave-owners in a free State; and the negroes were involved in a slavery on free soil harder than that they had run away from on the plantation. . . . [Martineau discusses blacks' contributions to Union army campaigns.]

The Sea Islands of South Carolina have maintained a denser slave population than perhaps any other region in the Southern States. After the battle of Port Royal, the white inhabitants fled, taking with them as many negroes as they could compel to go, and as much cotton and other produce as they could carry. More slaves were left behind than could be driven off. When the long-desired "Yankees" appeared on the plantations, they observed one half of the recommendations imposed on them from Washington: they collected what cotton was left, but they did not provide for the negroes. They carried off the mules wanted for the ploughing, and the rails for the fencing, besides the corn, the pigs, and the poultry. The collection of the cotton was done by agents, who suggested to Government that the estates should be let to be worked by speculators. As this would have left the negroes as much slaves as ever, and probably to a worse set of masters, the advice was opposed, and in good time set aside. The whole future of the freed negroes depended on their being now incited and encouraged to labour; and this could be done only by leading them to regard work as honourable in the eyes of free men, and the basis of the workers' own fortunes. It was proposed to the Government that associations should undertake the management of the deserted estates, for the benefit at once of the negroes and of the national treasury; and to this the Government assented. It agreed to furnish transport and rations for superintendents and teachers. Whatever else was wanted must be otherwise provided. The responsible person, the head of the Commission, was Mr. Pierce, a barrister of Massachusetts, selected for his well-trained ability, and his lawyer-like coolness and impartiality of temper, at a time when a pronounced abolitionist would certainly have had less influence over the minds of the timid and the hostile everywhere.[185]

Associations were formed in the chief Northern cities for providing clothes, in the first place, for these poor people; and next, the means of education, both in books and work. The Special Agent received his appointment in February 1862; and so early as the 9th of March a body of teachers and trainers landed at Beaufort. Forty-one men and twelve women, under Mr. Pierce's direction, went to work at once. These missionaries were not only clergymen and teachers, but farmers, mechanics, tradesmen, and physicians—all volunteers in the service, and selected with care from a larger number.

Nothing could be more forlorn than the scene in which they found themselves. The soldiery had stripped the estates, and overthrown all order; and they had terribly corrupted the negroes. Which way to turn themselves, the strangers did not know. Mr. Pierce traversed his dominion in the first place, making a survey which enabled him to assign stations to his assistants, and appoint their work. There were ten islands, containing 189 estates, and a negro population (before accessions from the mainland arrived) of 9,050. Before spring was over, there were seventy-four teachers and managers of the men, and nineteen women to take care of the women and children. The proportion of helpless persons among the heroes was, of course, very large, as the most burdensome were left on the hands of the Yankees; and the field-workers of all ages and qualities were less than half of the whole number. All of them were of a feeble habit of both body and mind. Their vegetable diet, their poor dwellings, their practice of sleeping on the floor in their day-clothes, their incapacity for any employment but the particular one to which they had been accustomed, their indolence, weakness of will and resolution, their levity, and the wretched destitution in which they were living, made up as desperate a case for missionary effort as could well be conceived.

First, they must all be vaccinated, for small-pox had broken out on many plantations. A hospital was opened, and six physicians worked at that job till it was finished. The missionaries, male and female, had much to do before they could open schools. They distributed clothing, visited the sick, tried to improve the household ways of the women, and soon were rich in eggs from the negro quarters—the slave-woman's form of paying compliments being a donation of eggs. The season was already six weeks late for sowing when the managers arrived, and there was a grievous deficiency of implements and stock. Each superintendent had to deliver in an account of the condition and appropriation of his lands before any arrangement as to tillage could be made. Yet it appears from the tables prepared for Government, dated June 2, that above 16,000 acres were bearing flourishing crops at that time. The cotton was then from six to twelve inches high, and properly thinned; and the corn, potatoes, rice, peas, and other vegetables all looking well. Though six hundred able-bodied men had been withdrawn from the plantations for military purposes, the energies of their comrades were by this time so awakened that they undertook nearly the whole work. Scarcely any of it was, in fact, abandoned. After going through these difficulties, and finding that some of the best lands could not be used, for want of fencing, and that the gang-system worked badly when wages were to be paid, and that four months of listless idleness had put the negro out of gear, it was really astonishing to the managers to reap such results as they did at the end of their first season. By that time the superintendents were taken into the service of the Government; a sufficient testimony of the value set upon their achievements at headquarters. The number of negroes under tutelage was eighteen thousand, and an increasing proportion was withdrawn on military service; yet those who remained behind had stored up corn enough for the whole community till the next harvest and cotton enough to pay the entire expenses of the experiment. Not many months later, the balance paid over to the United States Government was declared to be 40,000 dollars, after all expenses were cleared.

The opinion on the spot of the value of free negro industry is shown by the following paragraph of the First Annual Report of the Educational Commission for Freedmen (p.8.):—

> The success of one of our superintendents, in conducting two of the largest plantations for the Government, was so great, that he has, in connexion with some friends at the North, purchased eleven plantations, comprising about 8,000 acres, and is carrying them on this season by means of the old men, the women, and the children—most of the young and able-bodied men being now enlisted in the army of the United States. We are fortunate in having had among our superintendents one of sufficient means to enable him to undertake this operation upon business principles, with strict justice and fair, honest treatment of the freedmen.

Something of great importance is proved by the next passage. Our readers may have met with descriptions, in recent narratives of travel, of the intense eagerness of the freedmen and women to have a home of their own, and of the toil the men choose to undergo in building their own dwellings, working at the walls and the roof till a late hour in the night. How these men have arrived at building houses for themselves we may now see:—

> It is intended to sell a large portion of the plantations thus purchased, to the freedmen at cost, as fast as they shall prove, by industry and frugality, that such a course will be beneficial to them. Several plantations, amounting in all to about 2,000 acres, were purchased by the freedmen themselves, at the Government sale for taxes, they having combined the small savings of last season's work for that purpose: and these freeholds are being cultivated this season, in corn and cotton, by these men who, less than two years since, were slaves without hope of deliverance, the most isolated, and consequently the most ignorant of their class. (*Report*, p.9)

There is something more yet in the way of results. The supporters of this Commission looked beyond their own particular enterprise, and spared no pains to arouse the citizens of other parts of the country to do their duty to the freed negroes. The Report is able to say, at the end of the first year (p.9.):—

> From the statements recently received from the West, we have reason to believe that an entire reform has taken place in the treatment of the freedmen. They are now paid for their labour, and are eagerly sought for in all departments of the public service. A large number, who were suffering very much at Cairo, have been removed to Island No. 10, and the plantations of that island assigned them for cultivation. Measures have been taken by us to induce the formation of societies like our own, in several of the principal cities of the West.

As for the other functions of the missionaries, they opened schools on all the plantations, and taught the women to be clean, and to sew, to keep the clothes neat, to cook, wash, &c. The book-learning was sure to prosper: for it is a passion with freed slaves to share the white man's privilege of learning. The demand for spelling-books, and alphabets, and copy-books was enormous; and the shaky hands and dim eyes of the superannuated "darky" were as busy with the lesson as the brightest of the children. After a time, the aged scholars seem to have dropped off, more or less; but the children have prospered admirably. There were from two to three thousand of them, in high glee and credit, at the date of this Report; and the testimony of their teachers is this:—"The progress made by the children in their studies is generally fully equal to that of white children of the same age in our schools; and by many teachers is considered to have been more rapid than in any schools they had ever before taught." (p.13.) . . .

We have devoted some space to the South Carolina experiment because it was the first; but if we seek guidance in speculating on what the future of the great body of the slaves may be hereafter, we should look to the West, where, along the course of the Mississippi, seventy plantations were in full work with free labour within six months of the promulgation of General Banks's order for the Department of the South-west. This most significant story is worth the gravest attention.

When General Banks, at New Orleans, found himself compelled to form some plan for the great negro population under his charge, and for such of their masters as consulted him, the institution of slavery was virtually abolished throughout the region, and was apparently admitted by all parties to be so. The District of Columbia and the Territories had been decreed to be free soil for ever; and the newest event at the time we speak of was the President's Proclamation of Emancipation. Every slaveowner and every slave knew of these events; and all arrangements henceforth made were under that knowledge.

The negroes were flocking to General Banks and his officers by hundreds every day. They were in bad health and fell into bad habits. They huddled together in damp and dirty shanties, getting little work and food, but spirits and other bad things from the camps. At one station, 172 died in three months out of 1,000. General Banks offered to them the alternative of work on the levee or the roads for rations from Government, or work on some plantation (not necessarily the one they had escaped from) for fixed wages, which Government would guarantee on the security of the crop. The planters, on their part, understood that the negroes were to be treated as hired hands; the power of the whip was taken from everybody, but there was a provost-marshal within reach, to whom resort might be had when the negroes failed to fulfil their share of the bargain. No punishment was to be awarded which would not have been inflicted on whites in the same circumstances. If the negroes were willing to work, but shrank from intercourse with their old masters or their neighbours, they were to be placed on Government plantations. The plan took effect immediately. The planters were willing to make sacrifices to get their crop into the ground; and they bound themselves to pay wages, in kind and in money, well as they must have understood that their labourers could never be slaves any more. The negroes saw the advantage of getting pay as well as food, and of having a home on a plantation for their families. . . . [Here Martineau inserts the text of a notice declaring the slaves free and their labor to be compensated.]

From the moment the planter has signed the agreement which procures him this notice, his people are practically free beyond dispute. He cannot sell their persons or their services, nor obtain their labour without pay. On the other hand, he is not bound to keep them an hour in idleness. If he be ten minutes late in the morning, the labourer forfeits ten cents; and bad work is a reason for dismissal. What the benefit to the planter really is may be learned from a hundred incidents which show how the quality of the labour has improved. One of the planters, who had always insisted that negroes never would work but as slaves, hired negroes in February last in what he considered due proportion to his land. He presently found that his "force" was far too great, and he hired other deserted estates to occupy his surplus "hands." One of his managers has borne testimony in writing that the crop will exceed all former experience; that he manages three estates now with less trouble than one in past times, because the negroes work as if they had an interest in the crop; and that the fines for any sort of misconduct, on the three estates, did not amount to five dollars for the preceding month. . . .

General Banks's arrangements are avowedly provisional. A higher authority than his, he says, will hereafter settle the great questions involved in this department of his rule. But there is probably a universal conviction in that South-western region that slavery is at an end. Many of the negroes there did not come under the terms of the President's proclamation; yet their former owners are voluntarily employing them as hired labourers; and if the experiment goes on through a second season, it is in the highest degree improbable that there should be any prevalent or effectual desire for a return to the former system, even if it were possible.

Where, it may be asked, is all the devastation threatened in regard to this region above all the other regions of the Slave States, as a consequence of the Proclamation of Emancipation? The apprehension was a mistake altogether. A little more knowledge and reflection would have shown the most timid that the negroes do not burn and slay and ravish and lay waste when they have got what they demand, but, if at all, when they are disappointed and desperate. A little more knowledge still would have shown that the American slaves in particular were unlikely to break out into acts of revenge when their long trial was over. The same influence which kept them quiet under the yoke for the last thirty years of their bondage was not less powerful when the provocations of slavery had ceased. From the moment when they had the Abolitionists to look up to, the negroes rebelled no more: the same moral power, without any direct communication, trained and disciplined them for the great change which it promised; and no one who had any real knowledge of either the facts or the philosophy of the case can have felt any dread of evils which have occasioned as much virulent invective, and as much noisy menace, as if they had not been merely imaginary. . . . [Martineau discusses blacks in the military.]

Of the improvement of public feeling in regard to the people of colour, no stronger evidence can be afforded than the way in which the citizens of New York are now exerting themselves to compensate the sufferers from the violence of the Irish and the Southern faction in the New York riots. The best counsel have offered their gratuitous services for them, their suits of damages are promoted for them, and a careful estimate of their losses has been made by professional valuers, in order to the State paying the whole. This could not have happened at any time before the war.[186]

After all these transactions, after large numbers of fugitives had sickened and died, after the civil and military officers who had found it necessary to act in one way or another had taken their part, and had been alternately snubbed and countenanced, the Federal Government at length decided on one step in the way of its duty towards protecting the negroes. Last spring it appointed the American Freedmen's Inquiry Commission—the three Commissioners being men admirably fit for the duty—viz., Dr. Howe, well known in this country on many grounds, and everywhere as the educator of Laura Bridgman; Mr. Robert Dale Owen, of Indiana, the writer of some striking public letters in the course of the present war; and Dr. McKaye, who will do great things in the physiological study, as well as the sanitary management, of the negro and mulatto race. By their researches into the condition of the negroes these gentlemen rendered great service in the first weeks of their office, but their Circular, and the Questions they have prepared to go with the Circular, indicate a scope of inquiry which will do more than has yet been done to determine the destinies of that part of the negro race which has gone through the experience of slavery. . . .

The free blacks in the Northern States are shown by the Census and other returns to yield fewer criminals and fewer paupers, and to exhibit a lower mortality in proportion to their numbers, than any other class in the Republic. The love of a warm climate, and the attachment of the people to the soil on which they have lived from birth, afford the best promise that the negroes will not desert the territory where their labour is needed, and to which it is adapted. At the same time, it is plain to all eyes that slavery can never exist again where the labouring class has tasted freedom, and shown itself worthy of the freeman's privileges, and adequate to the freeman's duties. The territory which is now practically exempted from slavery is so large, and so rapidly augmenting, that it is already inconceivable that any remnant of it can preserve its "peculiar institution" after the close of the war, whatever the issue may be. The depressed race may be regarded now as having received an authorisation to try what it can do to obtain a free social position, after having gone through the discipline and training by which it can be raised. It has made a better beginning than could have been hoped; and its own manifestation of high qualities of mind and conscience has had a larger share than any working of events in releasing it from the contempt and dislike under which it has hitherto suffered in the freest States of the American Union. That species of oppression can never be renewed when colour ceases to be a badge of slavery; a consummation which we may now regard as nearly attained. . . .

These are some of the modes, called irregular, but thoroughly natural and inevitable, in which slavery has come to an end in the Southern States. The regular way, the method of compensation, our readers must know as much of as there is at present to be told. There has long been a Committee sitting at Washington to manage the compensation business for the District of Columbia. Missouri has accepted the terms of the Government, has decreed the

gradual emancipation of her slaves, and will doubtless give up the intermediate stages of servitude, as all emancipating countries do, because immediate liberation answers better. Delaware has few slaves, and does not desire to
have any. Maryland is not so "Southern," as a whole, as Baltimore is, with its
Southern commerce; yet the recent election is a clear decision in favour of
immediate emancipation. The other Border States are busy discussing the
case—selling their negroes to the Government for the army at the price of
volunteers (300 dollars each) or otherwise losing them from day to day. The
Federal Government has shown every readiness to pay, in order to facilitate
the process of emancipation.

We thus see how inconceivable it is that Slavery can ever again be an established and supreme institution in the Southern States; and unless
supreme, Slavery cannot exist. The Confederacy, aware of this, but apparently unaware of the certainty of failure in the then condition of their social
system, putting everything to hazard for assurance on this one point. Nothing better could have been desired by the friends of liberty and the deliverers
of the negro than that the end of the oppression should be brought about by
the oppressors themselves. Slavery would soon have become impossible except by a fearful social retrogression—an extension of its bounds, and a re-
opening of the negro trade. Such a retrogression has been rendered impossible, and the slaveholders have sought to avert the gradual disintegration of
their system by a sharp and perilous effort at isolation from outward influences. The result proves that they have miscalculated their chances, and
have precipitated the revolution in their labour system which they intended
to prevent. It is scarcely possible to conceive a more remarkable example of
that power which "shapes our ends, rough hew them as we will," than this
result of the American Revolution, opposed alike to the original intentions
of the Seceding States and of their antagonists. If it be true that the object of
secession was to extend and perpetuate slavery, that object has signally
failed; nay more, emancipation has been its direct consequence. If, on the
other hand, we are to believe that the seceding States are fighting not for
slavery, but for their own independence, then it becomes their first interest
to accept and complete the abolition of slavery, for it is that which cuts
them off from the sympathy of mankind. Of this their own statesmen are
aware. But the time is past when they had any option on the subject. Whatever be the political result of the war, President Lincoln declares in his last
Message that he abides by the policy of Emancipation. One million of the
four millions of men of colour who were slaves two years since are now free
under express Federal protection; many more have found their own way to
liberty; and now the distinct purpose of the Federal Government is to emancipate the rest as far as its power extends.

❖ ❖ ❖

APPENDIX

Itinerary of Harriet Martineau's American Tour

Martineau's path through America covered a representative portion of what was then considered settled or civilized land. Besides spanning the northern and southern states along the eastern seaboard, she explored as far west as the Mississippi and Ohio Rivers, including the plains area south of Chicago. Modes of transportation included train, coach, boat (on rivers, lakes, and canals), wagon, horseback, and on extremely muddy or bad roads, by foot. Some routes were through such uncultivated, wild country that roads were nonexistent. Occasionally, paths were so obstructed that the passengers were compelled to get out and walk, sometimes having to push the coach. Of the infamous "corduroy roads" made up of logs placed transversely, Martineau insisted the ride was smooth enough that one could write or draw, provided the coach skimmed over the logs quickly enough. Accommodations ranged from elegant mansions to log houses and farmhouses, with sleeping arrangements from four-poster beds to a bare floor, using luggage for a pillow and a cloak for a cover.

Of people and places, her experiences were no less varied:

> It would be nearly impossible to relate whom I knew, during my travels. Nearly every eminent man in politics, science and literature, and almost every distinguished woman, would grace my list. I have respected and beloved friends of each political party; and of nearly every religious denomination; among slave holders, colonisationists, and abolitionists; among farmers, lawyers, merchants, professors, and clergy. I travelled among several tribes of Indians; and spent months in the southern States, with negroes ever at my heels.
>
> I visited almost every kind of institution. The prisons of Auburn, Philadelphia, and Nashville: the insane and other hospitals of almost every considerable place: the literary and scientific institutions; the factories of the north; the plantations of the south; the farms of the west. . . . I saw weddings, and christenings; the gatherings of the richer at watering places, and of the humbler at country festivals. I was present at orations, at land sales, and in the slave market. I was in frequent attendance on the Supreme Court and the Senate; and . . . state legislatures. (1837, 1:52–53)

Added to the variety of such a tour is her surprisingly unconventional assertion that being a woman traveler not only did not limit her opportunities for cultural observation but indeed offered opportunities not available to even the most distinguished male traveler: "I was received into the bosom of many families, not as a stranger, but as a daughter or a sister. . . . I have seen much more of domestic life than could possibly have been exhibited to any gentleman travelling through the country. The nursery, the boudoir, the kitchen, are all excellent schools in which to learn the morals and manners of a people" (1837, 1:53). Martineau experienced both worlds—the feminine domestic sphere and the masculine public sphere—with an array of natural wonders and cultural artifacts in between.

By any standards, her access to political circles was remarkably broad, attesting to her fame following the publication of *Illustrations of Political Economy*. Of her associations in high political places, Martineau wrote that she and her companion were "handed on by the families of senators, to the care and kindness of a long succession of them, from the day we reached Washington, till we emerged from the Slave States at Cincinnati" (1983, 2:20). In Washington, Chapman notes, not only did she meet the major political figures of the day, she also "enjoyed the advantage of intimate and confidential intercourse with a class of men of whom none now remain,—the founders of the Republic and their immediate successors" (1877, 100). Throughout her life, Martineau's impeccable sense of timing repeatedly placed her in positions that were particularly fortuitous for a social-problem writer.

Of her choice to travel to America, Martineau wrote: "America was the right country . . . the national boast being a perfectly true one,—that a woman may travel alone from Maine to Georgia without dread of any kind of injury" (1837, 2:85). Perhaps—although not always without threat of lynching, should her politics prove too controversial.

Itinerary[187]

9 August 1834: Sails from England.

19 September: Lands in New York.

24 September: Meets Mr. Albert Gallatin, former secretary of the Treasury.

25 September: Meets Lewis Cass, secretary of war: a "[s]hrewd, hard-looking man."

Visits Paterson, New Jersey cotton mills and Passaic Falls.

Visits friends on Hudson River; then writer Catharine Sedgwick in Stockbridge, Massachusetts. The Sedgwicks provide Martineau with a letter of introduction to Vice President Van Buren.

6 October: Begins tour of New York State: Albany, Trenton Falls, Auburn, Buffalo, Niagara Falls.

Sails on Lake Erie to Pennsylvania, touring Meadville and Pittsburgh.

11 October: Crosses Allegheny Mountains to Northumberland on the Susquehanna River.

17 October: Leaves for Philadelphia for a six-week visit.

December: Visits Baltimore (three weeks). Meets Bishop White, Governor Barbour, and Mr. Latrobe.

Visits Washington, D.C. (five weeks). Visits Supreme Court, Senate and House of Representatives (in session), meets judges, senators, and representatives socially. Visits White House as guest of Andrew Jackson. Visits Washington's burial site in Mount Vernon. Hears Daniel Webster and Henry Clay debate the "French Question." Meets Webster, Calhoun, Colonel Preston, Judge Story, Edward Everett.

18 February 1835: Visits James Madison at Montpelier. Chief Justice Marshall a daily visitor.

Visits University of Virginia ("Jefferson's University"), Charlottesville.

Visits Virginia legislature, in session at Richmond.

2–11 March: Travels through North Carolina and South Carolina.

11 March: Arrives in Charleston, South Carolina (two weeks). Hosts: Governor Hayne and Senator Calhoun.

Visits Columbia, South Carolina (ten days), hosted by Colonel Preston.

Visits Augusta, Georgia (three days).

Visits Montgomery, Alabama (two weeks), then Mobile.

Visits New Orleans, Louisiana (ten days), escorted by Senator Porter, Chief Justice of Louisiana Supreme Court. Martineau is visited by Texas "adventurers" seeking to enlist her help to secure statehood.

Sails up Mississippi and Ohio Rivers to Cumberland River in Nashville, Tennessee.

Visits Mammoth Cave, Kentucky; then Lexington (three weeks), the guest of Henry Clay.

Sails Ohio River to Cincinnati, Ohio (ten days).

Returns to Virginia: Hawk's Nest, Sulphur Springs, Natural Bridge, Weyer's Cave.

14 July 1835: Arrives in New York.

August 1835: Visits Medford, Massachusetts.

Fall 1835: Stays at various villages in Massachusetts, visits Dr. Channing in Newport, Rhode Island.

Tours mountains of New Hampshire and Vermont.

Fall–winter 1835: Is in Boston, Massachusetts. Visits Massachusetts state legislature (in session).

Meets William Lloyd Garrison, Maria Weston Chapman, Ellis Gray Loring, Dr. Follen, Margaret Fuller. Is a guest of Charles and Ralph Waldo Emerson.[188]

18 November: Speaks at the BFASS meeting and is shunned by "polite" society.

22 December: Travels to Plymouth, Massachusetts, for "Forefathers' Day." Speaker Senator Sprague "abuses" England and, by implication, Martineau (sitting in the audience), in his speech.

Is guest of Massachusetts congressman Stephen Phillips in Salem, Massachusetts.

Spring 1836: Returns to New York (seven weeks). Is again shunned in society. Revisits writer Catharine Sedgwick in Stockbridge (one month).

Visits Saratoga and Lake George.

After receiving death threats for her professed abolitionism, alters her itinerary.

Summer 1836: Revisits Niagara; sails Lake Erie to Detroit and visits Michigan territory.

Sails Lake Michigan to Chicago. Visits prairies, returning to Chicago, Detroit, and Mackinaw via Lakes Michigan, Huron, and St. Clair.

13 July 1836: Lands in Cleveland, Ohio.

Tours Ohio, visiting Rapp's Settlement at Economy (Owenist Socialists).

Visits Pittsburgh and witnesses cruelties against free blacks.

Returns to New York from Pittsburgh via canal and railroad.

1 August 1836: Sails from New York for England. Is shunned on board ship for conversing with a "young lady of colour," an acquaintance from Philadelphia.

❖ ❖ ❖

NOTES

1. *Ed.* Martineau's original title for her most famous American travel journal, *Society in America,* was *Theory and Practice of Society in America.* She was quite disappointed when her publisher insisted on abbreviating the title in a way that downplayed the book's methodological agenda. As is evident in this discussion, the disjunction between theory and practice is central to understanding Martineau's critique of America.

2. *Ed.* The term "triangle trade" is rooted in the history of the Anglo-American slave trade. Slave trading ships originated primarily from Bristol and Liverpool, the first point in the triangle. Once in Africa (the second point), they traded European goods for slaves, which were transported to America (the third point). Americans bought the slaves with slave-produced goods that were returned to the originating British ports to be traded for the European goods that would fund the next round of trading. The abolitionist "triangle" was the alliance between British abolitionists, American abolitionists, and American blacks—free and enslaved.

3. *Ed.* Writing to abolitionist Abby Kelley, Martineau illustrated a popular analogy between America's slaves and Britain's industrial workers: "We have a population in our manufacturing towns almost as oppressed, and in our secluded rural districts almost as ignorant, as your negroes. These must be redeemed" (20 June 1838). Historian Henry Mayer adds, "the Americans faced a task and an opposition equivalent to what would beset British reformers who at once attacked the monarchy and the poor laws" (1998, 168).

4. *Ed. Illustrations of Political Economy,* published serially in twenty-five monthly numbers (London: Fox, 1832–1834). According to literary historian Louis Cazamian, each number sold at least 10,000 copies. Working at a furious pace, Martineau composed one novelette a month for two years, during which time she also wrote a four-part series for Lord Brougham's Society for the Diffusion of Useful Knowledge, *Poor Laws and Paupers Illustrated* (London: Charles Fox, 1833–1834), and the five-part *Illustrations of Taxation* (1834).

5. *Ed.* Unlike slavery in the United States, England's slavery system operated in its colonies. English plantation owners tended to be absentee landlords, often hiring overseers to run the plantation for them; as a result, many in England found reports of human rights atrocities in the colonies too fantastic to comprehend. The 1831 publication in England of the first narrative written by a black British female slave, *The History of Mary Prince,* began to make clear the cost of "civilized" luxuries in terms of the human lives that made them possible. Her own idea of slavery being "purely imaginary," Martineau had not personally witnessed slavery when she wrote "Demerara"; despite the tale's radicalism, what she saw in America convinced her she had not gone far enough.

6. *Ed.* The official emancipation of Britain's slaves was hardly the end of the matter, however. During her *Daily News* career, Martineau wrote many articles on the situations of blacks in the West Indies, continuing as late as 1867. See the appendix in Arbuckle 1994 for a listing. See also Martineau's *Daily News* articles on the illegal slave trade that continued throughout the century, primarily in the Caribbean markets.

7. *Ed.* My primary source for this discussion is *Harriet Martineau's Autobiography,* written and printed in 1855 and distributed posthumously in 1877. The autobiography is comprised of two volumes by Martineau; the third, entitled *Memorials,* is a biography by Maria Weston Chapman that relies primarily on excerpts from Martineau's private journals and correspondence. The two autobiographical volumes were reprinted by Virago Press in 1983, and this is the edition used here; volume three has not been reprinted.

8. *Ed.* The captain's concern with Martineau's landing in New York stemmed in part from the July anti-abolitionist riots in that city and from rumors of a death threat against British abolitionist George Thompson (1804–1878). Thompson had originally intended to sail to America on the same ship as Martineau, but was obliged to reschedule; it was feared that "if his [Thompson's] presence was known in New York, he would be a dead man before night" (Martineau 1983, 2:12). Thompson lectured for the London Anti-Slavery Society and was influential in the passage of Britain's 1833 emancipation bill; he came to America at Garrison's invitation. In the public mind, Martineau and Thompson were linked as "foreign incendiaries." It is a singular coincidence that they both spoke in Boston at the height of the mob violence against Garrison; Mrs. Thompson was among those present when Martineau spoke at the Boston Female Anti-Slavery Society meeting.

9. *Ed.* Ellis Gray Loring, a Unitarian Boston attorney who helped support Garrison's *Liberator.* Loring and his wife Louisa welcomed Martineau into the abolitionist fold (it was Loring who prompted Martineau to speak at the BFASS meeting) and were pained by her resulting public ostracization in the press. Martineau was accompanied by the Lorings for part of her journey.

10. *Ed.* Martineau originally intended to visit Missouri but death threats prompted by her professed abolitionism forced her to revise her itinerary. A chapter of *Retrospect of Western Travel,* entitled "Compromise," discusses the Missouri Compromise and its implications.

11. *Ed.* Martineau to Ezra Stiles Gannett, 15 December 1834, Houghton Library, Harvard University, ms am 1844.4 (25), item 27. Gannett was a Unitarian preacher affiliated with William Ellery Channing. It was in Gannett's home that she first met Garrison, although Gannett's attitude toward Garrison and his radical abolitionism has been described as "extremely hostile." As is typical of Martineau's approach to America, it was *because* she heard "every species of abuse" about Garrison that she was most keen to meet him (Mayer 1998, 208).

12. *Ed.* Harriet Martineau to Lord Brougham, 21 November 1858, University of Birmingham, hm18, Additional Letters. Martineau further distinguishes the abolitionists with whom she remained affiliated as the "Old Organization" or "primary Abolitionists"—those who resisted allowing party politics to supplant the moral issue of emancipation.

13. *Ed.* Colonization societies aimed to relocate American slaves in Africa. The American Colonization Society was chartered and subsidized by Congress in 1816. In 1824 the colony was named Liberia and its capital called Monrovia, after President James Monroe. In her *Autobiography,* Martineau records an episode in which American Eliot Cresson, traveling throughout England to collect money for the Colonization Society, raised suspicions by criticizing Garrison, who had exposed the society as a means for perpetuating both the slave trade and racism (see Garrison 1832). Money was raised to pay for blacks' passage to Africa; but once there, the settlers lacked resources for subsistence and were frequently imprisoned in barracoons and resold into slavery. Garrison

was initially interested in the idea of colonization and went to Baltimore to learn more about it; what he learned prompted him to become one of its most outspoken critics.

14. *Ed.* William Lloyd Garrison (1805–1879), Boston abolitionist and publisher of the *Liberator* (1831–1865). Garrison was the most prominent figure in the anti-slavery movement for over forty years. Martineau bought his portrait while in America and hung it over her mantle at home in England. Maria Weston (1806–1885) was born into a family of anti-slavery activists. She married Boston merchant Henry Chapman, who boycotted trade with slave states. Maria Chapman was, Martineau asserted, the "life and soul" of Boston's anti-slavery movement.

15. *Ed.* Fanaticism was a common accusation made against abolitionists. Many were pacifists and/or Quakers who employed passive resistance or symbolic acts of civil disobedience designed to convey a message rather than to damage property or injure people. Garrison, for example, publicly burned a copy of the Constitution because its wording permits slavery; this contrasts with the New York and Philadelphia rioters, who attacked abolitionists and free blacks and burned their homes and possessions. Martineau had yet to learn that rumors of abolitionist fanaticism were largely fictitious, although some abolitionist settlers in Kansas, for example, proved to be as violent as the pro-slavery Border Ruffians who opposed them.

16. *Ed.* Named after Virginia judge William Lynch (1742–1820), lynch law punished perceived offenders through mob violence, without a legal trial. Methods included tarring and feathering and hanging. Martineau was threatened with lynching several times; Garrison narrowly escaped this fate in Boston. Thousands more were not so fortunate: many blacks died by this means (slaves, runaways, and free blacks) as did whites, whether real or suspected abolitionists.

17. *Ed.* Henry Mayer notes that Martineau "heard 'very striking facts which had taken place in broad daylight vehemently and honestly denied' by local residents, whose 'ignorance and unconcern' she considered 'one of the most hideous features of the times'" (1998, 207).

18. *Ed.* Martineau apparently did not write for Garrison's *Liberator,* although she occasionally sent him money for its support (see Martineau to Garrison, 23 October 1850, Boston Public Library, ms.a.1.2, v. 19, p. 92). British abolitionist George Thompson was a prominent contributor, as was Parker Pillsbury of the London Anti-Slavery Society, yet Martineau's voice is, curiously, absent. The omission is odd, but I have found no contributions attributed to her other than excerpts from *Society in America* and *Retrospect of Western Travel,* although there are occasional notices announcing her books or reporting on the state of her health.

19. *Ed.* The full context of the quote is Martineau's denial of any intention to publish her American journals: "I can truly say that I travelled without any such idea in my mind. I am sure that no traveller seeing things through author spectacles, can see them as they are; and it was not till I looked over my journal on my return that I decided to write *Society in America*" (1983, 2:3). Her 1833 letter to Tait indicates otherwise. Although she was no opportunist, Martineau was incapable of seeing through anything *but* "author spectacles."

20. *Ed.* To Lydia Maria Child, Martineau wrote: "Some of my friends around you are grieved at the treatment I am receiving in Boston. I care nothing for newspaper abuse or the temporary prejudice of the multitude." Denying the charge that she gossiped about her American hosts, Martineau emphasized the differences between private relationships, which are confidential, and public figures, who can and should be critiqued for failure to represent the will of the people (10 January 18[?], Houghton Library, autograph file).

21. *Ed.* E. G. Loring to W. L. Garrison, 5 December 1835, Boston Public Library, ms.a.1.2. v. 5, p. 76.

22. *Ed.* Garrison to Samuel May, 5 December 1835, in Garrison 1971–1981, 6:232–33.

23. *Ed.* Clare Midgley notes that James Birney (who was later a presidential candidate for the Liberty Party) believed that Martineau's influence as a writer was better for the cause than her compatriot George Thompson's incendiary speech making (1992, 130). This is significant, considering that the Liberty Party resulted in part from the protest against women abolitionists and reformers.

24. *Ed.* Martineau's childhood hearing problems resulted in almost total deafness by early adulthood. She employed an ear trumpet, a hearing device that magnified sounds when people spoke directly into its tube. Her disability was frequently targeted by critics and used, along with her gender and spinsterhood, to discredit her political and social analyses. But she maintained a sense of humor: once, she quips, the trumpet was mistaken for a foghorn by the captain of a passing boat. She addressed the challenges of being a deaf traveler in the introduction to *Society in America,* where she outlined her methods for accuracy in communication, aided by her traveling companion, Louisa Jeffrey.

25. *Ed.* The controversial Martineau weathered many periods of censure throughout her life. In an 1866 letter to Henry Reeve, she responded to critics of her politics: "It is a very small fine to pay for the privilege of making the Americans and their country better understood in England than they might otherwise be. . . . If I were twenty years younger, and able to go I should probably find my second unpopularity got over as wonderfully as my first" [the 1835 BFASS meeting] (Sanders 1990, 206).

26. *Ed.* On 25 June 1836, Martineau wrote: "This is one of the most disgraceful stories in the history of usurpations. Whatever the Americans may be, they have been cruelly wronged, and all for the sake of the Southern Slave-holders, and a handful of land speculators. The efforts that we make against the slave-trade are and will be of little avail, while the great, new slave-market of Texas is open" (Bancroft Library, University of California at Berkeley, 5:43).

27. *Ed.* Although his presses had been destroyed by mobs twice before, clergyman Elijah P. Lovejoy persisted in publishing his abolitionist newspaper, the *Observer.* In November 1837, Lovejoy was lynched in his office for his anti-slavery politics. See *The Martyr Age of the United States.*

28. *Ed.* In all seriousness, apparently, Janet Courtney writes of Martineau: "If only she could have kept off abolitionism, she might have been quite popular in American society" (1933, 155).

29. *Ed.* Martineau considered herself fortunate to have avoided the standard expectation that all women must marry. Earlier, the sudden death of her fiancé freed her from what would have been a marriage of convenience rather than love, allowing her instead to pursue a literary career. But as a single woman, even a professionally successful one, she still had to negotiate the demands of her controlling mother and her brother, James. Their insistence on her docile obedience to maternal and patriarchal rule clashed with her radical, freethinking strong-mindedness. Further, in the literary realm, she defied convention not only by writing in genres and styles traditionally restricted to men but also by publishing under her own name, rather than a male pseudonym. Finally, by rejecting socialites' attempts to "lionize" her or otherwise exploit her fame, she challenged reigning standards of social practice—altogether, a risky business for a woman aiming to preserve her respectability.

30. *Ed.* Clare Midgley notes that the sections of *Society in America* addressing slavery were reprinted and distributed by the American Anti-Slavery Society as *Views of Slavery and Emancipation; from "Society in America"* (1837). The *AASS* also printed two thousand copies of *The Martyr Age* as a pamphlet; in addition to an 1839 British pamphlet edition, an 1840 British edition included Martineau's appeal to raise funds for the Oberlin Institute, an integrated (by both race and gender) college in Ohio, which survives today as Oberlin College (1992, 131).

31. *Ed.* Review of *Society in America* in *American Quarterly Review.* Frances Wright (1795–1852), a Scottish Owenite who established a socialist community in Nashoba, Tennessee, in 1826. Wright earned notoriety by advocating free love and birth control—which was typical of the utopian communities popular at the time—and by presenting a clear plan for the gradual emancipation of slaves.

32. *Ed.* Martineau to William Tait, 29 August 1833, University College of London, Special Collections. For a comparison of Martineau's travel writing with that of other nineteenth-century women, see Deborah Logan, "Harem Life, West and East," *Women's Studies: An Interdisciplinary Journal* 26 (1997): 449–74. "Hall" refers to Captain Basil Hall, author of *Travels in North America in the Years 1827 and 1828* (Edinburgh: Cadell & Co., 1829). Hall, she complains in her journal, draws sweeping general conclusions from solitary, isolated experiences: "What a traveller!" (Chapman 1877, 121). Frances Trollope, in *Domestic Manners of the Americans* (London: Whittaker, Treacher, & Co., 1832), declined to comment on blacks and slavery altogether.

33. *Ed.* Martineau to Charles Sumner, March 1839, Houghton Library, ms am 1301 (II), 85.

34. *Ed.* Martineau to William Fox, 13 May 1837, on the critical reception of *Society in America* (Bancroft Library, box 2, f. 63).

35. *Ed.* Martineau alludes to the scandalous practice of some travel writers (not de Tocqueville) who produced vivid accounts of foreign cultures from the comfort of their homes—they were, literally, "arm-chair travelers."

36. *Ed.* Notwithstanding this essential difference between the two, a comparative analysis of Martineau and de Tocqueville on American culture reveals that they agree on many points in their observations. See Lipset 1962.

37. *Ed.* Lipset notes that Martineau's 1853 translation of August Comte's *Positive Philosophy* made her "the first person to introduce sociology into England" (1963, 7 n. 4). But this suggests that *Society in America*, available sixteen years earlier, had little or no impact on sociology as a discipline, which is certainly not true. In fact, contemporary reviews demonstrate that it is her sociological seriousness to which reviewers most objected. Michael R. Hill posits that her translation of Comte was "overshadowed by the university academics who built and wrote the history of sociology since 1850" (1989, xi). A recent scholarly edition of Martineau's translation, for example, reprints her introduction but, curiously, excludes her entirely from the editor's introductory remarks. This too is odd, considering that Comte himself praised her lucid translation and skillful editing, which condensed an unwieldy nine volumes of theoretical discourse into a clear and crisp two-volume set. Comte in turn translated Martineau's version into French, which then sold as the definitive version.

38. *Ed.* C. A. S. Smith to Caroline Weston, 3 July 1837, Boston Public Library, ms.a.9.2.9 p.44.

39. *Ed.* In lieu of more serious analysis of her work, the *Times* printed a bawdy song ridiculing Martineau during the composition of the *Illustrations of Political Economy.* She locked horns with the *Times* throughout her career, charging that it promoted

its own aristocratic agenda under the banner of journalistic objectivity and "truth." As a social reformer, Martineau regarded the *Times* as a perpetual obstacle to social progress in its determination to maintain the status quo.

40. *Ed.* Dickens 1974, viii–ix; Thompson quoted in Chapman 1877, 171.

41. *Ed.* The marquis de Lafayette (1757–1834) was a French statesman and general known as a champion of republican values.

42. *Ed.* These images evoke Elizabeth Barrett Browning's radical anti-slavery poem, "The Runaway Slave at Pilgrim's Point," written for and printed in Chapman's annual the *Liberty Bell* over ten years later, in 1848. Browning's black woman narrator addresses the ghosts of the original Pilgrims, informing them of the atrocities daily perpetrated in their names and in the name of God.

43. *Ed.* As a political economist, Martineau argued that plantations reflected Britain's class structure, in which the privileged few were maintained by the masses of poor workers. The rise of the industrial middle classes radically altered that economic structure, in which work, once regarded as menial and degraded, came to define character and social worth. The South attempted to preserve an aristocratic economy that had been made redundant in the modern world; thus were working-class whites in the South even more reviled than slaves—as Martineau put it, "the lowest of the low."

44. *Ed.* One of the effects of such "unrestricted intercourse" is the ambiguous boundaries it created between the conditions of freedom and slavery. The children might be intimate friends, yet the ideology of the "peculiar institution" is quickly enough invoked when there is work to be done or leisure to be enjoyed. Children were thus early indoctrinated in a social arrangement that was presented as natural and normal, and which they in turn perpetuated as adults. The deception was an especially cruel one, as Martineau's sympathy for the mistress-poisoning slave demonstrates.

45. *Martineau.* The law declares that the children of slaves are to follow the fortunes of the mother. Hence the practice of planters selling and bequeathing their own children.

46. *Ed.* James Madison (1751–1836), fourth U.S. president (1809–1817). Martineau visited Madison during her American tour, proclaiming herself charmed by his conversation and delighted to have met the venerable statesman.

47. *Martineau.* I knew of the death of four men by summary burning alive, within thirteen months of my residence in the United States.

48. *Ed.* Martineau later amended both points. While many slaves were too exhausted to mobilize for insurrection, there were others, particularly runaway slaves ("the best of their kind") who excited her admiration. Further, she eventually conceded that war was the necessary, though least desirable, means for resolving the conflict.

49. *Ed.* Quakers Angelina and Sarah Grimké renounced their southern slaveholding legacy and became prominent in the northern abolitionist and feminist movements. In 1835 Angelina (1805–1879) wrote to Garrison that abolition was "a cause worth dying for" and soon after became a noted speaker and activist for the cause. She argued that woman's moral obligation was not to her own private home but to the reform of society, a stand that contributed to the eventual split in the abolition movement. Although she married Theodore Weld (she omitted the word "obey" when reciting her vows), she continued to be known as Grimké. Sarah Grimké objected to "the extravagance" of Martineau's "eulogies on American abolitionists" in *The Martyr Age of the United States* (Grimké to E. Pease, 5 January 1840, Boston Public Library, ms.a.1.2, v.9, p. 34).

50. *Martineau.* No notice is taken of any occurrence, however remarkable, in which a person of colour, free or enslaved, has any share, for fear of the Acts which

denounce death or imprisonment for life against those who shall write, print, publish, or distribute anything having a tendency to excite discontent or insubordination, etc.; or which doom to heavy fines those who shall use or issue language which may disturb "the security of masters with their slaves, (or diminish that respect) which is commanded to free people of colour for the whites."

51. *Ed.* William Ellery Channing, a Unitarian divine, represented the antithesis of his more flamboyant contemporary, Lyman Beecher. Channing resisted women's participation in the abolitionist movement, prompting one of his parishioners, Maria Weston Chapman, to rebel against her mentor. Channing's 160-page pamphlet, *Slavery* (Boston, 1835) revealed him to be more of a "fence-sitter" than an abolitionist: he condemned the ownership of humans but warned against abolitionist radicals—like Garrison—who demanded emancipation. Channing's stand anticipated an eventual split among the abolitionists, creating a conservative wing (without women and promoting gradual emancipation) and a radical (Garrisonian) wing that welcomed women reformists and urged immediate emancipation.

52. *Ed.* When Garrison was imprisoned in 1830 for libeling one merchant, another, Arthur Tappan, paid his fine and had him released from prison. Businessmen and philanthropists Arthur (1786–1865) and his brother Lewis (1788–1873) supported abolitionist endeavors, contributing funds to the *Liberator* and, in 1833, establishing the New York *Emancipator.* The Tappans were part of the 1840 split in the abolition movement and remained estranged from Garrison for years.

53. *Ed.* Martineau to William Fox, 1 October 1837, quoted in Burchell 1995, 46.

54. *Ed.* Modern scholars are as divided over the relative values of the two travel accounts as were Victorians. R. K. Webb claims, "the *Retrospect* is, flatly, the better book" (1960, 157), while Deirdre David argues, "*Society in America,* in my view, [is] the richer and denser text" (237 n. 3). Valerie Pichanick suggests that, had the writing been reversed so that *Retrospect* preceded *Society,* both accounts would have benefited (1980, 81).

55. *Ed.* This episode stems from Martineau's misinterpreting, because of her deafness, her host's meaning. As a result, she and her traveling companion subsequently exercised greater vigilance against potentially inflammatory social situations aimed at entrapping her. In terms of demonstrating Americans' interest in securing her support of various political agendas, the episode was instructive.

56. *Ed.* Part of the "liberality" Martineau experienced in the South had to do with southerners' desire to convince her of the efficacy of a slave-based economy as well as her own desire to give every group a fair hearing. But Martineau was not gullible, and she was aware that the moment she declared herself in support of any one agenda, the others would reject her as vigorously as they had previously courted her. Martineau's experiences reveal that violence against abolitionists—at this point, at least—was more prominent among northern pro-slavery capitalists than southern slave owners.

57. *Ed.* Martineau refers to the "long heel" several times, which seems to have been one of the physical characteristics used to determine questionable bloodlines. This is the racial equivalent of phrenology, a popular pseudo-science of the period that sought to determine character and intellect through the shape of one's skull.

58. *Ed.* The nullifiers rejected federal laws that conflicted with states' interests. In 1832, John Calhoun (S.C.) resigned his vice presidency under Andrew Jackson to protest a controversial protectionist tariff, bringing South Carolina to the brink of war with the Union. Working with Henry Clay, Calhoun formulated a compromise (1833) and averted war. The episode represents an early stage in the "states' rights" debates later dramatized by the Anthony Burns fugitive slave law case.

59. *Ed.* John C. Calhoun (1782–1850), vice president (1825–1832—first for John Quincy Adams and then under Andrew Jackson); later, he was a senator from South Carolina (1832–1850). He assured Martineau personally that slavery was a nonissue and would never be discussed in Congress.

60. *Ed.* General Andrew Jackson (1767–1845), seventh U.S. president (1829–1837). When Martineau visited "Old Hickory" in the White House, she apparently made a remark that displeased him; it was only later in the evening that he thawed toward her. She regarded Jackson as an army man, not a political leader.

61. *Ed.* Robert Hayne, governor of South Carolina. While a senator, Hayne engaged in a series of debates with Daniel Webster (Mass.) in 1830 in which he promoted states' rights and nullification while Webster argued that upholding the Constitution and the Union outweighed party concerns. During the nullification struggle, Jackson threatened to seal off Charleston harbor with federal troops; the state responded by calling for a volunteer army.

62. *Ed.* In a 7 July 1836 letter to Reverend Ware, Martineau wrote: "We are told that slaves are generally satisfied with being slaves, and refuse to be free when they have the opportunity. This is often true; but it proves nothing but the degradation of the slave. . . . Much more gladly would we restore the slave to his human privileges of hopeful toil, a free choice of objects for which to live, and the pleasures of brave struggle and deserved success" (Boston Public Library, ms. Eng. 244 [1–16]).

63. *Ed.* Catharine Sedgwick, writer and firm Unionist, hosted Martineau twice during her American tour. Although Martineau admired Sedgwick's ability to combine literary and domestic pursuits, she was less enthusiastic about her writing (see *Westminster Review* [October 1837] and Martineau 1983, 2:67). She was critical of Sedgwick's insistence that, although slavery was wrong, the Union was sacred and must be preserved at all costs—even at the expense of millions of slaves' lives. The distinction proved to be a crucial point as the conflict intensified.

64. *Ed.* Martineau notes that her description of Ailsie in *Retrospect* was read by the man whose wife had owned her before she died. When he wrote to Martineau asking her to adopt the child, "I accepted his proposal." Preparations for Ailsie's arrival in England included a fully outfitted bedroom, clothing, and arrangements for vaccinations and education, but she never came: her original owner demanded her back. In despair over her probable fate, Martineau wrote: "In her ripening beauty she was too valuable to be given to me. For what purposes she was detained as of course, there is no need to describe, . . . But she was never to be heard of more" (1983, 2:143–44).

65. *Ed.* Dr. Charles Follen was professor of German at Harvard until dismissed for his abolitionism. Follen died tragically in 1840 when the riverboat he was traveling on caught fire. Dr. and Mrs. Follen were close friends with Martineau, and the three traveled together during Martineau's American tour.

66. *Ed.* See Garrison's account of this episode (1971–1981 2:55–56).

67. *Ed.* Abby Kelley Foster, inspired after hearing speeches by Garrison and the Grimkés, became "abolitionism's most militant and indefatigable lecture agent" (Mayer 1998, 265). An aggressive activist, she attended the 1837 and 1838 women's anti-slavery conventions; at the tumultuous 1840 American Anti-Slavery Society meeting, Kelley's nomination as the only woman on the business committee crystallized the animosity that had long been brewing among the abolitionists. As a result, those male abolitionists who opposed "mixed" or "promiscuous" gatherings (those with women) broke from Garrison and his followers to form a politically oriented organization prohibiting women members.

68. *Ed.* After meeting Martineau, Garrison wrote to his wife Helen: "I can assure you, that we abolitionists need not fear that she will ever print any thing, either in this country or in England, inimical to us, or in favor of the Colonization Society" (7 March 1836, in Garrison 1971–1981 2:59).

69. *Ed.* Originally published in the *London and Westminster Review* 32 (December 1838): 1–59. George Thompson wrote to Richard Webb: "I have the *Westminster* with Miss Harriet's article here by my elbow. It is a glorious production. I should like to see it reprinted and widely scattered" (26 January 1839, quoted in Taylor, 1874, 44).

70. *Ed.* Martineau to Garrison, 25 June 1867, Bancroft Library, 3:2. Martineau's neighbor, Matthew Arnold, was a writer and critic; teacher Thomas Arnold and his school were the prototypes for the popular *Tom Brown's Schooldays*.

71. *Ed.* Several articles reprinted in this volume feature a list of titles employed in the author's discussion. The references, in other words, are listed at the beginning rather than the end of the article, as is now customary.

72. *Ed.* Named, apparently, for parliamentarian William Wilberforce (1759–1833), one of the founding voices of British abolitionism. He was a member of the Clapham Sect, comprised of evangelical Christians devoted to abolition, emancipation, and missionary work. He was instrumental in the passage of the 1807 bill abolishing the British slave trade and saw the emancipation bill that would free black British colonials pass just before he died.

73. *Ed.* See also Martineau's analysis of Garrison in Martineau 1861.

74. *Ed.* Samuel May, Unitarian clergyman and abolitionist, was a staunch supporter of Garrison, at whose marriage he officiated. May both praised and condemned Martineau's brand of abolitionism, ultimately lauding her as one of the two British abolitionists (George Thompson was the other) whose loyalty to American abolitionism never wavered (see Samuel May letters, Boston Public Library, ms.b.1.6v9). William Goodell, an abolitionist reformer from Providence, was conservative relative to Garrison. Lifelong friend Isaac Knapp (1804–1843), a printer and editor, sold Garrison his first press. Beginning with the first issue of the *Liberator* (1 January 1831), Knapp served as co-publisher.

75. *Ed.* David Walker was a free black whose 76-page pamphlet, *Walker's Appeal . . . to the Colored Citizens of the World* (1829), reflects his rhetorical powers as a fiery lay preacher. Walker's incendiary threats against white America and hints at bloody black insurrections, threats greatly enhanced by his race, prompted a campaign to suppress circulation of the pamphlet. Garrison's arrest for libel at this time reflects the high degree of anxiety prompted by anti-slavery writing and demonstrates the association between Garrison's *Liberator* and Walker's *Appeal* in the public mind. Although Martineau condemns Walker's tactics, she praises those of black Haitian liberator Toussaint l'Ouverture (with whom Walker has been compared), in her 1841 "historical romance," *The Hour and the Man*.

76. *Ed.* Also known as the Nat Turner Rebellion in 1831 (not 1832). A literate slave and "fanatically" religious lay preacher whose followers called him "the Prophet," Turner claimed that, in a vision of the second coming of Christ, a voice from heaven instructed him to "slay my enemies with their own weapons." Taking a solar eclipse as a sign from God, Turner led an insurrection that began with killing his owners and spread throughout the Virginia countryside; he was eventually caught and hanged. Over two hundred blacks were killed by state and federal troops in the confusion, although the debacle was blamed on the abolitionists, presumably for inciting slaves to insurrection with their talk of emancipation.

77. *Ed.* David L. Child, a Harvard graduate and editor of the *Massachusetts Journal*, early warned that the annexation of Texas was tantamount to adding another slave state to the Union. Martineau was misinformed as to his law career, although he did have several brushes with the law through libel suits. He was married to Quaker abolitionist, writer, and social reformer, Lydia Maria Child (1802–1880), whose *An Appeal in Favor of that Class of Americans Called Africans* (1833) resulted, as Martineau notes, in her social ostracization from "polite" society. Child avoided meeting Martineau, despite the latter's eagerness to make her acquaintance. Years later, Martineau wrote to her: "I thank you heartily for the openess with which you explain your former feelings towards me. [But] I cannot surrender my convictions to the opinion of the world. . . . What else have I,—what else have any of us to rely upon? What real evil can the opinions of the world do us?" (10 January 18[?], Houghton Library, autograph file).

78. *Ed.* Lewis Tappan, whose brother Arthur was responsible for Garrison's release from jail, was a successful merchant whose strong religious convictions prompted him to support social reform and philanthropic causes. In 1839, Tappan was a chief financial backer of the *Amistad* case—the defense of the African slaves whose revolt against their white captors resulted in a bloody shipboard mutiny, an event that galvanized the intensifying abolitionist movement.

79. *Ed.* The discussions were led by Theodore Weld, later married to southern abolitionist Angelina Grimké. The head of Lane Seminary, Dr. Lyman Beecher, a theologian and writer whose eloquence (he had "converted" Lewis Tappan, among others) was legendary, was the father of preacher Henry Ward Beecher and anti-slavery novelist Harriet Beecher (*Uncle Tom's Cabin*). Harriet Beecher married Calvin Stowe, also a Lane Seminary theologian.

80. *Ed.* Martineau was a vigorous supporter (through fund-raising) of Ohio's Oberlin Institute, which welcomed women, blacks, and other minorities. See Chapman 1877, "Consequences,—to Life Passive," pp. 226–51.

81. *Ed.* James Birney (1792–1857) emancipated his slaves and gave up his law practice in Alabama to promote the American Colonization Society. He published the abolitionist journal *Philanthropist* in Cincinnati and was executive director of Garrison's American Anti-Slavery Society. Birney ran for president as the Liberty Party candidate (1840 and 1844) on the abolition platform. The Liberty Party represented the political arm of abolitionism following the split of the Tappans and others from Garrison's organization in 1840.

82. *Ed.* E. S. Abdy, author of *Journal of a Residence and Tour in the United States of America* (1833–1834).

83. *Ed.* John Quincy Adams (1767–1848), sixth U.S. president and later congressman in the House of Representatives (Mass.). For most of his congressional career, Adams fought against the "Gag Rule," which prevented freedom of speech by prohibiting the right of petition in Congress. As Martineau notes, in 1838 Adams introduced 350 petitions to Congress, all of which were tabled under the Gag Rule. It was rescinded in 1844.

84. *Ed.* Broadcloth was worn by the merchant class, a reminder from Martineau that anti-abolitionist rioting was not perpetrated by low-class "roughs" or malcontents but by middle-class "gentlemen."

85. *Ed.* Martin Van Buren (1782–1862), eighth U.S. president (1837–1841). In 1848 he ran for president on the Free-Soil Party ticket. The party's slogan, "Free soil, free speech, free labor, and free men," reflected its opposition to the extension of slavery. Free-soilers did not, however, support abolition or emancipation.

86. *Ed.* Supported by early British abolitionists, dubbed the Clapham sect, slave James Somerset was legally freed in 1772 on the basis that "free soil makes free men" (Fladeland 1972, 20). The judgment was handed down by Lord Mansfield.

87. *Ed.* Quaker Lucretia Coffin Mott (1793–1880), abolitionist and gifted preacher. Mott was a founder and president of the Philadelphia Female Anti-Slavery Society; with the passage of the Fugitive Slave Bill, she turned her home into a refuge for runaway slaves. She attended the 1840 World Anti-Slavery Convention in London and the first women's rights convention in Seneca Falls, New York, in 1848.

88. *Ed.* Martineau alludes to the period's popular iconography, designed to symbolize acceptable gender roles. Whereas masculinity was represented as a tree or trellis (strong, virile, supportive, not easily swayed), proper femininity was imaged as a vine, with woman's "tendrils" wrapping around her masculine support, indicating her comparative weakness, dependency, docility, and pliability. Women abolitionists agitating for reform outside the domestic sphere were deemed unfeminine, unchristian, even "unsexed" since they demonstrated intellect and civil autonomy rather than dependency. The intense resistance to women abolitionists offers striking commentary on the political influence they wielded despite what Martineau calls their official "political invisibility."

89. *Martineau.* The prospectus of the *Liberator,* January 1838, has the following paragraph:—"As our object is *Universal* Emancipation—to redeem woman as well as man from a servile to an equal condition—we shall go for the Rights of Woman to their fullest extent. W. L. Garrison, *Editor.* I. Knapp, *Publisher.*"

90. *Ed.* On an April 1836 petition protesting the admission of slave states into the Union, Garrison's signature is followed by this statement: "It is thought advisable by the friends of the cause that as many signatures of ladies be obtained as possible, and therefore a blank is left in the printed remonstrance for the insertion of the words 'male' or 'female' as the case may require. Call on *all* whether members of your society or not. In behalf of the Boston Female anti-slavery society, Anne W. Weston." (Garrison 1971–1981 2:85).

91. *Martineau.* A resident of Boston was expressing to a European traveller one day, in the year 1836, his regret that strangers should be present in the country when its usual quiet and sobriety were disturbed. "I am glad," observed the traveller, "to have been in the country in its martyr age." "Martyr age! martyr age!" cried a clergyman, remarkable for the assiduity of his parochial visiting. "What *do* you mean? We don't burn people in Smithfield here." "No," replied the stranger, "because 'Boston refinement' will not bear the roasting of the bodies of men and women; but you come as near to this pass as you dare. You rack their consciences and wring their souls." "Our martyr age! our martyr age!" the clergyman went on muttering to himself, in all the excitement of a new idea.

92. *Ed.* Wendell Phillips, a Harvard-educated Boston lawyer who claimed to have been "converted" to abolitionism when he witnessed Garrison's near-lynching. He later served as president of the American Abolition Society and was an enthusiastic supporter of John Brown's actions at Harper's Ferry.

93. *Ed.* John Collins, American abolitionist who earned notoriety for traveling publicly with his friend, former slave Frederick Douglass. The two men were brutalized by "roughs" on several occasions when they resisted being separated by discriminatory practices on rail lines. Collins wrote *Right and Wrong among the Abolitionists of the United States* (1841) to record the 1840 split in the abolitionist movement. See also Martineau to Collins, 20 February 1841, Boston Public Library, ms.a.1.2, v. 11, n. 80;

Martineau to Collins, 9 November 1840 (Taylor 1974, 123); Collins to Chapman, 3 December 1840 (126); and Chapman to Elizabeth Pease, 30 September 1840, introducing Collins to Martineau (117–18).

94. *Ed.* Elisabeth Pease was a liberal Quaker, a British Garrisonian abolitionist, and an activist in the Chartist (working-class) movement of the 1840s. Pease and Martineau corresponded about the latter's needlework contributions to the anti-slavery fairs organized to raise money for the cause. Martineau to Elizabeth Pease, 2 February 1841, Boston Public Library, ms.a.1.2, v. 11, p. 91). For more on the "flagrant" proceedings mentioned in the letter, see Mayer 1998, chap. 13.

95. *Ed.* Martineau conducted several lecture series in Ambleside for the "workies." In 1853 she presented an anti-slavery lecture designed to prepare the "workies" for the arrival of three runaway slaves who were visiting the area, probably to raise funds for abolition societies by telling their stories (see note 182). "These things stir our sluggish folk here, and do more good than clergy and schools," she wrote to William Fox (26 February 1853, Bancroft Library, 2:95).

96. *Ed.* Termed "taxes on knowledge," stamp taxes raised revenue for the government but also controlled circulation (a form of censorship) by making the cost of newspapers—and thus knowledge and information—prohibitive to certain classes. Once the stamp tax was rescinded in 1855, periodicals like the *Times,* which aimed at upper-class audiences, declined in influence as papers like the *Daily News* benefited. As sales numbers demonstrated, readers from the increasingly literate lower and middle classes appreciated papers like the *Daily News* that addressed their concerns. According to Eugene Rasor, the repeal of such taxes "made possible the rise of a mass press" (Mitchell et al. 1988, 782).

97. *Ed.* See also Midgley 1992, 178–79 on Martineau's influence as a *Daily News* writer. A decade before the Civil War, Martineau was urging Britain to secure another source of the cotton so crucial to the country's manufacturing trades. As she predicted, cotton became a pivotal issue: wanting to protect their own interests, British capitalists favored trade with the southern states while British abolitionists called for a boycott of slave-produced goods. Arguing that alternative cotton sources would prevent England's culpability in perpetuating the American slavery system, Martineau was consistent in her claim that the product could and should be obtained elsewhere, thus keeping factories open and workers employed while forcing the South to restructure its economy by eliminating slavery. She wrote dozens of *Daily News* articles on this topic.

98. *Ed.* Illustrating her fierce loyalty to the *Daily News,* Martineau wrote to Garrison: "I am aware that passionate Americans in London hate and revile me for not worshipping their country and its political course as faultless. That does not matter in the least . . . but it is quite another matter to try to discredit a newspaper of the very highest character, and of proportionate influence" (Burchell 1995, 18).

99. *Ed.* Harriet Beecher Stowe (1811–1896) published *Uncle Tom's Cabin* serially in the *National Era* in 1851 and as a book in 1852. Its reception was unprecedented: the book sold 10,000 copies in the first week; 300,000 the first year; and 3 million in the United States alone, a figure probably doubled by translations and foreign sales. When Lincoln met Stowe, he (reputedly) acknowledged her as "the little woman" who wrote the book that started the Civil War. It is hardly surprising, as Martineau notes, that Stowe's name was "reviled" in the South. Clare Taylor attributes Stowe's approach in this novel to Martineau's "view of labour as a measure of value, and her trick of expounding classic economic doctrine through a didactic tale" (1995, 97). Although it was fashionable for a time to condemn *Uncle Tom's Cabin* for its sentimental

"romantic racism," in which blacks were portrayed as childlike and favored by the white, Christian God for their patience and docility, modern analyses of the novel recognize its seminal importance as an example of feminine—and feminist—writing. See, for example, Elaine Showalter's "Piecing and Writing" in Miller ed. (1986) and Jane Tompkins's *Sensational Designs* (1985). George Fredrickson (1971) discusses "romantic racialism."

100. *Ed.* The Fugitive Slave Act (1850), part of Henry Clay's "Omnibus Bill," provided for the return of runaway slaves to their owners and for the prosecution of anyone who assisted them. The law was drafted by James Mason (involved also in John Brown's "trial" and in the *Trent* affair). The law's bounty system allowed whites to collect fees on any black deemed an escaped slave. A plausible claim was so easily fabricated that even free blacks had no recourse once designated "slave" by a white.

101. *Ed.* Habeas corpus asserts Americans' constitutional right not to be imprisoned arbitrarily or held against their will without reasonable charges. During the Civil War, Lincoln suspended this right in order to detain those likely to act in ways detrimental to the Union. One source estimates that as many as 13,000 citizens were detained during the highly controversial suspension of habeas corpus.

102. *Ed.* Britain's Crimean War (1854–1856) was followed by conflicts with China (1856–1860) and the Indian Mutiny (1857).

103. *Ed.* On 15 June 1215, King John signed the Magna Carta at Runnymede. The document, the first of its kind in English history, guaranteed political liberties formerly granted only by a sovereign.

104. *Ed.* Introduced by Illinois senator Stephen Douglas (1813–1861), the Kansas-Nebraska Act (1854), with its provision for popular sovereignty, overturned the Missouri Compromise, making slavery possible in territory north of Missouri. Pro- and anti-slavery settlers quickly moved into the area, both sides seeking to establish a majority. The abolitionist faction was no less violent than the pro-slavers: funded by the Emigrant Aid Societies to settle in the territory, they were armed with rifles nicknamed "Beecher's Bibles" (after Henry Ward Beecher). Extreme violence throughout 1855–1856 earned Kansas its nickname, "Bleeding Kansas"; corrupt politicians conducted fraudulent elections; "Border Ruffians" attacked abolitionists (in Lawrence, Kansas, for example); and John Brown led a raid in which five pro-slavers were killed. More than two hundred people died in these conflicts. Douglas's bill also created a North/South split in the Democratic Party that allowed for the emergence of the Republican Party, from which platform Lincoln was elected.

105. *Ed.* John Charles Fremont (1813–1890), western explorer and travel writer, later a U.S. general and first presidential candidate for the Republican Party (1856) on a platform urging that Kansas be admitted as a free state; he lost to Buchanan. During the Civil War, Fremont boldly declared martial law in Missouri and freed its slaves (1861); Lincoln overturned the order and relieved him of his command. In 1864 Fremont again ran for president, this time against Lincoln as a candidate for the Radical Republicans; he later withdrew, not wanting to split the Republican Party.

106. *Ed.* As a slave owned by a Missouri doctor, Dred Scott traveled throughout the country, spending considerable time in free territory. Arguing that, under the terms of the Missouri Compromise, this made him a free man, in 1846 he sued for his freedom, after unsuccessfully attempting to buy himself and his wife. In order to try the case, New York abolitionist John Sanford purchased Dred (who was freed after the trial), and by 1855 the case had reached the Supreme Court. In 1857, Chief Justice Roger B. Taney (1777–1864) ruled that blacks were not citizens—and therefore could

not sue—but property—and therefore had no rights; he also declared the Missouri Compromise unconstitutional. Taney, a former Virginia slaveholder, was appointed by Andrew Jackson in 1835 to replace Chief Justice Marshall, an appointment that was vigorously opposed. Taney's judgment in the Dred Scott case so outraged people, especially those attempting to preserve neutrality, that it actually served to strengthen the abolitionist cause by swaying the undecided to their side.

107. *Ed.* Democrat James Buchanan (1791–1868) was the fifteenth U.S. president (1857–1861). By carrying all the slave states in the election, Buchanan defeated Fremont and Fillmore, setting an ominous tone for the anti-slavery cause. During his service as the American minister to England, Buchanan signed the Ostend (Belgium) Manifesto (1854), which pledged to offer to buy Cuba from Spain with the provision that, if Spain refused, America would simply take the island by force.

108. *Ed.* Franklin Pierce (1804–1869), the fourteenth U.S. president (1853–1857). Pierce (N.H.) opposed abolitionism and sponsored the Gag Bill. During his presidency, the Kansas-Nebraska act was passed, overturning the Missouri Compromise; runaway slave Anthony Burns became the scapegoat for the federal government's enforcement of the Fugitive Slave Act; Charles Sumner (Mass.) was beaten in the Senate chambers by Preston Brooks (S.C.); and the Kansas territory earned its nickname, "Bleeding Kansas."

109. *Ed.* The *Regina Coeli*, a French ship caught off the coast of Liberia with a load of blacks the French claimed were hired laborers. But once on board, the blacks were manacled like slaves. A mutiny ensued and the scheme exposed to British authorities patrolling the coast to prevent slave trading. The French claimed the "laborers" were expatriated Americans, prompting Martineau's observation that black Americans were "tricked" into deportation through Liberian colonization schemes only to be captured by French slavers to be resold into the market. See also Martineau's *Daily News* articles on the French slave trade: 1, 3, 7 July 1857; and 29 July 1858.

110. *Ed.* Radical abolitionist John Brown, who earned notoriety in 1856 for leading a raid in Kansas in which five pro-slavers were brutally murdered, raided a federal arsenal in Harper's Ferry, Virginia, in October 1859, determined to organize a slave uprising and end the slavery question definitively. But instead of the expected black reinforcements, federal troops surrounded Brown and his small band, many of whom were wounded or killed. Brown himself was quickly tried and hanged. Pro-slavers thought justice had been swiftly served; some abolitionists were appalled at the notoriety that threatened to compromise the platform of nonviolence. But others quickly lauded Brown as the great hero of the age for his readiness to die for abolition and to demonstrate his belief that bloodshed, not pacifism, and actions, not words, were necessary to purge America of its great "sin." The event shocked the world and, although condemned by some as a fanatic, Brown's death earned him almost instant martyrdom.

111. *Ed.* New York abolitionist Gerritt Smith, one of John Brown's financial backers for the Harper's Ferry raid. Initially a pacifist, Smith adapted a more aggressive approach to abolition as a result of his shock over the events in "Bleeding Kansas" by contributing large sums of money—$10,000 to the American Colonization Society and $40,000 to such "immediatists" as Garrison, whose *Liberator* he also helped subsidize (Mayer 1998, 216–17).

112. *Ed.* James Miller McKim, one of Garrison's inner circle of abolitionist friends. McKim's daughter Lucy married Garrison's son, Wendell.

113. *Ed.* Abraham Lincoln (1809–1865), sixteenth U.S. president (1861–1865), of the Republican Party. The Civil War began with southern secession and the formation

of the Confederacy following his inauguration and ended soon after his assassination by John Wilkes Booth, following his reelection and inauguration for a second term.

114. *Ed.* The Emancipation Proclamation, effective 1 January 1863, asserts that "all persons held as slaves" shall be set free. But the Union had no control over the Confederacy or the Border States, and it was not until passage of the Thirteenth Amendment (abolishing slavery, 1 January 1865) that emancipation began. Some responses to the proclamation emphasized that the motivation behind the Civil War was preservation of the Union, not the liberation of slaves. Presented with the possibility of immediate emancipation of millions of slaves, many feared retaliatory insurrections.

115. *Ed.* Martineau to Henry Reeve, 13 January 1859, quoted in Webb 1961, 327.

116. *Ed.* Nonetheless, Martineau's keen interest in Indian affairs prompted her to continue reading the *Spectator,* whose articles on India were so instructive that "one would bear with a good deal of vulgarity and bad temper about home affairs for the sake of them." She wrote two books on the Indian Mutiny, *British Rule in India* (1857) and *Suggestions towards the Future Government of India* (1858). Arbuckle notes that despite the *Spectator's* "flippant" tone, it maintained its "image of integrity and social purpose" (1994, 288 n. 2).

117. *Ed.* Martineau to Wendell Phillips, 29 December 1858, Houghton Library, ms am 1953 (866).

118. *Ed.* Martineau to Sarah Martineau, 4 November 1858, Kendal, Cumbria Record Office, HM papers #8.

119. *Ed.* Hinton Rowan Helper's *The Impending Crisis in the South* was banned in the South but 100,000 copies were distributed by the Republicans during Lincoln's presidential campaign. The book argues that the increase of poverty in the South was due to slavery, a political economy theory that Martineau heartily endorsed. Like Charles Sumner, Helper was "knocked down and beaten in the Capitol" by irate southerners.

120. *Ed.* The Know-Nothing Party reflects a time when American party politics were increasingly divided along geographical lines as slavery became a central issue. The party sought to exclude races, cultures, ethnicities, and religions other than that of white, Protestant Americans and earned its name because its members consistently denied knowing anything about certain people and issues. The Know-Nothing Party (later, the American Party) nominated Millard Fillmore for president in 1856; he lost to Buchanan.

121. *Ed.* Southern expansionists sought to annex Cuba and Nicaragua, either by diplomacy or by force, to expand the slave trade and the supply of available slaves.

122. *Ed.* Many believed that Massachusetts congressman Daniel Webster (1782–1852) relinquished his title as "dean of states' rights" when he supported Henry Clay's Compromise Measures of 1850, which included the Fugitive Slave Bill; he argued that these compromises were necessary to preserve the Union. In *The History of the American Compromises,* Martineau argued that Webster "committed political suicide" by aligning with Clay. She thought that Clay was brilliant but misguided and that his penchant for compromises merely delayed and further vexed the issues that would inevitably lead to war.

123. *Ed.* Democrat Lewis Cass (Mich.) promoted "popular sovereignty," which argued that slavery should be regulated (permitted or outlawed) by local governments. Cass was defeated by Zachary Taylor in the 1848 presidential election. Cass served as secretary of state under President Buchanan. Admiral Sir Charles Napier's (1786–1860) position in the British Navy made him instrumental in international efforts to control the slave trade.

124. *Ed.* Charles Sumner (1811–1874), an antislavery senator from Massachusetts, delivered a speech entitled "The Crime against Kansas" (May 1856), in which he condemned South Carolina senator Andrew Butler for embracing "the harlot Slavery" by his promotion of pro-slavery interests in Kansas. Two days later, Butler's nephew, Representative Preston Brooks (S.C.), avenged his uncle's honor by beating Sumner unconscious with a cane on the Senate floor. Other than a $300.00 fine, Brooks was not punished and was, indeed, reelected. Sumner, despite years of operations and recuperation, never fully recovered from the attack; he was reelected to the Senate during his absence. Of Sumner, Martineau predicted: "If he recovers, he will be President. If not, his career is over." Martineau to Henry Bright, n.d., Bancroft Library, 1:25. Her article mocks the South's valorization of Brook's cowardly act against a man she regarded as a personal friend, although she does question Sumner's brand of abolitionism—he was a Free-Soiler.

125. *Ed.* Martineau to John G. Palfrey, 20 December 1835, Houghton Library, ms am 1704 (601).

126. *Ed.* The earliest date that I found featuring an article attributed to Harriet Martineau is 9 April 1859. Although Chapman claims Martineau wrote "some ninety letters," I found only about sixty-two numbered letters between this date and 12 March 1862, when her contributions ceased. There are several pieces of anonymous writing, including occasional reprints from London's *Daily News,* that could be attributed to Martineau, but since the authorship is unclear I include only the writing featuring her byline, "Our European Correspondent" and signed either "H. M." or "Harriet Martineau."

127. *Ed.* Two exceptions are annual contributions to the *Liberty Bell* and two articles on sanitary reform to the *Atlantic Monthly* ("Health in the Camp" and "Health in the Hospital," both 1861). Webb points out that, given the limited audience of the *NASS*—abolitionists—and its small circulation, Martineau was in effect preaching to the already converted. Her message was unlikely to persuade the opposition to embrace the abolitionist ideology (1960, 331).

128. *Ed.* Samuel May to R. D. Webb, 25 February 1862, Boston Public Library, ms b.l.6., v. 9, n. 10). May proclaimed her objections to the Morrill Tariff "irrelevant." Nine years later May wrote, again to Webb: "I had always been an admirer of H. M. . . . She's a wonder, and a monument of what a human being . . . is capable. . . . I wonder what she herself would say of that sentiment or phrase, now, if she should happen to read it" (13 August 1871, Boston Public Library, ms b.1.6, v.11, n. 12).

129. *Ed.* Martineau to Charles Sumner, 2 August 1861, Houghton Library, ms am 1.4, v. 135;) and 14 November 1861, Houghton Library, ms am 1.4, v. 136.

130. *Ed.* Martineau to Dr. Combe, n.d., National Library of Scotland, ms 7265, f. 42.

131. *Ed.* In 1855 Martineau wrote to Garrison: "If slavery is an abomination, political corruption for the sake of slavery is an abomination also, with a lie to boot. If your countrymen permit your republic to decline into a dark despotism, for the sake of its one despotic institution, they will have perpetuated the most desperate crime, and created the most intolerable woe ever wrought by an association of human beings" (16 February 1855, Harris-Manchester College, Oxford).

132. *Ed.* Martineau to Florence Nightingale, 8 May 1861, British Library, shelfmark 47588; Martineau to Edward Flower, 21 February 1862, Bancroft Library, 1:72.

133. *Ed.* Joshua Giddings, Ohio Whig congressman supported by abolitionists. When powerful southern politicians tried to discredit Giddings, Garrison promoted him in the *Liberator,* resulting in his reelection. Giddings was later a Free-Soiler.

134. *Ed.* According to Chapman, as a Garrisonian and a pacifist, Martineau "deprecated" Brown's violent behavior, claiming that it put the North at a disadvantage, yet she was nevertheless "deeply moved with admiration for the saintly heroism of the man" (1877, 376). A comparison of her writing about Brown in the *Daily News* and the *NASS* is instructive of her shifting attitudes. Her poignant account of Brown's burial in the former is entirely sympathetic.

135. *Ed.* Although many northern abolitionists could not understand Martineau's objections to this protectionist tariff, her distress is understandable in view of her work for the Anti-Corn-Law League. It is worth remembering here her desire, expressed in an 1835 letter, for a closer relationship between America and Britain, so that the former could learn from Britain's past mistakes and Britain could learn from America's fresh perspective. Further, her understanding of political economy is far more acute than that of the men involved in this debate. Martineau has been accused of overreacting to this tariff, yet she rightly sees that the politics versus morality argument that split the abolitionist movement in 1840 continued to be played out in 1861, with the stakes considerably raised.

136. *Ed.* Lincoln formalized a Union blockade of Southern ports on the Atlantic seaboard and the Mississippi River (derisively termed the Anaconda Plan) on 19 April 1861.

137. *Ed.* Richard Davis Webb, Dublin abolitionist and printer, a strong supporter and lifelong friend of Garrison. In a letter to A. W. Weston, Webb attributes his interest in the American slavery question to reading Martineau's *The Martyr Age of the United States* (5 July 1859, Boston Public Library; see Midgley 1992, 131).

138. *Ed.* Unionists seemed to assume that Britain's avowed neutrality meant it would naturally side with them against the South's slavery interests—although mutual mistrust over the cotton supply was a constant factor. Similarly, the seceded Confederate states believed in their right to secure European alliances, and Martineau bitterly regreted that Britain's support of this right and preservation of its own neutrality seemed also to imply its support of slavery. She had been a guest of the Mason family during her American tour. Mason, who was instrumental in the passage of the Fugitive Slave Bill, also participated in John Brown's "trial."

139. *Ed.* William H. Seward (1801–1872), governor of New York and senator, also served as Lincoln's secretary of state. Seward was a founder of the Republican Party who himself had ambitions for the presidency; he was affiliated with Unionist Horace Greeley and, to Martineau, represented a hypocritical brand of abolitionism that valued the Union over emancipation. Seward was to have been murdered in the Lincoln assassination conspiracy, but he survived.

140. *Ed.* In May 1861, Britain declared its neutrality in the North-South conflict. It granted the Confederacy the status of a "belligerent," rather than a "rebel," which would have implied that the South was resisting the authority of the North and thus, by extension, acknowledged that the North did indeed hold that authority, but at the same time Britain did not recognize the Confederacy's independence. People on each side insisted that Britain's stance was tantamount to tacit support of the other side, emphasizing the same rejection of neutrality that Martineau had experienced in 1835.

141. *Ed.* Edward Everett (1794–1865), Massachusetts senator, American ambassador, secretary of state, editor, Unitarian minister, and president of Harvard University. Everett was a conservative whose aim to placate northern and southern interests earned Martineau's contempt, as did Henry Clay's compromises. The eradication of slavery was, for her, the only viable solution to America's civil strife.

142. *Ed.* The *Standard* of 4 January 1862 featured a column entitled "Mrs. Martineau's Recent Letters" signed by S.M. (presumably Samuel May). The writer refers to letter LIX of 28 December 1861 (printed above) and accuses her of siding with the South by not agreeing with Northern practices in the *Trent* affair. The writer also accuses her of "widening the breach between America and England" and concludes that England's "selfish greed of cotton and of trade" amounts to tacit support of slavery. If Martineau's comments are regarded as inflammatory, so too must comments such as May's.

143. *Ed.* On the editorial page of the 15 February 1862 *Standard,* a column entitled "Mrs. Martineau's Letter" observes: "The letter before us compels us to come to the unwelcome and unpleasant conviction that a mind always remarkable for its love of truth and the keenness of its logical insight, has suffered itself now to be beclouded by national prejudice, and carried away by a desire to establish a foregone conclusion."

144. *Ed.* Martineau's charge that the abolitionist movement was becoming derailed by politics was accurate, and the defensive condemnation of her strong stand—even by abolitionists—only validated her points. But she did not nurse grudges and rightly saw that the *Daily News* was the best platform for her writing on these issues. As a liaison between the British reading public and America, she continued to support the cause as vigorously as ever, maintaining friendships with the abolitionists until the end of her life. Fracturing among the abolitionists was characteristic of the movement, long before and after Martineau wrote for the *NASS.*

145. *Ed.* The editor's remarks recall Martineau's repeated insistence that the London *Times* did not represent mainstream public opinion in England. Although unmarried, she adapted "Mrs. Martineau," citing the eighteenth-century precedent of employing the term to denote an elderly woman and arguing that "Miss" was absurdly inappropriate for someone of her age and stature.

146. *Ed.* Martineau to unknown recipient, 10 August 1864 (Taylor 1974, 525).

147. *Ed.* Martineau refers to the *Trent* incident. See the *NASS* articles above.

148. *Ed.* Rumors that America wished to annex Canada added to England's irritation over the *Trent* affair.

149. *Ed.* See Martineau to Catherine Macready, 29 December 184[?], National Library of Scotland, ms 3713, f. 112; and Martineau to William Fox, 21 January 1843 (in Burchell 1995).

150. *Ed.* Martineau expressed disappointment that "Boz" failed to use his popular influence to speak out against slavery while in America. She also observed that his *American Notes* indicated he had little contact with ordinary citizens, an experience that she herself had found so culturally revelatory; she expressed a similar critique of de Tocqueville's account.

151. *Ed.* Letter to W. H. Wills, 6 January 1856, quoted in Dickens 1995, 9.

152. *Ed.* Martineau to Miss Estlin, 21 August 185[4?], Boston Public Library, ms.B.1.6, v. 4, n. 2.

153. *Ed.* Martineau wrote histories of England and India, and historical precedent informs all her writing on America, Ireland, and the Middle East. Similarly, she also wrote biographies, biographical sketches and obituaries, and a historical novel.

154. *Ed.* John Marshall (1755–1835), Chief Justice of the Supreme Court, 1801–1835. John Jay (1745–1829), first Chief Justice of the Supreme Court, 1789–1795. Bunker Hill, in Charlestown, Massachusetts, site of the first major battle of the Revolution in 1775. The 1815 Treaty of Paris required France to cease slave trading within five years.

155. *Martineau. Jefferson's Correspondence,* Letter cl., December 10th, 1819.

156. *Martineau. Ibid.* Letter clii., April 22nd, 1820. [Thomas Jefferson to John Holmes.]

157. *Ed.* Martineau was misinformed in her implication that Story retreated from public politics after the 1820 Missouri Compromise. In the 1841 *Amistad* case, when President Van Buren aimed to placate the Spanish government by handing over the African prisoners and J. Q. Adams joined their defense in protest, Judge Joseph Story (Mass.) ruled that the prisoners were not slaves and released them, arguing that they were free to decide their own fates. The decision rocked the political world nationally and internationally. Although the error may be explained by Martineau's near-fatal illness in the early 1840s, which resulted in close to seven years' seclusion, the omission is odd, given her usual scrupulous attention to historical detail.

158. *Martineau. Life and letters of Joseph Story,* vol. I, p. 362.

159. *Martineau. Life and Letters of Joseph Story,* vol. I, p. 366.

160. *Ed.* The Wilmot Proviso (1846), a bill introduced by Democrat David Wilmot (Pa.), prohibited slavery in the newly acquired territories of California and Texas, annexed as a result of the Mexican War. The proviso was supported by the Free-Soilers.

161. *Ed.* After both literary and monetary contributions to the periodical, Martineau later broke with the *Westminster Review,* charging that its article on the *Trent* affair constituted a "plea for slavery and the Slave States. . . . The Review has veered about, nearly all round the compass on the slavery question till now, when it points due South" (Martineau to unknown recipient, 22 February 1862, Bancroft Library, 5:59).

162. *Ed.* Martineau's point about slave mothers committing infanticide to save their daughters from the double degradation of sexual slavery anticipates Toni Morrison's 1987 novel, *Beloved.*

163. *Ed.* Historian James Rawley notes, "For the years 1811–1870, years of illegal trade for many Atlantic nations, Spanish America stood second only to Brazil, importing nearly 700,000 slaves" (1981, 52). Slave trading was legal in France from 1802 to 1815; in the first decade, notes Rawley, French ships transported an estimated 5,000 African slaves to its colonies and to the United States. The 1815 Treaty of Paris required cessation of French slave trading, but the practice continued illegally for decades. Contrary to the statistics recorded at the time, Rawley notes, more than ten times the number of suspected French ships were active in Caribbean slave trade, with an estimated 105,000 Africans traded between 1821 and 1832 alone.

164. *Ed.* Martineau to Wendell Phillips, 29 December 1858, Houghton Library, ms am 1953 (866).

165. *Ed.* Of her position at the *Daily News,* Martineau wrote to Charles Sumner, "I have made full use of my liberty since the atrocious and most disheartening 'disguised French slave trade' was set up" (23 June 1858, Houghton Library, ms am 1.4). On the slave trade, see *Daily News* articles: 17 November 1852; 24 August 1853; 16 June and 1, 3, 7, 8, 21 July 1857; 4 10, 11, 18, 22, 26, 29 June, 20, 29 July, 23 August, 2, 17, 25, 28 September, 14, 27 October, and 16 December 1858; 12 July 1859; 9 April, 16 June, and 9 August 1860.

166. *Martineau. Life of Wilberforce,* vol. III, p. 302.

167. *Martineau. Edinburgh Review,* vol. LXIII, p. 387.

168. *Martineau. The London Cotton Plant,* June 12th, 1858.

169. *Martineau. The London Cotton Plant,* June 26th, 1858, p. 37.

170. *Ed.* Martineau's use of the word "nigger," in our era a racist and derogatory term, reflected, for the Victorians, a distinction between free blacks and slaves. The difference between a "nigger" and a "negro" is thus economic—the latter is autonomous

and works for wages, the former is enslaved and does not. This distinction makes clear the inconvenience of the "mean-white" (non-slaveholding and thus themselves laborers) presence in the South, where whites justified slavery along racial lines; like aristocrats, slaveholding southern whites considered themselves superior to manual labor.

171. *Ed.* John Paul Jones (1747–1792), naval hero during the American Revolution, participated in the slave trade.

172. *Martineau.* It is feared, however, that since the withdrawal of the British squadron from the Western waters a considerable increase has taken place, and that from 20,000 to 30,000 negroes have been conveyed to Cuba this year under the American flag.

173. *Martineau.* Among the despatches is a letter from Lord Napier to Mr. Cass, detailing the following facts:—In the early months of 1857, ten vessels were captured, of which eight, carrying the American flag, were condemned as slavers. The two others—the *General Pierce* and the *Splendid*—were captured by Portuguese men-of-war; the *Splendid* being fitted for the stowage of 1000 slaves. Nineteen others, all Americans, follow on the list, one of which, the *North Hand,* was chartered by the notorious house of Figaniere, Reis & Co. of New York, for the ostensible purpose of conveying food to the starving inhabitants of the Cape de Verde islands! The recent capture of the *Echo,* with 384 slaves on board, by an American cruiser, is an encouraging indication of the effects produced by these disclosures; but the punishment of the slaver-captain is still uncertain, and the project for consigning these negroes to the agents of the Colonisation Society in Liberia deserves the liveliest reprobation.

174. *Martineau.* We are indebted to the Bishop of Oxford for the perusal of a letter of considerable importance which he has received from Dr. Livingstone, dated 22nd June, on board the *Pearl* steamer, in the Zambesi, on the east coast of Africa. Any such letter to one bearing the revered name of Wilberforce, must be interesting; but there are material statements of fact in it which lend an additional value to this communication. Of these facts, one of the one most worthy of attention is the travellers having found, on the banks of the river Laure, which they ascended some seventy miles, very fine cotton in the gardens of the natives; the flat fertile land, being within the influence of the sea-air, yields the plant almost without cultivation. These lands are supposed by Dr. Livingstone to be suited to the production of the celebrated Sea-Island cotton of the United States, the finest of any. The other fact of importance is, that the Slave-trade, to use the Doctor's expression, "is eating out the Portuguese power" in these parts. The Portuguese authorities at Tete and other points on the river who received Dr. Livingstone with so much kindness on his former journey, "have been expelled by the natives from every station," said those with whom the travellers had communication. "This," says Dr. Livingstone, "is the consequence of the Portuguese entering cordially into the notorious French Emigration scheme. The commandant of Tete stated in a letter that he had been a prisoner at Kilimane for the last six months, from a fear of passing between Mazaro and Senna. When we met the people of Mazaro, about two hundred were well armed, and ready to fight us, on the supposition that we were Portuguese; but when I called out that we were English, and pointed to the English ensign, they gave a shout of joy, and we saw them running off to bring bananas for sale." The bearing of these statements upon the African Question needs not be noted. It shows that the reappearance of slave-trading agents has at once affected the relations of the Portuguese and the natives in the most injurious manner; and unless the Cabinet of Lisbon takes energetic and effectual steps to crush this evil, the authority of the Crown of Portugal on the river is at an end. Its mouths cannot be held by a slave-trading power.

175. *Ed.* See also *Daily News,* 20 and 24 March 1857; 11 January and 23 December 1858; 14 January and 22 December 1860 on Buchanan.

176. *Ed.* James Monroe (1758–1831), fifth U.S. president (1817–1825). The 1823 Monroe Doctrine formalized the American opposition to European colonizing or other intervention in the western hemisphere.

177. *Ed.* Albert Gallatin (1761–1849), secretary of the Treasury (1801–1813).

178. *Ed.* While sailing on Lake Huron in 1836, Martineau wrote to Story: "I shall watch your country with intense interest, and some anxiety. . . . If every man would speak and act out his own mind, if the newspapers could be more decently honest, and your orators would cease to flatter the people, all would surely be well. And I have a strong faith that you will prosper; the bulk of your people are so good and true. They only want knowledge of the men they employ" (7 July 1836, Bancroft Library, 4:69). With its parting shot that she hopes Van Buren chokes on the Gag Bill, this early letter demonstrates her remarkable facility for prophetic—and political—insight and her ability to speak frankly to such an august personage as a judge.

179. *Ed.* Martineau to Henry Bright, 23 December 1865, Bancroft Library, 1:27.

180. *Ed.* Martineau was less confident that northern and southern whites will ever learn to live together. Recalling Charles Sumner's beating, she noted: "I don't see how they are to live, either as one nation or two. . . . Unless they can do this, they must accept the world's contumely for their weakness,—which is, in fact, the retribution on the North for its long complicity with the Southern oligarchy." After the war, she observed that southerners "have done mischief which it will take generations to repair,—created a barbarism which it will take a century or two to turn into a civilisation at all comparable with that of the North, which they have still to learn to understand" (Martineau to H. Bright, 30 November 1861 and 23 December 1865, Bancroft Library, 1:27).

181. *Martineau.* Sewell's *Ordeal of Free Labour,* ed. Rev. No. Ccxxxiii, p. 42.

182. *Ed.* Runaway slaves Frederick Douglass, William and Emily Craft, and William Wells Brown all became prominent activists in the abolitionist movement, particularly as lecturers on the abolition circuit. The Crafts were also noted for their ingenious escape from a Georgia plantation: light-skinned Emily, dressed as a man, posed as a master accompanied by "his" slave, William. With the passage of the Fugitive Slave Bill, the Crafts and Brown emigrated to Britain, where they became prominent abolitionist lecturers. According to Clare Midgley, Martineau arranged for their schooling in Surrey (1992, 142); they also, by arrangement, lectured to the "workies," or working classes, in Ambleside.

183. *Ed.* Contraband refers to goods smuggled illegally. Applied to runaway slaves, the term emphasizes the perversity of a system in which humans are regarded as material goods.

184. *Ed.* The 1860 presidential election featured four candidates: Abraham Lincoln (Republican), whose name was not on the southern ballot; his partner in the Lincoln-Douglas debates, Stephen Douglas (Democrat); John Breckinridge (Southern Democrat), who advocated individual and property rights; and John Bell (Constitutional Union Party), who urged compromise. Election analysts argue that the fragmentation of the Democratic Party resulted in Lincoln's victory.

185. *Martineau.* We have extracted the details which follow from the Official Reports, but some of them will be found set forth at greater length in Mr. Baptist Noel's *Rebellion in America* (pp. 348–377).

186. *Ed.* Martineau refers to the Draft Riots of 13–16 July 1863 in various northern states. The worst riots occurred in New York City, where blacks were lynched by

working-class Irish, requiring federal troops to restore order. Demonstrating yet again the prevailing confusion over the specific cause(s) being fought in the Civil War, many resisted the mandatory draft that would force them to fight on behalf of blacks (as opposed to restoring the Union).

187. *Ed.* It is difficult to determine exact dates with any precision. According to the itinerary provided in the introduction to *Society in America,* about sixteen days elapsed between Albany and Northumberland, yet she dates the former at 6 October and the latter at 11 October. The information provided here is what Martineau herself provided: a sequence of places visited, general (sometimes specific) length of stay, occasional arrival and departure dates.

188. *Ed.* Martineau seems not to have met the Alcotts while visiting New England. She does note that Bronson Alcott was in Philadelphia while she was there, but the two never met (1983, 2:79). Some New Englanders were offended by her attitude toward the transcendentalists, whose philosophy she dismissed as "fanciful and shallow conceits." Martineau objected to their aristocratic pretentiousness, "fancying themselves the elect of the earth . . . [while] the liberties of the republic were running out as fast as they could go" (1983, 2:71). Yet she admired Emerson, a friend and correspondent who subsequently visited her in Ambleside. Later, she notes, Emerson spoke "more abundantly and boldly the more critical the times became; and he is now, and has long been, completely identified with the Abolitionists in conviction and sentiment, though it is out of his way to join himself to their organisation" (1983, 2:63). She also admired Margaret Fuller, although the relationship was often strained. Martineau thought Fuller gifted but found her aversion to the slavery controversy offensive; in turn, Fuller was disgusted by Martineau's abolitionism. See also Martineau 1837, 3:175.

❖ ❖ ❖

WORKS CITED

The American Anti-Slavery Almanac for 1841. 1841. Vol. 1, no. 6. New York: S. W. Benedict.

Arbuckle, Elisabeth S. 1983. *Harriet Martineau's Letters to Fanny Wedgwood*. Stanford: Stanford University Press.

———. *Harriet Martineau in London's "Daily News."* 1994. New York: Garland Publishing.

Blackburn, Robin. 1988. *The Overthrow of Colonial Slavery, 1776–1848*. London: Verso.

[Boyle]. 1837. *A Review of Miss Martineau's Work on "Society in America."* Boston: Marsh, Capen & Lyon.

Burchell, R. A., ed. 1995. *Harriet Martineau in America: Selected Letters from the Reinhard S. Speck Collection*. Berkeley: Friends of the Bancroft Library.

Cazamian, Louis. 1973. *The Social Novel in England, 1830–1850*. London: Routledge & Kegan Paul.

Chapman, Maria Weston. 1877. *Memorials*. Boston: J. R. Osgood.

Courtney, Janet. 1933. *The Adventurous Thirties: A Chapter in the Women's Movement*. London: Oxford University Press.

David, Deirdre. 1987. *Intellectual Women and Victorian Patriarchy: Harriet Martineau, Elizabeth Barrett Browning, George Eliot*. Ithaca, N.Y.: Cornell University Press.

Dickens, Charles. 1974. *The Letters of Charles Dickens*. Vol. 3. Ed. Madeline House, Graham Storey, and Kathleen Tillotson. Oxford: Clarendon Press.

———. 1995. *The Letters of Charles Dickens*. Vol. 8. Ed. Graham Storey and Kathleen Tillotson. Oxford: Clarendon Press.

Fladeland, Betty. 1972. *Men and Brothers: Anglo-American Antislavery Cooperation*. Urbana: University of Illinois Press.

Frawley, Maria H. 1992. "Harriet Martineau in America: Gender and the Discourse of Sociology." *Victorian Newsletter* (spring): 13–20.

Fredrickson, George M. 1971. *The Black Image in the White Mind*. New York: Harper and Rowe.

Garrison, William Lloyd. 1971–1981. *The Letters of William Lloyd Garrison*. 7 vols. Ed. Louis Ruchames and Walter M. Merrill. Cambridge, Mass.: Harvard University, Belknap Press.

———. 1832. *Thoughts on African Colonization*. Boston: n.p.

Hill, Michael R. 1989. Introduction to *How to Observe Morals and Manners*, by Harriet Martineau. New Brunswick: Transaction Publishers.

Hoecker-Drysdale, Susan. 1992. *Harriet Martineau: First Woman Sociologist*. Oxford: Berg.

Lipset, Seymour Martin. 1962. "Harriet Martineau's America," introduction to *Society in America*, by Harriet Martineau. New York: Anchor Books.

Lohrli, Anne. 1972. *Household Words: A Weekly Journal, 1850–1859*. Toronto: University of Toronto Press.

Martineau, Harriet. 1832. "Demerara." In *Illustrations of Political Economy*. London: Fox.

———. 1837. *Society in America*. 3 vols. London: Saunders and Otley.

——. 1838a. *How to Observe Morals and Manners.* London: Knight.

——. 1838b. Letter from Harriet Martineau to Abby Kelley, 20 June. In Chapman 1877, 223–24.

——. 1838c. *Retrospect of Western Travel.* 3 vols. London: Saunders and Otley.

——. 1839. *The Martyr Age of the United States.* Boston: Weeks, Jordan & Co.

——. 1841. Introduction to *Right and Wrong among the Abolitionists of the United States,* by John Collins, 4–5. Glasgow: G. Gallie.

——. 1854. "Freedom or Slavery?" *Household Words* 9 (22 July): 537–42.

——. 1856. *A History of the American Compromises.* London: John Chapman.

——. 1857. "'Manifest Destiny' of the American Union." *Westminster Review* 68 (July): 76–98.

——. 1857. *The Manifest Destiny of the American Union.* Reprint. New York: American Anti-Slavery Society, 1857.

——. 1858. "The Slave Trade in 1858." *Edinburgh Review* (October): 541–86.

——. 1860. "The United States under the Presidentship of Mr. Buchanan." *Edinburgh Review* 112 (October): 278–97.

——. 1861a. "Representative Men: William Lloyd Garrison." *Once a Week* (8 June).

——. 1861b. "Representative Men: Alexis de Tocquiville." *Once a Week* (7 September).

——. 1862. "The Brewing of the American Storm." *Macmillan's Magazine* 6 (June): 97–107.

——. 1864. "The Negro Race in America." *Edinburgh Review* 119 (January): 203–42.

——. 1876. "Harriet Martineau. An Autobiographical Memoir." Obituary. *Daily News* (29 June).

——. 1983. *Autobiography.* 2 vols. Ed. Gaby Weiner. London: Virago.

Mayer, Henry. 1998. *All on Fire: William Lloyd Garrison and the Abolition of Slavery.* New York: St. Martin's Griffin.

Mesick, Jane. 1922. *The English Traveller in America, 1785–1835.* New York: Columbia University Press.

Midgley, Clare. 1992. *Women against Slavery: The British Campaigns, 1780–1870.* London: Routledge.

Miller, Nancy, ed. 1986. *The Poetics of Gender.* New York: Columbia University Press.

Mitchell, Sally, et al., ed. 1988. *Victorian Britain: An Encyclopedia.* New York: Garland Publishing.

Nevill, John Cranstoun. 1943. *Harriet Martineau.* London: Frederick Muller.

Pichanick, Valerie. 1980. *Harriet Martineau: The Woman and Her Work, 1802–76.* Ann Arbor: University of Michigan Press.

Posey, Walter Brownlow, ed. 1938. *Alabama in the 1830's as Recorded by British Travellers.* Birmingham, Ala.: Birmingham-Southern College.

Prince, Mary. 1831. *The History of Mary Prince: A West Indian Slave.* Reprint. Ed. Moira Ferguson. Ann Arbor: University of Michigan Press, 1997.

Rawley, James A. 1981. *The Transatlantic Slave Trade: A History.* New York: W. W. Norton.

Review of *How to Observe Morals and Manners,* by Harriet Martineau. 1839. *Quarterly Review* 63 (January–March): 61–72.

Review of *Illustrations of Political Economy,* by Harriet Martineau. 1833. *Quarterly Review* 49 (April): 136–52.

Review of *Society in America,* by Harriet Martineau. 1837. *American Quarterly Review* 22 (September): 21–53.

Review of *Society in America,* by Harriet Martineau. 1837. *Times* (London) (May 30).

Sanders, Valerie. 1990. *Harriet Martineau: Selected Letters.* London: Clarendon Press.

[Sims, William Gilmore]. 1838. *Slavery in America, Being a Brief Review of Miss Martineau on that Subject, by a South Carolinian*. Richmond, Va.: Thomas W. White.

Taylor, Clare. 1974. *British and American Abolitionists: An Episode in Transatlantic Understanding*. Edinburgh: Edinburgh University Press.

———. 1995. *Women of the Anti-Slavery Movement: The Weston Sisters*. New York: St. Martin's Press.

Tompkins, Jane. 1985. *Sensational Designs: The Cultural Work of American Fiction, 1790–1860*. New York: Oxford University Press.

Turley, David. 1991. *The Culture of English Antislavery, 1780–1860*. London: Routledge.

Webb, R. K. "Handlist of Contributions to *Daily News* by Harriet Martineau." University of Birmingham, Special Collections.

———. *Harriet Martineau: A Radical Victorian*. 1960. New York: Columbia University Press.

❖ ❖ ❖

I N D E X